A Practical Guide to Language Assessment

A Practical Guide to Language Assessment

How Do You Know That Your Students Are Learning?

Ildiko Porter-Szucs
Cynthia J. Macknish
Suzanne Toohey

WILEY Blackwell

For general information on our other products and services or for technical support, please contact our Customer Care Department within the United States at (800) 762-2974, outside the United States at (317) 572-3993 or fax (317) 572-4002.

Wiley also publishes its books in a variety of electronic formats. Some content that appears in print may not be available in electronic formats. For more information about Wiley products, visit our web site at www.wiley.com.

Library of Congress Cataloging-in-Publication Data

Names: Porter-Szucs, Ildiko, author. | Macknish, Cynthia, author. | Toohey, Suzanne, author.
Title: A practical guide to language assessment : how do you know that your students are learning? / Ildiko Porter-Szucs, Cynthia J. Macknish, Suzanne Toohey.
Other titles: How do you know that your students are learning?
Description: First edition. | Hoboken, New Jersey : John Wiley & Sons, Inc., [2025] | Includes bibliographical references and index. | Contents: Concepts–Qualities of test usefulness and the assessment use argument–Test design–Crafting assessments–Tools of the trade–Assessing young learners–PK-12 in the US & Canada: Assessment is not a dirty word–Assessing exceptional language learners–Assessing listening, viewing, representing, speaking, pronunciation–Assessing reading, vocabulary, grammar, writing–Grading, evaluation, feedback–Ethics, fairness, and security–Technology for language assessment–Improving assessments through statistics–Conclusion.
Identifiers: LCCN 2024040479 (print) | LCCN 2024040480 (ebook) | ISBN 9781394238736 (paperback) | ISBN 9781394238750 (ebook) | ISBN 9781394238743 (epub)
Subjects: LCSH: Educational tests and measurements–Design and construction–Textbooks. | Item response theory. | Language and languages–Study and teaching. | Language and languages–Ability testing–Evaluation. | Language teachers–In-service training. | Language teachers–Training of.
Classification: LCC LB3051 .P61459 2025 (print) | LCC LB3051 (ebook) | DDC 371.2601/4–dc23/eng/20241211
LC record available at https://lccn.loc.gov/2024040479
LC ebook record available at https://lccn.loc.gov/2024040480

Cover Design: Wiley
Cover Image: © Andriy Onufriyenko/Getty Images

SKY10096508_011725

Contents

Acknowledgments

We would like to thank several individuals and organizations, without whom this book would never have reached the light of day.

We owe a debt of gratitude to

- Ildi: my husband, Brian, children, and step-children for enduring my absence while I was working on the book, and my parents, Ilza and István, for passing on to me their love of languages
- Cynthia: my husband, Neil, as well as my students over the years who have all helped me to improve my skills in teaching and assessment
- Suzanne: my husband, Craig, for encouraging me to pursue my passions, and my parents for instilling a love of learning in me from a young age
- Eastern Michigan University for the 2019 Summer Research Award and the 2020–2021 Sabbatical Leave
- Avery H. Demond for the acronym VIP WAR.

For their assistance in research, statistical support, piloting, or feedback on the writing of this book, we are grateful to

- Ahmed Almosawi, Grigoris Argeros, Eliona Balilaj, James Cason, Damir Cavar, Malgorzata Cavar, Mark Chapman, Barry DeCicco, Lara El Khouri, Laura Hancock, Taña Hermosillo Huyck, Remy Jakeway, Wenbin Jia, Li Liang, Patrick McLain, Michael McLelland, Desiree Meisner, Shahbaz Nawab, James Pellerin, Lauren Prebenda, Rachele Stucker, Mary C. Tillotson, Hoda Zaki, Huda Yasan
- the students in the 2016–2024 cohorts of TSLN 420 and 520 at Eastern Michigan University.

For their invaluable guidance on improving this manuscript, we are profoundly grateful to

- Chih-Hsin Hsu of Arkansas Tech University
- anonymous reviewers
- the editorial team at Wiley

Acknowledgment

Introduction

Designed for educators in diverse contexts—whether domestic or international, spanning PK-12, post-secondary, or adult community settings—this comprehensive guide redefines the norm by introducing foundational concepts and bringing them to life through a deep exploration of test development and item-writing principles. Bridging theory and practice, it prepares the reader to create a test blueprint based on sound principles and to craft items and tasks tailored for diverse assessment purposes, including those for young learners. It also offers practical item-writer training, providing teachers and assessors with essential tools.

This textbook contains all the information and builds the skills that we would like teachers to have if we were to employ them to teach our students or children. This guide caters to a diverse audience, embracing pre- and in-service language teachers across age groups—from young learners to adults—operating in any educational context. It extends its reach to classroom-assessment professionals, item writers, assessment managers, directors of language programs, professors of language education, and other language experts.

Practicing language teachers, whether in world languages or English as a second or foreign language (ESL/EFL), will find this text invaluable for professional development courses. Moreover, content-area teachers from primary to tertiary institutions, assessment specialists in government, and policymakers will discover a wealth of insights within this indispensable resource.

The content within this textbook is curated from extensive research conducted in the field of language assessment. Every concept, principle, and skill-building exercise is grounded in the latest advancements and findings from academic research. This research-based approach not only adds credibility to the content but also aligns the material with the evolving landscape of language education.

Language assessment is an integral part of language education. When well chosen, administered, and interpreted, it is an indicator of student learning and proficiency. When an assessment tool is misaligned with the purpose, however, it can have serious unintended consequences. Results of assessments are also utilized by decision-makers to hold teachers, schools, and even entire school systems accountable. With such significant consequences, it is essential to prepare future language educators to make well-informed assessment decisions in their classes, schools, and professional decision-making bodies.

The term "assessment" carries a weight that often divides opinions. For many, it is a polarizing word that elicits reactions as varied as a spectrum. Some individuals equate assessment with testing. They view assessment as incompatible with teaching and learning. The various purposes of assessment elude them. In the realm of Teaching English to Speakers of Other Languages (TESOL) assessment courses, in-service teachers share tales of spending more time evaluating English learners[1] (ELs) than actually instructing them. Frustrations surface as they recount the delayed feedback from state-mandated tests, rendering scores outdated and inconclusive. Voices rise, questioning the validity of tests that yield disparate scores for the same student within a mere month. A select few, against the prevailing sentiment, may confess to being adept test-takers, harboring no aversion to assessment. Still, a prevailing sentiment lingers—why must they dedicate an entire course to language assessment when their passion lies in the act of teaching language itself? Yet, when the instructor of the assessment course asks for a show of hands: "How many of you would like to know if your students are learning?" most hands go up. The inevitable follow-up question is, "And how do you know if they are learning?"

Through multiple semesters of piloting and the invaluable feedback from students and colleagues, the authors have fine-tuned this volume, confident in its ability to cultivate assessment literacy among pre- and in-service second-, foreign-, and world-language teachers, empowering them for their future practices in any setting.

Most chapters follow the structure of theory-to-practice application; interspersed with Think-Pair-Share activities (after Kagan, n.d.), which invite the readers to deepen their engagement with the topic of the chapter; concrete examples from a variety of international contexts in the "Did you know?" sections; and a self-assessment quiz. We suggest that these chapters be studied one at a time, in the order presented.

Chapter 4 alone takes a different approach. Having learned about relevant theoretical concepts in the preceding chapters, going forward the readers learn to apply them to writing their own assessments and/or to evaluating those written by others. The authors intentionally do not place this content into the appendix, to emphasize its importance and to discourage its omittance when pressed for time. The chapter is divided into three broad item types: selected-response, constructed-response, and authentic assessments. Unlike the other self-contained chapters, this practical chapter should be studied progressively alongside them. For instance, in a 15-week semester, excluding the first and the last weeks for additional priorities, readers can integrate 10–15 pages of Chapter 4 into the remaining 13 weeks, depending on the workload each week.

One other piece of advice for readers on how to navigate Chapters 6 and 7: Chapter 7 is written specifically for primary and secondary school teachers in the United States and Canada. Teachers working in other contexts should instead study Chapter 6, as the latter is for those who may teach and assess young learners in other settings. In university programs where in one assessment class both groups of teacher-candidates are being trained, the professor may assign the two chapters concurrently. In the authors' program, for instance, all students read both chapters in the same week, but PK-12 teachers study Chapter 7 in depth and take the weekly achievement quiz on Chapter 7. Meanwhile, the other students do the same with Chapter 6. Readers outside the North American context may wish to skip Chapter 7 and replace it with material specific to the local context.

Readers will note the use of "he," "she," and the singular "they" pronouns throughout. The pronoun "they" has evolved into the default choice when referring to someone whose identity is

---

1 Throughout the text, we use the term "English Learner," because it aligns with the US federal definition, ensuring clarity and consistency in identifying students who are in the process of learning English, despite the availability of other asset-based terms such as multilingual learner and emergent bilingual.

unknown or deemed unimportant, and, for some individuals, it is a deliberate preference. Hence, the authors interchangeably use "he," "she," and "they" to reflect this diversity in addressing individuals.

We hope that users of this book will find it the practical guide to language assessment that we have intended it to be. We also hope that with its help, our readers will always be able to answer the question: *How do you know that your students are learning?*

1

Concepts

Chapter Overview

We begin this chapter with a diagnostic test (refer to Appendix A) that covers content from the entire book. Take it in a quiet setting, without external assistance. Your aim is to gauge your existing knowledge to set effective learning goals. After the self-assessment, engage in value-clarification exercises. Reflect on each question individually before discussing with others.

   To effectively use assessment language in this book, clarify commonly confused concepts and terms. This will enable categorization of assessments into different types.

1.1   Chapter Objectives

1. Express teaching and learning beliefs and align them with beliefs about English to Speakers of Other Languages (ESOL: English as a Second Language [ESL] and English as a Foreign Language [EFL]) or foreign-language (FL) testing and assessment
2. Explain important assessment concepts and terminology
3. Evaluate assessment practices in an ESL/EFL/FL setting you are familiar with by applying to it each of the key terms in this chapter
4. Distinguish between different types of assessment
5. Distinguish standards-based from standardized assessment

   STOP How assessment literate are you? Before reading this chapter, consider how much background knowledge you bring. Go to Appendix A and take the diagnostic quiz. After checking your answers, set learning objectives for yourself for the rest of the book.

1.2   Aligning Teaching, Learning, and Assessment Beliefs

In the following Think-Pair-Share value-clarification exercises, you will have the opportunity to verbalize your teaching and learning preferences on one hand and your assessment preferences on the other. You will also attempt to align them and consider potential conflicts between them. One question at a time, reflect on the issues. For example, if you believe that good teaching involves task-based learning, is your preferred assessment method, fill-in-the-blank grammar exercises, effective for this? Capture your thoughts in writing. Next, pair up with another teacher and discuss your thoughts. Once you have completed the first exercise, repeat the steps for the second and third exercises.

A Practical Guide to Language Assessment: How Do You Know That Your Students Are Learning? First Edition.
Ildiko Porter-Szucs et al.
© 2025 John Wiley & Sons, Inc. Published 2025 by John Wiley & Sons, Inc.

Think-Pair-Share 1.2a Value-Clarification Exercise—Part 1   Think back to the best and worst teachers who have ever taught you. What teaching strategies and techniques did they use? Make a list of the qualities that contributed to your judgment about them. What kind of teacher do you wish to be? Discuss.

Think-Pair-Share 1.2b Value-Clarification Exercise—Part 2   Think back to your most and least favorite ways of being assessed? What made them so? What goals did each of these ways try to achieve? Did these ways have any unintended consequences? To what extent did these forms of assessment contribute to your learning the subject matter? Discuss.

Think-Pair-Share 1.2c Value-Clarification Exercise—Part 3   Consider again the kind of teacher you wish to be. What assessment methods or tools can you employ to stay true to your pedagogical goals? What assessment methods run counter to your goals? Discuss.

Now that you have had a chance to explore your beliefs of teaching, learning, and assessment, consider the beliefs of the following pre- and in-service teachers. As you read, think about how internally consistent each teacher's beliefs are. Pay particular attention to how well each teacher's beliefs about teaching and learning match the needs of the students. Then compare how each teacher's beliefs about assessment match the teaching and learning beliefs and the needs of the students. How can you explain any inconsistencies you may find?

Teacher Profile: Han Mei Yin

Han Mei Yin tutors EFL students in China. Her students range in age from 8 to 18 years. They are motivated to study with Han Mei Yin to improve their grades in school, score well on the national college entry exam (Gaokao), and occasionally to improve their overall language proficiency.

Han Mei Yin wishes for her students to be able to communicate in English around the world. She believes teachers should develop not only their students' language proficiency but also their cultural competence, critical thinking skills, and autonomy. She's also intrigued by content-based instruction.

According to Han Mei Yin, assessment should show her students' progress. It should consist of various item types such as multiple-choice (MC) and short answer.

Teacher Profile: Kwang Bai

Kwang Bai teaches EFL students in a school in South Korea. His students range in age from 12 to 18 years. In his classes, he focuses heavily on accuracy to prepare his students for a national college entrance exam. For one year, he had an English teaching assistant co-teach his class, whose presence shifted the emphasis slightly onto communication.

Kwang Bai believes that the most effective and meaningful learning takes place when teachers, as facilitators, guide their students based on the students' needs. He wants to create a safe learning environment for the students and allow them to practice authentic language.

He knows that assessment affects what and how to teach. Assessments need to be practical for large groups of students but ideally should also allow for students to perform in various situations.

Teacher Profile: Joe Tremblay

Joe Tremblay teaches newly arrived immigrant adults in a community program in Canada. His students are developing language skills for immigration and employment. Joe Tremblay's philosophy of teaching and learning is guided primarily by his respect for his students. He asks his students whether they are learning English to find a job, to talk to their children's teachers at school, to write college essays, or for some other purpose. He feels it is his duty to teach the students what they want to learn.

Joe Tremblay assesses his students by asking for their opinion on their learning. He asks whether they think they are improving, whether the method of instruction is helpful for them, etc.

Teacher Profile: Steffi Wagner

Steffi Wagner teaches German in the United States to students aged 6 to 18 years. At the two schools where she teaches, world languages are taught through Comprehensible Input (CI) (Krashen 1982). Steffi Wagner's students across Levels 1–6 are a combination of heritage-language learners and those who are interested in the sciences and business. Her teaching philosophy favors the creation of a low-anxiety, input-rich environment, prioritizing listening, reading, and having fun. She shelters vocabulary but not grammar (Hedstrom 2017). Productive skills (speaking and writing) and grammatical accuracy emerge as the students are ready.

Steffi Wagner assesses her students' listening and reading comprehension by focusing on accuracy, while their speaking and writing skills by focusing on their fluency. Her beliefs are grounded in the idea that when students are motivated and eager to use the language, accuracy emerges naturally.

1.3 Concepts and Terminology

We need a common language to talk about assessment. Some terms will be new to most while others may appear to be familiar. We say *appear to be* because many related terms are widely used, yet poorly understood.

These include

- testing
- measurement
- assessment
- evaluation

In illustrating the relationship among these terms, a common representation uses concentric circles. Testing is the most specific term at the center, followed by measurement, which is a broader concept encompassing testing. Assessment is the broadest term, covering both testing and measurement.[1] Each of these terms can be followed by the step of evaluation. We would also add another step: feedback. These terms will be explored in this and subsequent chapters.

---

1 For visual depictions of these concepts, see Bachman and Palmer (2010), p. 22; Brown and Abeywickrama (2010), p. 6; Gottlieb (2016), p. 195.

The narrowest term is **testing**. Testing is the systematic administration and collection of instruments of learner (test taker [TT]) performance. Examples include the administration of tests with both high stakes and low stakes. High-stakes tests, in other words those that have important consequences for the TT, include the International English Language Testing System (IELTS 2024), Examination for the Certificate of Proficiency in English (ECPE), or the American Council on the Teaching of Foreign Languages (ACTFL) Oral Proficiency Interview (OPI 2024a), to name a few. These tests can determine employment, college admission, immigration, and certification. Low-stakes tests, such as in-class pop quizzes or chapter exams, may affect a course grade, but they carry fewer consequences for learners.

To measure something means to apply a scale or measuring instrument to the targeted object by skilled users of the instrument. Language assessments measure students' and TTs' performance in the target language. **Measurement**, then, "is the process of quantifying the observed performance" of TTs (Brown and Abeywickrama 2010, p. 4). Measurement of receptive language, for instance, may include the administration of an MC vocabulary test (Internet-Based Test of English as a Foreign Language [TOEFL iBT] and the TOAFL test of Arabic) or of matching names to pictures following verbal commands (Cambridge English's Pre-A1 Starters). The responses are then scored by computer or a human, based on an answer key. Productive language includes the writing of a report, as in the World-Class Instructional Design and Assessment (WIDA) ACCESS for English Language Learners (ELLs) (WIDA 2024b) or a conversation with an examiner about a problem, as in the Examination for the Certificate of Competency in English (ECCE; Michigan Language Assessment 2024). TT responses of productive language are measured with the help of rating scales, rubrics, and benchmarks specifically to measure the targeted language production. Measurement feedback can be quantitative or qualitative. Quantitatively, the observed language performance is converted to a numerical score, such as 25 out of 30 or a grade or a percentile, such as the 75th percentile, below which a given percentage of scores falls. Qualitatively, the feedback is a written or oral description of the observed language proficiency, tailored to the student, elaborating on strengths and growth opportunities.

Tests are a type of **assessment**. Therefore, all tests are a form of assessment but not every assessment is a test. Assessment is an appraisal or judgment of observed behavior. In second- or foreign-language assessment, the target of observation is language-related behavior. Assessment is, for instance, when a teacher looks at the students' body language and notices that nobody wants to be called on to answer a question. Assessment is also when the teacher makes a mental note that she should teach the difference between [θ] and [s] upon hearing a student say "*I don't sink so.*" But assessments can also be when a five-year-old brings his favorite teddy bear to a "show and tell" at school and the teacher writes in his notebook that little Pedro did the assignment with both enthusiasm and clarity. Assessment also comprises peer- and self-assessment: classmates may peer-review each other's essays and each student may comment on his/her individual contribution to a group project.

Evaluation can be understood as the *Now what?*, or the value judgment with consequences that is placed on the measurement. Take, for instance, a language school where 20% of the students fail a teacher's final exam. Assuming that the teaching was effective and the exam is not flawed, there will certainly be consequences for those students: at the very least their final grade will drop unless they are given a chance to retake the exam; that, too, has consequences of time and effort for the students. There may also be a variety of consequences for the teacher. Perhaps the teacher's reputation as being unreasonably strict or ineffective will spread and students will avoid her class. If her performance evaluation at the school is tied to her students' success, as defined by the class's pass rate, then her supervisor's opinion of her may thus be shaped. Consequences could go even further if student pass rates are made public. Language schools may compare themselves to each other and prospective students may choose to study at a competitor's school. If the accrediting agency bases its evaluation of the school on its students' pass rate, the school's accreditation may be in danger. The ripple effects may be endless. Often it is because of the evaluation placed on assessment practices (and their misuse) that assessment and testing earn a bad reputation and the stakeholders are ready to abolish any form of assessment. Therefore, it is essential to remember to separate assessment tools from their various uses and misuses. The decisions associated with evaluation may result in intended, unintended, or potentially unknown consequences for individuals, programs, institutions, and beyond. This underscores the importance of incorporating an examination of consequences as a key element in the Assessment Use Argument (Bachman and Palmer 2010).

To summarize, a test is a common way to measure language proficiency, but it is just one of several forms of assessment. It is important for someone using an assessment to determine which form of assessment best meets the needs of the specific context. When measurements are taken, quantitative or qualitative feedback can be given to TTs on the results. These results may have a variety of consequences for the TT, the teacher, and the school, as determined by evaluative judgment.

1.4   Assessment Purposes and Types

Remember the four teachers introduced at the beginning of this chapter: Han Mei Yin, Kwang Bai, Joe Tremblay, and Steffi Wagner? Their profiles demonstrate that students study a language for a variety of purposes. Han Mei Yin's and Kwang Bai's students study for college entrance exams. Joe Tremblay's students study to communicate with their children's teachers at school or to secure a job. Steffi Wagner's students study either to nurture their families' heritage language or to prepare for prospective employment opportunities. Han Mei Yin wants to track her students' progress, as does Joe Tremblay. The various purposes can be accomplished by different types of assessment. Assessments can be classified in a variety of ways. According to their purpose, they can mainly be placement, diagnostic, progress, achievement, proficiency, and certification.

1.4.1   Placement

Imagine a prospective language learner walking through the doors of the *School of World Languages*. Which level course should she enroll in? If she has never studied the language before, the decision is easy: Level 1. But what if she reveals that she has studied the language for 2 years already? That is hardly sufficient information to place her in the right course level. In 2 years, some learners make immense progress while others very little. What if the prospective student helpfully adds that she was in an intermediate class at another school? Do we have enough information now to recommend a level? At best, we might be able to eliminate the lowest and highest levels but we might still be left with several in the middle. What at one school is considered intermediate at another school may be some other level. This is where a placement test can be useful.

> A **placement test (Screener)** sorts TTs into as many proficiency levels as needed at the school/ institution.

A placement test (in US K-12 contexts called a *screener*) contains questions at various levels of proficiency. In a language program with four levels, absolute beginners (or novices) may not need to take the test but could immediately be directed to the beginner level. Everyone else would be placed into one of the remaining three levels based on their score on the placement test. Students who answer almost all the questions correctly can test out and not have to take any of the courses based on the placement test. The line drawn between the different levels depends on the institution and is the result of a standard-setting study. Each institution must determine for itself where the lines, or **cut scores**, between levels are drawn.

Standard setting involves establishing descriptions for achievement levels and determining the *minimum scores* required for each level, known as **cut scores**. Panels for standard setting comprise diverse educators and assessment specialists. Panelists are responsible for recommending the *minimum acceptable performance levels* for classifying students/TTs into each achievement level. These cut scores serve as the baseline for categorizing examinees into specific performance levels rather than the next lower level. "While there are numerous methods for setting performance standards, all include a combination of technical considerations and expert judgment" (New York State Education Department n.d.).

Did you know?   The Kindergarten WIDA Screener and the WIDA Screener are placement tests in many primary and secondary schools in the United States.

From a test-development perspective, the questions, also known as *items*, appearing on a placement test span a wide range of proficiency levels: from very easy to very hard. Imagine item difficulties as several sieves placed into each other. The goal of each is to sort.

 The top sieve has very large holes. Only students whose familiarity with the language is rather rough or rudimentary are stopped at this first level. All others pass through the first sieve and into the second one (*Source:* OpenClipart-Vectors / Pixabay).

 Here, those who can use some language (for example, can talk about personal, well-rehearsed topics) are retained and all others pass to the third sieve (*Source:* Open Clipart-Vectors / Pixabay).

 At the third level, those students who can express themselves in finer details of the language (for example, can talk about both personal and professional topics as long as they are familiar) are identified, and the rest pass through to the fourth sieve. Here, almost everyone is filtered out because the holes are tiny. Only those whose proficiency is at a high level would pass through the last sieve because they cannot learn anything new at this example institution (*Source:* WikimediaImages / Pixabay).

From a test-development perspective, a placement test contains a wide range of item difficulties. However, there is a limited number of items at each level in order to keep the length of the test manageable. Thus, some target elements may not be assessed at all (for example, a point of view that the author of a listening passage would agree with), while others may receive some coverage (for instance, the main idea and significant details in a listening passage). Because of this limitation, there is always a chance that a student may be misplaced and procedures should be in place to change the initially allocated level if appropriate. In order to achieve its purpose, a placement test is a somewhat crude instrument that assesses the big picture rather than a finely tuned one as will be demonstrated by some of the other types of assessment.

1.4.2 Diagnostic

Let's assume that all new students at the *School of World Languages* have now been sorted (placed) into appropriate course levels. In each course, there is a syllabus, containing the target elements to be taught in that particular course. For instance, in the novice Level 1 course, the Simple Present, the Present Progressive, and the Simple Future are taught. In the high beginner course, these verb tenses are reviewed and new ones are added: Simple Past (regular and irregular) and Past Progressive.

> The **diagnostic test** diagnoses TTs' knowledge of language specific to a particular class or unit or topic.

A diagnostic test[2] assesses (diagnoses) the students' knowledge and/or use of the specific language to be covered in that course. Such assessment is administered before any instruction takes place; in other words, it's a pre-test. It reveals each student's familiarity with the concepts specific to that course. The assessment may reveal that students are unfamiliar with something they should know, such as the Present Progressive in the Level 2 course. Based on the diagnostic results, the teacher and/or the school administrator may determine that some students have been misplaced by the placement test and should be in the Level 1 course. Or the teacher may decide to back up and start the course by re-teaching, rather than reviewing, what the students have not yet mastered. It is much like a mechanic conducting a diagnostic test on your car to determine how well it is performing. The diagnostic results will indicate what service needs to be done on the car to improve its performance.

Think-Pair-Share 1.4.2a Analysis and Application   Knowing what you know about the level of difficulty and distribution of items on placement tests (see Section 1.4.1) and what you know about the purpose of diagnostic tests, think about the difficulty and distribution of items on diagnostic tests. Discuss. (Do not read the next paragraph until you have completed this application exercise.)

From a test-development perspective, diagnostic tests are the opposite of placement tests. If placement tests are shallow and broad, then diagnostic assessments are deep and narrow. Only items at a specific proficiency level are represented (for example, only high beginner, or WIDA Level 2, or CEFR Level A2, or ACTFL Level Novice High), and within that level, even more narrowly, only those target elements which are taught in that particular course. Unlike on a placement test, on a diagnostic, multiple items may be designed to assess the learners' knowledge of each target element. For example, in a high-intermediate course on the diagnostic test, there may be 12 questions about the Simple Past tense. Two of them may be on statements of regular verbs (for example, *walked, danced*), two negatives of regular verbs (for example, *didn't play, did not paint*), and two interrogatives (for example, *did he open, didn't she like*). The rest may be on irregular verbs in the affirmative (*saw, got*), negative (*weren't, didn't buy*), and interrogative (*did they sing, didn't we know*).

---

2 In US K-12 (and in Michigan as required by Read by Grade Three), teachers are required to use a diagnostic reading assessment with any K-3 student scoring below the benchmark on the reading screener.

Diagnostic assessment may be administered at the beginning of the entire semester on all the topics to be covered in that course during that semester. However, a diagnostic test may be even narrower and conducted just before a specific unit on a subsection of the semester is taught.

An issue sometimes arises when an institution, in an effort to save time and money, uses the same test for both placement and gaining diagnostic information. Unfortunately, using a test for an unintended purpose like this can result in the use of misinformation for decision-making. Ironically, even more time will then be needed to sort out the resulting problems.

1.4.3 Progress

> **Progress assessment** measures how much students are improving. It is administered at various points during a course.

If we follow our imaginary group of students enrolled in the high-beginner course at the *School of World Languages*, we see that they are moving towards achieving the learning objectives for the unit on the Simple Past tense. The teacher would like to assess whether they're on track to reaching their goal in a timely manner. The students are curious how they would do on the test if it were today. Thus, the teacher administers a progress assessment. The content of this mock or practice test is essentially that of the achievement assessment (see Section 1.4.4), but no results are captured for a progress report. It is only for formative, interim purposes.

1.4.4 Achievement

> An **achievement** assessment assesses what the students have learned after the target element has been introduced, taught, practiced, and mastered. It could occur repeatedly during the instruction to inform teaching and learning (formative) and also at the end of instruction for evaluation (summative).

The students at the *School of World Languages* have just completed the unit on the Simple Past tense (regular and irregular). Throughout the unit, the teacher had tracked the students' recognition, understanding, controlled production, guided production, and free production of the target element. She had assessed the students daily in a variety of ways: observing the students' participation and body language, responses to questions, thumbs up/sideways/down, exit tickets, gap-fill exercises, sentence transformation, listening to the description of a historical event and responding to comprehension questions about it, pair work, oral and written picture description, journal writing, etc. Each of these measures had informed the teacher of how well individual students and the class in general were acquiring/learning (achieving) the targeted material. This is called **formative assessment**. Keeping the course schedule and syllabus in the back of her mind and her students' mastery of the material, the instruction had been informed by a recursive cycle of teaching → learning → assessment → more teaching → more learning → more assessment. She had even administered a practice assessment to track the students' progress from the beginning to the end of the unit. The evaluation of students' work, up until this point, had been mostly on effort and completion and less on quality. The purpose of assessment thus far had been to inform, shape, form (see formative) student learning, and improve instruction.

At the end of the unit, the students' mastery (achievement) of all the target elements taught were assessed. This is known as **summative assessment** because it sums up what the students should know (also see elsewhere in this chapter). The teacher did so with a combination of multiple-choice questions (MCQs), personal written narrative about a family tree, oral presentation of the same, and skit writing and performance in pairs. Each of these assessments was graded: some quantitatively, some qualitatively, and some both.

Think-Pair-Share 1.4.4a Analysis and Application There are two distinct types of achievement assessments discussed in Section 1.4.4: formative and summative. Reflect on your language teaching and/or learning experience. List specific examples of each type. Who created these assessments? Who administered them? Who evaluated them? How were they used? How easy was it to detect change in the amount of language the students knew?

1.4.5 Proficiency

After several semesters of study at the *School of World Languages*, some students would like to have official proof of how much language they know. Some would like to submit their test results to their employer to receive a raise or promotion. Others need the score for educational purposes, either to be admitted to a competitive-admission school or to receive course credit for the language they know. Still others would like to immigrate to a country where the studied language is spoken broadly. And some students would just like tangible proof of their knowledge.

> **Proficiency test:** independent of a particular course or instruction received, the overall competence of multi-skill language is assessed in a high-stakes, standardized manner, with a professionally developed test.

Did you know? The following are well-known proficiency tests: ACTFL APPT (2024b), TOEFL iBT, IELTS (2024), TOEIC, Michigan Language Assessment exams, CELPIP, Cambridge English Language Assessment qualifications, CAEL, CELPIP, OET (Cambridge Boxhill Language Assessment), AVANT STAMP (2024a), ACTFL OPI (2024a), Linguaskill, PTE, TrackTest, Eiken, CET China (Zhang 2022), China TEM (Yang 2017), WIDA suite of tests (WIDA 2024b), MSU Exams, Duolingo English Test, and many more.

Unlike achievement assessments, proficiency tests are typically not produced by the teacher or even the school itself—although they can be if the school has the requisite resources. Mostly, they are produced by high-stakes standardized testing agencies, where professional test developers specialize in creating large-scale assessments. Such tests are usually researched, developed, assessed, improved painstakingly so as to maximize the balance of the core assessment qualities of validity, reliability, practicality, authenticity, interactiveness, and washback (for more on the qualities of test usefulness, see Chapter 2). The results of recognized proficiency tests transfer across institutions. This means that the test is issued and administered by one institution and its results are accepted at multiple others. This is in contrast with achievement tests, which are developed in/for/ by the specific course. A score of 78% on an achievement test at school *A* may not be accepted at school *B* as a 78%. There exist, however, proficiency tests that are developed by a testing agency for in-house administration. If the test is computerized and scored by the testing agency, then the results of such tests may or may not be transferable across institutions. However, if the test is scored in-house, then the results will likely not be accepted by other institutions since crucial elements of test security and standardization (i.e. test administration and scoring) cannot be vouched for by the testing agency. Standardized proficiency tests are increasingly computerized (e.g. TOEFL iBT, WIDA ACCESS for ELLs 2.0,) although test components may occasionally still be administered face-to-face (e.g. IELTS speaking test).

Proficiency tests may cover a broad spectrum of proficiency levels or just a narrow band. Most proficiency tests, similarly to placement tests, cover several levels of proficiency: from beginner to advanced (for instance, IELTS). Proficiency tests can usually be used for placement purposes because of the breadth of items required by both test purposes. One notable proficiency test is the IELTS by the British Council, IDP: IELTS Australia, and Cambridge University Press and Assessment, spanning 9 bands, which align with A1 (beginner) to C2 (advanced) levels on the Common European Framework of Reference (CEFR). IELTS has both a general training test for immigration or general purposes and an academic test for university admission or acceptance into a professional association. Another example is the TOEFL iBT by the Educational Testing Service, spanning approximately A2 (high-beginner) to C1 (low-advanced). These proficiency tests often double as placement tests. They cannot be passed or failed. It is the test user (such as a university) that determines the minimum acceptable score for particular purposes.

Some proficiency tests, however, are designed to determine whether the TT is or is not at a particular level of proficiency. Such is the ECPE by Michigan Language Assessment (2024), aimed at the C2, or highest, level of the CEFR. Another example is B2 First by Cambridge English (2024a), aimed at the B2, or high-intermediate, level of the CEFR. Such tests can be passed and failed, the targeted proficiency certificate achieved or not. These tests, therefore, often double as certification tests.

Think-Pair-Share 1.4.5a Analysis and Application Do you have any experience with a proficiency test (language or other subject) either as a TT, a teacher, test administrator, or item writer? Conduct informal research on one such test that is most applicable to your current or future work setting. What information is gained by this test type that cannot be gained otherwise? What advantages and disadvantages are you aware of for this test type? Discuss.

1.4.6 Certification/Licensure/Qualification

A few of the students at the *School of World Languages* are hoping to sit for exams that certify their English proficiency for specific occupations. One student would like to be a nurse in Australia, another a pilot, and a third a teacher. To prove their language proficiency for these purposes, they must take the appropriate assessments.

Some proficiency tests lend themselves for certification, or licensure, or qualification. They certify the TT's language proficiency at a specific level, such as at the B2 (high-intermediate) level of the CEFR. For example, the following tests accomplish this: the ECCE by Michigan Language Assessment (2024) and B2 First for Schools by Cambridge English Assessment. The minimally proficient, or passing, score in such cases is determined by the assessment organization designing the test.

There exists another category of proficiency tests for certification, licensure, and qualification: those where typically the organization accepting the score sets the minimal standard. Numerous occupational licensure exams fall into this category. Examples include ETS's Praxis Tests (2024a), which certify non-native-English-speaking teachers' subject-matter and content knowledge for classrooms where English is the medium of instruction. The International Civil Aviation Organization (ICAO) requires ICAO Level 4 English proficiency as minimum for all aviation professionals. Exams aligned with the ICAO proficiency descriptors include the Benchmark Test of English for Aviation (b-TEA) by Mayflower College, the English Language Proficiency for Aeronautical Communication (ELPAC) by Eurocontrol, and the ICAO English Test. Another example is the Occupational English

Test (OET) created by Cambridge Boxhill Language Assessment for healthcare professionals in Australia and other countries.

1.4.7   Other Common Assessment Classifications

In addition to their purpose, assessments can also be classified according to various additional criteria. According to the use of the assessment results, they can be *formative and summative*. Formative assessments can also be referred to as *interim measures*. Additionally, some assessments blend formative and summative elements.

Think-Pair-Share 1.4.7a Review   Recall the two types of classroom-based achievement assessments described in Section 1.4.4. At what point in the learning cycle were they used and to what end? Discuss.

1.4.8   Formative

If you answered *formative* and *summative*, congratulations. Formative assessments, as described above, are—or definitely should be—the most common type of assessment in the classroom. They are used to develop (form) the students' knowledge and skills and thus inform the teaching–learning process as it is happening. For example, the teacher engages in formative assessment when he listens to students negotiating meaning with each other. As he hears one student circumscribing *mittens* as *gloves with one finger*, the teacher assesses for communicative competence and accuracy. He then offers the correct word—*mitten*—to the students, who can continue their conversation. However, formative assessment can also resemble a test. For instance, a practice/mock, or progress test, before the final exam may be formative. The students may take a timed MC test under strict testing conditions, then find out what their score would be if this were the actual test. The teacher then uses the test results to see which learning objectives have not yet been met and provides additional explanation and practice. Students can also be trained to assess themselves and others in this way. They can monitor their own language production, compare it to the target, self-correct, and incorporate the correction into future production.

Formative assessment, thus, shapes or forms learning as it is taking place and all attentive teachers engage in it. The purpose of formative assessment is not to evaluate the students' knowledge but rather to improve it.

1.4.9   Interim Measures

A special type of formative assessment are interim measures, a term commonly used in the public school system in the United States, for instance. These are essentially practice progress tests for high-stakes standardized tests. They are typically created, and sometimes even administered and scored, by the same test development organization that does the high-stakes, semester-end achievement, or proficiency assessments. The interim measures are administered at predetermined and regular intervals (such as at the beginning, middle, and near-end of the instructional period). Their purpose is to track students' progress toward achievement or proficiency and to determine skills needing re-teaching for struggling students. If the student is identified as excelling, the interim assessment may be used as a data point to justify moving a student into a different level or course. The report accompanying the results also provides school administrators beneficial data at the school, classroom, and student levels.

1.4.10 Summative

Summative assessment is usually contrasted with formative assessment. Its purpose is to evaluate the students' attainment of the learning objectives after the teaching and learning have concluded. Examples include a final exam in a course or a chapter test on what the students have mastered. Once the test is graded, the class moves on to the next level in the case of a course final exam or to the next learning unit in the case of a chapter test.

Not all summative assessments are tests though. Some are projects, presentations, performances, demonstrations, scenarios, essays, book reports, portfolios, etc. Summative assessments may be created, administered, and scored by the classroom teacher (see Figure 1.1). They can also be co-created by teams of teachers at the same school or school district, as well as administered and scored by the team. These in the public schools in the United States are commonly referred to as *common assessments*. Summative assessments may be created by the publisher of the instructional materials used in class, when, for instance, course textbooks are accompanied by a test bank. Finally, in some innovative, student-centered programs, students contribute to the development of the summative assessment, e.g. by suggesting exam questions.

After these assessments are administered, even if the correct answers are discussed and the students receive feedback from the teacher, they are considered summative assessments because they occur at the end of the course or unit and the purpose is not to inform teaching and learning but to evaluate what the students have achieved.

1.4.11 Multiple Measures

When assessing language, good practice dictates that judgment should not be made based on a single measurement, such as a final exam. Students may have a bad day, the type of assessment may not suit their learning style, the topics may be more or less familiar, the assessment may be poorly designed, and no single assessment is capable of capturing something as complex as language proficiency. Assessment should mirror learning: sustained repetition over a long period of time. Formative and summative, receptive and productive, individual and group, low and high stakes, etc. should be taken together—as multiple measures—to capture the students' language learning for decision-making.

1.4.12 Assessment *of, for,* and *as* Learning

Both similar to and distinct from summative and formative classifications is the categorization of classroom assessment by its purpose as **assessment *of* learning, assessment *for* learning,** and **assessment *as* learning** (Earl 2006, Gottlieb 2016). **Assessment of learning** is another term for summative classroom assessment, "used to confirm what students know and can do, to demonstrate whether they have achieved the curriculum outcomes, and, occasionally, to show how they are placed in relation to others" (p. 26). This includes chapter tests, final exams, and presentations of projects. **Assessment for learning** is another term for formative classroom assessment, "designed to give teachers information to modify and differentiate teaching and learning activities" (p. 25). It is based on the learning objectives for the daily lesson and a note whether each student has met the objectives. For instance, a checkmark can be placed in a chart for each student who can explain in the target language how they conducted an experiment. In **assessment as learning,** the focus is on the language learner developing metacognition and reflective ability necessary to turn assessment opportunities into learning opportunities. "When students are active, engaged, and critical assessors, they make sense of information, relate it to prior knowledge, and use it for new learning" (p. 25). Self-(and peer-) assessment tools such as journals, reflection papers, checklists, the muddiest point (Mosteller 1989), and monitoring self in relation to a linguistic role model are examples. For more on self-assessment and co-construction of success criteria, see Chapter 11.

The following two terms—learning-oriented and scenario-based assessment—transcend traditional categories and effectively incorporate assessment of, for, and as learning, even though they fall outside the previously mentioned nomenclature.

1.4.13 Learning-oriented Assessment

In learning-oriented assessment (LOA), the primary goal of assessment is to enhance learning. It goes even beyond bringing about positive washback, by centering the learning process and examining how assessment can enhance learning (Turner and Purpura 2016). This can be achieved through framing educational goals and evaluating outcomes. The latter can be accomplished by either formative or summative assessment (or assessment for, as, of learning). The second key component of LOA is student involvement, such as through self- or peer-assessment (or assessment as learning). Third, learners need to receive feedback, "which they can use to 'feedforward' into future work" (Carless 2007, p. 59). This iterative process is an exemplification of the planning–teaching–learning–assessment cycle outlined in Chapter 3.

1.4.14 Scenario-based Assessment

Scenario-based assessment (SBA) is akin to task-based and performance-based assessment, where participants complete a series of interconnected, learning-oriented tasks to achieve an end goal situated in a real-world context (Purpura 2021; Turner and Purpura 2016). A scenario can involve any situation requiring authentic information gathering, negotiation, and presentation. This approach allows for the concurrent assessment of, for, and as learning (Purpura 2021).

1.4.15 Discrete vs. Integrative Skills vs. Multiliteracies

Depending on the number of skills assessed at once, we can further classify assessments. *Discrete* means separate skills, while *integrative* (or *integrated*) means that the skills are combined during the assessment. *Skills* traditionally refer to listening, speaking, reading, and writing (while vocabulary and grammar are often referred to as *subskills*). A *discrete-skills test* assesses each skill in isolation. For example, there is a separate section just for speaking: learners are given a picture and asked to describe it. Similarly, there is a separate section for writing: learners may be asked to write about a picture or given a brief prompt and asked to write about it using their background knowledge. Note that it can be difficult to assess receptive skills (reading, listening) without the use of a productive skill (speaking or writing), although those may not be the focus of a discrete-skills test. An *integrative-skills* assessment of speaking does not separate speaking from other skills. Thus, the learner first has to receive information receptively (through reading and/or listening/viewing) and then speak about it. Likewise, an integrative writing assessment is based on what the learner first reads and/or hears/views.

Did you know? Trinity College London's Integrated Skills in English (ISE) test has two exam modules: Reading & Writing, where TTs first read and then write about it, and Speaking & Listening, where TTs speak about what they first listen to.

Integrative assessment is considered more authentic because in real life we often speak or write about something we first heard or read, such as a book or movie review. Admittedly, it is possible for a discrete-skill assessment to be authentic as well; take, for instance, writing a letter or telling a personal story. Other notable integrative assessments described by Brown and Abeywickrama (2010) are cloze and dictation, both of which will be discussed in the item-writing chapter (Chapter 4). Integrative vs. discrete-skill tests have implications for validity. (For more on this, see elsewhere in this volume.)

1.4.16 Multiliteracies

Language learning has expanded from the traditional emphasis on the skills or domains of reading, writing, listening, and speaking to account for the more culturally and linguistically diverse societies and the more globalized and technologically advanced world we live in. To this end, the New London Group (1996) advocated another important concept: multiliteracies. Multiliteracies pedagogy includes two aspects of language use: instruction to promote awareness of the social, linguistic, and cultural contexts in which texts are embedded and instruction to promote skills in various modes of communication (e.g. video, sound, websites, visuals, images, gestures). Both of these aspects include skills in critical thinking, creativity, and digital technology. The caveat here is that multiliteracies pedagogies are not necessarily accessible to all populations. Even in developed countries, there are areas that lack sufficient resources or adequate internet infrastructure to provide a full multiliteracies education. Indeed, Cope and Kalantzis (2017) in revisiting the 1996 pedagogy of multiliteracies claim:

> Beneath these practices of literacy and pedagogy, schooling continues to serve and even to amplify social inequality. The school itself maintains an institutional insistence on inequality so long as its systems rely on norm-referenced, summative assessments. Learners are brought into the class with the expectation that all can perform, but assessment mandates that only the few can excel while the many do moderately well at best, or not very well (p. 20).

COVID lockdowns exacerbated the disparities even more, yet taught us the importance of socioemotional wellbeing, networking, and digital collaboration. To advocate for an "education for justice," while maintaining the importance of a multiliteracies pedagogy, teachers need to navigate the disparities and create differentiated and scaffolded approaches to instruction and assessment. The focus can shift from a final product biased towards literacy (summative assessment) to the process and development of multiliteracies (formative assessment) through more diverse assessments, including self- and peer-assessment with scaffolded peer feedback. Cope and Kalantzis (2015) suggest "CGScholar" (https://cgscholar.com/home/), a multimodal writing space where "help credits" can be awarded for contributions to the learning of others and to the learning community. Such approaches encourage individual agency and differentiation over lockstep instruction and learning, and standardized assessments.

While we promote multiliteracies, for logistical purposes the chapters of this book are organized by the traditional skills of speaking, listening, reading, and writing.

1.4.17 Informal vs. Formal

Assessments can also be classified based on levels of formality. As the name suggests, *informal assessment* is unofficial, casual, often unplanned. It is classroom-based, formative, assessment for learning, but may include assessment as learning as well. Examples include *"on-the-run" assessment*, when students are working independently (alone, in pairs, small groups, or as a whole class) and the teacher circulates around the classroom, listens in and responds to observed needs. Students might be writing the script for a podcast on the life of a teenager in their neighborhood. They might be searching for a particular word and ask the teacher as he walks by. The teacher offers the word, asks the students to explain what part they are working on, praises the students for making steady progress, and moves on. Another example might include monitoring the progress towards a particular learning objective of the day: *upon completion of this class, students will be able to make a suggestion to someone in a higher position of power using appropriate vocabulary and grammar.* As students are role playing such situations with their partners, the teacher walks around with a checklist containing each student's name and the learning objective. As she hears a student make the targeted suggestion pragmatically correctly, she checks it off on her checklist. An issue that arises here is that individual students may meet the objective, but not at the moment when the teacher is observing. Depending on class size, there may not be enough time for the teacher to adequately attend each group or pair. To this end, teachers must create multiple opportunities for this type of assessment.

Informal assessment may simply comprise quick check-ins with students. After an explanation, the teacher might ask the students, *Who understands?*, to which students who do will raise their hands. One way to encourage participation is to prime the expected behavior; in this case the teacher would raise his hand while asking the question. Alternatively, the teacher may ask a yes-no question, *Is that clear? Yes? No? Maybe?* and wait for a response. Another option, particularly popular with young learners, is the nonverbal equivalent of the above: thumb-up 👍, thumb-down 👎, thumb-sideways 🤚, or another culturally appropriate gesture (*Source:* https://tinyurl.com/thumb supdown). Again, priming the response with the thumb gestures is likely to increase participation. The issue with this type of assessment is that it relies on self-reporting and some students may be too shy to admit they don't understand, or simply gesture the same way that their peers are gesturing. One way around this is to ask more targeted questions (e.g. *Why don't we just tell the boss to buy the software?*) or ask for follow-up explanations, such as *Which part is easiest for you to understand? Why?* or *What makes this clear for you?* or *Explain why we use different words and structures with the boss than with our family members.*

Another informal assessment technique is the instant MC quiz. With advanced preparation, this can be done online. Even without technology, however, the teacher can quickly present a question to the students and ask them to indicate their responses using their fingers held close to their chests. The teacher can assess the class's response in general or even individual students' specific responses just by scanning the class. For instance, after having explained the difference between phrases, dependent (subordinate) clauses, and independent (main) clauses, the teacher writes on the board the following: *which is a cold month.* Next, he asks the class to show one finger if this is a phrase, two fingers if this is a dependent clause, and three fingers if this is an independent clause. Since students cannot see how many fingers their neighbors are holding up close to their chests if they keep their eyes on the teacher, within seconds the teacher can assess whether the targeted concept is sufficiently well understood to move on or whether further explanation is needed. Informal assessment is not necessarily ungraded. The teacher may award extra credit to anyone who is able to solve a particular challenge. Sometimes, extra points are given if students make corrections in response to formative feedback on assignments or drafts. Participation might be graded if it is considered an effective discussion contribution.

Remember! Informal and formative assessment should dominate the language classroom. In fact, if there is just one takeaway from this book, we hope it will be that **the vast majority of assessments in the language classroom should be informal and formative because assessment cannot be decoupled from teaching and learning**.

Formal assessment should always be planned. Formal assessment carries with it higher stakes for the students, teacher, institution, and other stakeholders. They may be classroom assessments lasting a few minutes to several-hour-long assessments taken at an authorized test center. Analogously, formal assessments can vary in the severity of stakes they hold for the stakeholders. They may range from relatively low-stakes pre-scheduled chapter tests, through higher stakes midterm and final exams, all the way to high-stakes proficiency and certification tests. Therefore, they should not be approached lightly. During development, steps described in the chapter on test design (Chapter 3) should be followed. Predetermined steps should also be followed during the administration and evaluation of the assessment instrument.

Formal assessments do not necessarily have to be inauthentic, written tests. Rather, they can include formal authentic assessments such as oral presentations, written lab reports, multimodal **projects**, portfolios, and role plays (as in the international teaching assistant assessment, described in Chapter 2).

> **Projects** are extensive, in-depth, student-initiated, student-directed, collaborative, authentic/real-world, purposeful explorations of topics that are focused on both process and product and are presented to an audience in the target language (Alan and Stoller 2005, as cited in Beckett and Slater 2018; Debski 2006). Through projects, language learners acquire both content and language meaningfully, while developing academic and social skills (Beckett 1999; Beckett and Slater 2018). Example projects include authoring a children's book, website development, creating a YouTube video for non-specialists and research report for specialists of a scientific topic, multimodal presentations, writing music and lyrics, or interviewing travelers.

Formal assessments are almost always summative but they do not necessarily have to be. Interim measures can be both formative and formal, as are any major assessments taken in a context where no grading or other form of evaluation occurs. When formal assessments are inauthentic, they are often disruptive to the teaching-learning cycle. Thus, the prevalence of inauthentic formal assessments in the classroom should be rare. (For more information on authenticity, see elsewhere in this volume.) Admittedly, with national or state-mandated tests, this may sometimes be out of the teacher's control.

1.4.18 Direct vs. Indirect

The final dichotomous classification of assessments is direct and indirect. *Direct assessments* measure the target element through the use of language, while *indirect assessments* approximate it through another measure. For example, a written essay would assess grammar use directly, while a MC test would assess grammar use indirectly, though many would argue that what a selected-response test assesses is grammar knowledge rather than grammar use. Receptive skills (listening and reading) are measured indirectly because we cannot observe comprehension as such in the brain. Comprehension can be assessed from the inferences made from a productive skill (speaking, writing, drawing, or acting). A concern over direct testing emerges with productive skills since they are cumbersome to assess. Time, effort, and money are required to design the assessment and rating scale, to train the examiners in test administration, to train the evaluators in scoring, and to actually score. Due to this low practicality, indirect measures are sometimes used to infer proficiency in a productive skill.

Did you know? Compass ESL (Academic Success Media 2018) is a computerized placement test, consisting of three sections: listening, reading, and grammar. It is used to place non-native English speakers into college ESL classes.

The assessment of pronunciation yields an excellent example of the difference between direct and indirect modes. A direct and authentic assessment of this subskill would have the TT produce spontaneous and/or prepared language and, based on a rubric, the tester would evaluate the pronunciation aspect of the speech stream. A less authentic but still largely direct assessment would have the TT listen and repeat utterances. An indirect assessment would have the learner match written words that rhyme with each other, as in the following example. (Note that not all words will have a pair depending on regional accents.)

slay	taught
paw	grey
thought	shah

It is not irrational to conclude that knowing which words rhyme suggests knowledge of pronunciation. And short of a direct assessment of pronunciation, this might be a reasonable proxy. However, knowing *about* pronunciation and being able to pronounce words accurately are not the same. A direct assessment, whenever possible, is preferable to an indirect one.

1.4.19 Summary of Assessment Purposes and Types

In Chapter 1, we introduced some common ways to classify assessments (see Figure 1.1). It is crucial to know the purpose of an assessment before selecting or designing it because the use of assessment data is important and can have consequences. Think carefully about your beliefs about teaching and learning as you select or design assessments. Consider the issues raised in this chapter before implementing an assessment.

Think-Pair-Share 1.4.19a Analysis and Application Evaluate the assessment practices in an ESL/EFL/FL setting you are familiar with (or another if you are new to the field) by applying to it each of the key terms in this chapter. Emphasize what is and what is not in line with good language assessment practices.

a. Specifically, what types of testing, measurement, assessment, and evaluation take place in this setting? Discuss each one.
b. Which types of assessment tools are used there? Do they align with the descriptions provided in Sections 1.4.1–1.4.6? Are these assessments integrative? How do you know?
c. In the same setting, how are students assessed formatively, summatively?
d. Apply the labels assessment *of, for*, and *as* learning to this setting. Explain each example.
e. What, if any, interim measures are used there? Do final evaluations result from the recommended multiple measures?
f. Considering one of the four teachers introduced in the teacher profiles, analyze the assessments they believe in vs. actually use using the terms formal-informal and direct-indirect. Explain.

Summary Table of Assessments

Features of Assessment Types		Placement/ screener	Diagnostic	Progress	Achievement	Proficiency	Certification/ licensure
				Purposes of Assessment			
	Formative/assessment for learning	✓	✓	✓	✓		
	Summative/assessment of learning	✓			✓	✓	✓
	Assessment as learning			✓	✓		
	Development	In-house or commercial (testing agency or publisher)	In-house or commercial (publisher)	In-house or commercial (testing agency or publisher)	In-house or commercial (publisher)	Commercial (testing agency)	Commercial (testing agency)
	Administration	In-house	In-house	In-house	In-house	Commercial (testing agency) occasionally in-house	Commercial (testing agency)
	Scoring	In-house	In-house	In-house	In-house	Commercial (testing agency) occasionally in-house	Commercial (testing agency)
	Score transference among institutions	Maybe	No	No	No	Yes, if commercial No, if in-house	Yes
	Use of results	In-house	In-house	In-house	In-house	In-house, education, immigration, employment, legal, personal	Education, employment, legal
	Direct/indirect items	Both	Both	Both	Both	Both	Both
	Discrete/integrated-skills items	Both	Both	Both	Both	Both	Both
	Formal/informal	Formal	Formal	Both	Formal	Formal	Formal
	Interim measures	✓	✓	✓	✓	✓	

Figure 1.1 Summary table of assessments. *In-house* refers to assessments produced and used by the institution or teacher.

1.5 Standardized or Standards-Based

Standardized and *Standards-based*: two similar-sounding terms that need clarification. Simply put, *standardized* has undergone a process of standardization and *standards-based* is based on standards. We will now examine each term in detail.

1.5.1 Standardized

> **Standardized** assessments require "all TTs to answer the same questions, or a selection of questions from a common bank of questions, in the same way" and are "scored in a 'standard' consistent manner, which makes it possible to compare the relative performance of individual students or groups of students" (The Glossary of Education Reform 2015, para 1). Although a standardized assessment does not by definition have to be a test which has been created, administered, and scored by a high-stakes standardized testing agency, most of the time it is.

Examples of well-known standardized assessments include the following tests of English: Cambridge Placement Test (Cambridge English 2024a), CELPIP, College English Test, EIKEN, IELTS, TOEFL iBT, and WIDA Access for ELLs (WIDA 2024b). For languages other than English, the following are all standardized exams: TOAFL for Arabic, various FIAF exams for French, various Goethe Institut exams for German (2024), ELTE Origó for Hungarian, JLPT for Japanese, HSK for Mandarin Chinese, Certyfikat Polski for Polish, and Diploma of Spanish as a Foreign Language (DELE) for Spanish.

1.5.2 Standards-Based

Think-Pair-Share 1.5.2a Background Schema Activation   For this exercise, think of a setting that you know best. This may be a language school, a university, primary/secondary school, an adult education program, etc. Now imagine that there are no language classes offered at this institution but that you have been put in charge of starting and teaching a new ESL/EFL/Spanish/Korean/ etc. program in this setting. How would you know what to teach? Discuss.

Think-Pair-Share 1.5.2b Background Schema Activation   Imagine that within your country of residence, each school can set its own curriculum. A student who is attending the second year of elementary school transfers to another school in the middle of the school year. What problems for this student might stem from the lack of coordinated curriculum among schools? Discuss.

According to a study of OECD members, countries around the world approach educational standards differently. In many, there is a national curriculum set by a government agency such as a national ministry of education. Such is the situation for example in Australia, Brazil, Chile, Germany, Korea, Mexico, Norway, New Zealand, Singapore, and the United Kingdom (Pont 2013). In some other countries, while there are no mandatory national content standards, there are other models. In the United States, the Common Core State Standards have been adopted by four-fifths of all the states; nevertheless, individual state departments of education do enjoy a certain degree of autonomy (Common Core State Standards Initiative n.d.). Meanwhile, Canada's educational system is decentralized, with provinces and territories establishing their own curriculum as they deem appropriate (Councils of Ministers of Education n.d.).

Standard is a term with many meanings. According to a report by The Organization for Economic Co-operation and Development (OECD), in some contexts, it is used to mean a goal; in others, "it is used as the criteria to judge whether a particular performance can be considered appropriate" (2013, p. 14); in others the level descriptors in a particular content area are defined. Standards may even be synonymous with curriculum and learning outcomes (OECD 2013).

Learning Standards: In the United States, according to one commonly accepted definition, "learning standards are concise, written descriptions of what students are expected to know and be able to do at a specific stage of their education. Learning standards describe educational objectives—i.e. what students should have learned by the end of a course, grade level, or grade span—but they do not describe any particular teaching practice, curriculum, or assessment method" (The Glossary of Education Reform 2014, para. 1).

1.5.3 Language Standards

Apart from the national standards in various subject matters mentioned above, language-learning standards for particular settings have also been developed. In addition to the term *standards*, there are other common related terms such as *framework, benchmarks, can do statements, proficiency guidelines, models, descriptors,* etc. We will use the term "standards" to refer to them collectively.

On the following pages, we will introduce five notable language standards, which are used in a variety of countries, with various languages and age groups, and in different institutional contexts.

CEFR = Common European Framework of Reference for Languages: Learning, Teaching, Assessment

"The CEFR was developed to provide a common basis for the explicit description of objectives, content and methods in second/foreign language education" (Council of Europe 2018). The descriptors are worded as can-do statements of what the language user can do in a variety of skills at six levels of proficiency: Basic user (A1, A2), Independent user (B1, B2), and Proficient user (C1, C2). There exist CEFR scales for adult and young learners (7 and older), as well as for sign language. The CEFR is used not only in Europe but all over the world. Now most assessment organizations link their scores to the CEFR scale.

They are the CEFR, ACTFL, CLB, WIDA, and CASAS.

In addition to the so-called Global Scale, which provides general descriptions of overall language proficiency, the CEFR volume contains dozens of other scales that are specific to particular language-use situations. Figure 1.2 depicts what language users at any given proficiency level can do in overall listening comprehension. This scale is then further broken down by the specific listening situation, such as understanding conversation between other speakers (Council of Europe 2018, p. 56), listening as a member of a live audience (p. 57), listening to announcements and instructions (p. 58), and many more.

Spoken Reception

Overall Listening Comprehension

C2	Can understand with ease virtually any kind of spoken language, whether live or broadcast, delivered at fast natural speed.
C1	Can understand enough to follow extended speech on abstract and complex topics beyond his/her own field, though he/she may need to confirm occasional details, especially if the accent is unfamiliar.
	Can recognise a wide range of idiomatic expressions and colloquialisms, appreciating register shifts.
	Can follow extended speech even when it is not clearly structured and when relationships are only implied and not signaled explicitly.
B2	Can understand standard spoken language, live or broadcast, on both familiar and unfamiliar topics normally encountered in personal, social, academic or vocational life. Only extreme background noise, inadequate discourse structure and/or idiomatic usage influence the ability to understand.
	Can understand the main ideas of propositionally and linguistically complex speech on both concrete and abstract topics delivered in standard speech, including technical discussions in his/her field of specialisation.
	Can follow extended speech and complex lines of argument, provided the topic is reasonably familiar, and the direction of the talk is sign-posted by explicit markers.
B1	Can understand straightforward factual information about common everyday or job-related topics, identifying both general messages and specific details, provided speech is clearly articulated in a generally familiar accent.
	Can understand the main points of clear standard speech on familiar matters regularly encountered in work, school, leisure, etc., including short narratives.
A2	Can understand enough to be able to meet needs of a concrete type, provided speech is clearly and slowly articulated.
	Can understand phrases and expressions related to areas of most immediate priority (e.g. very basic personal and family information, shopping, local geography, employment), provided speech is clearly and slowly articulated.
A1	Can follow speech that is very slow and carefully articulated, with long pauses for him/her to assimilate meaning.
	Can recognise concrete information (e.g. places and times) on familiar topics encountered in everyday life, provided it is delivered in slow and clear speech.
Pre-A1	Can understand short, very simple questions and statements, provided that they are delivered slowly and clearly and accompanied by visuals or manual gestures to support understanding and repeated if necessary.
	Can recognise everyday, familiar words, provided they are delivered clearly and slowly in a clearly defined, familiar everyday context.
	Can recognise numbers, prices, dates and days of the week, provided they are delivered slowly and clearly in a defined, familiar everyday context.

Figure 1.2 CEFR overall listening comprehension scale. *Source:* https://tinyurl.com/spokenrubric

ACTFL = American Council on the Teaching of Foreign Languages

The ACTFL Proficiency Guidelines "describe an individual's language skills in terms of proficiency: the ability to use language to accomplish communication objectives" in terms of listening, speaking, reading, and writing. In each skill, proficiency is defined by four criteria: functions & tasks, accuracy, context & content, and text type (ACTFL 2024c).

For each of the four skills, five main levels of proficiency (distinguished, superior, advanced, intermediate, and novice) and within the last three main levels, three sublevels (high, mid, low) are identified. The Guidelines are available for learners of English as well as a variety of other languages. The ACTFL Guidelines are primarily used in the United States by teachers of world languages although, to a lesser extent, ESL programs also align themselves to this set of standards.

CLB = Canadian Language Benchmarks

"The Canadian Language Benchmarks (CLB) standard is a descriptive scale of language ability in English as a Second Language (ESL) written as 12 benchmarks or reference points along a continuum from basic to advanced. The CLB standard reflects the progression of the knowledge and skills that underlie basic, intermediate, and advanced ability among adult ESL learners" (Centre for Canadian Language Benchmarks 2012, p. V). The CLB places adult immigrants to Canada in the four skills on a proficiency scale ranging from Stage I (Basic Language Ability) to Stage III (Advanced Language Ability). Within each stage, it distinguishes four levels: CLB 1 Initial, 2 Developing, 3 Adequate, and 4 Fluent.

Before further discussion of standards and benchmarks, it is necessary to introduce a multivalent term—domain—and clarify its meanings.

Domain: This term has multiple meanings relevant to education.

In psychological sciences, *domain* refers to cognitive, affective, and psychomotor ways of learning. See, for instance, Bloom's Taxonomy of educational domains.

In WIDA (2024b), a popular US K-12 educational and assessment framework, *domain* has for decades been equivalent to *skill*.[3] For instance, listening, speaking, reading, and writing have been called language domains.

Elsewhere in assessment, *domain* refers to the setting where language is used. Examples include academic/educational, public, personal, occupational/business domains. Within academia, classroom, office hours, library, parent–teacher conference, laboratory, gym, study group, etc. are examples of domain.

---

3 The 2020 Edition of the WIDA ELD Standards Framework has moved away from the use of the term Language Domains and has instead started referring to Modes of Communication: Interpretive (Listening, Reading, and Viewing) and Expressive (Speaking, Writing, and Representing).

Think-Pair-Share 1.5.3a Reflect in writing or verbally on which meaning of *domain* you are familiar with. And what other terms do you use for the other definitions of *domain* listed here?

WIDA

"WIDA English Language Development (ELD) Standards Framework provides a foundation for curriculum, instruction and assessment for multilingual learners in kindergarten through grade 12. The ELD Standards Framework is centered on equity and fosters the assets, contributions and potential of multilingual learners" (WIDA 2024b).

The framework consists of four components, ranging from broad to narrow in scope:

- WIDA ELD Standards Statements
- Key Language Uses (KLUs)
- Language Expectations
- Proficiency Level Descriptors

These components are interrelated and form a complete picture of English language development.

The five WIDA English Language Development standards provide educators with a connection between language development and academic content. They are:

Standard 1: English language learners (ELLs) communicate for Social and Instructional purposes within the school setting

Standard 2: ELLs communicate information, ideas, and concepts necessary for academic success in the content area of Language Arts

Standard 3: ELLs communicate information, ideas, and concepts necessary for academic success in the content area of Mathematics

Standard 4: ELLs communicate information, ideas, and concepts necessary for academic success in the content area of Science

Standard 5: ELLs communicate information, ideas, and concepts necessary for academic success in the content area of Social Studies

Four Key Language Uses (KLUs) represent prominent language uses across disciplines: narrate, inform, explain, and argue. KLUs bring focus and coherence to the language of schooling, helping educators prioritize and organize curricular planning for content and language integration. KLUs represent the most prominent ways students use language as they investigate and explain phenomena, support claims with evidence, and share stories about their experiences (WIDA 2024b: ELD Standards 2020).

Language Expectations, which are written for all grade-level clusters (K, 1, 2–3, 4–5, 6–8, 9–12), point to common, visible ways students need to use language to meet grade-level academic content standards. Educators can use language expectations to set curricular priorities in order to support students in expanding what they can do with language (WIDA 2024b: ELD Standards 2020).

Proficiency Level Descriptors (PLDs) are a detailed articulation of multilingual learners' growth in interpretive and expressive language across levels of English language proficiency (WIDA 2024b: ELD Standards 2020). Written on a continuum of skill development, the PLDs describe skill development at the word/phrase, sentence, and discourse levels.

(Continued)

(Continued)

The former WIDA Standards Framework included two additional performance-related components that many educators found (and continue to find) helpful, the Can Do Descriptors and the Model Performance Indicators (WIDA 2024b: ELD Standards 2012). The **Can Do Descriptors** are aligned to the WIDA Performance Definitions and further describe the skills the students should be able to do with mastery in each of the domains of language and across the levels of the WIDA Performance Definitions. Both EL and general education teachers use the Can Do Statements to set realistic learning targets for students. WIDA **Model Performance Indicators (MPI)** (see Figure 1.3) have three components: (1) language verb, (2) content stem, and (3) language support/scaffold. The "content stem" component of the MPI is generally taken from a content area standard (e.g. Next Generation Science, CCSS [Common Core State Standards] ELA, Mathematics). MPIs are situated within a content area task and the task is differentiated across the WIDA Performance Definitions and suggested scaffolds are provided for each level. WIDA provides only a sampling of MPIs for each grade span and content area. High-quality examples of MPIs written for mathematics content, 3rd grade through Algebra II, can be found in the Oakland Schools ATLAS mathematics curriculum units in each unit in the resources section in documents titled "Language Supports for Mathematics."

Think-Pair-Share 1.5.3b Application

a. Familiarize yourself with the 2020 edition of the WIDA Framework (WIDA 2024b: ELD Standards 2020). Read Section 2 (starting on p. 21) to a) understand and b) explain to a colleague how the document accomplishes the following goal: "The WIDA ELD Standards Framework is like a map in that it offers language expectations as destination points, as well as road signs to set goals for curriculum, instruction, and assessment for multilingual learners" (p. 23).

b. Next, read Section 3 (starting on p. 37); select a grade level (for example Kindergarten) and an annotated language sample (such as the WIDA ELD Standard 2 Language for Language Arts "Narrate" on p. 55); analyze the annotated language sample (p. 55); analyze the corresponding components (p. 48). Help a colleague understand your specific example.

c. Using the writing sample of a language learner you know, employ the Grade-Level Cluster Materials in Section 3 for its analysis. Explain your analysis to a colleague.

Figure 1.3 depicts what Model Performance Indicators (MPIs) might look like if created by a classroom teacher, based on WIDA. This is an integrated strand broken down into components. In the domain of Listening, a student at Level 2 Emerging proficiency is able to do the following. Note that the various font styles in the first row refer to the respective font style in the MPI sentence.

Language function	Content stem	Support/Scaffold
Categorize information on *the stages of the life cycle of the butterfly from video, interactive presentations, and guest speakers* <u>using graphic organizers</u>.		

Figure 1.3 MPI deconstructed.

WIDA's 2012 Amplification of the ELD Standards for Kindergarten-Grade 12 visually depicts numerous Model Performance Indicator (MPI) integrated strands. For one example, see p. 19. The column headers are the five proficiency levels, the row headers are the four skills/domains, and the content-area context where students might use such language is on green architecture, which is one of the topics within the content standards.

Think-Pair-Share 1.5.3c Application

a. Look at Figure 1.3 and p. 19 of the WIDA 2012 Amplification of The English Language Development Standards (WIDA 2023). Locate the MPI for the Level 2 Emerging student in Listening. Identify the three components within the sentence: (1) the verb denoting the language function (i.e. categorize); (2) the part of the MPI that describes the content (i.e. components of green architectural plans from video, interactive presentations, and guest speaker); and (3) the support that helps the learner achieve the objective (i.e. using graphic organizers). Make a note of the Example Context for Language Use, the Cognitive Function, and the Topic-Related Language. Note that all students, regardless of language proficiency, will achieve the same content objectives (i.e. relating to components of green architectural plans from video, interactive presentations, and guest speakers); what scaffolds the students receive are contained in the verb and support.

b. In the 2012 Amplification of The English Language Development Standards (WIDA 2012), select a (horizontal) strand of MPI. Analyze how "language may look as a progression from one level of language proficiency to the next" (p. 10). Explain this progression through proficiency levels to a colleague.

c. Set up a scenario by thinking of a specific language learner (age, class, language proficiency) within a specific content-area class (e.g. mathematics). From the relevant content standards, select a content objective for a specific lesson. Identify the cognitive function needed to meet this objective (e.g. "to analyze"). Write your own MPI for the appropriate language expectation, given the scenario you have designed. With a colleague, analyze each other's MPIs whether the three components (verb, content stem, language support/scaffold) are present and appropriate.

CASAS = Comprehensive Adult Student Assessment Systems

The English-as-a-Second-Language Model Standards for Adult Education Programs "describes general standards, defines language proficiency levels, and identifies possible tests for measuring language proficiency. The language proficiency levels are sequenced from ESL beginning literacy through advanced-high" (California Department of Education 1992, p. V.). The CASAS standards are used in adult basic education, specifically by government agencies, businesses, community colleges, literacy organizations, and correctional facilities in the United States, Singapore, and El Salvador.

Figure 1.4 depicts an example chart from a legible version of the original CASAS model standards document (CASAS 1992, p. 8, ESL Model Standards Key). The columns contain beginning proficiency divided into adult ELs with low literacy skills and literate adults with low and high English proficiency. The higher proficiency levels are not depicted in this figure. The horizontal row headings not only show the four skills but also language proficiency in a general and work setting as well as the learner's comprehensibility to English speakers.

Appendix A: Levels of Language Proficiency

Proficiency	ESL Beginning Literacy	ESL Beginning	
		Low	*High*
General	Possess limited or no oral proficiency in English Cannot read or write in English May not read or write in primary language	Unable to function unassisted	Possess limited functioning related to immediate needs
Work	Unable to function unassisted in any situation requiring reading or writing in English	Can handle routine tasks that are easily demonstrated	Can handle routine tasks that involve basic oral communication skills
Listening	Unable to understand conversation in English	Can comprehend isolated words and phrases	Can comprehend range of high-frequency words used in context
Speaking	Depend on gestures or primary language to communicate	Depend on gestures, a few English words, and primary language to communicate	Communicate survival needs using learned phrases and sentences
Reading	Unable to read English	Recognize letters and numbers	Get limited meaning from print with successive rereading and checking
Writing	Unable to write any English other than own names and addresses	May be able to write own names and addresses	Copy words and phrases and write sentences based on previously learned materials
Comprehensibility To English speakers used to dealing with nonnative speakers To English speakers not used to dealing with nonnative speakers	Unable to make selves understood	Not able to make selves understood	Make basic needs understood when context supports interaction

Figure 1.4 CASAS proficiency levels. *Source:* https://tinyurl.com/casaslevels

1.5.4 A Word About Assessment in Content and Language Integrated Learning (CLIL)

Many of the aforementioned standards/frameworks/benchmarks (CEFR, ACTFL, CLB, CASAS) focus either entirely or primarily on language. However, increasingly content is taught alongside language. This happens not only in native-language contexts but also internationally, where learners are taught academic content in a foreign language. Content and Language Integrated Learning (CLIL) can be defined as "the teaching of any non-language-subject through the medium of a language which is not the mother tongue" (Quartapelle and Schameitat 2012, p. 29).

Integrating language and content is common practice in ESL/EFL instruction, whether in an intensive ESL skills course or an immersion course, or to be more inclusive of ELs in a mainstream course. With a few exceptions (e.g. math equations, limited picture tasks), some level of language proficiency is required in order to demonstrate content knowledge. The question is, should teachers assess language and content together or separately? Indeed, should they assess language with content at all? There is no one-size-fits-all answer because CLIL models can range on a continuum between language-driven and content-driven foci (Snow 2001). In some European contexts, the target language may not be the language of instruction, and the focus of CLIL tends to be more on content than on language (Coyle et al. 2010). In other contexts, the focus is evenly split between content and language. In immersion programs, the focus is more on content, while sheltered or pull-out programs are more language focused. To this end, the decision of how to assess CLIL **tasks** varies.

> A classroom **task** can be defined as "an activity that: (1) is goal-oriented, (2) is content-focused, (3) has a real outcome, and (4) reflects real-life language use and language need" (Shehadeh 2018).

Other factors also influence decisions about content and language assessment, such as the age and proficiency level of the learners, the purpose and nature of the task, as well as types of errors. For example, for teachers to accurately assess performance, they need to determine whether an inaccurate response or weak performance is a result of a language barrier, or a lack of content knowledge. A relevant concept to consider is Cummins' (1979) theory of BICS and CALP (Basic Interpersonal Communicative Skills and Cognitive Academic Language Proficiency) because a learner's strong proficiency in everyday communication skills may hide weaker skills in academic communication. Mistakenly penalizing a learner for a content error, when the real issue is one of language, makes that assessment invalid and unfair. From a European perspective, Coyle et al. (2010) suggest that CLIL teachers avoid giving formative feedback on language every time content is assessed because this can undermine the learners' confidence in their content knowledge and application. Instead, they advocate "language clinics" within a class lesson to address frequent errors observed by the teacher over a period of time.

Barbero (2012) presents a three-tiered framework for formatively assessing language and content. The framework integrates concept knowledge, thinking skills, CALP functions (e.g. classifying, summarizing, explaining, organizing), and vocabulary and language structures. The author stresses that formative assessment must align with learning objectives and feedback must be provided to learners. As such, the framework can be useful for determining progress and ways forward, as well as the basis for more formal rubrics for authentic assessments. This is reminiscent of the LOR assessment discussed earlier in this chapter.

In summary, language instruction can and should be integrated with relevant content, but due to the highly contextualized purposes and approaches used, teachers need to use their professional judgment to determine how and when to assess them.

1.5.5 Summary of Language Standards

Language learning standards are created by teams of language experts to inform all stakeholders of what learners can and cannot do with the language at any given proficiency level. Standards inform curriculum developers, teachers, assessment experts, lawmakers, and even learners themselves. Linking curricula, lessons, assessments, policies, etc. to the same set of standards promotes consistency in outcomes across time and space.

Think-Pair-Share 1.5.5 Analysis Compare–contrast the terms *standardized* and *standards-based assessment*. Is the curriculum in a language program known to you based on standards? Which ones? Are the assessments utilized in that same language program standardized? How do you know? Discuss.

1.6 Chapter Conclusion

This chapter started with a diagnostic test to assess your current understanding of language assessment, providing insights for your learning journey. We covered fundamental assessment concepts such as testing, measurement, evaluation, and various assessment types, emphasizing frequent low- or no-stakes assessments. We distinguished between standardized tests and language standards, frameworks, and benchmarks. The chapter concluded with an overview of content and language assessment. To reinforce your learning, complete the achievement quiz and engage in Think-Pair-Share exercises throughout the chapter. These activities build a strong foundation for further exploration in language assessment.

Appendix 1 – Achievement Quiz of Chapter 1

(For discussion or writing prompts, see the Think-Pair-Share tasks in this chapter.)

Directions: Select the response that best answers each question below. Each question is worth 1 point.

1. All students who are new to your school have to take a test to see which language class (Levels 1–6) they should enroll in. This is a(n) _____ test because it _____.
   a. certification ... certifies what the students know at each level
   b. diagnostic ... diagnoses what the students need to learn at each level
   c. achievement ... contains many items at one level of difficulty
   d. placement ... contains a few items at each level of difficulty

2. Which of the following is a key reason for using multiple measures when assessing language proficiency?
   a. to reduce the assessment workload for teachers at the end of the year
   b. to build students' endurance, such as toward a single, comprehensive test
   c. to account for variations, such as bad days, learning styles, and familiarity with topics
   d. to emphasize the importance of individual assessments over group assessments

3. The vast majority of language assessments should be _____.
   a. summative
   b. formative
   c. achievement
   d. indirect

4. Which of the following best describes the role of language standards (including frameworks, benchmarks)?
   a. They primarily focus on content in language education.
   b. They serve as prescriptive rules for language assessment.
   c. They provide a structure for lesson planning and assessment.
   d. They function as a descriptive scale of language ability.

5. True (T) or False (F): In second-language and CLIL settings, it is important for teachers to know whether they are assessing content, language, or both simultaneously.

2

Qualities of Test Usefulness and the Assessment Use Argument

Chapter Overview

This chapter explores the qualities of effective assessment based on Bachman and Palmer (1996, 2010) and Bachman and Damböck (2018). It discusses essential attributes such as validity, reliability, practicality, authenticity, washback, and interactiveness. While some qualities can be measured directly, others require estimation. The primary focus is on maximizing validity and reliability, which are crucial for assessment credibility. The Assessment Use Argument (AUA) framework guides the development of context-specific assessments and offers a structured approach to justify assessments to stakeholders convincingly.

2.1 Learning Objectives

1. Define the six qualities of test usefulness
2. Demonstrate how the six qualities can be applied to two different language assessments
3. Propose a change to one assessment you are familiar with to maximize the six qualities
4. State the rationale for the AUA
5. Describe the steps involved in making an AUA

2.2 Qualities of Test Usefulness

Effective language tests have six desirable characteristics, referred to as qualities of test usefulness: you can remember them from the mnemonic *VIP WAR*:

Validity (see Sections 2.2.1–2.2.7)

Interactiveness (see Sections 2.2.18 and 2.2.19)

Practicality (see Sections 2.2.14 and 2.2.15)

positive **W**ashback (see Section 2.2.17)

Authenticity (see Section 2.2.16)

Reliability (see Sections 2.2.8–2.2.13)

Let us consider them one at a time, although not quite in this order.

A Practical Guide to Language Assessment: How Do You Know That Your Students Are Learning? First Edition.
Ildiko Porter-Szucs et al.
© 2025 John Wiley & Sons, Inc. Published 2025 by John Wiley & Sons, Inc.

2.2.1 Validity

Think-Pair-Share 2.2.1 Activating Background Schema   What does it mean when someone exclaims, "That's a valid point (or question)"? Or what do we criticize when we say, "That's not a valid reason"? And what may be true of an assessment tool when it has validity?

> **Validity** is the extent to which a test measures what it claims to measure.

Valid points, questions, and reasons, according to the Merriam-Webster dictionary, are "well-grounded, justifiable, logically correct" (2024). In terms of assessment, validity is more complex. A *valid assessment*, a question of degrees rather than absolutes, is an assessment whose quality users can have confidence in. This confidence can only be gained after careful evaluation from various dimensions: What is the purpose of the test? What domain and skills are tested? Who wrote the test and for whom? Is the test appropriate for the context it is used for? How will the results of the test be interpreted and used? etc. In other words, the claim that a test is valid should be accompanied by further explanation: for example, valid with this age group and in this setting.

It is helpful to distinguish different types of validity:

1. content
2. construct
3. criterion-related: concurrent and predictive
4. face
5. consequential

2.2.2 Content Validity

> **Content validity** refers to the extent to which the content of the assessment reflects the content of the course, domain, and general use of the target language.

Recall from Chapter 1 our high-beginner imaginary students at the *School of World Languages*. They have just completed a unit on the Simple Past tense. An end-of-unit assessment with content validity would sample the real-life use of the Simple Past at the high-beginner level, as taught in the course. Therefore, it would include the most frequent verbs (rather than most obscure ones), both regular and irregular verbs, in affirmative and interrogative, and in questions and statements, which were all taught in class. There would probably be ample examples of *BE, GET*, and *HAVE* due to their frequency in everyday use. Such a sample of the content would likely have high content validity. However, if there were an overabundance of *LIE* vs. *LAY* that would be an example of low content validity because while these oft-confused verbs may be a favorite of teachers and testers, their relative infrequency in everyday use does not warrant special representation on the assessment. Thus, for content validity, either "teaching to the test" may be necessary or testing what has been taught.

2.2.3 Construct Validity

> **Construct** is the characteristic you are attempting to measure. When assessing the learner's grammar through a grammar item, then *grammar* is the construct. When measuring writing proficiency, then *writing* is the construct. Chapelle (1999) defines *construct* as "the learner's underlying competence" (p. 32).

Construct validity refers to the extent to which scores on an assessment instrument indicate underlying language ability (Cohen 1994). Evidence for construct validity can be provided only through research. It is not possible to make construct-validity judgments by simply looking at the assessment or developing a "feel" for it. Let us examine a business Japanese-speaking test's construct validity argument. The construct of speaking in this situation shall be defined as *expressing oneself fluently, coherently, with unambiguous grammar and vocabulary, and with clear pronunciation in business negotiation over price.* A construct validation study would need to show to what extent each of the pieces of the construct (i.e. fluency, coherence, unambiguous grammar, unambiguous vocabulary, clear pronunciation, while negotiating price) impact the TT's score. The desirable outcome would show that stronger performance in the aforementioned areas would correlate with a higher score. An undesirable outcome would show no such (or inverse) correlation but instead a correlation, for example, between the gender, nationality, and creativity of the TT. The latter factors are not what the test claims to assess; therefore, research should show that they have no effect on the TT's score.

2.2.4 Criterion-related Validity

> **Criterion-related validity** measures the positive correlation between the TT's score in a skill on a well-established assessment against a new assessment tool.

This validity argument becomes important when the introduction of a new assessment instrument is being considered. For instance, the language department at a college is considering replacing the current placement test with a new one. In order to assess the criterion-related validity of the new assessment, the language team decides to conduct a study in which the old test serves as the external criterion against which the new test's validity is measured. All current students are invited to take the current placement test as well as the newly proposed placement test back to back. In order to lessen the effect of sequencing, half of the volunteers are randomized to take the old test first and the new test second, while the other half the other way around. The expectation is that students who score high on one test would score high on the other in each of the skill areas (listening, speaking, reading, writing, grammar, vocabulary) and vice versa: students who score low on one do so on the other. Where such a positive correlation (high-high, low-low) exists, the argument can be made that there is criterion-related validity. This example demonstrates the **concurrent** type of **validity** because the two assessment instruments are taken concurrently. Another type of criterion-related validity measure is used to predict the TT's performance in a future situation. An assessment instrument has **predictive validity** if it positively correlates between the TT's score on one assessment and the TT's performance in a future situation. Most commonly, the future situation is grades in college (grade point average [GPA]).

Did you know? High-stakes standardized assessments required for college admission worldwide continue to rely on their predictive validity. Their proponents argue that such tests can predict the TTs' success (as measured by their GPA) once admitted to college. One study on the predictive validity of the TOEFL iBT showed a general pattern that students with higher test scores tended to earn higher grades in college although according to the authors, the "predictive validity expressed in terms of correlation did not appear to be strong" (Cho and Bridgeman 2012). Another study on the predictive validity of the IELTS on first-year grades at an English Medium University in the United Arab Emirates was found to be a "meaningful predictor," whereby a higher IELTS score was positively correlated with a higher GPA in the first year

(Schoepp 2018). Concerns over the predictive validity of other high-stakes standardized tests have also been raised for years. For example, challenges made to the claim that ETS's Graduate Record Exam (GRE) is able to predict success in graduate school are numerous though the exact nature and severity of the arguments vary (see Clayton 2016; Fair Test 2007; Klieger et al. 2018; Moneta-Koehler et al. 2017).

Think-Pair-Share 2.2.4 Analysis and Application   On your own, conduct an online search of any published predictive-validity studies conducted on assessment instruments you are aware of. Share your findings. Discuss what they mean for the use of these instruments for the purposes that they are used.

2.2.5   Face Validity

> **Face validity** is whether the assessment appears to measure what it claims to measure.

"What does this have to do with anything?"—This exasperation gets to the heart of face validity. A test that has face validity physically looks the way it is supposed to, so nobody will ask what this test has to do with the construct it claims to assess; it is clear at first glance that the test does what it claims to do. Thus, a multiple-choice test of vocabulary looks like it assesses vocabulary, so on the face of it, that is what it assesses.

For instance, the Versant English Test, a computer-delivered and scored test frequently used to assess the spoken English of call center employees, contains a task called Sentence Builds. The TT hears three phrases in scrambled order and has to rearrange them into a complete sentence without writing them down. The TT hears:

<< *to their leader / listened carefully / the young men* >>

Then immediately, the TT is expected to say: *The young men listened carefully to their leader.*

The face validity of the Sentence-Build item type can reasonably be called into question. On the face of it, unscrambling decontextualized sentences in one's mind appears to have little to do with speaking and listening proficiency. From Versant's own validity summary, however, this item type measures the TT's "syntax and pragmatics" (Pearson 2022, p. 6). "The Sentence Builds task involves constructing and articulating sentences. As such, it is a measure of candidates' mastery of sentences, in addition to their pronunciation and fluency" (p. 7).

Face validity is simultaneously the most and least important type of validity. To the casual observer, if the test looks the way it is supposed to, then no other validity matters, and vice versa: if the test does not look the way it is supposed to, then it matters little that other types of validity may be strong. Thus, face validity increases TTs' and other test users' support for and acceptance of the assessment as legitimate and is important to consider. But as the above examples demonstrate, there is more to a test or technique than meets the eye.

2.2.6   Consequential Validity

> **Consequential validity** concerns all the consequences of the use of an assessment, such as "its accuracy in measuring intended criteria, its impact on the preparation of TTs, its effect on the learner, and the (intended and unintended) social consequences of a test's interpretation and use" (Brown and Abeywickrama 2010, p. 34).

Consequential validity is akin to the concept of test **impact**. And it encompasses the narrower concept of **washback** (or **backwash**), which will be discussed later in this chapter.

Assessments have consequences. Students usually study for and teachers often teach to the test; in other words, teachers teach (at times exclusively) the material or constructs needed for tests; therefore, assessments often drive classroom instruction. Assessments, especially high-stakes ones, even drive the curriculum. The most obvious examples are test-prep courses for various language proficiency tests: for English, Certificate of Advanced English (CAE), EIKEN, functional capacity evaluation (FCE), Origó, TOEFL; for French, Diploma in Advanced French Language (DALF); for German, Goethe-Zertifikat; for Spanish, DELE and International Spanish Language Evaluation Service (SIELE); for Chinese, Hanyu Shuiping Kaoshi (HSK); for dozens of world languages, ACTFL OPI; etc. Teachers' job security may depend on their students' results on tests. Results of national examinations, e.g. Singapore's Primary School Leaving Examination (PSLE), can determine students' educational paths, such as streaming and secondary-school accessibility. Other assessment results, such as those from A-level examinations in the United Kingdom and Singapore, and China's Gaokao (Chen 2018) determine eligibility for higher education. In some US states, results of student performance on required third grade reading assessments determine whether a student must be retained, i.e. to repeat third grade. School rankings are created to a great extent based on test results: in Poland based on the Matura secondary-school exit exam and in Germany based on the Abitur. In turn, the rankings can affect school funding, staffing, resources, enrollments, school and individuals' reputation, and more. There are also societal consequences of assessments. For instance, governments and departments of education worldwide await with great anticipation results of the Programme for International Student Assessment (PISA), which "tests 15-year-old students from all over the world in reading, mathematics and science" every 3 years (OECD n.d.). These data are then used to form educational policy.

2.2.7 Summary of Validity

In summary, validity refers to the inferences drawn about the instrument, it depends on many types of evidence, and it is specific to a particular use. Thus, no argument should be made that a particular assessment instrument is *valid. period. no further qualification needed*. Rather, evidence (content-, construct-, criterion-, consequences-related) should be collected, from which validity can be inferred. What we can then say is that a particular assessment instrument has a fairly high (or low or moderate) construct validity, etc. For more discussion on validity, please see Chapter 14.

Think-Pair-Share 2.2.7a Analysis and Application Revisit the distinction between direct and indirect testing introduced in Chapter 1. What implications for the four aspects of validity (content, construct, consequential, and face) may direct vs. indirect assessments have? Demonstrate through a concrete example of each.

2.2.8 Reliability

Think-Pair-Share 2.2.8a Activating Background Schema Do you know someone who is reliable? Unreliable? What qualities make them so? How do these qualities apply to an assessment tool?

> **Reliability** is when the test score is consistent, repeatable over time, and free from inconsistent fluctuations.

The Merriam-Webster Dictionary defines reliable as "dependable" (2024). The same can be said for assessments. When test results are reliable, they are dependable; they are repeatable over time; they do not fluctuate significantly.

We distinguish different types of reliability:

- rater reliability
- learner-related reliability
- instrument-related reliability

2.2.9 Rater Reliability (Scorer or Assessor Reliability)

> **Rater reliability**: in constructed-response assessments (for definition, see elsewhere in this volume), the score should remain consistent regardless of who rates the same performance and when.

Achieving reliability in assigning scores (ratings, grades, marks) stems from thorough rater training. The following example of rater reliability will come from our personal experiences as teacher-examiners. At predetermined times in the school year, language teachers at our respective institutions are called upon to rate so-called written exit exams (proficiency assessments taken by students in writing classes to qualify for the next level). All teachers gather to assign scores to each piece of writing using a rating rubric. In order to score reliably, the raters first engage in a **norming** exercise. Once the norming session has resulted in satisfactory scoring, each piece of writing is scored by two teachers. This way, the students can rest assured that it will not matter which two teachers read and rate their essays; the scores will be consistent. The reliability between the raters (**inter-rater reliability**) will be high. In other words, the raters will, optimally, be in close agreement with each other. Typically, when there is disagreement between any two raters of an assessment (weak inter-rater reliability), a third trained rater serves as the tiebreaker.

> **Norming (aka calibration)** is the process of achieving reliability among raters of constructed responses (written or oral production of language). It consists of four stages: (0) **rating-scale analysis** (raters familiarize themselves with the evaluation criteria and the rating scale; (1) **benchmarking** (every rater discusses the same examples of target performance—at each level of the rating scale—in order to understand how to apply the descriptors of the rating scale to the specific examples of learner work); (2) **calibration** (raters individually rate some prescored papers without knowing the previously assigned score; this is then followed by a reveal of the previously assigned score and a discussion); and (3) **qualification** (a test of rating accuracy: this a repetition of the calibration stage with higher stakes; raters who pass are allowed to score constructed-response assessments while those who do not, may get a second chance to pass the qualification stage).

Whenever there are multiple raters using a rubric, it is necessary to norm them to achieve reliability in their rating. Without it, raters would be likely to interpret the rating rubric differently, effecting different scores. Then the scores would not be consistent but would rather depend on which rater produced them. In a school context, norming helps to avoid the problem of one teacher gaining a reputation of being a "hard marker, or grader," while another teaching the same course becomes known as an "easy marker, or grader."

Another type of rater reliability is **intra-rater reliability**. Here, the internal consistency of one rater's scores is concerned. The descriptors of the rating scale, or rubric, should be applied to the learner's work consistently, regardless of when the rating occurs. It should not matter whether the rating takes place on a Friday morning or a Tuesday afternoon or whether it is the second paper scored or the fortieth after fatigue has set in. The same (written or oral) language sample produced by the learner should receive the same score from the same rater. In other words, the rater should be in (near) perfect agreement with him-/herself.

A classroom teacher can conduct such an intra-rater reliability experiment in the following way. Grade (without commenting) a pile of (15–20) student writing samples using the rating rubric. Write the grades on a separate sheet of paper. Shuffle the papers and put them away for 3–4 weeks. Repeat the grading process and compare the second set of grades to the first set. Examine any discrepancies. The goal is to reach a perfect agreement with oneself. In order to prevent low intra-rater reliability when scoring a large number of student performances, coffee breaks help, as does note-taking of how unexpected errors were dealt with in case they reappear. Chances are that despite your best efforts, you will not be able to reach a perfect agreement or intra-rater reliability. It is normal to become uncalibrated due to forgetfulness, influence of particularly strong or weak performances, and other factors. Therefore, even when there is just one rater (such as the classroom teacher), the teacher should conduct a brief norming session before reaching for a stack of student papers or presentation videos. The rater should at least refamiliarize themselves with the benchmark performances and only then begin rating new pieces of student work. Without this step, the rater may one day assign an essay one score and a week later a different score, which again would introduce inconsistent fluctuations into the scoring.

In addition to the aforementioned norming, other strategies to maintain rater reliability are also common. These include marking one question at a time on every paper (rather than the whole paper for each student), making notes while marking on how a particular response or use of language was assessed in case it occurs again in another paper, flagging similar problem areas and sorting the papers so they can be marked together, etc. The notes can be helpful for subsequent cohorts or for the design of future assessments.

Naturally, rater-reliability concerns arise only with assessment tasks requiring raters, i.e. constructed response. This is not a concern with selected-response items with an answer key, such as multiple-choice, true/false, matching, blank fill, etc. For information on bias (such as rater bias due to gender, first language [L1], ethnicity, familiarity with L1, handwriting, etc.), see Chapters 3, 8, 12, and 13.

2.2.10 Learner-related Reliability (Person-, Test-taker-, Student-, Situational)

> **Learner-related reliability**: in constructed-response assessments (for definition, see elsewhere in this volume), the score should remain consistent regardless of factors related to the learner (or TT) other than proficiency in the language skills being measured.

Just as examiners fail to produce internal consistency all the time, so do students (or TTs). One reason may be factors that can be summarized as the *good-day effect*. Health, sleep, hunger, nutrition, thirst, fatigue, anxiety, self-confidence, amount of preparation done, comfort with the examiner, etc. may all influence whether the TT is having a good day, which may influence their success on the assessment. Such physical and situational factors may be influenced but never entirely controlled.

Students' familiarity with the assessment format may also impact their results. For example, if students do not understand that wrong answers on some MC tests are penalized, they may guess some answers and receive a lower-than-normal score. Furthermore, if one day a TT is given an assessment that is long enough where they cannot remember all their answers and the next day asked to retake it, it is very likely that their answers will differ from day to day.

Learners' language production may also vary considerably depending on how it is being assessed. If they have traditionally taken selected-response examinations and arrive to a new class that requires performance assessments, the students' results may be inconsistent. Learners may produce language of varying quality if the speech is rehearsed or not, monologic or dialogic, requiring short or long production, on a personal or professional/academic topic, on a familiar or unfamiliar topic, etc.

Our own research on 100 language TTs investigated whether the mode of delivery of a speaking test produced different scores depending on whether it was direct (face-to-face) or indirect (audio-delivered) (Porter-Szucs et al. 2016). Our findings indicated that there was no statistically significant difference in our adult TTs' scores depending on the mode of delivery. These findings do not mean though that with a different population of TTs (for example, children) or under different circumstances the mode may not influence learner-related reliability.

2.2.11 Instrument-related Reliability (Test Factor)

> **Instrument-related reliability** exists when the test score is consistent, repeatable over time, and free from inconsistent fluctuations due to the assessment instrument and its administration.

The assessment instrument and its administration are yet another factor that needs to be controlled in order to maximize the reliability of the scores. Examples include controlling the environment (e.g. room temperature, noise, seating arrangement), the clarity of testing procedures and instructions; keeping the mode and format consistent; and including multiple measures. One example is if a recorded text is played during a dictation in one class, but then the audio player breaks, and in the next class, the teacher reads the text during the dictation; in such cases, the results may be inconsistent. Another example is if one speaking test is dialogic while another is monologic, then we cannot expect consistent results. Finally, students' language proficiency might be rated differently depending on the instrument used to measure it, such as a multiple-choice test, a written/oral proficiency test, or a task-based/performance-based test. Each instrument can only assess an aspect of the learner's language ability, and thus, depending on the instrument, the information gained about the learner may fluctuate. Consequently, while some fluctuation in scores is to be expected and it is impossible to eliminate inconsistencies related to the assessment instrument, steps can be taken to reduce them.

2.2.12 Summary of Reliability

The reliability of an assessment tool concerns the consistency of the scores it yields. Low reliability can occur due to the instrument, the learner, and the rater. Therefore, measures must be taken to reduce the chances of fluctuations in scores for any reason.

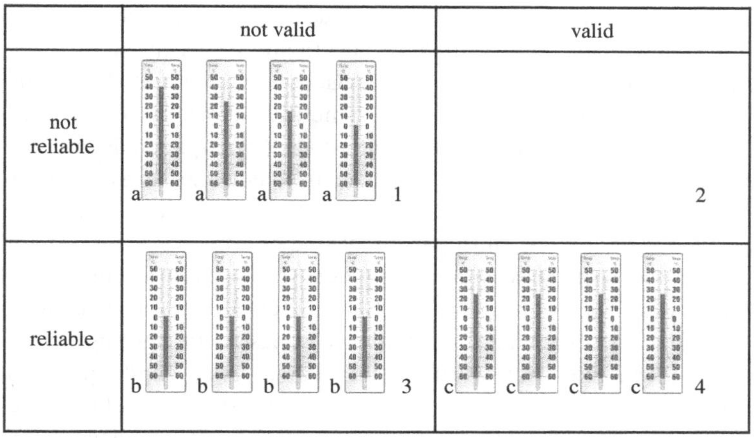

Figure 2.1 Validity vs. reliability. *Source:* Unknown author / Pixabay

2.2.13 Validity vs. Reliability

The concepts of validity and reliability are commonly confused. To illustrate the distinction, refer to Figure 2.1. Picture a scenario where the temperature in your vicinity remains constant for half an hour. You have three thermometers (*a, b, c*), but you are uncertain whether any of them are both accurate and reliable. In an experiment, you take each thermometer, reset it, and measure the temperature repeatedly in quick succession. In Quadrant 1, you observe that when you repeatedly measure the temperature with thermometer *a*, the readings are inconsistent, ranging from a high of 40°C to a low of 0°C. Consequently, you label the result as unreliable, and therefore, inaccurate, or invalid. Thermometer *b* consistently shows 0°C each time (see Quadrant 3), indicating reliability. Thermometer *c* consistently reads 25°C (see Quadrant 4), suggesting reliability as well. To establish whether *b* or *c* is also accurate, an external measure is necessary—something known to be accurate, like the weather service for the area. In this case, thermometer *c* in Quadrant 4 is found to be both reliable and accurate in measuring the temperature. Thermometer *b* in Quadrant 3 is reliable but not valid since it consistently displays the wrong temperature. Since there is no thermometer that is unreliable yet valid when conditions remain constant, Quadrant 2 remains empty.

Applying the above analogy to a language assessment instrument, such as a test, if all conditions remain constant, the test should consistently and accurately assess the knowledge of the same group of learners, demonstrating a high degree of reliability and validity, as in Quadrant 4. However, there is no validity without reliability (see Quadrant 2). Consequently, reliability is often viewed as a component of validity rather than a distinct quality.

2.2.14 Practicality

Think-Pair-Share 2.2.12a Activating Background Schema Think of language assessments that are impractical. What qualities make them so? Now think of some that are practical. Why is that so? Discuss.

Practicality equals "available resources minus required resources" (Bachman and Palmer 2010, p. 262). It comprises the money, time, personnel, and effort required for the construction, administration, and evaluation of assessment.

The exercise of imagining a practical assessment for the overworked language teacher may conjure up images of something ready-made that the students take themselves without the teacher's involvement and that provides valid and reliable scores with just the right amount of constructive feedback for the students. This description may translate into a multiple-choice or computerized test. And until the remaining qualities of test usefulness are introduced, multiple-choice or computerized assessment is the panacea for the overworked teacher's problems. Let us examine the components of practicality in detail though. Practicality means that the required resources do not exceed the available resources in terms of money, time, personnel, and effort.

Money: Creating an assessment tool costs money. Designing the test (especially a standardized one) and writing the items have a price tag. Revising, pilot testing, and publishing the assessment cost money. So does administering the assessment. The facilities (e.g. classroom, lighting, soundproofing device such as room dividers, and a quiet heating and cooling system) and equipment (e.g. computers, noise-canceling headphones, software, pen, and paper) cost money. The salaries of the teacher, examiner, invigilator, clerk, etc. have to be paid. Evaluation costs money as well. This may only include the teacher's salary if the teacher provides instantaneous feedback to the students during formative assessment. But other expenses may incur if the scoring and commenting take place at a later time. In the case of high-stakes assessment, score reports and certificates are issued at an additional cost.

Time: This is a resource many classroom teachers around the world have lacked for decades. Yet many aspects of assessment take time. Commercially designed assessments save teachers' valuable time but must be evaluated carefully. Teachers and/or examiners have to be trained in administering the assessment, which also takes time. Further considerations include scheduling time, dates, and durations for the assessments (e.g. exam periods must work around instructional schedules and availability of resources and examiners). Also, individual oral presentations in a class take an enormous amount of time away from instruction compared to a written essay that all students sit at the same time. The higher the stakes of the assessment, the more in-class time is spent preparing the students for the test. Depending on who evaluates the assessment, scoring and the provision of feedback may take time as well. In fact, who has not spent evenings and weekends hunched over a pile of papers?

Personnel: Assessment requires personnel. Each stage of the process (from conception, design, creation, coding, administration, analysis, management, to marketing) requires people with expertise. These experts must be recruited, trained, and managed so they are available when and where they are needed. Technology is displacing people to some extent and increasing practicality, but we are still a long way from being able to disregard practicality.

Effort: Assessment requires effort. Each of the aforementioned steps (design and/or selection of assessment, preparation of students, administration of assessment, scoring, etc.) requires the effort of teachers, staff, and students. Ongoing, formative, in-class assessment in particular requires additional effort from the teacher, in that they have to assess on an ongoing basis the extent to which each student is meeting the daily learning objectives. Even online assessment resources require effort from the teacher, who has to stay abreast of the ever-expanding list of e-resources. Be it Quizlet or WriteReader, new apps and websites pop up daily. Language teachers invest effort to seek them out, learn to use them, set them up for the latest assignments, administer assessments, and score them. Then again, summative assessments also require effort. Determining assessment specifications, strategically selecting what content to cover in a limited time, and creating an adequate number of items to maximize validity are important. For example, while multiple-choice items are very practical to mark, creating effective items requires enormous effort.

2.2.15 Summary of Practicality

In summary, assessment tasks with high practicality include self-assessment and peer-assessment checklists, multiple-choice and other selected-response tests developed by a third party, computerized assessment where computers are ubiquitous, and informal, so-called *on-the-run* formative assessment in the classroom. Assessments with low practicality include human-graded essays, oral presentations, selected-response tests developed by the teacher, and assessment where technology is lacking. An assessment's practicality hinges on numerous factors that begin well before the learner ever sees the assessment and that end long after. Yet an assessment that has high validity and reliability and low practicality will frequently meet with resistance from stakeholders.

Think-Pair-Share 2.2.15 Analysis and Synthesis   Analyze formative and summative, low- and high-stakes assessments you are aware of in terms of the three aspects of practicality presented in this chapter. Offer ways to increase their practicality without compromising validity and reliability. Discuss.

2.2.16 Authenticity

Think-Pair-Share 2.2.16a Activating Background Schema   What does authenticity mean? What does inauthentic assessment look like? Choose one of the four teachers whose profile was introduced in Chapter 1. Given their beliefs about teaching, learning, and assessment, what would authentic assessment look like? How does it compare to the actual assessment their students take? Discuss.

> **Authenticity** means that the assessment task closely resembles a real-life task, outside of the teaching–learning–assessment situation.

If you've ever exclaimed, "but this would never happen in the real world," then you have complained about inauthenticity. Merriam-Webster defines *authentic* as *real, actual, done the same way as an original* (2024). Thus, authentic assessment is that which could credibly occur in the real world. It is contextualized in a real-world setting and has a logical reason, flow, and outcome.

> **Task-based language assessment (TBLA)**, or "the process of evaluating, in relation to a set of explicitly stated criteria, the quality of the communicative performances elicited from learners as part of goal-directed, meaning-focused language use requiring the integration of skills and knowledge" (Brindley 1994, p. 74, as cited in Choi 2020). TBLA centers on the students' ability to use their language to accomplish the task (see Chapter 1 for a definition of *task*.)
>
> TBLA is an example of **performance-based language assessment (PBLA)**, "which focuses on evaluating examinees' actual performance of practical skills rather than their abstract knowledge of language systems and structures" (Wigglesworth and Frost 2017, as cited in Choi 2020).

Written examples include writing an email, a blogpost, a play, a letter to the editor, a book review, a report, a lab report, a critique, an analysis, a recipe, a fictional or nonfictional story, taking down dictation, etc. Oral examples include giving a presentation, acting in a play, narrating an event, telling a story, dictating, negotiating, buying and selling, interviewing, providing a description, etc.

Scenario-based assessment (SBA), as introduced in Chapter 1, is related to TBLA and PBLA. Purpura describes a scenario where participants share "information at a science fair on the prevention and spread of invasive plant species" (2021, p. A75). Another scenario involves creating a three-video presentation to address community problems such as graffiti or trash, which will be shown at the next City Council meeting, followed by a Q&A session (Purpura 2021, p. A79). An additional scenario might involve choosing between vacation destinations. The string of interconnected learning-oriented tasks in a computerized assessment might proceed as follows. The TT learns about each destination through provided reading passages, discusses the options with simulated peers (artificial intelligence chatbot), receive guidance from a simulated teacher on how to write a summary, writes a scaffolded summary, engages in further discussion, writes another summary without assistance, synthesizes understanding and plans the final presentation with simulated peers, makes an oral presentation, and answers questions. The TT is assessed at each of these steps.

These steps might sound familiar to those acquainted with the paired speaking task of Michigan Language Assessment's ECPE (video). However, SBA includes additional elements, such as computerization, interaction with the computer rather than live TTs, and guidance from the computer rather than a live examiner. A key feature in this learning-oriented framework is that TTs must learn new information (e.g. destinations) and skills (e.g. summarizing) and are assessed on them both in a discrete and integrated manner.

TBLA, PBLA, and SBA are prime examples of authentic assessment formats. Inauthentic assessments are multiple-choice, true/false, blank fill, cloze, listen-repeat, etc. Generally speaking, selected-response items lack authenticity, while constructed-response tasks are considered authentic.

Think-Pair-Share 2.2.16b Analysis and Synthesis   Recall the assessments you analyzed in Think-Pair-Share 2.2.12b. Consider the one you found to have high validity, reliability, and practicality. How authentic is it? And what about the one that, in your previous analysis, lacked one or more of validity, reliability, and practicality? How authentic is it? Discuss the conflict between authenticity and the other qualities of test usefulness.

Assessment of project-based language learning (for definition of project, see Chapter 1): Projects should be carefully organized to prevent students from feeling torn between wishing to complete the project and earning good grades (Smith 2005, as cited in Debski 2006). Evaluations should comprise self-, peer-, and teacher-assessments. Debski (2006) emphasizes that criteria should be student-centered and include criteria related to not only language (grammar, vocabulary, pronunciation, function) but also problem-solving, investigation, and academic and social skills (such as evidence of research, analysis and synthesis of ideas, quality and quantity of individual contributions toward the group project, creativity and originality, format and presentation, preparation, reflection on language use, etc.).

Final project outcomes may include portfolios, presentations, interviews, annotated bibliography, websites, etc. Besides final outcomes, interim and process-focused criteria should also be included in the evaluation, such as observations, student communication logs, questionnaires, checklists, diaries, and journal entries.

For design suggestions of project-based lessons—including lesson plans, outcome expectations, and evaluation criteria with weighted percentages—see Debski (2006).

2.2.17 Washback (Backwash)

Think-Pair-Share 2.2.17a Activating Background Schema   Recall what you learned about consequential validity under Section 2.2.6. Now explore your experience—either as a teacher or a student—with *teaching to the test*.

Washback is the effect assessment has on teaching and learning.

Starting from the broader definition of consequential validity, the narrower concept "washback" refers to the assessment's intended and unintended consequences on the students, teachers, and institutions. One unintended consequence of assessment, as alluded to in Think-Pair-Share 2.2.17a, is the practice of teaching to the test. This occurs when students face high-stakes assessments, leading to the reverse domino effect of turning the instruction into test preparation. Students request practice tests and test-taking strategies to "beat the test," while parents often demand that schools ensure good performance. Teachers, feeling obligated to cover both the structure and content, make pedagogical decisions based on the assessment. Of the infinite number of target elements that could be taught in class, the teacher may steer the students toward what will help them on the test.

All of the aforementioned scenarios have shown *negative washback*, where the effect of the assessment on teaching and learning is negative. Furthermore, feedback on student performance is often not provided, and areas of strengths and weaknesses are not always shared. And because most high-stakes standardized assessments rank low on authenticity, when an inauthentic test drives the instruction, it usually drives instruction away from authenticity, whereby students end up practicing multiple-choice or fill-in-the-blank exercises rather than using the language for communicative purposes. They practice clicking on the screen or circling *A, B, C*, or *D* instead of formulating sentences to communicate their intended meaning.

Washback does not have to be negative though. *Positive washback* means that the assessment has a positive impact on teaching and learning. Teaching to the test can be positive for content validity. Washback can also help a teacher to reflect on the cause of the results. For example, overall weak scores may suggest that students did not prepare, but it could also indicate a problem with the test design, administration, or teaching of the material. Results can just as well confirm for the teacher that the assessment is well designed or indicate that something went wrong with the test design or instruction of learners. Teachers can then investigate the issue and improve their teaching and design of assessments.

Task-based and project-based language assessments are also examples of an assessment having positive washback, as the following demonstrates. The Graduate Student Instructor Oral English Test (GSI OET) (a high-stakes oral exam of spoken proficiency for international teaching assistants [ITAs] administered at the University of Michigan by Michigan Language Assessment) is a performance test with positive washback. This authentic assessment has a positive washback because teaching to the test and preparing for it allows learners to improve the language needed not only during the assessment but also in an authentic language use situation. The test consists of four stages: (1) making small talk, (2) giving a lecture, (3) holding office hours, and (4) answering short questions from students on video. Since each stage of the assessment is authentic, test preparation essentially means practicing the language that ITAs are likely to need in the performance of their work duties and doing so in an authentic way. Not only the content but also the method of assessing the language needed by ITAs rank high in authenticity.

Perhaps a note should be made about the variability of learners' reactions to assessments. Students may have positive or negative reactions to assessment results. A good score may motivate some students and make others complacent. A bad score may motivate some but demotivate others. In this sense, even authentic assessment may trigger a negative reaction in a learner who received a bad result. As assessment designers seek to maximize positive washback and minimize negative washback, they should keep individual variability in mind.

Hughes (2003, pp. 53–55) makes a series of recommendations for achieving beneficial washback.

- "test the abilities whose development you want to encourage"—turning this recommendation around, if you test choosing from multiple options, students will become experts at selecting from options rather than in using the language itself
- "sample widely and unpredictably"—the more predictable the test is, the more directly its content and format will encourage a narrowing of the curriculum to focus on the predictable features
- "use direct testing"—(for more on direct–indirect testing, see Chapter 1) if you want to assess speaking ability, have the TTs speak rather than listen to one line in a dialog and select from among responses the most appropriate to complete the dialog; the former is considered direct and the latter indirect testing
- "make testing criterion-referenced"—(for more information on criterion- vs. norm-referenced testing, see Chapter 14 on Improving Assessments through Statistics) the evaluation and scoring criteria should be set in advance against a performance standard rather than depend on the performance of other TTs
- "base achievement tests on objectives"—the focus of study shouldn't be on *covering the textbook* but on achieving the learning objectives demonstrated in the curriculum; then the objectives will drive the curriculum.

2.2.18 Interactiveness

Think-Pair-Share 2.2.18 Activating Background Schema   Think of engagement. Based on your personal experience either as a learner or teacher, compare three to four assessments in terms of how engaging they are. What makes some engaging while others not? Discuss.

> **Interactiveness** describes the degree to which the learner's individual characteristics (language ability, topic knowledge, attitude, emotions, background schemata) are positively engaged by the assessment task (Bachman and Palmer 1996). It is similar to engagement, as long as the learner's language ability is being engaged and the learner is not on autopilot during task execution.

Interactiveness is a quality of the assessment task. The way the task is set up determines the extent to which the task will interact with/engage the learner's language ability and affect. Thus, the following would be examples of **high-task interactiveness** at various proficiency levels:

- **Paraphrasing steps in a recipe**: In language classes, students at all levels frequently teach recipes to each other or learn the recipes of the country whose language they are studying. However, just reading the steps in a recipe may or may not engage the learner's language ability. A simple or highly familiar recipe can be understood and followed as if on autopilot. However, if the learner is asked to paraphrase the steps, then describing even the simplest recipe becomes highly interactive. Note that the interaction is not necessarily among the learners but between the learner's language ability and the execution of the task.
- **Helping shoppers locate food items in a grocery store**: On a simulated shopping trip in the language classroom, learners role-play a shopper looking for ingredients to a recipe and an employee giving directions. The employee may have a drawing of the grocery store with the large categories of items written on the drawing (i.e. bakery, dairy, greengrocer, etc.).

The shopper has a recipe and is asking about the aisle where all the ingredients can be found. This beginner-level task has high interactiveness for both shopper and employee.

- **Writing a letter of complaint**: An intermediate-level task may be to write a letter of complaint. The topic may be to dispute a parking ticket or to pretend-post a critical comment on the website of a business where the letter writer had a negative experience. Note that in some cultures complaining is rarely, if ever, done, so this assessment task would need to be preceded by a class discussion on the sociocultural and linguistic aspects of complaining in the target language.
- **Debating the pros and cons of autonomous vehicles:** This is an advanced-level task. It may follow a study of the topic, issues, and language; in this case, it would be an achievement assessment. It may, however, be part of SBA, as illustrated in Section 2.2.16.
- **Writing a summary of an article:** Summarizing, like paraphrasing, is a highly interactive task. It requires that the learner understand the article, distill it into its main ideas, put the main points in their own words, and write them down coherently.

In all the above cases, the learner would need to engage their linguistic resources to be able to perform the task. In contrast, the following tasks at various proficiency levels have **low interactiveness**:

- **Showing movers where to place pieces of furniture:** This may be a highly engaging task because the office employee or homeowner has to make decisions where the furniture should be placed as it is being brought in by the movers (or the task simulated in the classroom). At the same time, it is not necessarily a *linguistically* engaging task as the learner can evaluate the consequences of each decision (table in the corner, bookshelf against the wall) in their first language (L1). So, the target language linguistic resources of the learner are not necessarily engaged. The learner–decision maker can simply point at the right location or say "over there."
- **Visually depicting the balcony scene in Shakespeare's *Romeo and Juliet*:** In classrooms where this play is read, instructors may wish to evaluate the learners' comprehension of the play through a task or project. However, depicting a scene—such as the famous balcony scene—visually (having the students draw, paint, make a collage, build a set) is low in linguistic interactiveness. While the learner is doubtlessly engaged in this art project, their linguistic ability remains dormant. To increase the interactiveness of the task, students would either need to collaborate in the target language while making the project or present their work in writing or orally.
- **Addressing envelopes from a list of addresses:** This and any copying task, while on the surface relies on language ability, can be performed mindlessly, or even in a language the student has no proficiency in.
- **Repeat-after-me exercises:** This is a staple of language classrooms and occasionally it is necessary. However, it is not engaging and learners could almost do it in their sleep.
- **Multiple-choice grammar tasks:** Compared to tasks in which the learner must directly produce language and use it to create meaning, multiple-choice items are passive, assess the recognition of form, and promote guesswork.

2.2.19 Interactiveness vs. Authenticity

Interactiveness and authenticity are closely linked, though not identical, concepts. Both link characteristics of the assessment task with something else. That something else in the case

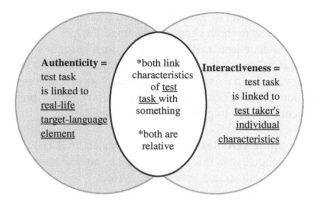

Figure 2.2 Interactiveness vs. authenticity.

of authenticity is the language used in a real-life situation (for instance, lecturing for an ITA or making a reservation at a restaurant). In the case of interactiveness, it is the extent of engagement by the learner. The following situations and Figure 2.2 should clarify the difference.

Scenario 1: At an English-medium hospitality school, a final exam may ask students to perform the task of polishing silverware. The authenticity of this task may be high in terms of content or skill knowledge, but the interactiveness, or engagement with the target language, is probably low since the learner can do it on autopilot and without using the target language.

Scenario 2: As part of the same hospitality exam, before cooking a dish, explaining how the learner will prepare it and why is probably high in interactiveness. The authenticity may be considered high in that the learner is required to cook and occasionally while training others or broadcasting a cooking show, explain the cooking procedure aloud, but more commonly it may be moderate since typically cooks do not narrate their actions aloud. At most, they ask others to hand them ingredients.

Scenario 3: As part of the same hospitality exam, the learner has to write down from memory food safety rules such as at what temperature different foods can be stored and for how long. This task may be considered relatively high on interactiveness because the learner must recall a series of important details. This does not mean that the learner may find the task interesting or exciting but the learner's mind, language ability, and topical knowledge are engaged. The authenticity of the task, however, is low because it is unlikely that a hospitality employee will ever have to write these facts down. It is much more likely that they can consult a handbook on food safety when in doubt.

Note that interactiveness does not mean that learners necessarily need to interact with (converse, engage with) another person. It is the task that they need to interact with in an engaged manner.

A final word of caution on interactiveness: so far, we have focused on task characteristics that engage learners but not those that engage individual learner characteristics. The teacher-assessor would do well to avoid situations on assessment that might confuse or emotionally shut down learners, hindering their engagement with the task. Examples include the introduction of an unfamiliar assessment task (multiple-choice where selection of a distractor is penalized, group exam, peer review), relying on cultural assumptions that not all learners share (like references to snow or typhoons), or bringing up potentially upsetting topics (like a prompt about parents for a refugee student who lost theirs or a natural disaster for students whose home may have been destroyed). In classroom assessments, teachers should ensure that topics and tasks are comfortable for all learners. Otherwise, construct-irrelevant variance (see elsewhere in this volume) will hinder the interpretation of assessment results. In a high-stakes standardized setting, test designers can be expected to take reasonable precautions not to upset the TTs. They can also ensure that task types will be familiar to the TTs by releasing a sample test to the public.

Think-Pair-Share 2.2.19a Analysis and Synthesis

a. Recall the assessments you analyzed in Think-Pair-Share 2.2.15. Consider the one you found to have high validity, reliability, and practicality. How high would you score it on interactiveness?
b. And what about the one that, in your previous analysis, lacked one or more of validity, reliability, and practicality? How interactive is it?
c. Do interactiveness and authenticity go hand in hand in these cases?
d. Discuss any conflict among all the six qualities of test usefulness.
e. Propose a change to one of these assessments to maximize the six qualities.

Think-Pair-Share 2.2.19b Analysis Think of engagement. Based on your personal experience either as a learner or teacher, compare three to four specific assessments in terms of how engaging they are. What makes some engaging while others not? Discuss.

2.3 Assessment Use Argument (AUA)

> The **Assessment Use Argument (AUA)** is a documentation of the development, use, and justification of an assessment. It is a detailed, integrated approach designed to assist with the development of well-thought-out and defensible language assessments. It "consists of a set of claims that specify the conceptual links between a test taker's *performance* on an assessment, an *assessment record*, which is the score or qualitative description we obtain from the assessment, an *interpretation* about the ability we want to assess, the *decisions* that are to be made, and the consequences *of using the assessment and of the decisions that are made*" (Bachman and Palmer 2010, p. 30). Assessment designers can demonstrate that their assessments work in the real world with the help of the AUA.

In the following, we outline the main elements of this conceptual framework. These elements are to be considered and carefully documented throughout the process. For an in-depth look, we recommend Bachman and Palmer (2010) and Bachman and Dambröck (2018), which have served as sources for this information.

1: Setting
The process of assessment design begins with a description of the setting, in which the test designer or teacher or program director would like to develop an assessment for a particular group of learners for particular purposes. All stakeholders are identified.

2: Initial planning questions about key elements

a. What beneficial consequences does the assessment hope to achieve? Examples might include improving teaching or enhancing learning.
b. What decisions are to be made to bring about these beneficial consequences?

    c. What information does the assessment designer need to have about the learners' language ability? How does the assessment designer interpret the language needed for the target language use situation?

3: Assessment Use Argument

Once a decision has been made that an assessment needs to be developed,[1] the assessment designer methodically analyzes each element through a modified Toulmin's model of argumentation (2003). The motto here is "Show your work!" In other words, one's argument must be explicit and traceable.

> Based on Toulmin's model of argumentation, Bachman and Palmer's approach to practical reasoning consists of **claim, data, backing (supporting evidence), warrant (inferential links from data to claims), rebuttal (statements weakening the claim), rebuttal backing, and rebuttal counterclaim.**

    a. Foreseeable (and unforeseeable) *consequences* of step 2(a) are examined with the Toulmin approach. Based on *data*, a *claim* is made that such consequences will be beneficial for the various stakeholders. Supported by *backing*, a series of *warrants* are formulated. As applicable, *rebuttals* supported by *backing* and *rebuttal counter-claims* are identified.

    b. Any decisions that need to be made by the assessment designer or decision-maker about step 2(b) are examined with the Toulmin approach (see step 3(a)).

    c. A claim is made regarding the meaningfulness, impartiality, generalizability, relevance, and sufficiency of the interpretations about language ability (see step 2(c)). This claim is examined with the Toulmin approach.

    d. The assessment record, such as a score or description, is examined with the Toulmin approach.

Note that some backing for the above stage (steps 3(a)–(d)) may be provided by the subsequent design statement.

4: Design statement and blueprint

"The Design Statement is a document that states what one needs to know before actually creating an assessment ... Its primary purpose is to guide the test developer in the last three stages—Operationalization, Trialing, and Assessment Use—in the process of assessment development and use" (Bachman and Palmer 2010, p. 143).

    For an example blueprint, see Appendix 2 in Chapter 3.

5: The assessment, instructions, prompts, and rating scales

The final element of the conceptual framework is the assessment itself with all of its components.

2.3.1 Summary of the AUA

This framework rests on four pillars: justifying language assessment uses and consequences to stakeholders; clearly articulating a coherent AUA, which links assessment performance to its interpretation and intended use; providing evidence to support statements made in the AUA; and collaborating among stakeholders during the development and use of the assessments.

---

1 To explore alternatives to creating your own test, refer to Bachman and Palmer (2010).

2.4   Chapter Conclusion

In this chapter, we explored six key qualities of effective tests. Test usefulness remains crucial as it introduces concepts like reliability and validity, familiar across assessment experts, educators, administrators, policymakers, and the public. However, achieving an assessment that maximizes each quality simultaneously is challenging because they interact. For instance, increasing validity can compromise reliability, and enhancing authenticity may reduce practicality. Such trade-offs necessitate informed decisions aligned with assessment goals and contexts, which inherently involve subjective judgments by developers. These qualities are interconnected and must be considered throughout test development and administration.

Understanding local conditions and constraints is equally vital for language assessors. Decisions made in assessment—for accreditation, improvement, resource allocation, or research—carry consequences, intended or unintended. Assessors bear the responsibility to identify interested parties, consult with them, anticipate outcomes, and mitigate potential drawbacks. An effectively articulated AUA, developed collaboratively and supported with evidence, serves as a potent tool for guiding assessment practices and ensuring accountability to interested parties.

Appendix 1 – Achievement Quiz of Chapter 2

(For discussion or writing prompts, see the Think-Pair-Share tasks in this chapter.)

Directions: Select the response that best answers each question below. Each question is worth 1 point.

1. Every semester, two teachers teach two separate sections of the same language class: *Arabic for Academic Purposes Level 4*. They teach the same syllabus from the same textbook and use the same assessments year after year. What should they do before evaluating any speaking or writing assignments?
    a. establish their intra-rater reliability
    b. conduct a norming session on sample student work
    c. anticipate instrument-related reliability problems
    d. minimize negative test impact

2. Seven-year-old children are asked to bring to their low-intermediate French-as-a-foreign-language class a favorite toy and tell the class about it in French. The teacher evaluates each student's speech as they speak. What can be said about the authenticity and interactiveness of this assessment?
    a. high authenticity, low interactiveness
    b. low authenticity, high interactiveness
    c. low authenticity, low interactiveness
    d. high authenticity, high interactiveness

3. A language teacher usually has 10 students in her class. Her favorite assessments elicit lots of oral and written production from the students. Suddenly her class size increases to 30. If she makes no changes to her teaching and assessment as a result of the new class size, which quality of test usefulness will be the most affected?
    a. validity
    b. washback
    c. practicality
    d. reliability

4. Why is the Assessment Use Argument (AUA) considered a crucial component in the development of language assessments?
   a. to emphasize the importance of test usefulness and its interaction with various qualities of effective assessments
   b. to provide evidence supporting statements made in the AUA and demonstrate the real-world effectiveness of assessments
   c. to guide the test developer in the initial planning stages and help in identifying stakeholders
   d. to minimize the subjectivity involved in decision-making by evaluating the qualities of language assessments objectively

5. What is the primary purpose of the Design Statement in the Assessment Use Argument (AUA) framework?
   a. to guide the test developer in the stages of Operationalization, Trialing, and Assessment Use
   b. to justify language assessment uses and consequences to stakeholders
   c. to provide evidence supporting the statements made in the AUA
   d. to analyze the foreseeable and unforeseeable consequences of assessment decisions

3

Test Design

Chapter Overview

This chapter discusses the creation of a test blueprint (or test specification, specs) for classroom and standardized assessments. The chapter is organized around the Wh-questions to help think through all the details of test design.

3.1 Learning Objectives

1. Explain the need for a needs analysis
2. Explain why only standardized assessment results can be transferred across institutions
3. Explain what should not be assessed and why
4. Distinguish raw scores from scaled scores
5. Explain the procedure and justification for test equating
6. Write a blueprint for a classroom assessment situation you are familiar with

3.1.1 Foreword on Terminology

By *classroom assessment*, we refer to any assessment administered in a classroom, by instructors, intended to see how much their students are learning. By *standardized*, as defined in Chapter 1, we mean any assessment created, administered, and scored in a standardized and systematic manner. We will treat them as separate categories, although they can overlap.

Assessments for the classroom are by and large created by the classroom teacher. However, they can also be created by a group of teachers, administrators, or a learning specialist at the same school. At times, a consortium of schools functions together and creates common assessments for all schools in the system. Quite frequently, the textbooks that are adopted by schools have test banks, which are used for classroom assessment. These sources can be very useful but should be approached with great caution because although many publishers are quite diligent about hiring assessment experts to create these exams, not all do. Another caution would be that these publisher-produced questions are often written to assess only the shallowest depth of knowledge. Every instructor and administrator should have the requisite familiarity with good assessment practices and apply these skills to determine the quality of the test used in their own classroom.

Standardized assessments can be so-called *secure* or *institutional*. Both are created by testing agencies. And both can colloquially be secure such as when an institutional test is stored and

A Practical Guide to Language Assessment: How Do You Know That Your Students Are Learning? First Edition.
Ildiko Porter-Szucs et al.

administered very securely. The main differences are in the test administration, scoring, and score reporting. So-called **secure tests** are administered by the trained staff of authorized test centers. The procedures at these test centers are then monitored by the test creator. After test administration, the results are then returned to the testing agency and scored there. Score reports are then issued by the agency to the TT and/or any stakeholder authorized by the TT. This may include an educational institution, a workplace, or a government agency. These scores are recognized widely and can be transferred from institution to institution because the test creator vouches for the standardization of the process, security of the forms, and accuracy of results. Forms of **institutional tests**, although developed by the testing agency, are then sold to institutions to be administered and scored there. These institutions include language schools, colleges, and workplaces. The same test form may be in use at any given school for even decades. Even if at one institution the test form, or compilation of test questions, is stored securely and administered rigorously, there may be other schools that are not quite so scrupulous in their storage and administration practices. Additionally, test questions that are used over and over, time after time inevitably become known to students and lose security at the user end. Thus, because the test developer can only vouch for the standardization of the test form but not for that of the test administration and scoring, the resulting scores are usually not recognized beyond the institution where the test is taken.

In our discussion, all standardized tests—secure and institutional—will be discussed together even though schools may use institutional tests for a variety of purposes in the classroom, such as a pre-test, a progress test, and a post-test within the same semester.

3.2 Test Design

Think-Pair-Share 3.2a   Think of a concrete assessment you have created for a specific setting and purpose. Now imagine administering it to a different group of students. Think of different age, country, school setting, purpose, etc. What if any adjustments would you need to make to the original assessment before you could administer it to the new group of students? Why? Discuss. (If you have not created any assessment instruments before, think of your experience as a student in a language class taking an assessment while considering these questions.)

As the above exercise demonstrated, the same assessment tool cannot be administered to different test-taking populations without revision because validity would be compromised. For instance, a test for adults may not be appropriate for 9-year-old children; a test designed for students in a monolingual environment may assume cultural knowledge that students around the world may not share; a grammar achievement test will be inadequate for placement into speaking proficiency levels. In this chapter, we will look at the considerations that go into designing both classroom and standardized assessments. These principles can also be followed when evaluating commercially designed assessments for a particular setting.

3.2.1 Test Design Considerations

Figure 3.1 summarizes the major factors to be considered when designing an assessment instrument. In this modified Venn diagram, the middle oval, where the left and right circles overlap, depicts factors necessary for both classroom and standardized assessments. Factors only in the left circle pertain to classroom assessments alone while those only in the right circle pertain to just standardized assessments. Let us begin with the process of designing classroom assessments (left and middle areas).

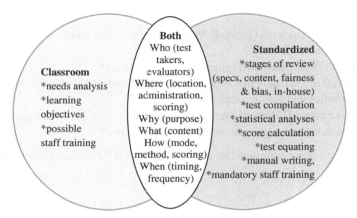

Figure 3.1   Test design considerations for classroom and standardized assessments.

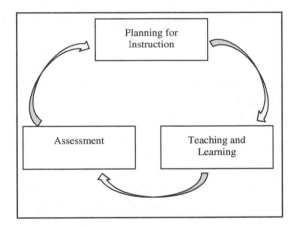

Figure 3.2   The PTLA cycle for classroom assessment.

3.3   Designing Classroom Assessment

Assessing student work and providing constructive feedback are essential parts of what we call the planning–teaching–learning–assessment (PTLA) cycle (see Figure 3.2).

Guided by standards, the teacher (occasionally assisted by other stakeholders, such as school administrators, department heads, instructional coaches, and students) plans the instruction. Afterwards, the teacher facilitates the students' learning. And concurrently and/or subsequently, the teacher (at times complemented by the learners themselves) assesses the students' learning. The information gained from the assessment then informs further planning for teaching and learning. And the PTLA cycle continues. Without assessment, the feedback loop is incomplete. The student lacks information on whether they are on the right track. Thus, the results of classroom assessment need to be fed back to the student appropriately.

A **test blueprint, test specification, or spec** is the design document of the test. Assessment creators arrive at it by asking and answering a series of questions. Although in a blueprint these questions are asked and answered in a different order, we are grouping them here by the *Wh* question as a mnemonic device.

1. **Who** is being assessed?
2. **Where** are the TTs (students) located? **Where** are the assessments administered? **Where** are the assessments scored?
3. **Why** are students being assessed (purpose of assessment)?
4. **What** is to be tested? **What** is **not** to be tested? **What** are the directions for the students (TTs)? **What** are examples and non-examples of items/tasks?
5. **How** are skills assessed? **How** are scores determined?
6. **When** is the assessment administered? **When** is it scored?

See Appendix 2 for a more complete list and Appendix 4 for references to two complete specification documents.

3.3.1 Who?

Classroom assessments are designed with a specific group of students in mind. In addition to the language-proficiency level of the students, teachers need to know their students' age, maturity level, life experiences, educational background, first language (L1), culture, aspirations, special needs, interests, and hobbies.

Think-Pair-Share 3.3a   Consider the following vocabulary item, designed to assess the verb *to fast*. Discuss why it may or may not be appropriate for a classroom setting you are familiar with.
   Instructions: Write the missing word in the blank.
   During religious periods such as Ramadan, many people [fast] from sunrise to sunset.

The vocabulary item in Think-Pair-Share 3.3a may have generated the following discussion points. If the students had just learned about Ramadan practices in class or if the classroom is located in a context where the students would reasonably be expected to know about Ramadan and its traditions, then this is a fair vocabulary item. Otherwise, the students' lack of familiarity with the culture would interfere with their ability to demonstrate their knowledge of the word. Thus, it is essential for the teacher to examine his/her own cultural background in relation to those of the students and the target culture (if in a second-language setting). Something as innocuous as lack of familiarity with snow, Boxing Day, Santa Claus, el Día de los Muertos, Diwali, a wedding ring, or a school uniform, etc. may unfairly disadvantage certain students during assessment. Since the above vocabulary item contains all text, it would not be appropriate for younger children. Not only would pre- and semi-literate students struggle to decipher the writing but they would likely struggle to understand the content cognitively as well. The concepts of fasting and religious rituals are abstract; thus, this item would not be appropriate for the youngest of learners. Furthermore, the age of the student will influence the length of the assessment as well, as very young learners cannot concentrate or sit for long. Assessments for children must keep the children's need for increased movement and limited concentration in mind. For more on assessing young learners, see Chapter 6.
   The students' culture and L1 also have a bearing on assessment design. Related to culture, assessment designers must keep in mind students' familiarity with or expectations about assessment. Some students may not be used to certain assessments, e.g. group conversations or MC tests where points are deducted for wrong answers; therefore, teachers need to train students in assessment formats in order to increase interactiveness and reliability. Some target elements become less difficult if the L1 is related to the target language (TL). For instance, *precarious* is a late-acquired, infrequent word in English and thus should be assessed on advanced tests. However, students with Romance L1s may find it easier than others because of its Latin etymology (see Figure 3.3).

Spanish and Italian	Portuguese	French	Romanian
precario	*precário*	*précaire*	*precar*
https://www.spanishdict.com/translate/precarious https://www.wordreference.com/enit/precarious	https://en.bab.la/dictionary/english-portuguese/precarious	https://dictionary.reverso.net/english-french/precarious	https://www.definitions.net/translate/precarious/ro

Figure 3.3 Etymology of *precarious* in romance languages. *Source:* Author created.

Another possible aspect of *Who are the students?* is familiarity with the students' background. For instance, if teachers know that a refugee student has lost both parents in war, it is not advisable to use speaking or writing prompts related to parents. Here interactiveness and reliability could be affected.

Less relevant in classroom assessments are other possible questions with *Who*. *Who* designs the assessment? *Who* administers the assessment? *Who* evaluates the students' responses? *Who* stores the assessment? The answer to these questions is typically the classroom teacher.

3.3.2 Where?

Once the exact characteristics of the students taking the assessment have been established, the location of the assessment administration and scoring must be thought through. Several components of the previous section—*who* the students are—overlap with *where* they are. Such is the instructional setting: preschool, primary, secondary, post-secondary (college, university), graduate (post-graduate) school, language school, adult education, refugee resettlement, vocational, and other specific settings. These are students of various ages, focusing on different aspects of the target language, depending on their purposes. The setting determines whether the students are taking classes for credit or not and whether the assessments are formative, summative, both, no stakes, low stakes, or high stakes.

Example 1: Bilingual daycare center
In a bilingual daycare center, where the children are 3–5 years old, for instance, assessment may take the form of the children singing *Head, Shoulders, Knees, and Toes* while touching their body parts in accordance with the song. At the end of the school year, the children may stand on a stage and perform for the audience and receive a certificate of completion. There are no stakes but the teacher assesses each child's achievement or proficiency, nevertheless.

Example 2: Community ESL citizenship class for refugees
In a community ESL class in the US made up of refugees, adult students might be preparing to pass the citizenship exam. Among the students, several have medical conditions that impact learning and assessment. Some are hard of hearing, others have visual impairment, while others have post-traumatic stress disorder. During class they learn to understand and respond to written and oral questions. During formative assessment, the students' achievement on each learning objective is tracked by the teacher in a low-stakes manner. The high-stakes summative assessment—the citizenship exam—is administered by an official government entity. In-class accommodations are provided depending on the possibilities of the teacher and the resettlement agency. Accommodations

during the naturalization exam for applicants with disabilities are provided by the US Citizenship and Immigration Services. Other countries also provide accommodations.

In addition to the previous location-related aspects of classroom assessment that overlap with TT-related aspects of the setting, further location-related considerations were briefly touched on in Chapter 2 as part of the discussion on practicality. They include seating, the proximity of TTs, temperature, noise level, and access to technology (to the requisite amount of space and technical support to utilize the technology).

Example 3:   High-tech college French as a second language class
At a college in Canada, for instance, a learning management system (LMS), such as Moodle, Blackboard, Brightspace, or Canvas may be used. In it, the instructor may design a daily quiz for the students to take in class. This requires a sufficient number of computers with laptops, possibly speakers and headphones, an adequate layout for the students to take the quizzes in privacy, and the space to house the hardware since not all students have access to their own personal devices.

Example 4:   Low-tech EFL rural elementary school
At a less high-tech school, such as a rural elementary school in Mozambique with 50 students in attendance, classroom assessment design must adjust to the setting. The teacher may design whole-class, paired, and individual tasks. In large language classes, receptive skills (listening and reading) can be assessed fairly easily, as long as for test-security purposes, multiple parallel forms of the same paper-and-pencil test are created. The challenge with large classes entails assessing productive skills (speaking and writing). Here the teacher will need to balance a variety of factors for both administration and evaluation. As for writing, even if multiple parallel prompts can be created and administered during class time, the writing samples will have to be graded by the teacher, which is a time-consuming undertaking. Self-assessment and peer-assessment are an option in formative and low-stakes situations, but not in high-stakes midterm or final exams. Therefore, the teacher's ability to rate a large number of multi-page writing samples sets a limit to the nature, frequency, and extent of authentic, written assessments. Speaking, including pronunciation and fluency, will pose an even greater challenge for test administration. It is time-consuming for the teacher to conduct one-on-one conversations with each student in class. In-class presentations take time away from instruction as well. Out-of-class time is also limited for the teacher. Therefore, in a low-tech school, the teacher may choose to assess the students in pairs or small groups formatively on an ongoing basis so as to maximize practicality. If spoken language can be recorded and evaluated later, it presents the same challenges as the evaluation of written work. The most efficient way, therefore, may be the concurrent administration and evaluation of students' speaking. This, however, has implications for rater training, which was discussed in Chapter 2.

Other location-related considerations not yet discussed are specifically related to whether the instruction is taking place in a second-language, foreign-language, or online setting. In a second-language setting—where in the greater society the target language is spoken by the population—(such as English is in England or German in Austria), assessment can incorporate the world beyond the classroom. Students can be asked to call a local business for information, write a petition to the school or a letter to local politicians and send it off. On the other hand, in a foreign-language setting (such as Hebrew in Brazil), assessment is restricted to the classroom, technology, materials, or invited visitors. An online class is further limited to technology-mediated interaction for both learning and assessment.

3.3.3 Why?

Many would argue that the purpose of assessment is the place to start designing a test. We started with the *Who* and the *Where* because we believe that it is necessary to envision a specific group of students before we can design an assessment for them for any purpose.

Think-Pair-Share 3.3b Do you remember from Chapter 1 the fictional *School* of *World Languages*? Now, recall the various assessments their students had to take from the time they first walked into the school until some of them took a test of international English for healthcare workers. What were these assessment types and purposes? Which ones can be considered *classroom* assessments?

Of the assessments discussed in Chapter 1—placement, diagnostic, progress, achievement, proficiency, and certification—the following can be considered classroom assessments: diagnostic and achievement. The rest are more appropriately categorized as standardized and will be discussed in the second half of this chapter. Of the other classifications, both formative and summative assessments can be used in the classroom.

The purpose of assessment, to a great extent, determines the design of the assessment. It determines the construct, the types of items, the number of items, the mode of elicitation and response, the use of assessment results, etc. As discussed in Chapter 1, a *diagnostic assessment* is specific to the target element, or instructional focus. It is a pretest whose purpose is to see how much the students know about the topic prior to any instruction. The proficiency level (beginner, intermediate, or A1, A2, B1, or Novice Mid, Novice High, etc.) that the items target matches that of the target language elements studied in the class. For instance, if in the next chapter students will learn to give a formal persuasive speech at a conference on climate change, then a direct, authentic diagnostic assessment may have students record themselves giving a 2-minute prepared speech on this topic, which would be evaluated based on a rubric. The evaluation criteria of the rubric might include formality of address, fluency, range of vocabulary, etc. An example opening line might sound *"Ladies and gentlemen, I have come to speak to you today about a matter of utmost urgency."* An indirect, practical diagnostic assessment may have students take a multiple-choice test with the subjunctive mood after verbs and adjectives of urgency (*It is imperative that the world take/takes/will take action*). The assessment would be at an advanced (C1-C2) CEFR level of proficiency in either case and would assess only the language targeting the construct definition. A diagnostic assessment is by definition formative. Its results are used to influence teaching and learning. If students display superior prior knowledge on the diagnostic, then potentially the entire unit may be skipped or only briefly touched upon. Conversely, if the diagnostic reveals gaps in prerequisites, the instructor may need to modify her instructional plan and pre-teach the missing information.

Between the diagnostic and achievement assessments, numerous *formative assessments*, or interim measures, will be administered to the students. Their purpose is to track the students' progress on daily learning objectives. These assessments consist of mostly informal, on-the-run, assessments, observations, checklists, self- and peer-assessments, as discussed earlier. Once the instruction period concludes and the teacher is satisfied that the students have mastered the target elements, formal, summative (achievement) assessment may be administered.

The *achievement assessment* is the post-test following the instruction. Often it is nearly identical to the diagnostic assessment. In other settings, practices might vary depending on available instructional materials. In the above example of students preparing a speech for a climate-change conference, a direct, authentic achievement assessment would require that the students speak for 3–4 minutes on the topic in front of an audience. The teacher may evaluate the speech in real time but record it for future verification. In the case of the multiple-choice diagnostic, which is indirect yet practical to administer and score, the achievement test takes a similar format. The actual items are slightly changed so that students cannot memorize the pre-test and excel on the post-test. So instead of *"It is imperative that the world take action,"* a student may encounter *"It is urgent that each country act."*

To summarize the role that purpose plays in assessment design, the purpose of the assessment—be it formal–informal, formative–summative, diagnostic–achievement, etc.—in conjunction with the other factors is that it determines the assessment's format, length, item types, etc.

3.3.4 What?

A. What should be assessed?

In answer to the previous questions, we have already offered aspects of the "what" question. In other words, who the students are, where they are taking language classes, and why they are doing so influence the content of the assessment. However, in addition to all of that, it is important to consider what content will be included in the classroom assessment. Classroom assessment can be informal and formal. Let us return to the four example settings from Section 3.3.2 and understand what the content of *informal assessments* could be in each setting (for a definition, refer to Chapter 1).

Example 1: Bilingual daycare center

Taking for example a bilingual daycare center with ten 4-year-olds, as the children are learning *Head, Shoulders, Knees, and Toes*, the content of the assessment can be whether the children can point to the body parts named in the song. Assuming that this is culturally appropriate, the teacher may put the children in pairs (ask them to turn to their "elbow partner") and say *point to your partner's nose* and then watch if the children can perform the command. On a matrix of students' names vs. body parts, the teacher checks off which student can identify which body part. This is an informal, formative, checklist assessment. The content is derived from the learning objective: *Students will be able to identify the body parts from the song by pointing at their classmate's correct body part.*

Example 2:   Community ESL citizenship class for refugees

With the ultimate goal of passing the US citizenship test, today the refugees are learning about the Supreme Court. After the teacher introduces the Court and the number of justices sitting on it, an informal, formative assessment may be to answer the relevant question from the Civics Practice Test (US Department of State n.d.), as illustrated below.

1. How many justices are on the Supreme Court?
   a. nine (9)
   b. ten (10)
   c. eleven (11)
   d. twelve (12)

The teacher displays the question on the screen and the students respond by holding up close to their chests 1 finger for response A, 2 fingers for response B, 3 for C, and 4 for D. At a glance the teacher sees how many and which students did not identify the correct answer (A=1 finger). She can then decide to reteach the topic as necessary. Thus, again, the content of the assessment is directly linked to the learning objectives of the lesson.

It is not uncommon, particularly in settings that are responsive to the needs of the students, to include a needs analysis. A **needs analysis** is a brief survey of students' interests, strengths, and needs. It is usually administered in voluntary (rather than mandatory) classes with self-directed learners. It can be administered at the beginning of the semester in order to guide the design of the syllabus and all future assessments. It can also be administered as frequently as each class session, especially in drop-in settings where there is no guarantee that the same students will attend from week to week. Classroom assessments are, thus, designed based on topics, from which the teacher creates learning objectives, but the topics themselves may be suggested by the students. For example, students may choose the topic of *going to the doctor.* The teacher translates this into a learning objective: *Upon completion of today's lesson, students will be able to explain, as if to a doctor, their medical symptoms about a studied disease.*

Did you know?   Through a cooperative initiative in Ypsilanti, Michigan, USA, various community entities such as a literacy organization, university teacher-training program, and faith-based group collaborate to deliver weekly language classes. TESOL students from the university take on the role of instructors, utilizing a space provided by the church to teach students recruited by the literacy organization. In these classes, the teachers conduct a daily needs analysis of the adult students, who in turn select topics they would like to learn to talk about in English, such as visiting the doctor, eating out, holidays, etc. The teachers tailor the lessons and learning objectives to the students' needs.

Example 3:   High-tech college French as a second language class
In the Canadian French for Academic Purposes class, in the academic speaking and listening class students are learning about the process approach to listening (see Porter-Szucs 2018). The learning objective states that *Students will be able to predict with 80% accuracy an upcoming point in an audio-recorded lecture by selecting from among four multiple-choice answers on Edpuzzle* (Edpuzzle n.d.). After the students have been practicing, the process of listening, stopping, predicting, verifying, and revising for the last two days, the teacher prepares a five-item quiz for them on the Edpuzzle educational software. The students sit at their individual computer terminals, put on their headphones, and take the quiz. The new lecture is divided into six segments; following the first through fifth segments, the recording stops and students answer one quiz question about the next point that they predict. The teacher uses the results of this planned but formative assessment to inform her next instructional steps.

Example 4:   Low-tech EFL rural elementary school
In the Mozambican fourth-grade English class, students are practicing speaking, listening, geometric shapes, and prepositions. After whole-class practice where the teacher draws an abstract figure using circles, squares, triangles, etc. on the board, students in pairs describe to each other what they see. One student in the pair sits facing the board and describes the drawing to the other, who sits with their back to the board but facing their partner. Now for individual assessment, the teacher describes another abstract drawing using the same shapes and each student draws it privately. The teacher then collects the drawings and while the students practice the same activity in pairs with abstract drawings of their own design, the teacher checks the students' work.

As the aforementioned four examples demonstrate, the content of assessments should be guided by the learning objectives. And the learning objectives of the day should make up the ongoing, formative assessment. Feedback can then be given as soon as possible—instantaneously if appropriate—to inform the cycle of teaching, learning, and assessment.

The content of *formal classroom assessment* is determined by the course objectives and the unit's learning objectives (for a definition of formal assessment, see Chapter 1). Formal assessments typically occur at predetermined points in the instructional cycle, such as every Friday, every month, or twice a semester. They are longer, planned, and more comprehensive than their informal counterparts. Let us again return to the four example settings and consider what formal, summative assessments could be administered there.

Example 1: Bilingual daycare center

The teacher would like to assess whether all children can name their body parts verbally and identify them from listening. Thus, the names of the body parts constitute the assessment. The teacher gives each student a black-and-white drawing of a child and five different colored pencils. In the listening portion of the assessment, the teacher first picks up a red pencil. After she ascertains that each child is holding their own red pencil, she asks them to color the shoulders red in the picture. She repeats this with the remaining colors and body parts. At the end, she collects each child's drawing to check later and to record the students' achievement. In the speaking portion of the assessment, the teacher assesses each child in so-called centers. Students are working on different projects at various stations, or tables, in the classroom. Each group of children remains at each table for a set period of time before rotating to the next one. One of the centers has the teacher in it and the teacher does the mini-assessment when the students move through her center. She points at the body parts of a teddy bear and asks each child: What is this? Each child responds by identifying a different body part, such as *knee, head*, etc. The teacher then records the students' accomplishment of the unit learning targets and invites the next group to her table.

Example 2: Community ESL citizenship class for refugees

The topic of the Supreme Court is part of the larger topic of the three branches of the US government (USA Government Contact Center). A unit test may have a verbal and written part. On the verbal part, the teacher schedules 5-minute oral interviews with each student, has the student draw a question from a pile of questions already covered in the unit, reads the question aloud, and has the student respond verbally. Answers can be checked immediately from a list of acceptable answers. The written questions are projected to the whole class onto a screen and students respond in writing on a piece of paper.

Example 3: High-tech college French as a second language class

In this French immersion academic class, the process approach to listening is part of a larger unit on listening strategies in an academic environment. Since the immersion students will specialize in a variety of fields after completing their intensive language study, the teacher uses both student-supplied and teacher-supplied materials to teach from. For the listening portion, however, a topic from the textbook or a TED Talk on a generic topic of global appeal, such as the environment or technology, will likely be appropriate. Lack of content knowledge should not pose a barrier, and the listening strategies should be demonstrable. To demonstrate understanding of the main idea, after listening to the whole passage, students write a title for what they heard. To demonstrate inferencing, students select from a four-option multiple-choice item the statement (none of which was mentioned in the listening) that the author is most likely to agree with. Since the class is equipped with computers for each student, the test can be taken on the computer, through the learning management system, and be entirely or at least partially evaluated automatically.

Example 4: Low-tech EFL rural elementary school

The lesson on geometric shapes and prepositions in this integrated-skills class is part of the larger topic of describing visual information orally and capturing aural information pictorially. The content of the assessment comes from the context: the world that surrounds the learners. During the unit, the children learned about how information is often organized spatially: (a) from center outwards, (b) outside in, (c) left to right, (d) right to left, (e) top to bottom, (f) bottom to top, and also (g) general to specific. Thus on the listening portion of this unit assessment, the teacher creates three different forms of the test paper. All students listen to the same aural descriptions read by the teacher but perform different exercises, depending on their form of the test paper. For instance, while group A may draw the picture being described, group B may identify differences in a same-different picture, and group C may answer True/False questions based on what they hear. Then for the next exercise, the task rotates as the picture to be described changes. The three different forms of the test are not to differentiate ability levels or to increase complexity. The assessment is designed this way to efficiently maintain test security in a class where students are sitting in close proximity to each other.

In the speaking portion, the teacher can probably not afford to assess speaking directly, personally, and individually more than a few times during the marking period. What is manageable though is if the teacher pulls out a set number of students during each test for individual assessment until all students have been assessed by the teacher at least twice. Thus during this particular unit assessment, the teacher may employ peer-assessment of the type the students are familiar with as a no-stakes exercise. The method should not be given much grading weight because of the high possibility for rating inconsistency. One way the speaking task can be executed is that the teacher puts the students into pairs and creates three parallel forms of descriptions. In each description, one student receives the picture while the other student receives an acceptable description. The speaker describes their picture and the listener follows along by reading the description silently. If the speaker's description is reasonably close, the listener awards a point and if it is not, then no point is awarded. Students who do not receive points can then appeal to the teacher and perform this activity in front of the teacher. See Figure 3.4 for an example.

Form 1 *Student A describes a picture to student B.*	*Student B listens to A's description and compares it to the following written description.*
	*In the picture there are ten fish. They are lying on a plate (on a table, in a pan).* *They are the same kind of fish. Some (four) are big, and some (six) are small.* *The big fish are on the bottom, and the small fish on the top (on top of the big fish).* *The fish are silver (grey/brown/shiny).* *They have big round eyes.* *They have long bodies.* *Each fish has a head and a tail.* *Nine fish are looking (facing) left. One fish is looking (facing) up.*

Figure 3.4 Peer-assessed picture-description task. *Source:* Unknown author / Wikimedia Commons / CC BY-SA 4.0.

How close the description would need to be for a point to be awarded will depend on how oral description has been taught, e.g. overview statement + systematic (sequential) description. And some students might identify the fish by its name while others will say *silver fish*. Perhaps a rubric could be used with descriptors such as the total number of fish, use of adjectives of size and color, specific studied terms, such as *similar to, different from, bigger/smaller than*, etc. It is important to highlight that peer-assessment, as illustrated in the example above, is a skill that students of all ages need to be taught. Furthermore, it is essential to consider cultural appropriateness. Even if students receive instruction in peer-reviewing, deducting points from a peer might violate cultural norms and should not be attempted. For more information on peer-assessment and peer-feedback, see Chapter 11.

There can be numerous variations on this technique, allowing the teacher to balance practicality with the other qualities of assessment described in Chapter 2. Students' (even children's) speaking could be teacher-assessed and peer-assessed through speeches, oral reports, and oral share-outs. The teacher could use a well-established speaking rubric (such as the WIDA Speaking Scale, the CEFR Speaking Scale, or the International Baccalaureate rubric). If the goal is to assess both listening and speaking, then the teacher would use the rubric and the classmates would respond in writing to a few questions prepared by the teacher. The students listening would answer about the student who was speaking. For example, if students were giving presentations on a famous person they researched, the other students would receive a form to complete as they listened; each form would have the same questions, and students would have to listen to their classmate's speech to understand; their written responses, in turn, would help the teacher gauge listening comprehension. Questions might include, "What was the most interesting fact you learned about during the speech?" or "What was confusing to you about the speech?" or "What else would you like to learn about the topic?" Answers to these questions help the teacher get a general idea of each student's listening comprehension, holistically.

The level of difficulty of items and tasks on diagnostic and achievement assessments should be appropriate for the proficiency level of the class. There should be sufficient items that would challenge the more proficient learners but there should also be enough items so the less proficient students within the same class do not feel defeated. Items should never be tricky. The goal is not to trick students, but rather to determine if they know the given material. The wording of the items should always be clear. (For more information on item design, see Chapter 4.)

B. What should not be assessed?

In addition to what is to be assessed, it is important to consider what is not to be assessed. In classroom assessment, with a few notable exceptions, diagnostic and achievement assessments are appropriate. Whatever is taught and learned in class is what should be assessed. Conversely, whatever is not taught and learned should not be assessed. Exceptions are test-preparation classes. In a TOEFL or IELTS test-prep class, students prepare to pass proficiency exams, whose content extends beyond any leveled language class. For more information on the content of proficiency tests, see elsewhere in this chapter.

C. What are the instructions for the students?

Instructions, or directions to classroom assessments should be well known to the students prior to the assessment. The wording should be used during everyday classroom activities when clarifications can be provided and the activities can be modeled. When possible, the directions may even be given in the first language of the students. By the time of assessment, the students should not have to spend time working out the meaning of the directions. Nevertheless, it is important to note that the directions should be short and clear. The assessment designer must be clear on the assessment construct: if the assessment is supposed to assess a target element, then the wording of the instructions should not interfere with this goal. If it does, then the assessment no longer assesses the students' performance on the construct—such as their ability to write an argumentative essay—but rather their ability to comprehend and follow complicated directions. For example, if the instruction is to describe, then the student should write, and the teacher should expect a description, not an explanation. Thus, when test items are pre-tested, so should be the directions.

3.3.5 How?

How are skills assessed? In the preceding sections of this chapter, we alluded to this question to some extent. The identity of the students, location of the class, purpose of assessment, and content have a bearing on *how* the assessment takes place.

Considerations are numerous.

- Preliterate learners (very young or low-literacy learners, such as many SLIFE[1] or LESLLA[2] learners) cannot be assessed through written text.
- Deaf or hard-of-hearing learners may need to skip listening tasks or may need a sign-language interpreter.
- Visually impaired learners may need to avoid visual material and might need Braille and/or text translated to speech.
- Young learners may need shorter and more engaging tasks to accommodate their developing attention span.
- The environment beyond the classroom may be more conducive to incorporating authentic assessment in a second- rather than foreign-language setting.
- Online classes necessarily incorporate technology in all tasks as well as TTs' comfort with using it.
- Low-tech or no-tech teaching environments necessitate corresponding classroom assessments.
- Direct and authentic assessment of productive skills in large classes raises practicality concerns.
- The qualities of test usefulness need to be maximized through every test-design decision.
- It is best practice to document the development, use, and justification of the assessment in the AUA, which includes the assessment blueprint.

We will now consider other aspects of the *How?* of assessment.

Two important terms to introduce are the ***elicitation*** and ***response*** formats.

> **Elicitation (input) format** is the way the assessment question or prompt is posed to the test taker. It could be oral, written, or multimodal. For instance, if a test taker receives a paper test with written instructions to read a passage and to speak about it for 2 minutes, then the elicitation format is written because the passage and the instructions are written. However, if the test taker both reads a passage and listens to a lecture, then the elicitation formats are multimodal because two modes are used.

---

1 Students with Limited or Interrupted Formal Education
2 Literacy Education and Second Language Learning for Adults

> **Response format** is the way the test taker produces language in response to the assessment question or prompt. It could be oral, written, nonverbal, or multimodal. For instance, in the above example, the 2-minute monologue produced by the test taker in response to the written passage and prompt requires an oral response. In Asher's (1969) Total Physical Response (TPR) language learning method, the response format is nonverbal. An example is the Simon Says game (see Shukla 2019).

Did you know? On the TOEFL iBT, there is an integrated essay task. First, TTs read an article; next, they listen to a lecture on the same topic but with an opposing viewpoint; finally, they write an essay about the relationship of the content in the article and the lecture. In this integrated-skills task, the elicitation formats are written and oral and the response format is written. For detailed instructions on how to write the most common item types of various elicitation and response formats for both classroom and standardized assessments, see Chapter 4.

Another *How?* question to be asked when designing any assessment is how scores will be determined. Much of classroom assessment is for formative purposes and is ungraded. In other words, students do not receive a grade on the quality or quantity of their work. The purpose of such evaluation is to see whether the students have reached the learning objectives or are making sufficient progress toward them and frequently also to provide feedback to the students. For such purposes a simple checklist (objective met: Yes/No) may suffice. Alternatively, target elements mastered vs. not mastered could be entered into the evaluation rubric. In other cases, it is the students' effort that counts. For instance, one fluency-building task is journaling. It is usually considered counterproductive to assess journal entries based on accuracy, so the evaluation may be tied to page length and the timely completion of the task, instead.

The evaluation of summative classroom assessments, however, requires a different approach. The instructor must weigh the importance of each individual assessment relative to the final grade. For instance, what percentage of the final grade is made up of homework vs. in-class work? Formal vs. informal assessment? Quality vs. effort? Midterm and final exams vs. everything else? Sometimes the classroom instructor has the autonomy to make all the above grading decisions alone. In other cases, all these decisions are made for the instructor. For more on grading, evaluation, and feedback, see Chapter 11.

3.3.6 When?

There are a few time considerations for classroom assessments. **When** is the assessment administered? **How much time** is required for its administration? and **When** is it scored? Here we must further break down classroom assessments into informal and formal ones. *Informal* classroom assessments can take place at any time in the instructional cycle. In fact, we would argue that a good teacher never stops assessing. Did the student arrive on time? early? late? Did they arrive with a smile on their face? crying? despondent? Is the student attentive? distracted? mentally or emotionally absent? Do you detect signs of comprehension on the student's face during instruction? signs of confusion? Does the student participate in whole-class activities? small groups? pairs? individual ones? How fluent and/or accurate is the students' language?—An attentive teacher notices and makes mental or written notes on all of the above; in other words, **the attentive teacher assesses continually**.

Beyond the aforementioned continual assessment, more deliberate efforts must be taken to assess learning objectives on an ongoing basis. In Chapter 1, Section 1.4.17 we discussed at length various types of informal and formal assessments. Here we will focus on their time implications. On-the-run assessment can truly be implemented on the spur of the moment: the teacher explains something and would like to check whether further explanation is needed, so he asks students to indicate verbally or nonverbally how well they understand. He can ask the students to self-assess—thumbs up, sideways, or down about whether they understand—or, to get a more accurate assessment he asks the students to apply the information and then checks for accuracy. An example of the latter occurs when the teacher just explained and demonstrated the form, meaning, and use of "used to" and then asks the students to complete the following sentence in their own notebooks or on mini-whiteboards: *When Juan was little, he _____ (not used to) eat spicy food but now he does.* The teacher then walks around and checks the answers, based on which he knows whether more practice is needed or not. These detours may take a couple of minutes away from class time but could also save unnecessary practice time on something that has already been mastered.

The rule about provision of feedback on assessment is that, as long as the learners' affective filter allows, it should be provided with minimal delay. In particular, formative feedback should be given immediately if possible. Ideally, the class focuses on a target element, assessment takes place (teacher-led, self-, peer-, or computerized assessment), and feedback is given right away. With some types of assessment, feedback can be provided the next time the class meets. This includes exit tickets, low-stakes quizzes, etc. The former is explained in the Glossary and the latter is exemplified in Example 4 of the high-tech college in Canada in this chapter. For a discussion on feedback, see Chapter 9. Whenever designing assessment, it is essential to consider the resources (such as time) required of the students and the teacher to administer and evaluate the assessments.

Formal classroom assessments also have **time implications**. They must be

a. scheduled with some regularity
b. created and piloted in advance
c. announced to the students and prepared for in and out of class by the students
d. administered in class (or sometimes outside of class)
e. scored and then the results evaluated usually by the classroom teacher or a team of teachers
f. feedback must be prepared and delivered to the students

a. Formal classroom assessments typically occur at the end of a chapter or unit, as well as mid-term and at the end of the term. They usually take place when the teacher has evidence through formative assessment that the learning objectives for the unit have been met by the majority of the learners. If the class has a syllabus, this type of assessment is typically announced in it.

b. Formal classroom assessments are created in advance. As we will see in Chapter 4, writing test tasks is a time-consuming undertaking. It consists of the matching test tasks with the learning objectives and the group of learners.

   i. For instance, imagine that the class has just completed the study of the imperative mood. In a class of adults that follows a traditional structural syllabus, the instruction probably focused on how to create the imperative (infinitive without *to*); thus, the assessment will contain a written fill-in-the-blank or multiple-choice test.

   ii. In a more communicative classroom, the situational syllabus may have been used. During class, the instructor may have introduced various situations in which people tell each other what to do. Thus, the assessment in this class may entail having each student write a recipe for a traditional dish. So a student from the Ivory Coast may teach her classmates how to make Kedjenou.

    iii. Children studying science in English, on the other hand, may have been exposed to the imperative while being told how to conduct scientific experiments. Thus, the assessment may have the students write the steps of one of the experiments based on picture prompts. However, in order to ensure that the assessment accomplishes the objectives, does so in the time limit, and is error free, it is highly advisable to ask another teacher who is familiar with the students to pilot the assessment. Ideally, the students should only be given the test after an impartial party has had a chance to critique it and any typos or other problems have been resolved. The higher the stakes, the more important pilot testing becomes. This additional step, however, takes time, and it is acknowledged that classroom teachers rarely have this luxury.

  c. Formal classroom assessments are such because they are announced in advance and the students have a chance to prepare for them. The higher the stakes, the more essential this step becomes. In-class review activities or even review days may need to be scheduled. Practice tests may be assigned for homework. It is not uncommon for the teacher to create a study guide or an additional test form as a practice or mock test for in-class or out-of-class practice. In some settings, review sessions are scheduled outside of class, when interested students and the teacher make time for additional practice.

  d. The administration of the assessment usually takes a substantial amount of the class period. Receptive skills and writing can be administered concurrently for all the students, with no additional time commitment. In-class speaking, however, and task- or project-based learning require more of the instructor's and/or the class's time. Thus, this aspect must be planned for. One alternative, if technology is available, is for students to be placed in sound-proof audio labs or receive headphones and speak directly into the microphone. Another alternative is for several teachers to administer the speaking portion of the assessment to different sets of students and video- or audio-record it for later evaluation. A third alternative, if test security is of low priority, is for students to record their speeches at home.

  e. **and f.** We don't know a single teacher who chose this profession so that they could spend time grading. Evaluating assessments is among the least favorite parts of most teachers' jobs.

> A **stale joke on grading**: *If you're overwhelmed by the amount of grading you have to do, just throw the whole pile of papers down the stairs. Those that go the furthest down must be the heaviest, so they deserve the best grade. The ones that land on the top are the lightest, so they get the worst grade.* (One version of this joke by Ross 2008.)

Most likely, every teacher ever tasked with checking student work has been tempted to take a shortcut: if not exactly following the stair method. Assessing and providing constructive feedback are time consuming and should be accounted for in the test blueprint, or specifications. One helpful perspective for the busy teacher is to perceive grading as an opportunity to celebrate little achievements that students demonstrate rather than a daunting chore. Additionally, employing the following **time-saving devices** can also be beneficial:

- learning management systems (such as Moodle, Canvas, Blackboard, etc.) where selected-response items are graded automatically (see Chapter 4)
- automated essay scoring technology (more in Chapter 13)
- automated reading-annotation scoring technology, such as Perusall
- automated speaking-scoring technology, such as Pearson's Versant
- commercially and freely available apps, programs, websites, and other forms of technology that deliver and score assessments
- checklists and coded errors

- rating scales and rubrics
- self- and peer-assessment
- student-teacher conferences
- written and spoken (face-to-face or recorded) feedback

Depending on the setting, the time required for the entire assessment process will range widely. For more on grading, evaluation, and feedback, see Chapter 11.

3.3.7 Summary of Classroom Assessments

The assessment blueprint must consider all relevant questions: Who are the learners? Where are they? Why are they learning? What are they learning, and what needs to be assessed? How is the instruction and the assessment? When does the assessment cycle take place? The importance of a well-documented AUA and test blueprint grows with the stakes of the assessment. Informal classroom assessments do not require an AUA or formal blueprint, though teachers should consider these questions informally. Formal classroom assessments do need such documentation, despite practical constraints. In the next section, we will discuss standardized assessments, where a test blueprint is essential.

3.4 Designing Standardized Assessments

We trust that by the time the reader reaches this section of the book, it has become clear that assessment does not equal high-stakes standardized testing and that there are many different forms of assessment, as discussed in Section 3.3 under Classroom Assessment. We also hope that by now it is clear that in particular informal and formative classroom assessment should be most prevalent, followed by formal summative assessment. High-stakes standardized tests should play a limited role in most language classes (excepting those that specifically prepare learners for such tests).

Think-Pair-Share 3.4 Think of a time when you had to take an important test. It may have been a school-completion or entrance exam. It may have been to earn a certificate or license such as a driver's license. What was the experience like? Where were you? How did you feel? How did you do? How many times did you take the test? What did the test look like? Who created the test? How was it similar to/different from a classroom assessment? Discuss.

In this section of the chapter, our focus will be limited to the design of standardized assessments. Similar to the considerations that enter into the design of classroom assessments, the test blueprint, or test specifications of professionally prepared assessments will be outlined. Of the Venn diagram in Figure 3.1, the grey circle on the right and the white overlap in the middle will be relevant to our discussion.

3.4.1 Who?

Designers of standardized tests frequently start by considering *who* is being assessed. The TTs, however, are not confined to a homogenous group of students in a limited area but are often spread around the world. They are young and old, have various genders, speak numerous first languages, hail from diverse religious, cultural, and ethnic backgrounds, and have different strengths, weaknesses, abilities, and aspirations.

Think-Pair-Share 3.4.1a Write one language test question for the teaching-learning setting you are most familiar with. Return to this exercise once you have completed this step. **STOP** Now that you have written this one test question, imagine that students unknown to you in three different countries are also going to take this test question. How successful would they be? For instance, if you are most familiar with teaching EFL in a South Korean primary school to 12-year-olds and you wrote the test question for them, how successful would 12-year-olds in Haiti, Kazakhstan, and New Zealand be? Discuss.

Think-Pair-Share 3.4.1b Despite the diversity of the target TT population, some commonalities can be identified among them. Examine the following two *Did you know?* facts and identify the target TT population of each assessment.

Did you know? In China, the College English Test (Zhang 2022) is a high-stakes standardized assessment taken by undergraduate students who are not English majors as a prerequisite for a bachelor's degree.

Did you know? WIDA (2024b) is an assessment organization that specializes in pre-kindergarten through 12th-grade English language assessments administered in schools in 40+ US states and 400+ international schools around the world.

CET is designed for college students in China whose L1 is Chinese (Zhang 2022). These students major in a variety of subjects other than English because English majors must pass a more rigorous proficiency test. WIDA assessments, on the other hand, are created for young learners of various ages (approximately from 5 to 18), mostly for students who live and attend school in the United States. However, some of the target TTs live outside the United States and study at English-medium international schools. Therefore, it is safe to assume that they will all be familiar with American English and US customs to some extent. Testing agencies conduct multiple stages of review in order to ensure that test items are accessible to the target group of TTs, that they do not discriminate against them, and that scores reflect language ability rather than irrelevant factors, such as confusion about the test. Other population-related considerations include the TTs' ability. Many large assessment organizations produce alternate forms for TTs with disabilities. This includes large print, Braille forms, or magnified screens for blind TTs; listening portions replaced by written scripts for deaf TTs; and other accommodations for TTs with documented disabilities. (For more information on students with special-needs, see Chapter 8 on exceptional language learners.) The test designer's task is considerably more challenging when only limited information is available on the TTs. This makes it increasingly important for the user to do due diligence before adopting a standardized assessment.

3.4.2 Where?

In the above section on the TT population, we discussed the geographic location of the TTs to some extent. Let us consider further where the TTs are located, where the assessments are administered, and where they are scored. The location of the TTs has implications for access to test centers as well as sample and practice materials. Secure assessments, as stated before, are administered in approved test centers. They are usually in major population centers, potentially far away from some TTs. A further consideration is whether the test center is equipped to administer paper-based tests or computerized ones, and if the latter is the case, whether the test occurs at a designated center or remotely from the TTs' homes.

Did you know?   While IELTS can be taken online worldwide, there are certain locations where it is administered in a paper-based format (IELTS 2023). As a test with a global reach, it is provided in a format that is accessible to the TTs even in geographic locations without widespread computer access or reliable internet.

The location of not only the TTs but also of the evaluators must be considered when designing the blueprint. Assessments can be scored by the computer automatically. Such is the case with computerized assessments, for instance, the Versant Arabic Test by Pearson. They can also be administered locally, at the test center, but scored centrally, at the assessment organization. This is the case with the IELTS writing test. Finally, tests can be both administered and evaluated locally, at the test center. The IELTS Academic and General speaking test is one such example.

3.4.3   Why?

Think-Pair-Share 3.4.3a   Recall for what purposes classroom assessments are typically used. In Think-Pair-Share 3.3b you identified these tests within the context of the fictional *School* of *World Languages*. Discuss. And which assessments taken by these students were standardized? Which ones were administered at the institution (the language school) and which ones at a secure test center? How do you know? Discuss.

Of the assessments discussed in Chapter 1—placement, diagnostic, progress, achievement, proficiency, and certification—diagnostic and achievement tests are typically classroom assessments while the placement, proficiency, and certification tests are typically standardized. Placement tests are commonly administered and scored locally; proficiency and certification tests are administered centrally at approved secure test centers. However, there is a growing trend among testing agencies to create proficiency tests that can be taken remotely in the TT's home. Note that progress tests are not mentioned in either category. This is because depending on its purpose, progress can be measured with an achievement or a proficiency test.

The purpose of an assessment determines the kinds of items that it will include. A **placement test**, as discussed in Chapter 1, will contain items targeting a range of proficiency levels so that it can sort TTs into level-appropriate groups. Thus, at the testing organization, sufficient test items at each level must be commissioned from item writers, pretested on the target TT population, and compiled into test forms.

Did you know?   The Cambridge Placement Test (Cambridge English 2024) is an online test of general English, which is used to place students into pre-A1 to C2 levels of proficiency.

A **proficiency test** can be of two kinds. One kind is frequently the same type of test as a placement test and thus requires a breadth of items to be able to distinguish language abilities or proficiency levels. Proficiency tests also must have sufficient breadth, i.e. items at adjacent levels of difficulty, to be able to detect changes in proficiency. At the same time, they must also have some depth, i.e. items at the same level of difficulty, for stakeholders to have confidence in sampling a range of TTs' language knowledge. Otherwise, TTs may feel that they just got lucky or unlucky with the types of questions that were asked, which would have implications for reliability and validity. Such are the TOEFL and IELTS. They measure levels A–C on the CEFR. Another kind of proficiency test is similar to a certification test (see below). It targets specific language proficiencies rather than a range. Therefore, items are concentrated at or below the proficiency level and it is possible to pass or fail the test. Such are the Examination for the Certificate of Competency in English (ECCE) aimed at the B2 level on the CEFR and B1 Business Preliminary aimed at B1 proficiency.

Did you know? The EIKEN test is a series of tests of practical English proficiency in Japan. It is akin to a certification test in that it is offered at seven levels: from Grade pre-1 to Grade 5, ages 6–11.

Certification (Licensure, Qualification) tests, as discussed in Chapter 1, are often designed as pass/fail assessments. They are frequently situated in a specific context: law, medicine, aviation, maritime, and international teaching. The test is designed to assess whether the TT possesses the minimally acceptable *threshold* competence that is needed to perform the duties required by that context. Therefore, the breadth of the proficiency levels is quite narrow. Most items are concentrated at or below the threshold or cut-off. While other score points may be identified as well, they are usually for informational purposes although it is possible for the test user to accept a lower or higher cut-off score. For instance, in the Test of Legal English Skills Advanced (TOLES Advanced) by Global Legal English although six score bands are identified from green to gold, the descriptors make it clear that the assessment organization recommends that the cut-off be at red, or "GOOD legal English skills" although they do allow that some employers may wish to be satisfied with purple, or "satisfactory legal English skills."

Did you know? The Graduate Student Instructor Oral English Test (GSI OET) by Michigan Language Assessment qualifies international students to serve as teaching assistants. There are four score points (*A, B, C, D*) and the cut-off between pass and fail is at *B*.

Progress tests, as the name suggests, measure progress, or improvement. Progress may be measured in a specific target language area or in general proficiency. In the former case, an interim achievement assessment may be administered in the classroom halfway through the learning cycle. In the latter case, a proficiency test may be administered as an interim measure. This could be an institutional test administered locally or a secure test administered at an authorized test center. An assessment instrument can only measure progress if it has a sufficient number of items targeting the specific proficiency level of the TT and if the scoring allows for small incremental changes to be reflected. Otherwise, if the instrument is not fine-tuned enough, even if the TT continues to improve, the scores may not reflect the change. (For more on scoring, see Chapter 9).

In summary, the purpose of an assessment, in other words, why a TT sits for it, fundamentally influences test design. The types of tasks, their difficulty, and their number are all determined by their intended use. This is why it is crucial for stakeholders to use assessments for purposes for which they were intended, rather than the not uncommon practice of getting as much mileage out of a single assessment as possible. For example, to save time and money, an institution may use a proficiency test as a placement test. Using (abusing) assessments for purposes that they were not designed for is akin to misusing the household chemical bleach. Just because it effectively removes some stains and cleans some surfaces does not mean that using it to remove discolorations on our skin or washing our food with it is wise.

Think-Pair-Share 3.4.3b Consider the following situation. At a language school where the semesters are between 7 and 14 weeks long, parallel forms of the same institutional proficiency test are used for the following purposes:

- to verify placement in each class at the beginning of the semester (called a pre-test),

- as an interim, or progress test (called a practice exit test three weeks before the end of the semester), and
- as a high-stakes proficiency test (called an exit test), where a cut-off score must be reached for a student to advance to the next class.

The proficiency test used is designed to measure TTs' proficiency from A2-B2 on the CEFR. The students at the college range from novice (below A1) to B2. Discuss what recommendations you would make to the language teachers and administrators at this school if you had the opportunity. Explain.

3.4.4 What?

So far, we have mentioned the content of standardized assessments in the context of *who* the TTs are, *where* the TTs are located, *where* the evaluators are located, and *why* the assessments have been created. In this section, we will further investigate *what* constitutes the content of standardized assessments.

Some language tests are for general purposes (e.g. IELTS General Training, Avant STAMP in multiple languages (2024a), ACTFL in multiple languages), others for academic (TOEFL, IELTS Academic, CAEL), and others for occupational (OET by Cambridge Boxhill and CELBAN for healthcare professionals, TOLES for legal professionals, Maritime English Test for sea professionals, TOEIC for the workplace, ETS 2024b). Some tests include a range of domains (Michigan English Test by Michigan Language Assessment). There are tests for children (WIDA ACCESS, Cambridge English: Schools). It is these domains (personal, public, educational, academic, occupational, workplace) that serve as the content for the language tasks.

A **general test** lends itself most easily to proving everyday language proficiency for adults, for instance, for immigration because the topics of the items on the test are from the domains most commonly encountered in everyday life. Thus, a listening passage may be on traffic lights, a reading topic on paying bills, vocabulary on public transportation, a grammar item on air pollution, a speaking prompt on the public library, and a writing prompt on planning an event. A typical adult is likely to have experience with these topics and will, thus, have the requisite background schema to be able to focus on the task at hand rather than being preoccupied with their lack of background in the specific topic.

A **test for young learners** will similarly be based on topics that the learners will have experience with and the age-appropriate cognitive abilities to comprehend. The listening may be on two friends talking about homework, the reading passage on birds, vocabulary related to school, the speaking prompt on extracurricular activities or a picture description, and the writing on school uniforms.

An **academic test**, aimed at adults or older teenagers, assumes an interest in university studies. Therefore, all the topics will be on university life and university-level content. There may be an academic lecture on hydroponic aquaculture, a reading on the psychological concept of flow, vocabulary on research, a grammar item on office hours, a speaking prompt on the advantages and disadvantages of delaying the start of school for teenagers until 10 a.m., and a persuasive essay on gender-segregated instruction.

Tests for professional purposes may be general and highly specific. In the former case, topics will include conversations among coworkers, between managers and their subordinates, and customers and business people; concerns over delayed shipment; management of human resources; responding to emails; creating sales presentations; and complaining about price hikes. In the latter case, topics will be specific to the occupational situation at hand. A medical language assessment will assume that the TTs are trained medical professionals in another language already and the test serves to assess the TTs' familiarity with the terms and context in countries where the target language is spoken. Similarly, a test of legal language will contain specific vocabulary used in the legal profession, assuming that the TTs have been trained in the concepts in their first language. **Test specifications** (see Appendix 2) state which domains/topics and how many items each assessment is to contain. For instance, 10 items will be distributed in the following way: 5x office, 3x homework, and 2x transportation.

The test blueprint also extends to the following aspects of the test content:

- number and order of skills assessed (e.g. writing before speaking)
- whether skills are assessed separately or in an integrated fashion (e.g. listen and answer with multiple-choice questions, i.e. only listening is assessed or listen and write about what you heard, i.e. both listening and writing are assessed)
- number of listening and reading passages
- how many words each passage may contain
- readability level of each passage (more on this in Chapter 5)
- if any, number, size, and nature of illustrations accompanying passages
- number of items assessing each skill
- word count range of items in each skill
- word frequency of vocabulary used (more on this in Chapter 5)
- number and types of speaking and writing prompts (more on this in Chapter 4)
- whether TTs have topic options in speaking and writing prompts (e.g. narrative about favorite movie or about the most pleasantly memorable day of the TT's life)
- whether TTs receive preparation time before speaking or if speaking is extemporaneous
- how many TTs and how many examiners are present during a speaking test (e.g. 1 on 1, 2 TTs on 1 examiner, 2 on 2, 3 on 2)
- how long each section lasts (e.g. 45 minutes for writing, 2 minutes for each speaking prompt, 30 minutes for grammar, etc.)
- weightage of each section
- how quickly audio or video recordings should deliver the content

The test blueprint also specifies what content is <u>not</u> included in the assessment. It is in particular important to avoid upsetting TTs. Anger, fear, and other negative emotions are not conducive to demonstrating one's true ability. Even more so than during classroom instruction when learners encode and store information, during assessment when learners retrieve information their affective filter should be low enough to allow them access to their encoded and stored information (for more on the affective filter, see Krashen 1982). In a classroom, discussing with students controversial and taboo topics is a favorite discussion topic. Students usually have strong feelings on all sides of the issues. Such topics tend to generate lively discussions. If any students take offense during the discussion, the teacher can respond appropriately to the elevated emotions. Not so during assessment. The interlocutor's role is different. While a teacher can attend to the students' emotions in class, during assessment the examiner cannot go off script. She must simply wait for the TT to calm down sufficiently to be able to access their language, which usually deserts speakers of second languages at times of anxiety. This is why keeping the topics positive and friendly is both the test designer's and the examiner's task.

Think-Pair-Share 3.4.4a Imagine that you are working for an assessment organization that writes language tests for secondary school students who have immigrated to your country from all over the world. The following narrative essay topic comes across your desk on one of the test forms. *Write about a time when you recently traveled. Describe the trip with specific details.* What is your opinion about this topic? Discuss.

The item writer's linguistic goal with the above essay topic must have been to elicit a past-tense narrative, which seems appropriate. Maintaining an entire essay in the various past tenses is a challenging task and will no doubt put the TTs' linguistic ability on display effectively. This topic is also appropriate for the age group. Most secondary school students have taken a trip that they will remember, even if just a school trip to a local attraction. However, given that these students have all immigrated to the country where the assessment is given, there is a possibility that some of them have been refugees, that they have escaped war, and that their journeys have been traumatic. One of our former students, for example, as a child had escaped with his family from a war-torn country in the middle of the night while his city was being bombed. They walked for 30 hours nonstop until they crossed into a neighboring country. There they stayed in a refugee camp for 5 years in squalid conditions and without the opportunity for the children to attend school. Finally, his family was resettled to the United States, where he became our student. Imagine if he were asked to write on this topic and had to prove his language proficiency by reliving the details of his journey! An innocent-looking topic could inadvertently rekindle his traumatic memories. A simple revision, however, could make this topic acceptable: *Write about a fun trip you recently took. Describe with specific details why you enjoyed it.*

3.4.5   What are the instructions for the TTs?

The instructions to the whole test and each item type must be worded carefully. Similarly to the directions of classroom assessments, it is essential that the directions of standardized assessments be simply worded, short, and clear to the TTs. While students in a classroom have the advantage of hearing the directions from the teacher during everyday instruction, TTs do not. This is why the directions also need to undergo vetting before they become part of a live test.

3.4.6   How?

All limitations mentioned so far also apply to standardized assessments. Thus, TTs' literacy, ability, age, environment, comfort with technology as well as the available technology at the test center will shape how assessments are created and delivered. So will whether the assessment is administered at a secure test center or at an institution and whether the scoring takes place locally or centrally. We have discussed all these questions before.

We have not yet addressed how the assurance of quality in standardized assessments is achieved. Test designers document the process of test development, use, and justification in the AUA. The blueprint, a component of the AUA, guides the development of test items and compilation of test forms. However, before any item is added to a test form, it undergoes multiple **stages of review**.

1. First it is examined whether it meets the specification for the given item type.
2. Next its content is examined, specifically whether the TT population would be likely to understand it based on their expected background knowledge.
3. At another stage of review, the item is considered from a fairness and bias (FAB) perspective. This reviewer considers the TTs' known first languages, home countries, ethnicities, cultures, religions, political situations, etc. It would be the FAB reviewer who would flag the essay topic in Think-Pair-Share 3.4.4a as inappropriate and return it to the item-development team for revisions. Topics that are best avoided on assessments make up the acronym PARSNIP (Politics, Alcohol, Religion, Sex, Narcotics, -Isms, and Pork) (Oxford University Press, as cited in Gray 2006). To this, we would add any topic that, depending on the student or TT population, may be considered negative, upsetting, or controversial. When test items are compiled onto a test form (according to specifications), they continue to go through further stages of review. At this *in-house-review stage*, staff members take the test as if they were real TTs. They note any

concerns from any of the perspectives mentioned before (not meeting specifications, concerns with content, violating FAB guidelines). Other concerns might be that two items that are in close proximity to each other may provide clues about each other. For instance, below, item 1) assesses the words that collocate with "look forward" while item 2) provides this information in the stem because it assesses a different point.

1. *Thank you for your introductory letter, Ms. Khan. I'm looking forward* (to meeting) *you in person soon.*
2. *We are looking forward to hearing from you* (at your) *earliest convenience.*

Here item 2 keys item 1. Even if a TT does not know how to complete item 1 (i.e. does not know that "BE looking forward" is followed by "to" and a gerund), by looking at item 2, they can do so. Item 2 assesses a different target element (i.e. the collocate of "earliest convenience," which is "at your"), but the answer to item 1 "BE looking forward to" is provided in the stem. Thus, the arrangement of the items on the test form causes a problem, which the in-house reviewer can intercept.

4. After a newly developed item is accepted by all reviewers, it is pilot-tested. Piloting is like a dress rehearsal for the test item. It does not yet count and it does not affect the TTs' score but information is gathered about the performance of the item. There are various ways this can happen. Sometimes TTs are recruited specifically to pilot the items. Ideally, these are TTs from the same demographic as the actual TTs. They complete the exam and offer feedback on the items. For instance, they may comment in writing or verbally on the clarity of the speaking prompt. In other cases, the pilot-test items are included on live test forms, hidden so they become indistinguishable from those test items that do count toward the TTs' score. The TTs, not knowing which items matter and which ones do not, approach each with equal earnestness. Later the results of the piloted items are analyzed statistically to inform test developers about the items' performance. (For basic statistics, see Chapter 14.)

5. Item-performance statistics are then used to either accept or revise or reject items. Accepted items become operational in the future. Rejected items are used in training manuals as mistakes to be learned from. Items requiring revision are sent back to the item-writing team and go through the development–review–piloting process again until they are accepted or rejected.

The route of a test item from the planning to a live test is long. And this route is prescribed by the test blueprint. Similarly long is the route of a rating scale's validation. The difference lies in the fact that a rating scale is created once, when a new assessment is created. At that time, various aspects of the rating scale must undergo validation. The research and statistical team analyze the rating data, examine the raters' processes, and analyze the spoken or written language output of the TTs (Chan 2017). In Chapters 4 and 5, we will discuss the creation of a rating scale, but its validation is beyond the scope of this volume, even if it should be specified in the blueprint.

Another important consideration is how test scores are arrived at. The exact steps involved in score calculation require knowledge of statistics that goes beyond the scope of this volume. However, there are a few concepts that we can introduce here. **Raw scores** are the actual scores TTs achieve on a form of a test. So, as Schweitzer (2019) explains, if a TT answers 80 questions correctly out of 100, then the raw score is 80 points or 80%. This, however, is not necessarily the score that is reported to the TT and other stakeholders. Instead, this score is converted in an equating process to a so-called **scaled score**. This is necessary to be able to equate different forms of the same test. As Schweitzer explains, "Scaled scores allow for accurate comparisons and ensure that people who took a more difficult test are not penalized, and people who took a less difficult test are not given an unfair advantage" (2019, para.10). In addition, assessment organizations need to ensure that the scaled scores maintain their meaning over time. Despite the item writers' and test designers' best efforts (such as writing to the same test specifications), no two test forms that contain different items can be identical. Some will be harder than others, yet TTs' scores should not be influenced by such unintended factors as the accidental difficulty of the form they might be taking. A common solution is **test equating**. "A primary goal of test equating for testing programs is to eliminate the effects on scores of these unintended differences in test form difficulty" (Holland et al. 2006, p. 169). One common test-equating method is described below. On a live test form, not only are there pilot-test items and operational items, as described above, but also so-called anchor items. A subset of operational items that has had excellent performance statistics over time is used in subsequent adjacent test administrations as *anchors*. Any new items' performances are compared to the anchor items and the difficulty of the test form is calibrated to the difficulty of the anchors.

Imagine two forms (such as January and February) of the same language test. Each form has been written to the same test specs. The items that appear on each test are *operational items* (already pretested items, which count toward the final score), *pretest items* (new items which are being tried out for the first time and do not count toward the final score), and *anchor items* (pretested, true and tried items with great statistical properties). Operational and pretest items will be different between the January and February forms but anchor items will be the same. The TTs' performance on the anchor between the two forms can be compared and from this the overall difficulty of the two forms is calculated. If the latter form is found to be easier or harder than the former one, then the scores on the February form can be adjusted accordingly. Thus, with this method of equating, statisticians are able to *equalize the difficulties of the two test forms* but still *measure the abilities of the TTs* who took the tests. This way *scores that are issued by the testing organization for any given test have the same meaning across time and form.* So a score of 20 in January has the same meaning as a 20 in February. For an in-depth discussion on equating, we recommend *Equating Test Scores* by Holland et al. (2006).

We have discussed how classroom test scores and secure standardized scores are arrived at. What remains is how *test scores on institutional tests* are calculated. Institutional tests are created by assessment organizations and multiple parallel forms are sold to institutions (such as schools and workplaces) to be administered and scored locally on site. The scores are predetermined centrally by the assessment organization. The test forms are usually accompanied by a raw-to-scale conversion chart. This guides local test administrators in their calculation of scores. For instance, if in September form *K* is administered to the students, then their raw scores (how many correct answers they received on the test) is looked up on the conversion chart that corresponds to *K*. This converted scaled score is reported to the students. In December if form *L* is administered to them, their raw scores are again looked up on the chart that contains information about *L*. The student receives this scaled score. The scaled scores are comparable across time and forms.

Each institution that uses tests that have been purchased from a vendor or that has created assessments for its own use needs to conduct a standard-setting study. For more information on standard setting, see Chapters 1 and 4.

3.4.7 When?

We have touched on numerous time-related aspects of test design already. These include how long each section of a test should be and how fast the listening recordings should be. We have also noted that secure tests are usually administered locally and scored centrally at a later time, while institutional tests are both administered and scored locally. What we have not yet stated explicitly but the description of the item-review process in the previous section may have suggested is that test development is a lengthy process. High-stakes standardized test forms are started approximately 6 months before use. The development of new assessments takes even longer. Another time-consuming aspect of assessment is when TTs and other stakeholders receive official scores. Computerized assessments are gaining popularity because they can return scores relatively quickly. The Versant speaking test, which is automatically scored by an algorithm, makes scores available within 24 hours. Other computerized assessments that assess multiple skills, such as the computerized Avant STAMP test (2024b), make results available in approximately one week. This is in contrast with the paper-based version of the IELTS, where results take up to 2 weeks. Since standardized assessments are used summatively rather than formatively, a quick turn-around time is not essential pedagogically; it is, however, anxiously awaited by stakeholders for occupational, educational, immigration, and personal reasons.

3.5 Chapter Conclusion

In conclusion, the test specifications (test blueprint) are essential to any assessment, whether in classrooms or standardized settings. Intentional planning is crucial, especially for high-stakes assessments. Teachers and professional test developers should use the Wh-questions from this chapter to guide their blueprint design. Appendix 2 provides a sample test blueprint for reference.

Think-Pair-Share 3.5a 1-Write a blueprint for a classroom assessment situation you are familiar with. Be so specific that if you gave the blueprint to another language teacher, they could recreate your assessment. 2-Exchange blueprints with a colleague. Recreate each other's assessments solely from the blueprint. What ambiguities arose? Revise your and/or your classmate's blueprint where ambiguity led to discrepancies.

Appendix 1 – Achievement Quiz of Chapter 3

(For discussion or writing prompts, see the Think-Pair-Share tasks in this chapter.)

Directions: Select the response that best answers each question below. Question 1 is worth 6 points if entirely correct or 1 point partial credit for each correct question. Questions 2–5 are worth 1 point each.

1. Write at least one of each of the guiding Wh-questions that serve as a guide in developing classroom assessment.
    a. Who _____ ?
    b. Where _____ ?
    c. Why _____ ?
    d. What _____ ?
    e. How _____ ?
    f. When _____ ?

2. A needs analysis is used as _____.
    a. part of the application for a standardized test
    b. end-of-semester assessment in mandatory classes
    c. a pre-instruction survey with self-directed learners
    d. a form of placement test in institutional assessment

3. You are a FAB reviewer for a global language assessment company. Critique the following test item.
   Good Friday is the name of the Friday _____
   a) after Thanksgiving   *b) before Easter*   *c) after Labor Day*
   d) before Christmas
   a. This is a well-written item because it is clear and accurate and the options are parallel.
   b. Option C is the only three-word option, so it should be revised to achieve parallelism.
   c. Without the context provided in the test specifications, one cannot critique this item.
   d. This is a culturally biased item because only Christians will be able to answer it.

4. In classroom and standardized language testing situations, what is a crucial factor to consider as to which topic should be avoided?
   a. the popularity of the topic among students
   b. the upsetting nature of the topic to students
   c. the level of difficulty the topic presents to students
   d. the alignment of the topic with test preparation classes

5. Based on the chapter, what is the primary purpose of converting raw scores to scaled scores in the context of test equating?
   a. to favor individuals who take more challenging tests
   b. to penalize individuals who take less difficult tests
   c. to ensure consistent scores for test takers across forms and over time
   d. to accommodate unintended differences in difficulty between test forms

Appendix 2 – Classroom Assessment Blueprint

1. **Plan**
   a. Who are the Ss and what needs do they have? Who administers? Who evaluates?
   b. Where are the Ss? Describe the setting. Where are the evaluators?
   c. Why are the Ss assessed, or what is the purpose of assessment?
   d. What are the learning objectives/course goals? What constructs are assessed? What is the proficiency level assessed? What content might also be assessed? What is the test structure like? What tasks/item types does the assessment contain? What is the length of the entire test? What is the length of each part? What is the assessment delivery mode (paper-pencil, computer, internet, etc.)? What is the input format? What is the response format? What are the instructions to the Ss? What are the instructions for test administration? What are the instructions for test evaluation/scoring/marking/grading?
   e. How many parts are there? How many items/tasks are there in each part? How are the items/tasks designed? How is the order of the items/tasks? How is the assessment administered? How is it scored (if constructed response, is there a rating scale)? How important is each part (weighting, point value)?
   f. When to assess? How frequently? When to evaluate?

2. **Write**
   a. Write out the answers to the above questions.
   b. Write the test outline as in the following example.

Instructions for the Ss.

Section 1: Writing: 30 minutes total, choose one of two topics and write an expository essay without a dictionary or other form of assistance

Section 2: Multiple-choice listening: 20 items, of which 10 items are about 5 short dialogs (2 items each) and 10 items are about 2 lectures (5 items each)

Section 3: Multiple-choice reading: 10 items about 2 passages (5 items each), 15 vocabulary items, and 15 grammar items

Section 4: Speaking: 10 minutes total, one-on-one face-to-face interview, three tasks: picture description (3 minutes), narrative (4 minutes), persuasion (3 minutes)

   c. Write the entire test form, instructions for the test administrator and for the test evaluator.

3. **Assemble** the test.

4. **Administer** and ensure evaluation/scoring is accurate.
   a. Pilot the test on a similar S population, if possible. If not, pilot it on other Ss. If not, pilot it on colleagues. At the very least, pilot it yourself.
   b. Analyze pilot responses and test statistics.
   c. Revise based on pilot.
   d. Administer to Ss, ensuring similar test conditions.
   e. Analyze actual responses and test statistics. Analyze scores over time if items are reused.
   f. Revise, keep, and discard items as needed.

5. **Build** all future assessment forms (pre- and post-test, forms *A, B, C*) to the same blueprint specifications.

Appendix 3 – Standardized Test Blueprint

The blueprint of a standardized assessment closely mirrors that of classroom assessments (see Appendix 2).

Bachman and Palmer identify the following main components of a blueprint:

1. Assessment specifications
2. Task specifications (for each task type)
3. Procedures for setting cut scores and making decisions
4. Procedures and formats for reporting assessment record, interpretations, and decisions
5. Procedures for administering the assessment

For a more comprehensive explanation of each of the aforementioned steps, see Bachman and Palmer (2010).

For a detailed guide on writing test specifications, see Davidson and Lynch (2002).

Appendix 4 – Two Detailed Examples of Test Specifications

1. For an example of an academic writing test specification based on Popham's adaptable template (1978, available on Glenn Fulcher's website n.d.), we recommend Walters' work (2016).
2. For a specification of a speaking test linked to the CEFR, we recommend Mewald et al. (2009).

4

Crafting Assessments

Chapter Overview

When writing or evaluating assessment items, it's crucial to follow sound item-writing principles and practices. Whether you are a full-time test developer or a classroom teacher, the goal is to create high-quality assessments that can be justified using an Assessment Use Argument and exhibit good test properties as discussed in Chapter 2. Building on theoretical concepts covered earlier, you will learn to apply them practically in creating or assessing assessments.

This chapter categorizes assessments into selected-response, constructed-response, and authentic types. It concludes by outlining steps beyond item design, guiding readers through the entire assessment-design process. Unlike other chapters, this practical chapter should be studied alongside others, section by section.

4.1 Learning Objectives

1. Recognize common item-writing terminology
2. Recognize sound item-writing principles
3. Write well-crafted items, prompts, and rating scales
4. Critique assessment items
5. Offer corrective feedback on assessment items in accordance with best practices

4.2 What to Assess?

Taking into consideration the learners/TTs, the purpose of the assessment, the context, etc., develop an assessment blueprint (more on the blueprint in Chapter 3). Arguably, the most essential element of the blueprint that is responsible for the quality of an assessment is the quality of the items, prompts, and rating scales. Therefore, the vast majority of this chapter provides guidance on their creation.

> **Test Taker (or candidate):** The test taker (TT) is the person whose language is being assessed. In a teaching–learning situation, this person is referred to as the student (learner, pupil) while in an assessment situation, as the TT.

A Practical Guide to Language Assessment: How Do You Know That Your Students Are Learning? First Edition.
Ildiko Porter-Szucs et al.
© 2025 John Wiley & Sons, Inc. Published 2025 by John Wiley & Sons, Inc.

> **Student, Learner, Pupil, Test Taker, Candidate**: In a classroom, we typically refer to an individual of any age who is studying/learning a language as a *student* or *learner*. In this volume, we do not use the term *pupil* for young learners. In a classroom setting, when a student or learner participates in assessment, we usually continue to refer to them as *student* or *learner*.
>
> In contrast, when someone participates in assessment in a high-stakes setting, they are referred to as a *test taker*. Although the term *candidate* is often used synonymously with *test taker*, it is not used in this volume.
>
> We may use the following abbreviations:
>
> S = student (learner)
> Ss = students (learners)
> TT = test taker
> TTs = test takers
> T = teacher
> Ts= teachers

4.3   General Item Writing Guidelines

1. **Start with the assessment blueprint**. Be clear on the Who? Where? Why? What? How? When? of assessment creation (see Chapter 3).
2. **Identify a relevant situation or target element** (structure, feature, concept, standard, etc.) that you wish to assess.
3. **Determine how best to assess the target element**. Is the skill to be assessed productive, receptive, or integrated? Is it best to assess it with task-, project-, performance-, scenario-based assessment?
4. **Assess only what is worth assessing**. Depending on the purpose, setting, context, TT, etc. of the assessment, assess only elements that are commonly used so as to optimize washback. Given that teaching, learning, and assessment have a recursive relationship, TTs should not have to devote a considerable amount of time preparing to master concepts that are rarely used at a particular proficiency level and in a given context. For instance, in an adult-education or community setting or in a Spanish-for-tourists class, students are going to benefit from spending more time on yes/no or WH questions than on embedded questions. In an English for Academic Purposes (EAP) class, however, embedded questions can be beneficial.
5. **Avoid assessing language features that would force a decision about prescriptiveness vs. descriptiveness**. Again, circumstances may override this recommendation, but in general you should assess what will truly help your students/TTs. This means, for example, that assessing the prescriptive use of *lie* vs. *lay* should give way to a target structure that will serve the students/TTs more.
6. **Provide even coverage of the material. Don't over assess one area of language to the detriment of others**. Keeping the purpose of the assessment in mind, maintain a balance. For instance, in an intermediate ESL/EFL class, where you are studying all the verb tenses, be sure to assess all the times and aspects in a way that reflects their use in the language and their usefulness to the students. The assessment should reflect what the students are learning, so the Present Perfect vs. the Simple Past, for instance, should occupy proportionally as much of the test as it does of the time spent learning it. Try to keep in mind that you want to give TTs an opportunity to demonstrate their language ability and show how much they have learned, rather than confuse them with tricky items.

7. **Avoid knowledge items on an assessment of skills**. On an assessment of English language proficiency, it is best to emphasize principles, scenarios, and usage rather than trivial facts. For instance, instead of asking the TTs to list the US presidents from first to last, assess language skills (listening, speaking, etc.). For example, in a paragraph, describe a major achievement of one US president or show how the policies of one president related to those of his predecessor. If the facts appear in a listening or reading stimulus passage, then they could be sparingly assessed. Of course, if the subject matter of the course is the history of a country or another content area rather than use of the language itself, the assessment should mirror the course content.

8. **Document the sources**. Whenever possible for item-writing inspiration and for accountability, document the references/sources behind each item, the best answer, and a rationale for it. For example: *Option B is correct because the stem says _____; C and D are not effects but rather causes and A actually contradicts the main idea because _____. See page 123 of Jackson (2000).*

   a. **Consider the proficiency level**. Ensure that the item/topic is at the appropriate level of proficiency/difficulty. Consult the Tools of the Trade (Chapter 5) for ideas on how to achieve this.

   b. **Study this chapter carefully**. While crafting items, be sure to follow both the general and item-type-specific item-writing guidelines from this chapter.

Think-Pair-Share 4.3a   Reflect on the definition of "construct" introduced in Chapter 2. Provide a specific example of how the construct of *fluency* is defined in a language teaching/learning context you are familiar with.

The way the construct is defined will determine how the test item is constructed and evaluated. Consider, for example, the construct of writing a composition. *Composition* in different contexts may be defined in vastly different ways.

4.3.1   Example Construct Definition A of Composition

Composition ability means expressing oneself clearly, coherently in writing on a particular topic.

4.3.2   Example Construct Definition B of Composition

Composition ability for academic purposes means writing an argumentative essay on a particular topic in the following way: clear, coherent, grammatically and lexically correct, as well as mechanically accurate.

Think-Pair-Share 4.3b   Reflect in writing or verbally on the differences between the two construct definitions. What features of writing do they emphasize? What might the rating scale look like for each one?

Think-Pair-Share 4.3c   Think of two different contexts. Write two construct definitions for *speaking*. Evaluate them as in 4.3a.

Each test item should test just one construct; otherwise, conclusions about the TT's mastery of the construct will be difficult to draw. Consider, for instance, the following item on a vocabulary test of young ELs (6–10 years old).

Claire bought three dozen eggs. How many eggs did she buy?

a. *36**   **b.** *30*   **c.** *13*   **d.** *3*

On a vocabulary test of young learners, the only construct assessed should be the meaning of vocabulary, i.e. the meaning of *dozen*. In this item, however, the TTs' ability to do math is also assessed (3 × 12). Considering the TTs' young age, we cannot assume that this is a fair or valid question.

Think-Pair-Share 4.3d   Why might it be problematic that the vocabulary item about a *dozen* eggs tests more than the targeted word? Discuss.

Construct Irrelevance (or Construct-Irrelevant Variance): An irrelevant factor that hinders the interpretability of the TT's mastery of the construct because the item may measure something more or other than the targeted construct.

In the exercise about a *dozen* eggs, the TT's ability to answer the question about the three dozen eggs depends not only on knowing the meaning of *dozen* but also on the ability to multiply 12 × 3. Given that the target test-taking population is 6–10 years old, this may cause construct irrelevance; TTs may answer incorrectly not because they do not know the meaning of the assessed word but because of their developing knowledge of mathematics.

Construct irrelevance, thus, may occur when the score does not reflect the TT's mastery of the construct due to an irrelevant element introduced in the item. However, the item may also be unnecessarily easy due to the TT's familiarity with the assessed topic or due to the presence of helpful clues. Examine the following reading-comprehension test item.

During the month of Ramadan, Muslims ___ from dawn to dusk.

a. *party*   **b.** *feast*   **c.** *fast**   **d.** *pray*

TTs with background knowledge on this topic will be able to identify the correct answer, or key, without reading the passage.

Assessment item writers should take care to minimize construct-irrelevant variance.

Think-Pair-Share 4.3e   Sometimes teachers and item writers would like to challenge students and TTs in order to differentiate students' language ability. Why is introducing construct irrelevance into test items not the right way to increase the challenge? Discuss.

Test Item (or Item) is the assessment question to be answered, the writing prompt to write or speak about.

Based on response attributes, there are two broad categories of test items: selected response and constructed response.

Selected-Response Item (SR): These are items where the TT selects from among options provided by the item writer. Examples include multiple-choice, true/false, matching, and fill-in-the-blank from a word bank.

Constructed-Response Item (CR) (or supply-type): These are items where the TT supplies, or constructs, an answer to the question or prompt. Examples include fill-in-the-blank without a word bank, short answer (verbal or written), essay, and oral presentation.

The following sections examine the most common item types and describes how to write them. Sections 4.4 (4.4.1–4.4.20) discuss the most common selected-response item types. Sections 4.5 (4.5.1–4.5.16) discuss the most common constructed-response items.

4.4 Selected Response

4.4.1 Multiple-Choice Question (MC or MCQ)

The MCQ is perhaps the most common item type in many language-learning contexts around the world. It most commonly assesses knowledge-recognition of grammar, vocabulary, formulaic language, reading comprehension, and listening comprehension. Its popularity can be ascribed to its ease of test administration and scoring and relatively high objectivity. Its disadvantages include the lengthy and challenging test development process, the low interactiveness and authenticity, that it assesses recognition, the ease of guessing and cheating, and the frequently negative washback.

Example MCQ
A multiple-choice item consists of the following parts (see Figure 4.1): the stem, which is the statement or question that provides the context for the question and the actual problem to solve, and the options, which typically consist of one correct answer (known as the *key*) and one or more incorrect answers (known as the *distractors*). In Figure 4.1, there are four options (a, b, c, d), of which only one is the key (d) and three are the distractors (a, b, c). MCQs can have three, four, or more options. Most MCQs have just one key and the rest are distractors although it is possible to craft items where two or more options are correct. In computerized tests, options may appear in a drop-down menu.

Did you know?   Omnibusek, a standardized elementary-school English proficiency test in Poland, contains MCQs with multiple keys. For instance, there may be a picture of a little boy sitting and a little girl standing and the TT must select all statements that are true of the picture. The statements might be

a. *The boy is sitting.*
b. *The girl is sitting.*
c. *The boy isn't standing.*
d. *The girl isn't sitting.*

In this case, there is no stem, the keys are *a, c,* and *d,* and the distractor is *b.*

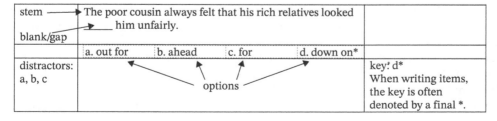

Figure 4.1   Sample multiple-choice item.

4.4.2 Guidelines for designing MCQ

1. Design each item to measure a single construct.
2. Minimize the reading load on the TT. State both stem and options as directly as possible. Put as much wording in the stem as possible rather than in the options. Therefore, the following item can be revised:

The back part of a ship _____.
a. *is called the stern**
b. *is called the bow*
c. *is called the hull*
d. *is called the starboard*

The repeated "is called the" should be moved to the stem and the options should remain the unique words only.
The back part of a ship is called the _____.
a. *stern**   **b.** *bow*   **c.** *hull*   **d.** *starboard*

3. State the stem in the positive form whenever possible. Avoid *not, never, no, except, all but* whenever possible. If not possible, be sure to highlight the negative words clearly and group all items containing a negative stem at the beginning or end of all MCQ items. Negatively worded stems may introduce construct-irrelevant variance when the TT gets confused by the wording. Options containing *all of the above* and *A and B only* are also confusing and should be used sparingly.

See the following undesirable item.
Which of the following cities is NOT in Australia?
a. *Auckland**   **b.** *Canberra*   **c.** *Sydney*   **d.** *Melbourne*

Rephrase this item to avoid the negative stem.
Which of the following cities is in Australia?
a. *Canberra**   **b.** *Johannesburg*   **c.** *Auckland*   **d.** *Vancouver*

If you can't think of any plausible distractors, try flipping the stem and the options.
Canberra is in which country?
a. *Australia**   **b.** *New Zealand*   **c.** *Canada*   **d.** *USA*

4. Whenever possible avoid words of extreme—*always, never, everybody, nobody, all*—because of the possibility of rare unanticipated cases. When a stem contains such a word, it is usually a distractor, unless it references someone's specific opinion, as in "according to the author." Conversely, stems containing qualifiers such as *usually, mostly, rarely, many, most*, etc. tend to make the item correct. These test-taking tips are well known to savvy TTs.
5. Ensure that the key smoothly completes the stem in both meaning and form. Note in the example in Figure 4.1 that all the options are lower case because they fit into the middle of the stem. If the missing word started the sentence, then the options would start with a capital letter.
6. Place the blank towards the end of the stem rather than the beginning. This way, as TTs read the stem, they can understand the context and by the time they reach the blank, the key is at the tip of their tongue. In other words, ideally, TTs could even complete the stem without looking at the options. When they do look at the options in search of the key, they can confirm their initial guess.

See the following incorrectly worded stem.

The secretary _____ be on vacation since he never misses a day of work; that's the only possible explanation for his absence.

a. *must**   **b.** *might*   **c.** *can*   **d.** *should*

Rephrase the stem to move the blank towards the end.

Since he never misses a day of work, there is just one possible explanation for the secretary's absence: he _____ be on vacation.

a. *must**   **b.** *might*   **c.** *can*   **d.** *should*

7. Do not let the key stand out in any way. Make all options parallel in length, part of speech, form, capitalization, punctuation, etc. In other words, if the key is a verb, ideally all options should be verbs.

See the following undesirable reading-comprehension item.

Based on the story, what do you think Carlos will do next?

a. *walk the dog*
b. *He will call his friend.*
c. *to watch television*
d. *do his homework*

Rephrase this item to make all the options parallel.

Based on the story, what do you think Carlos will do next?

a. *walk the dog*
b. *call his friend*
c. *watch television*
d. *do his homework*

If it is not possible to keep the options parallel because, for instance, the key is a verb but at least one distractor must be a noun, then in a four-option MCQ test, two options (the key and one distractor) should be verbs while the remaining two options should be nouns. If the key is a phrase, then ideally all options should be phrases. Again, if the ideal isn't possible, then balance the options any way you can to protect the key.

8. Avoid accidental double keys. In poorly crafted items, there may be two correct options by accident.

For instance, according to a listening passage, the dough should be cut into approximately 2-inch squares. If the item is as follows, then there is a double key.

Cut the dough into _____-inch squares.
a. *1-2*   **b.** *2-3*   **c.** *3-4*   **d.** *4-5*
Both *a.* and *b.* could be keyable since the stimulus states "approximately 2" inches.

9. Avoid lopsided options that naturally group together and essentially reduce the number of available options. For instance:

An airplane that travels faster than the speed of sound is _____.
a. *sonic*
b. *supersonic*
c. *hypersonic*
d. *interstellar*

Savvy TTs know that the key is one of the three options with the same root *(sonic)*, so construct-irrelevance can thus be introduced into the item.

10. Items should be written in such a way that in isolation each option should be plausible. Only when substituted back into the stem should the key emerge as the only correct option. For example:

The fresh paint made it appear _____ new.
a. *as if the building were**
b. *although the building was*
c. *like this building is*
d. *similar to how this building*

Each of the options (*a., b., c., d.*), when read in isolation, sounds like it could be part of an English sentence. However, when read within the stem, then all but the first option create ungrammatical sentences.

11. Avoid leaving unwanted clues for the TT. For example, the following would be a bad listening or reading item. For example:

Excuse me, may I have an _____?
a. *banana*　　　　b. *melon*　　　　c. *orange** 　　　d. *plum*

Grammatically only the key, option c., would be correct because the indefinite article *an* must be followed by a vowel sound while options *a., b.,* and *d.* start with a consonant. Thus, even if the TT didn't understand what the speaker asked for in the stimulus, the inadvertent clue would tip off the TT. One way to correct this item is to move the indefinite article from the stem to the options (*a banana, a melon, an orange, a plum*); another way is to change the article in the stem to *a(n)* or *a/an*.

12. Distribute the key evenly among the possible options. It is tempting to make *a.* the key because when crafting the item, the item writer always writes the correct answer first and only later creates the distractors. Nowadays online quiz makers, learning management systems, and randomizer programs can select random keys. However, short of an electronic solution, pulling *a., b., c., d.* out of a hat or rolling a die repeatedly is still the best key-randomizing method.

13. On a vocabulary test, create options that are of similar frequency. For instance, if the key is 20 occurrences/million on the COCA,[1] then the options should also be in the 15–25/million range. Or if the key is 1–5/million, so should be the key and distractors.

See the following undesirable item at the advanced level.
An antonym for the word "agreeable" is _____.
a. *violent** 　　　　　　b. *easygoing*　　　　　　c. *serene*
agreeable (2.048/million), violent (43.83/million), easygoing (1.62/million), serene (3.75/million)

Rephrase this item to avoid the overly frequent lexical choice: *violent*.
An antonym for the word "agreeable" is _____.
a. *aggressive** 　　　　　b. *easygoing*　　　　　c. *serene*
aggressive (1.54/million)

---

1 For a thorough discussion of the Corpus of Contemporary American English (COCA), see Chapter 5.

4.4.3   Other Examples of Multiple-choice Item Types

Figure 4.1 depicts a typical multiple-choice item type. The Omnibusek example from Poland depicts another one. Let us examine several more and apply the aforementioned guidelines to them.

A. Odd word out: Identify the odd word out by crossing it out.

  1. a. *exhibit*   **b.** *disguise*   **c.** *display*   **d.** *expose*

The key is b., Options a., c., and d. are all verbs meaning *to show* but option b. means *to hide*. Despite the lack of context, there is only one key. Another plus of this item is that two of the options begin with the prefix *ex-* and two with *dis-*, so the options are parallel and the key does not stand out.

However, the frequency of the assessed vocabulary is quite broad: *exhibit* 23/million, *disguise* 6/million, *display* 43/million, and *expose* 45/million. In particular, the key stands out as infrequent. If this item appeared on a general proficiency test or on a certification test for a particular language proficiency level, then this frequency gap would be suboptimal. However, if this were an achievement test, after the students had studied all four words, then that would be acceptable.

  2. a. *cats*   **b.** *dogs*   **c.** *mice*   **d.** *rain*

This is a badly written item. Due to the lack of context, a convincing argument can be made for either c. or d. being the odd word out, or the key. *C* can be the key because the remaining words comprise the idiom *It's raining cats and dogs*. *D* can be the key because the other words are all animals.

3.

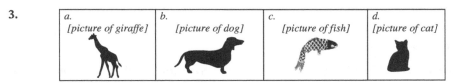

a. [picture of giraffe]	b. [picture of dog]	c. [picture of fish]	d. [picture of cat]

Figure 4.2   Sample picture item: odd word out. *Sources:* gdakaska / Pixabay, Clker-Free-Vector-Images / Pixabay, gdakaska / Pixabay, OpenClipart-Vectors / Pixabay

With the proper instructions, item 3 (or Figure 4.2) could become usable. The instructions would have to state that the TTs are to focus on the number of syllables in each word rather than where the animals live or whether they are mammals. Therefore, if this were a pronunciation item, then the key would be *a.* since *giraffe* is pronounced as two syllables while *dog, fish*, and *cat* contain one syllable each.

B. True/False/Not Given (Not Stated)
"True/False/Not given" items are three-option multiple-choice items. A statement about the stimulus may either be true, false, or not mentioned in the text. As an illustration, let us examine the passage and items below.

> *Directions: Read the passage below. Then, based on the reading, answer the questions that follow as T (True), F (False), or NG (Not Given).*
>
> *Party-supply stores around the United States are closing. Has demand for party hats, balloons, and costumes fallen? Are Americans perhaps not in the mood to party? Quite the opposite: it's the global shortage of the second-most common element, helium, that's the culprit.*

  1. *T/F/NG*   *Americans are less interested in partying.*
  2. *T/F/NG*   *Helium is the second-lightest element on Earth.*
  3. *T/F/NG*   *Party stores cannot purchase enough helium.*

The answer to the first question is *False*, to the second *Not Given*, and to the third *True*. Although from background knowledge, some TTs may know that helium is the second-lightest element on Earth after hydrogen, this information is not mentioned in the text. And since this is a test of reading *comprehension* rather than scientific background knowledge, statement #2 must be *NG* rather than *T* or *F*.

C. Insert the missing word/phrase/sentence/paragraph

In reading comprehension tests, coherence and cohesion can be assessed by asking the TTs to insert missing information where it logically belongs. Typically, during assessment development, the item writer writes a reading-comprehension passage with all the information. Next, parts of the passage are removed and moved into the items. These parts may be individual words (such as adjectives, adverbs, and transitions), phrases, or even complete sentences. The passage should sound complete with or without the missing text. In the remaining passage, typically four spots are marked *a., b., c.,* and *d.* where the removed text could be inserted. One spot is the key while the remaining spots are the distractors. The item stem prompts the TTs to insert each missing text into one of the *a., b., c.,* and *d.* spots.

Building on the previous example passage from B about helium:

*Directions: Read the passage below. Then, indicate where the **bold-faced** sentence could be added to the passage: to spot a), b), c), or d).*

> ***a)*** *Party-supply stores around the United States are closing.* ***b)*** *Has demand for party hats, balloons, and costumes fallen? Are Americans perhaps not in the mood to party?* ***c)*** *Quite the opposite: it's the global shortage of the second-most common element, helium, that's the culprit.* ***d)***

> **1.** *Look at the **a), b), c),** and **d)** spots in the above passage. Indicate where the following sentence could be added to the passage.*

While the element itself is plentiful in the ground, there is an insufficient amount mined to meet the demand.

a. before the first sentence
b. between the first and second sentences
c. after the third sentence
d. after the last sentence

The correct answer is *d) after the last sentence*. The bolded sentence refers to "the element," which was identified as *helium* in the previous sentence; it also identifies the reason for the global helium shortage as a problem of mining the gas. In order to key this item, the TT must understand the logic and flow of the entire passage and how the ideas cohere.

D. Find the error

In most MCQs, TTs look for the correct answer, but in this item type, they seek to identify the incorrect option. The Paper-Based TOEFL test employed this item type extensively. Here, the stem is a complete sentence with three to five elements underlined, boldfaced, or otherwise highlighted. The *a, b, c, and d* options are the three to five highlighted elements. These can be grammatical, lexical, or mechanical (spelling, punctuation, capitalization). Examine the following examples for each.

1. ___Had___ I known you ___are___ coming, I would ___have___ ___cooked___ your favorite meal.
     a.   *b.*   *c.*   *d.*

2. Tokyo, Delhi, and Shanghai are ___among___ the most ___densely___ ___populated___ cities in the ___globe___.
                            a.   *b.*   *c.*   *d.*

3. Let's meet on ___Thursday___ at ___Noon___ at ___Café___ ___Anna___.
            a.   *b.*   *c.*   *d.*

The key in item 1 above is *b.* (it should be *were*), in item 2 it's *d.* (it should be *world*), and in item 3 it's *b.* (it should be *noon*). A variation on this item type is to ask TTs to correct the error after having located it.

E. Dialogic items

An item may contain a dialogue either in the stimulus or in the stem itself. Listening comprehension items are frequently based on a conversation between two or more people, such as a librarian and a library user, a tourist and a tour guide, two students, and two coworkers. Having listened to the conversation, the TTs then respond to questions. These questions may be comprehension questions about the dialogue. TTs may also be prompted to provide alternative or additional turns in the dialogue. The speakers are typically identified as *M for man, W for woman or M for male, F for female, B for boy, G for girl, 1 for older*, and *2 for younger speaker*. Take the example in Figure 4.3.

  2. *Listen to the conversation again. Then choose the best response.*
    M1: Have you seen Katie recently?
    W2: She's been out since the party last week.
    M1: a. I guess I'll have to call her.
         b. I agree that's a good idea.
         c. I'll go outside and look for her.

In the first item above, the dialogue involves a conversation between two coworkers in a small office. The question about the conversation assesses the TTs' comprehension of the second turn, in which the woman says that Katie *has been out since the party last week*. The key is option *a.* because *being out* means out of the office, so Katie has not been in the office this week.

In the second item above, the task is to continue the stimulus dialog by selecting from among the three options the most plausible third turn. The best response is *a*, for the man to decide to talk to Katie by calling her on the phone. In this item not only the stimulus was dialogic but also the options.

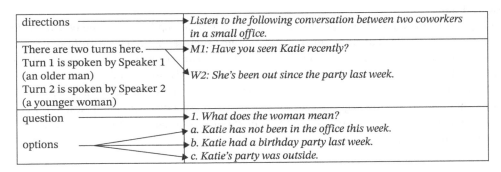

Figure 4.3 Sample dialogic item.

a. b. c.

Figure 4.4 Sample multiple-choice item: pictures as options. *Sources:* https://tinyurl.com/directorchairpic; https://tinyurl.com/rollingchairpic; https://tinyurl.com/beachchairpic

F. Pictures as options

Pictures can be used in place of written options. They are often used with less proficient, young, or low-literacy TTs. Learners whose literacy skills in the target language would be an impediment to being able to engage fully with the assessment should not have to do so. Otherwise, the test may introduce construct-irrelevant variance. Also, asking TTs to use a productive skill (writing or speaking) when assessing a receptive skill, like listening can lessen validity. When selecting pictures, make sure they are age-appropriate, e.g. not too juvenile for an adult assessment, and be aware of any copyrights[2] that may prevent your use of images.

See the following pictorial MCQ following a brief listening stimulus.

After hearing a stimulus passage—a description of three chairs someone is considering buying—the narrator asks which chair the woman will buy. The options are the three chairs in Figure 4.4.

In the case of color images, it is important not to disadvantage TTs with color blindness or color deficiency; thus, the three options should differ in more than just color. The description of the three chairs in the stimulus should also mention the various distinguishing features. For instance, the shopper may say that the beach chair looks as comfortable as a bed, the office chair with the five wheels looks the most practical, but the four thin legs of the movie director's chair do not feel strong. So at the end, the shopper chooses the office chair.

Did you know?   On the WIDA Screener for grades 1 to 3, TTs look at a large picture and read a sentence about it. The picture, for example, may depict a classroom and the sentence may describe an element of the classroom. Three boxed-off sections of the classroom appear, and the TT is to select from among the boxed answers one that the written sentence describes. In another version of the same task, on the large picture is a small picture fragment. The TT is to drag the fragment box to one of the answer boxes in the picture.

G. Minimal pairs

Technically this is not a new item type but rather a very common application of the typical MCQ. Minimal pairs are words that differ in only one sound, such as *hat-hot, ball-call*, and *Polish* (nationality)-*polish* (make shiny). The options in this item can be depicted as symbols of the International Phonetic Alphabet (IPA), or as pictures, or in regular orthography. To turn it into a low-stakes interactive activity, students or TTs, in pairs, can take turns reading the assessed words to their partners. As a kinesthetic group activity, TTs can even use a fly swatter and swat at the correct option, which is depicted on the board or the wall. (See the internet for tutorials on the flyswatter game in a language class.)

---

2 Royalty-free sites available on the internet include Creative Commons (n.d.) and Public Domain Vectors (2024).

Below are depicted two versions of the typical minimal-pair MCQ.
Version 1—Directions: Listen and circle the word you hear.

1. *hit*   *heat*   *hate*
2. *fit*   *feat*   *fate*
3. *sim*   *seem*   *same*

or

Version 2—Directions: Listen and circle the sound you hear.

1. / ɪ /   / iː /   / eɪ /
2. / ɪ /   / iː /   / eɪ /
3. / ɪ /   / iː /   / eɪ /

In both versions, the TT hears only one of the three words pronounced in each item. For instance, in *1. hit*, in *2. fate,* and in *3. seem*. The only difference is that in the first version, the TT circles the word that is read, while in the second version, the TT circles the IPA symbol of the minimal pair. Ideally, the words should be played from a quality audio recording so the assessment administration can be standardized.

H. Select Cloze, or Cloze with multiple-choice options

A cloze, also known as the *cloze-deletion test*, is a fill-in-the blank passage. Unlike the typical MCQ item, where the blanks in isolated sentences are to be completed from the answer choices, a cloze passage consists of connected sentences with blanks. Based on the occurrence of the blanks, there are different types of cloze. In one type—*fixed ratio, or systematic*—the deletion typically occurs anywhere between every 5th and 10th word in each sentence. For instance, every 7th word is deleted. The more frequent the deletion, the more challenging the task.

In another type—*rational, or unsystematic*—specific parts of speech are deleted (such as three nouns, two verbs, and four adjectives). Deletions may also occur purposefully when a concrete number of micro (or local) and macro (or global) items are deleted. Keying local items simply requires understanding the immediate vicinity of the blank. Keying global items requires looking beyond the sentence where the blank occurs. It may even require the careful re-reading of another paragraph, such as a pronoun referring to someone who was mentioned in a previous sentence or a cohesive device (a transition) that shows the relationship between sentences or paragraphs. The difficulty of the cloze passage needs to match the TTs' proficiency.

The *conversational cloze*, the third type, wherein words are missing from a dialogue, will be discussed with the constructed-response item types.

Regardless of the type of deletion, the first and last sentences of the passage must remain intact. In other words, no word should be deleted from the first or last sentence. There should also be at least three to four intact words between two blanks.

The most common skill assessed by a cloze is reading comprehension. However, even listening can be assessed through a cloze if what is being assessed is whether the TT can hear/decipher sounds or words.

4.4.4   Example Rational Select Cloze

When you accidentally cut your finger, your skin heals itself after a few days. Wouldn't it be wonderful if other materials could heal (1)_____ too? This wish could soon become a (2)_____. Researchers have created a rubber-like material that can do (3)_____.

To demonstrate their invention, the scientists 3D-printed (4)_____ piece of the material in a few minutes. (5)_____ they cut it in half. At room temperature, the material (6)_____ itself in 6–8 hours. With increased heat (140°F/60°C) the healing (7)_____ shrank to 2 hours.
Possible applications include the soles of shoes, toys, and car tires.

(1) a. them	*b. their*	*c. theirs*	*d. themselves**
(2) a. true	*b. reality**	*c. happen*	*d. fact*
(3) a. just that*	*b. that's it*	*c. it's so*	*d. so that*
(4) a. the	*b. that*	*c. an*	*d. a**
(5) a. Then*	*b. Thus*	*c. Though*	*d. Third*
(6) a. developed	*b. produced*	*c. repaired**	*d. improved*
(7) a. distance	*b. power*	*c. time**	*d. energy*

In the rational-deletion cloze above, both local and global items have been deleted. **Local items** are *(1), (2), (3), (4)*, and *(7)*. These items can be keyed just by examining the phrase, clause, or sentence in which the deletion takes place. **Global items** are *(5)* and *(6)* because finding the correct option requires that the TTs think beyond the immediate sentence. In item *(5)*, for example, each option by itself is possible. When placed back into the gap, it's necessary to examine the entire sentence structure and even the previous sentences to eliminate all the distractors. Option *b.* is incorrect because the relationship between that sentence and the preceding one is not cause-effect. Option *c.* is incorrect because the relationship is not that of concession or contrast. Option *d.* is incorrect because the sentence with the gap is not the third but the second step. Therefore, option *a.* is the key since the connection between the sentences is chronological. In item *(6)*, all four options have similar meanings and grammatically fill the gap. However, only option C makes sense in the context of the entire passage. The second and penultimate sentences mention healing and the whole passage reinforces this idea. The key—*repaired*—is a synonym of *healed*.

Proponents of cloze assessments argue that TTs must attend to the larger context beyond the sentence level, it's possible to test discourse features, and it's possible to assess a variety of constructs in one passage: one item can test grammar, another vocabulary (including collocations), another a cohesive device, etc. These advantages have been demonstrated in the example passage above. Opponents of cloze assessments argue that they take a long time to develop, they may be confusing to TTs, and attempts at validating the effectiveness of cloze assessments have largely failed because it is unclear what constructs specifically cloze tests measure. About the debate over the extent to which vocabulary in a cloze contributes to TTs' performance, Read (2000) concludes that a cloze is a highly *"embedded* assessment of vocabulary" (p. 115), and therefore, the distinct contribution of vocabulary is difficult to measure.

4.4.5 Guidelines for Designing Cloze Assessments:

- Write or select a passage that is suitable to the TTs' proficiency level and the purpose of the assessment. It should not be too technical for the TTs.
- Check the readability of the completed text. (For more on readability programs, see Chapter 5.)
- The length should be such that a suitable number of items can be included. Remember that the first and last sentences should remain intact. Also, remember that blanks should be spaced every 5–10 words apart. The closer the blanks are to each other, the more challenging the task.

- Depending on the type of cloze being crafted, follow the specific instructions for the rational-deletion, fixed-ratio, or conversational cloze.
- When designing the MC items, follow the general guidelines for MCQs.

I. Cross-text items

The typical reading-comprehension MCQ is based on the stimulus passage directly preceding it. Cross-text items, however, refer to more than one stimulus passage. A well-designed cross-text item can only be keyed if the TT understands the assessed information from all the targeted passages.

Cross-text items are similar to integrated test items in that more than one source of stimulus is necessary to answer them. They differ, however, in that integrated items assess information delivered through various modes—written and spoken, i.e. from both reading and listening passages—while cross-text items assess multiple texts from the same mode.

4.4.6   Example Cross-text Item

Imagine that the following two excerpts have been taken from longer reading passages.
Directions: Read the passages below. Then answer the questions. Question 1 may refer to more than one passage.

Reading A
Fingerprinting, iris recognition, face recognition—once straight out of science fiction are now widely used techniques for recognizing or verifying a person. Face recognition, in particular, has been used widely due to its noninvasive nature.

Reading B
There are fewer than 2000 giant pandas living in the wild, all of them in China. Recently, the Chinese government has increased its conservation efforts by building the Giant Panda National Park. The tracking of the animals over 27 000 square kilometers will be made easier by facial recognition technology.

1. *According to Readings A and B, what are some advantages of tracking pandas with facial recognition technology?*
   a. *It is an automated process.*
   b. *It can be implemented quickly.*
   c. *It is more precise than other forms of identification.*
   d. *It can be done without direct human contact with the animals.*

The correct answer is d., based on the two texts. TTs need to understand the first text to learn that face-recognition technology is noninvasive, in other words requires no direct contact with the subject of the surveillance. TTs need to understand the second text to know that this technology is being applied to pandas.

Did you know?   The Michigan English Test (by Michigan Language Assessment) contains cross-text items in the reading section. TTs read three passages on the same general topic, first answer comprehension questions specific to each passage, and finally answer cross-text questions, which refer to two or more of the texts.

4.4.7 Dichotomous Response

Dichotomous items contain two options. Most commonly, these are True (T) and False (F). T/F questions are often used in reading and listening comprehension assessments. Other types of dichotomous items are Yes/No, Up/Down, and Left/Right, choosing between two pictures, minimal pairs when the choice is between two options. Dichotomous items share the same advantages as MCQs: ease of test administration and scoring as well as relatively high objectivity. Its disadvantages include the low interactiveness and authenticity and that it assesses recognition. TTs have a 50/50 chance of locating the key, which may further ease guessing and cheating.

Example dichotomous item: T/F
The typical dichotomous item will be used following a reading or listening passage. The above example follows a reading passage about Jane Austen's novel *Emma*. The passage is also referred to as the *stimulus* because it stimulates responses to the test questions.

Think-Pair-Share 4.4a Synthesis   Sometimes each line of the stimulus or reading text is numbered and the items require TTs to select true or false AND the line in the text that indicates that it is true or false. Why do you think test designers would require TTs to do this?

4.4.8 Guidelines for Designing Dichotomous Items

Similar principles apply to this item type as to the MCQs and a few new ones.

1. The wording of the items should be simple and clear. Negatives should be used sparingly and double negatives should be avoided if possible: e.g. *It is **not uncommon to** ....* They make the stem unnecessarily convoluted. Our goal is to assess the TTs' comprehension of the passage and not whether they can follow the twists and turns of the stem. A TT may miskey item 3 in Figure 4.5 not because they misunderstand the stimulus passage but because they get confused by the question about it.
2. Ask questions about meaningful and important parts of the passage. Again, item 3 fails in this regard. While it is true that Emma was often kind to Miss Bates, the more significant element of the plot is that she was often rude to her. Thus, item 3 should be revised as *Emma was often unkind to Miss Bates*, which would make the statement True.

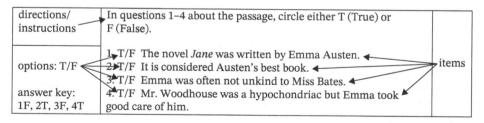

directions/ instructions	In questions 1–4 about the passage, circle either T (True) or F (False).	
options: T/F	1. T/F The novel *Jane* was written by Emma Austen. 2. T/F It is considered Austen's best book. 3. T/F Emma was often not unkind to Miss Bates. 4. T/F Mr. Woodhouse was a hypochondriac but Emma took good care of him.	items
answer key: 1F, 2T, 3F, 4T		

Figure 4.5 Sample dichotomous item: true/false.

3. The item should assess the stimulus rather than the stem or the options. In other words, the more challenging concepts and vocabulary should be in the stimulus and the less challenging synonym in the item assessing the TT's comprehension of the stimulus. The following is a bad example. The stimulus uses the word cow and the T/F item aims to assess it.
   T/F The cow is a dairy producing mammal.

If the word to be assessed is *cow*, then all the other words used to define it should be more frequent than it. At print time, the frequencies in the Corpus of Contemporary American English (COCA) (BYU, n.d.a) of the central words in this definition are as follows.

cow	25.3/million
mammal	8.9/million
dairy	9.7/million
produce	187.1/million

We see that a relatively frequent word (*cow*) is defined with much less frequent words (*mammal, dairy*). Therefore, even if a TT may understand the target word, they may answer the question incorrectly because of not understanding the words that explain the target word. This item, in its current form, assesses less the meaning of *cow* and more those of *mammal* and *dairy*.

Revised, this item reads as follows.

T/F The cow is an animal that gives milk.

All the key words—*animal, give,* and *milk*—are more frequent than the word the item purports to assess.

4. Items should be independent of each other. The example in Figure 4.5 is correct in this regard. Whether or not a TT correctly keys one item will not influence their chances of correctly keying another item. An incorrect example would be if between items 3 and 4, we inserted the following item:

The heroines of Austen's other books are less masterfully written.

If the TT chooses that it's true that Emma is Austen's best book, then they're likely to answer *True* about this new question, and vice versa because the two questions are related to each other.

5. Items should not key each other. The example in Figure 4.5 does violate this item-writing principle though. Item 1 asks whether the author's name is *Emma Austen* and whether her novel's title is *Jane*. Let us assume that a TT cannot find the correct answer to this question by reading the stimulus passage. When the TT reaches items 3 and 4, it should become obvious that the main heroine's name is *Emma*; therefore, item 1 must be False. TTs should not be able to answer a question without reading and understanding the stimulus, and most of all they should not be able to guess correct answers because other items give them away.

6. In item 4, the word *hypochondriac* can be assessed if it was specifically taught in class, and on an achievement assessment, the teacher is trying to assess whether the students have learned its meaning. It occurs 0.4/million times in COCA, which is extremely infrequent. If it appeared on a proficiency assessment, then TTs who speak a language that uses this Greek word would have an advantage over those TTs who do not.

4.4.9 Other Examples of Dichotomous Item Types

Figure 4.5 about the novel *Emma* depicts a typical dichotomous item type. Let us examine several more and apply the above guidelines to them.

A. Dichotomous Keys in US K-12 Settings:

This is essentially a decision tree of yes/no questions, similar to the game *Twenty Questions*. It is frequently used when trying to identify something or someone based on the presence or absence of certain characteristics. At the end of the series of forks in the decision tree, the identification is made. Let us examine the following example of one student trying to guess a sport that the other student is thinking of.

> Student A: *Do you play this sport with an animal?*
> Student B: *No.*
> A: *Do you play it with a ball?*
> B: *Yes.*
> A: *Is the ball round?*
> B: *Yes.*
> A: *Is the ball soft?*
> B: *No.*
> A: *Do you kick the ball?*
> B: *No.*
> A: *Do you throw the ball?*
> B: *Yes.*
> A: *Do you play it in the water?*
> B: *Yes.*
> A: *Is it water polo?*
> B: *Yes.*

This can be a successful teaching–learning activity as well as an assessment. It can be conducted with students taking turns in pairs or groups. From an item-writing perspective, the wording of the questions should be simple and comprehensible to the student/TT. This includes a deliberate choice of vocabulary, sentence structure, and sentence length. The options typically follow a dichotomous pattern, such as *Yes/No* and *Go To* whichever next question allows for the dichotomous pattern to continue.

B. Same/Different

The same/different dichotomous item is commonly used in listening discrimination, similarly to 4.3 G) Minimal Pairs. The TT hears two sounds/words/phrases/etc. one after the other and decides whether they are the same sounds/words/phrases/etc. or different. For instance, the recording may play:

1. *[steam – steam]*
   and the TT marks (*) on the answer sheet
   same*   *different*

In contrast, the recording may play

2. *[steam – stem]*
   and the TT marks
   same   *different**

As with any listening assessment, a consistent, high-quality delivery is best for standardization.

4.4.10 Matching

Matching items typically comprise two lists, where pairs of items (one from each list) need to be connected. Matches can be made between words and their definitions, words and corresponding pictures, categories and examples, words and specific sounds that they contain, words and their synonyms or antonyms, profession names and their functions, abbreviations or acronyms and their meanings, male–female equivalents of nouns, etc. The possibilities for matching items are virtually endless. Matches are typically made by drawing a line between the paired items. However, they can also be solved through filling in blanks, whereby items from the list are written/typed/ copy-pasted/dragged to their match. Matching items share many advantages of MCQs: ease of test administration and scoring, as well as relatively high objectivity. Its disadvantages include low interactiveness and authenticity and that they assess recognition.

Example Matching Item

A matching item consists of the following parts (see Figure 4.6): the so-called *premises* in one column and the answers, or options, in another column. The premises are typically numbered from *1*; the answers (options) are typically marked with letters starting with *a*.

4.4.11 Guidelines for Designing Matching Items

Similar principles apply to this item type as to the MCQs, with a few additional guidelines:

1. The wording of the item should be simple and clear to efficiently test the TTs' comprehension of the premises.
2. If pictures are used, they should be unambiguously clear, age appropriate, and diverse to represent the breadth of the TT population. Since matching items lack context, TTs cannot rely on context clues to key the item.
3. It is advisable to have more options than premises. Otherwise, if the number of premises equals the number of options, TTs can easily guess the last few matches by elimination. Alternatively, there can be fewer options than premises. In this case, one premise may be unmatched, or options may be matched with more than one premise. Directions should state whether all premises will be matched with options and in what way. See the Other examples of matching items.

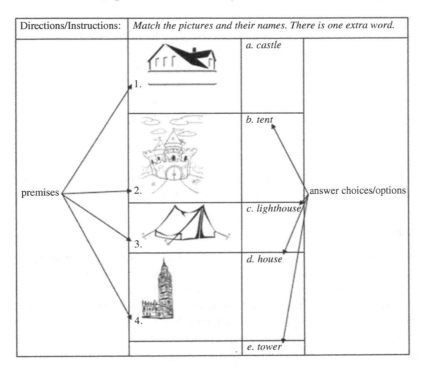

Figure 4.6 Sample matching item: pictures and labels. *Sources:* https://tinyurl.com/housesihlouette; https://tinyurl.com/castledrawingpic; https://tinyurl.com/campingtentpic; https://tinyurl.com/towerdrawing

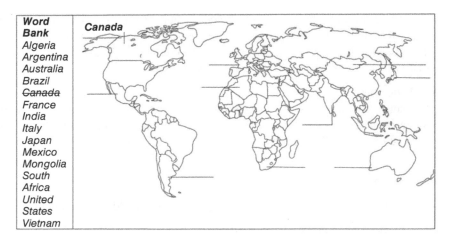

Figure 4.7 Sample map labeling with a word bank. *Source:* https://tinyurl.com/worldmapdrawing

4.4.12 Other Examples of Matching Items

Figure 4.6 depicts a common matching item type. Let us examine several more and apply the above guidelines to them (Figure 4.7).

A. Map labeling task using a word bank:
Look at the map. Using the word bank, write the names of the countries on the lines. One example has been done for you. Four names are extra and have no match on the map.

B. Letter–Number Matching:
This is one of the most common matching item types, in which TTs match the numbered sentence starters with the correct sentence ends denoted by letters.
Directions: Write the letter that completes the numbered idiom. One option is extra and has no match.

1. *Better late*	a. *don't make a right.*
2. *Two wrongs*	b. *don't fix it.*
3. *There's no such thing*	c. *than never.*
	d. *as a free lunch.*

The answer key is *1-c, 2-a*, and *3-d*. Option *b.* has no match. This item type is often used for words and their definitions, general concepts and their specific examples, etc.

4.4.13 Sequencing or Ordering

The sequencing item type is often used with processes and narratives. It involves the TT reading, listening to, or viewing a stimulus where processes or events are presented in a particular order. TTs then rearrange pictures, words, and statements about the stimulus to match the correct order. This step can stand alone or may be followed by a production task where TTs describe the sequence verbally or in writing. Care should be taken though to separate the constructs of stimulus comprehension from production (sequence description). TTs should not be penalized when the production task is scored for describing the sequence out of order if they misunderstood the comprehension task. With longer listening passages, some assessments may allow TTs to take notes while listening and use their notes while answering questions.

Sequencing items share the same advantages as MCQs: ease of test administration and scoring as well as relatively high objectivity. Its disadvantages include low authenticity and that they assess recognition.

4.4.14 Example Sequencing Item on a Computerized Test

Directions: Listen to internet chef Hoda describe how to make the perfect Egyptian falafel.
[*The following italicized part is the recording script. The TT only hears it.*]
Welcome to Hoda's Recipes. Today we're going to learn to make delicious falafel. Look at the list of ingredients on the screen. Stop this recording while you gather them. Ready? Now follow the steps with me.

	a. Form balls the size of golf balls.
	b. Add the wet ingredients to the food processor.
	c. Bake the balls at 200 degrees Celsius (or 400 Fahrenheit).
	d. Mix until a crumbly mixture is formed.
	e. Add the dry ingredients to the food processor.
	f. Add the chickpeas to the food processor.

Figure 4.8   Sample sentence sequencing item.

1. *Mix the dry ingredients (parsley, cilantro, onion, garlic, flour, baking powder, cumin powder, ground coriander, sea salt).*
2. *Mix the wet ingredients (lemon juice, olive oil).*
3. *Add the chickpeas to the food processor.*
4. *Add the wet ingredients to the food processor.*
5. *Add the dry ingredients to the food processor.*
6. *Mix until a crumbly mixture is formed (about 1 minute).*
7. *Transfer the mixture to a bowl and form balls the size of golf balls.*
8. *Flatten the balls and place them on an oily baking tray.*
9. *Bake the balls at 200 degrees Celsius (or 400 Fahrenheit) until golden brown.*
10. *Flip them over for a few more minutes.*
11. *Serve in pita bread with tahini sauce.*
Mmmm. They smell delicious. Enjoy your meal!
Now rearrange the main steps by dragging each step to the correct box.
The correct order is *1-f, 2-b, 3-e, 4-d, 5-a*, and *6-c*.

4.4.15 Guidelines for Designing Sequencing Items

1. The wording of the steps in the sequence should be simple and clear.
2. Transitional expressions indicating sequence (first, finally, at 9 o'clock), should be omitted from the items. They may be included in the stimulus passage itself. If included in the items themselves, TTs could rearrange the steps without comprehending the stimulus, turning the task into a reading rather than listening exercise.

3. The number of steps in the sequence can match the number of slots, unlike in matching, where the number of premises should differ from the number of answers. In sequencing, each step depends on the previous and subsequent ones, making the process of elimination less helpful than in matching.

4.4.16 Other Examples of Sequencing Items

Figure 4.8 depicts a common matching item type. Let us examine several more and apply the above guidelines to them.

A. Word Scramble
Unscrambling letters can arguably be viewed as a form of sequencing. This is a common assignment for young learners and a favorite pastime for adults. For instance, the Bronze level Michigan Young Learner Exam (MYLE) (Michigan Language Assessment 2018), designed for beginner elementary and lower secondary students, contains such a section. A picture might depict a pencil alongside the jumbled letters *(C E I L N P)*, which spell the word *pencil*. The learner is then tasked with spelling the word *pencil* correctly.

4.4.17 Miscellaneous Selected-Response Item Types

Selected-response (SR) items are, by definition, distinguished from constructed-response (CR) items by whether the response options are given by the test developer or whether the TT has to produce them without relying on the supplied options. Therefore, listen-repeat and copying are two additional SR item types.

4.4.18 Listen-Repeat

In this item type, the examiner, teacher, or recording pronounces utterances (sounds, words, sentences) and the TT repeats them as closely as possible.

Example Listen-Repeat
Directions: Listen carefully and repeat the words you hear. You will hear each group of words once and you will repeat it once. Speak clearly and fluently.
  [TT hears: a brown pillow]
  [TT repeats:] a brown pillow

4.4.19 Guidelines for Designing Listen-Repeat

1. The length of the target utterance should match the TTs' proficiency level (shorter for less proficient learners).
2. The phonemic and phonological features included in the utterance should reflect the makeup of the test-taking population and common challenges for speakers of those first languages. For instance, a listen-repeat assessment designed for Japanese students of English will likely contain the phonemes /l/-/r/.
3. The pronunciation of the speaker should be standard for the target test-taking population and reflect the purpose of the assessment. For instance, an assessment designed for immigrants to Quebec will feature Québecois French pronunciation likely to be encountered by immigrants.

Did you know?   The Versant Professional English Test (Pearson Education 2023) and the Versant English Placement Test (formerly Phone Pass) (Pearson Education 2019) contain a *Repeat* task. In both, TTs are asked to repeat sentences they hear.

4.4.20   Copying

In this item type, the TT handwrites or types exactly what is displayed in the task. For instance, a LESLLA[3] learner copies a sentence from the board. This exercise can be beneficial for TTs with limited literacy and target language skills, regardless of age.

4.5   Constructed-Response (Supply) Item Types

Unlike selected-response items, where all the language is provided to the TTs, in constructed-response (CR) items, TTs produce, supply, or construct their answers. The language produced can range from single words to multiple utterances/sentences/paragraphs. Advantages of CR assessments include high authenticity and interactiveness, positive washback, assessment of production, and reduced guessing potential. Disadvantages include difficulty of test administration, labor- or technology-intensive scoring, and reduced objectivity.

4.5.1   Composition (Essay)

The most common CR item types are written compositions and speaking exams in response to a prompt. To ensure fair and consistent evaluation of constructed responses, they must be scored using a rubric, either holistic or analytic. Figure 4.9 depicts a holistic rating scale for composition. Rating scales must be developed carefully and pilot-tested on a representative sample of the target TTs before use in assessment and decision-making. Cut scores must also be established through standard-setting studies. Users of rubrics for evaluative purposes, such as raters, must be trained in the consistent use of the rubrics through norming or calibration. For more information on cut scores and standard setting, see Chapter 1 of this volume and this guide on norming/calibration (Washington State University Office of Assessment for Curricular Effectiveness 2020).

> **Rubric / Rating Scale / Scoring Guide**: A rubric is "a scoring guide used to evaluate the quality of students' constructed responses" (Popham 1997, p. 72). It contains assessment criteria describing the construct at a range of performance levels and is typically presented as a table. With its use, scorers aim to ensure reliable scoring. Rubrics can commonly be classified as holistic, analytic, single-point, primary-trait, and multiple-trait. Although we, in this volume, do not, some sources in the literature make a distinction between rating scales and rubrics. See, for instance, Plakans and Gebril (2015): "A rating scale has the main goal of determining a score on a performance, while a rubric is often used in educational settings to provide feedback to students" (p. 42).

---

3 Literacy Education and Second Language Learning for Adults (LESLLA) "aims to support adults with little or no home language schooling or literacy, who are now learning to read and write for the first time in a new language" (LESLLA 2019). In other words, these learners have little or no formal education in their first language.

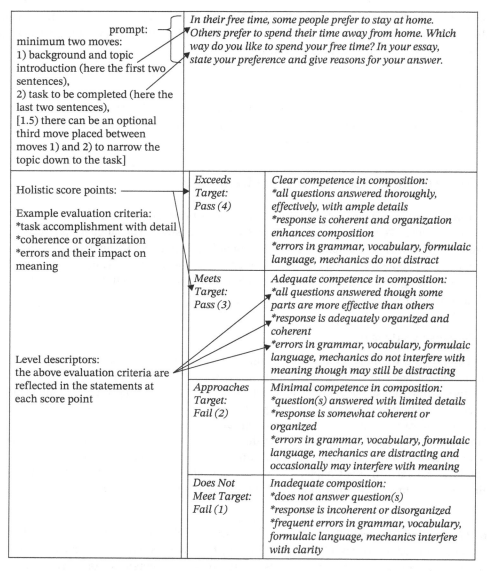

prompt: minimum two moves: 1) background and topic introduction (here the first two sentences), 2) task to be completed (here the last two sentences), [1.5] there can be an optional third move placed between moves 1) and 2) to narrow the topic down to the task]	*In their free time, some people prefer to stay at home. Others prefer to spend their time away from home. Which way do you like to spend your free time? In your essay, state your preference and give reasons for your answer.*	
Holistic score points: Example evaluation criteria: *task accomplishment with detail *coherence or organization *errors and their impact on meaning	*Exceeds Target: Pass (4)*	*Clear competence in composition: *all questions answered thoroughly, effectively, with ample details *response is coherent and organization enhances composition *errors in grammar, vocabulary, formulaic language, mechanics do not distract*
Level descriptors: the above evaluation criteria are reflected in the statements at each score point	*Meets Target: Pass (3)*	*Adequate competence in composition: *all questions answered though some parts are more effective than others *response is adequately organized and coherent *errors in grammar, vocabulary, formulaic language, mechanics do not interfere with meaning though may still be distracting*
	Approaches Target: Fail (2)	*Minimal competence in composition: *question(s) answered with limited details *response is somewhat coherent or organized *errors in grammar, vocabulary, formulaic language, mechanics are distracting and occasionally may interfere with meaning*
	Does Not Meet Target: Fail (1)	*Inadequate composition: *does not answer question(s) *response is incoherent or disorganized *frequent errors in grammar, vocabulary, formulaic language, mechanics interfere with clarity*

Figure 4.9 Holistic writing rubric explained.

Holistic scoring: TT performance is condensed in a single score based on a holistic rating scale. In this type of scale, evaluation criteria are general and listed together for each score band. Trained evaluators score using the detailed definitions of the construct and evaluation criteria as well as the holistic rating scale. Advantages include that it is easy to use and is cost-effective to create. Disadvantages include reliability and validity concerns and the limited information about language performance they provide.

Did you know? The ACTFL (2024a) (OPI), available in over one hundred languages, uses holistic scoring, as does the International Baccalaureate (IB) Middle Years Programme's (2014) language acquisition assessment. The speaking and listening portions of STANAG 6001 (NATO 2010), a military proficiency test and the Spanish DELE exam (2019), are also scored holistically.

Although the Test of Written English (TWE) (English 1988) is no longer administered by the Educational Testing Service (ETS 2024c), it remains a common institutional test worldwide and is scored holistically.

Analytic scoring: Each criterion is awarded a separate score. Evaluation criteria are described separately and in detail. Knoch (2009) found that the analytic scale was associated with greater reliability. More finely grained rating scales can capture smaller changes in language ability and provide more targeted feedback on TTs' strengths and weaknesses. Nowadays, most high-stakes standardized assessments of English are analytic.

Did you know? The TOEFL iBT by ETS (2023) assesses both the independent and integrated speaking tasks with analytic rating scales, as does the IELTS speaking test. The Michigan English Test (MET) by Michigan Language Assessment (2024) evaluates all writing tasks with analytic scales. Additionally, the German immigration test Deutsch-Test für Zuwanderer A2-B1 (Goethe-Institut 2009a) is scored analytically.

Single-point rubric: This is a variation on the analytic rubric. Separate assessment criteria are displayed and awarded separate scores, but only the target proficiency is described; the score points below and above are not described. The main advantage includes brevity, so TTs are more likely to consult it. Single-point rubrics are commonly used for self-assessment.

Primary-trait scoring: The primary trait is the assessment criterion deemed most important. Such scoring rubrics evaluate a single component of writing or speaking analytically. For example, a primary-trait writing scale may focus solely on *topic development*. The evaluation criterion may be phrased as *The thesis is fully developed, with details, facts, and personal examples.*

Multiple-trait scoring: Similarly to a primary-trait scale, occasionally a secondary, tertiary, etc. trait is also assessed analytically. In such cases, the primary trait may be weighted more heavily than the other traits or all may be weighted equally. Fulcher (2009) states that these traits are typically prompt-specific. The advantage is that test users may receive rich data on the TTs' performance. A disadvantage, however, is if each trait is not really evaluated separately but if the first score determines the subsequent scores, which Fulcher, citing Thorndike, called the Halo Effect (Fulcher 2009).

Example Holistic Rubric for Writing Assessment

The rubric in Figure 4.9 is for a writing assignment. The construct of good writing in this case could be defined *as an opinion essay on a particular topic written in a way that is thorough, effective, detailed, coherent, organized, and grammatically, lexically, and mechanically error-free.* This construct definition is then manifested in the rubric through the evaluation criteria, which appear at each level.

The development of rating scales should begin with a clearly defined construct. The construct is then broken down into proficiency levels, or bands. The most important decision is what is considered good enough and not quite good enough. Depending on the decision to be made, the rating scale may only have two score points: pass and fail. For example, on an exit exam, the only decision to be made is whether the student can exit the language program or not. However, typically several score bands are needed, like in the rubric in Figure 4.9. A placement test will require as many score bands as there are levels of language class. The placement test needs to determine whether a prospective student should take language level 1, 2, or 3 at the language school. It should also determine when someone is proficient enough that they no longer need to take a language class at that school. The highest score band, therefore, will allow the prospective student to "test out" of language classes altogether.

After the construct and the rating scale have been developed, writing or speaking prompts can be crafted. In Figure 4.9, the writing prompt consists of two moves. The first move provides the background and mentions the topic. Here, the topic is *spending free time*. The background states that different people prefer to spend their free time in different ways: either at home or away from home. The final move gives instructions about the task to be accomplished. It usually suggests a way to accomplish the task as well. There may be reference to specific rhetorical moves in the wording, such as *compare, contrast, analyze, define, argue, persuade, narrate, tell about a time when,* and *discuss*. The final move also emphasizes essential elements of the response such as *details, examples, specific, concrete, personal, and cite at least five reputable sources.*

It is important that the rhetorical move in the prompt align with the expected response. For example, it would be unfair to ask TT to describe something and then expect an explanation. Note, however, that often a comparison might require similarities AND differences, and in some disciplines, expectations differ, e.g. a definition might include an explanation. It is best to advise students to clarify specific assignment instructions with an instructor.

4.5.2 Guidelines for Designing Constructed-Response Prompts

1. Prompts should provide as much and as little information as necessary. Unnecessarily lengthy prompts increase the TTs' seat time and consume their mental energy on reading instructions rather than producing language. If the prompt is in the target language, it also includes language that TTs can use in their response. The more language that is provided in the prompt by the assessment designer, the harder it is for the TTs to produce original language unless the prompt is given in the TTs' first language. Unnecessarily brief prompts, however, may lack sufficient context and clarity.
2. The words used in the prompt should be chosen carefully. Their readability level should match the least proficient TT who is anticipated to take the test. Remember that in this item type, we are assessing the TT's speaking or writing rather than their comprehension of the unnecessarily convoluted prompt.
3. Include the two moves: a) background and topic, b) task.
4. Determine in advance, and through pilot testing verify, the appropriate time limit for the response. Decide whether additional time will be given for preparation and/or review.
5. Determine whether dictionary use will be allowed.
6. Determine the guidelines for full and partial credit.

Written responses to prompts can be given in a variety of forms. Essays are just one of them. Others include role plays, summaries, summary-responses, letters to the editor, lab reports, and research papers. The aforementioned principles of prompt- and rubric-creation apply to them as well.

4.5.3   Oral Interview with Analytic Rubric

Constructed-response items are also commonly used in speaking assessment, such as an oral interview, oral presentation, picture description, or role play. TTs respond to prompts that are delivered by a live examiner or that are mediated by technology (from a computer or another device, such as a telephone, CD, or DVD). The prompt may be based on a pictorial, verbal, or written stimulus. The prompt may also be available in written form in addition to audio form. The TTs may be given preparation time before responding. The live examiner may also serve as a scorer, or scoring may take place concurrently by another examiner who is present or later by a rater from a recording, since speaking tests are frequently audio or video recorded. Scoring takes place with the use of a rubric, where the examiner circles the relevant level descriptors for each evaluation criterion. The rubric used may be holistic or analytic.

Let us examine a speaking test using an analytic rubric. Note that the example analytic scale has not been pilot tested, nor has it undergone standard setting.

Neither rubric (Figure 4.9 or 4.10) contains another essential element of rubric creation: a thorough explanation of each evaluation criterion. This is important for rater training so that all raters, scorers, and evaluators have the same understanding of how each performance translates into scores.

Directions:	*In this task, you will look at a picture and answer some questions about it.*
Prompts 1 & 2:	1. *Describe the picture.*
	2. *In your opinion, what happened before this picture was taken?*
Stimulus picture:	
	Source: https://tinyurl.com/constructionguy

Figure 4.10   Oral interview with analytic rubric explained.

(Continued)

Evaluation criteria:	Rating Scale / Rubric				
		Task Accomplishment	**Fluency**	**Pronunciation**	**Language Use**
*Task accomplishment (answering questions, detail, organization, coherence) *Fluency *Pronunciation *Language use (grammar, vocabulary, formulaic sequences)	*Exceeds Target: Pass (4)*	*competent speech, all questions answered thoroughly, effectively, with ample details, response coherent and organization enhances speech*	*response fluent and rate of fluent speech, which varies to enhance message*	*pronunciation does not interfere with meaning and is not distracting*	*errors in grammar, vocabulary, formulaic language, mechanics do not distract*
	Meets Target: Pass (3)	*on topic, all questions answered though some parts more effective than others, response adequately organized and coherent*	*fluent speech with few hesitations, false starts, and self-correction, which do not interfere with communication*	*pronunciation does not interfere with meaning though occasionally may still be distracting*	*errors in grammar, vocabulary, formulaic language do not interfere with meaning though occasionally may still be distracting*
	Approaches Target: Fail (2)	*mostly on topic, limited details, somewhat organized and coherent*	*response too slow or too fast*	*pronunciation distracting and occasionally may interfere with comprehension*	*errors in grammar, vocabulary, formulaic language distracting and occasionally may interfere with meaning*
	Does Not Meet Target: Fail (1)	*off topic, disorganized, incoherent answer*	*response halting*	*pronunciation interferes with comprehension and causes listener to work hard*	*frequent errors in grammar, vocabulary, formulaic language interfere with clarity*

Figure 4.10 (Cont'd)

4.5.4 Gap Fill or Fill in the Blank

In addition to the essay and oral interview, gap-fill items are the best-known examples of CR items. Gaps can occur in several turns of a conversation, in what is also called a *conversational cloze* item. Gaps can vary from a single word to a phrase. They are similar to the already familiar MC items discussed in Section 4.3, but here the TTs supply the missing words. Techniques for scoring include *exact-word scoring* and *acceptable-word scoring*. The former means that only one answer is accepted; the latter means that there are several acceptable answers. Compared to SR,

CR items are time-consuming to score for humans, in particular when acceptable-word scoring is used; however, students/TTs do have the opportunity to produce language, which is an advantage. Compared to scoring other constructed-response item types or tasks, scoring gap-fills is more reliable, particularly when only exact words are accepted; however, the relative difficulty of item writing is a disadvantage.

Did you know?   In the IELTS listening section, the Form Completion task involves filling in gaps. Usually only exact answers are accepted though to some extent acceptable-word scoring is also used.

Fill-in-the-blank items are common when assessing listening comprehension, dictation, reading comprehension, grammar, and vocabulary.

4.5.5   Example Gap-Fill Item

Directions: Write the missing words in the English idioms/proverbs. Between one and three words are missing in each statement.

1. *Better _____ than never*
2. *Your guess is _____ mine*
3. *To play the devil's _____*
4. *The pot calling the _____*

Answer key: *1-late, 2-as good as, 3-advocate, 4-kettle black*

4.5.6   Guidelines for Designing Gap Fill/Fill in the Blank

1. See the MCQ item-writing considerations in Section 4.4, as they mostly apply here as well.
2. When determining scoring options, consider the purpose of the assessment (proficiency, achievement, etc.). On an achievement assessment, on the one hand, the exact word may be expected. On a proficiency assessment, on the other hand, the acceptable-scoring method is preferable unless there is only one acceptable answer.
3. When determining scoring options, also consider the item type. In a listening, dictation, or reading task, where the TT has a chance to locate the correct answer, exact-word scoring can be fair. Otherwise, acceptable scoring may be more appropriate.
4. Decide how spelling, capitalization, and punctuation errors will be treated. If the purpose of the task is to assess vocabulary or grammar alone, determine in advance whether mechanics are part of the construct definition or not and score accordingly. The construct definition should guide scoring decisions.

4.5.7   Supply Cloze

Similar to the select cloze item type (see H under Section 4.4.3), the *supply cloze* is a cloze test, where TTs complete the missing words in a continuous written passage. Unlike a select cloze, however, no MC answer choices are provided in advance. Rather, TTs supply the missing words themselves, hence the name. Deletions—rational or fixed-ratio—are handled similarly to the select cloze. Receptive assessment of conversations, reading, and listening are the most common skills assessed this way.

Advantages of the supply cloze include increased production, possibility to assess beyond the sentence, and compared to other constructed-response item types, increased difficulty and relative ease of scoring, especially if only exact words are accepted as answers. Disadvantages include the complex item-writing process. Also, multiple unexpected responses must be anticipated.

4.5.8 Example Rational Supply Cloze

Directions: Read the following passage and complete it with the single word missing from each blank.

When you accidentally cut your finger, your skin heals itself after a few days. Wouldn't it be wonderful if other materials could heal (1)_____ too? This wish could soon become a (2)_____. Researchers have created a rubber-like material that can do (3)_____. To demonstrate their invention, the scientists 3D-printed (4)_____ piece of the material in a few minutes. (5)_____ they cut it in half. At room temperature, the material (6)_____ itself in 6–8 hours. With increased heat (140°F/60°C) the healing (7)_____ shrank to 2 hours. Possible applications include the soles of shoes, toys, and car tires.

Key list, or list of acceptable keys:

1. *themselves /autonomously / automatically / spontaneously / naturally*
2. *reality / possibility / feasibility*
3. *self-healing / that / it /this / likewise*
4. *a / one*
5. *Then / First / Subsequently / Afterwards / Next / Immediately*
6. *fixed / healed / repaired / glued / regenerated / restored / mended / reconstructed / rebuilt*
7. *time /period /duration / interval / timeframe / cycle / process*

When compared to the same passage in Section 4.4.4, it becomes apparent that without the MC answers for the TTs to choose from, the task becomes harder. In fact, the first slot probably cannot even be filled until the entire passage has been read and the main topic ascertained. From a scoring standpoint, most blanks can be filled with a large variety of options (see items *1, 5, 6,* and *7*).

4.5.9 Guidelines for Designing Supply-Cloze Tests:

- See the guidelines for designing cloze tests in general in Section 4.4.5.
- In addition, it is essential that the teacher or test developer pre-determine which exact evaluation criteria will be scored. In the case of the supply-cloze passage in Section 4.5.8, for instance, would word form, spelling, and capitalization be assessed as well or only word choice?
- Prepare detailed scoring instructions.
- Prepare a complete list of keys.
- Prepare a rating scale if necessary.

4.5.10 Short Answer

Short-answer tasks can vary in length from a single word to a few sentences. The prompt may be written, aural, or visual. Responses may be written or oral. Unlike gap-fill or supply-cloze items where students choose from options, short-answer items require students to generate their own answers without any prompts. This makes them more similar to essay questions but without the

Directions: Look at the two pictures. Read the true statement about the first picture; then write a true statement on the same topic about the second picture. Write complete sentences. Follow the example. (1 point each for correct spelling, capitalization, punctuation, content, and language use. 0 points for answers containing errors. No partial credit for partially correct answers.)

A: a square in a circle	B: a triangle and a rectangle in a circle
Source: https://tinyurl.com/vectorsquare	Source: https://tinyurl.com/vectortriangle

Example: There is a square in a circle. → *There is a triangle in a circle.*
→ *There is a rectangle in a circle.*
→ *There is a rectangle under a triangle.*

1. The square is white. → _____
2. The square has four sides. → _____
3. The square has four angles. → _____

Key list (acceptable answers):
1. The triangle is white. / The rectangle is white. / The circle is grey.
2. The triangle has three sides. / The rectangle has four sides. / The circle has zero sides.
3. The triangle has three angles. / The rectangle has four angles. / The circle has zero angles.

Figure 4.11 Sample short-answer item: picture comparison.

structured gaps. Advantages include increased production and reduced recognition or guessing. Disadvantages include less reliable scoring, potentially decreased validity, lengthier rating scale development and scoring, longer response time, and so fewer items on test.

Example Short-Answer Item Type: Picture Comparison

The example in Figure 4.11 depicts a short-answer picture-comparison task, where the response is given in writing. The list of acceptable answers as well as scoring guidelines are provided in the bottom row of the figure. Scoring specifics should be given careful thought and made known to the TTs in advance. The TTs should not be caught by surprise that, in order to earn a point, not only does the content and language of their answers have to be correct but so do the mechanics. Similarly, when the response is given orally, it is essential that the teacher or assessment developer pre-determine which exact evaluation criteria will be scored. In the case of Figure 4.11, for instance, would word choice, word form, sentence structure, pronunciation, fluency, and volume be assessed as well or only whether the TT identified that the shape was a triangle or a rectangle?

4.5.11 Information Gap

The information gap is a classic classroom activity with a built-in self- and peer-assessment component. Each pair receives two versions of the same handout. This can be a story, a schedule, a map, a picture, etc. The two versions contain different details, which when put together create one complete whole. Below are three examples of this item type.

4.5.12 Typical Information Gap

Directions: *You and your partner are classmates and your teacher announced to the class the schedule for Thursday's excursion to the Art Museum. There is a problem though: you each wrote down some of the information but not all of it. Ask each other for the missing information and complete your own copies of the schedule. (Discuss but do not show your schedules to each other!)*

Partner A	*Partner B*
*8:00 am—meet in front of the school by the school bus	**_____ am—meet in front of the school by the school bus*
*_____ am—arrive at the Art Museum	
*9:00 am—meet with the museum tour guide for a tour	**8:40 am—arrive at the Art Museum*
	*9:00 am—meet with the _____
*9:05 am—check _____	**9:05 am—check bags and coats in the coat check*
*12:30 pm—pick up bags and coats from the coat check	**_____—pick up bags and coats from the coat check*
*_____—walk to the Artist Restaurant	**12:45 pm—walk to the Artist Restaurant*
*2:00 pm—meet in the restaurant lobby to walk back to the Art Museum	**_____*
	*2:15 pm—painting workshop at the museum
*_____	**_____—meet _____ go back to the school bus*
*3:50 pm—meet in the museum _____ bus	**_____—leave the museum and ride back to the school*
*4:00 pm—leave the museum and ride back to the school	
*_____—arrive at the school	**4:40 pm—arrive at the school*

4.5.13 Innovative Textual Information Gap

Directions: *Yesterday morning a suitcase disappeared in front of the train station. The police are still investigating. You and your partner are detectives and you are each reading eye-witness testimony. Read the information you each have, discuss each detail, and compare it with your partner's details. Pay attention to any differences and similarities. Later, you will write a report about what the witnesses agreed on and what you still have questions about.*

Partner A	*Partner B*
Eye-Witness Report 1	*Eye-Witness Report 2*
I'm a taxi driver and I was parked in front of the train station. It was exactly 9 am. I remember the station clock chiming 9. Then suddenly I heard a man scream. I got out of the cab and saw that a middle-aged man was yelling and pointing toward the train station.	*I work at the coffee shop at the train station, right by the taxi stand. Yesterday my shift started at 10 am but I was a few minutes late because usually I hear the big clock chiming ten. I was just opening up the store, when I suddenly heard a man scream. I quickly ran out of the coffee shop and bumped into someone pulling a large white suitcase. I think it was a woman. She had a brown hat on, so I couldn't see her hair, but I did see her grey coat and red pants.*
Then I got back in my cab because it was cold and raining. But I looked around and saw a young woman (or a man with long hair?) running inside the station, pulling a large silver suitcase. It was a very nice, expensive suitcase.	*I looked in the direction of the screaming and I saw an old man. He was pointing at the woman with the suitcase. He asked me to call the station police, so I did.*
The woman had long light brown or dark blonde hair. She was wearing a blue jacket and red pants. That's all I remember.	

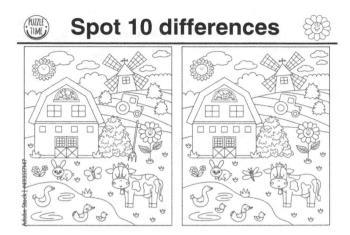

Figure 4.12 Sample spot the difference. *Source:* Lexi Claus / Adobe Stock

4.5.14 Spot the Difference Information Gap

The picture (as in Figure 4.12) can be created to include the vocabulary of objects or actions under study. After one copy is created, a specific number of details can be altered (for instance, a chair moved, a book removed), and the two versions of the picture finalized. Each pair of students receives either version A or version B.

These information gap activities are effective because each student is fully engaged and collaboration is essential to complete the task. If the students miscommunicate, they notice it themselves when they check their answers. Self- and peer-assessment and feedback are immediate.

4.5.15 Mixed-Up Texts

In this reading-comprehension item type, the teacher selects or writes a longer text and a shorter one. The shorter text is then mixed into the longer one. Care should be taken to insert words where they are grammatically possible, but at the same time where they sound out of place. As the reader crosses out each out-of-place word from the longer text, they write them in order in the space below the longer text. This way the shorter text is reassembled. Figures 4.13 and 4.14 depicts the task as the students would receive it. Note that capitalization rules may be violated in the process.

4.5.16 Guidelines for Designing Short Answer

1. Determine when the short-answer item type is more appropriate than the selected-response or another supply-type item.
2. State the prompt or stem precisely but without providing too many clues. Be sure that there is just one acceptable answer if only the exact word is accepted as a response. Conversely, if multiple correct answers are possible, either narrow the prompt sufficiently so that only the desired response is plausible or—preferably—change to *acceptable-word scoring*.
3. Prepare detailed scoring instructions such as a complete key list and rating scale as necessary.

> *Read the story below. Cross out all the words that do not fit and write them in the blanks below. The removed words will create the beginning of a famous poem. After you have copied the words into the blanks, correct the capitalization and punctuation.*

How to Draw a Dog

First, draw a horizontal oval shape. This will be the shadows snout. On top of the oval, draw an upside-down on the U. This will be the head of the dog wall. Inside the snout but close to noises the head, draw a big round nose. Now draw two ears. They can be pointing down up or hanging down. The above the nose, on the face, draw two eyes and two hall eyebrows. Under the nose, draw a life mouth. Next, under the horizontal oval, doesn't draw a large vertical oval for the body. It is time to frighten draw the two front legs. To finish the dog, draw me at all a tail. Now give your new friend a name.

_____ _____ _____ _____
_____ _____ _____ _____
_____ _____ _____ _____ _____ _____

(Maya Angelou)

Figure 4.13 Mixed-up texts: the student task.

> *Read the story below. Cross out all the words that do not fit and write them in the blanks below. The removed words will create the beginning of a famous poem. After you have copied the words into the blanks, correct the capitalization and punctuation.*

How to Draw a Dog

First, draw a horizontal oval shape. This will be the ~~shadows~~ snout. On top of the oval, draw an upside-down ~~on the~~ U. This will be the head of the dog ~~wall~~. Inside the snout but close to ~~noises~~ the head, draw a big round nose. Now draw two ears. They can be pointing ~~down~~ up or hanging down. ~~The~~ above the nose, on the face, draw two eyes and two ~~hall~~ eyebrows. Under the nose, draw a ~~life~~ mouth. Next, under the horizontal oval, ~~doesn't~~ draw a large vertical oval for the body. It is time to ~~frighten~~ draw the two front legs. To finish the dog, draw ~~me at all~~ a tail. Now give your new friend a name.

Shadows on the wall
Noises down the hall
Life doesn't frighten me at all
(Maya Angelou: Life Doesn't Frighten Me)

Figure 4.14 Mixed-up texts: the answer key.

4.6 Authentic Assessments, Alternatives to Tests

The two previous sections introduced sound principles of writing selected- and constructed-response items. Most of these item types commonly appear on high-stakes tests, on standardized tests, and on assessments in traditional settings. Increasingly, though, authentic alternatives to tests are gaining ground worldwide. In this section, we will focus on how to write such item types.

4.6.1 Self-Assessment

O'Malley and Pierce (1996) write that "[i]f we see ELL students as active learners who construct their own knowledge, then surely asking students to map their route and check their progress along the way are part of the learning process" (p. 38). This is what Gottlieb (2006) calls assessment *as learning*. Students who are not used to assessing their own progress and proficiency may find the practice alien, so teachers may need to teach their students the benefits and steps of self-assessment. Self-assessment evaluation criteria are frequently linked to the course or unit objectives although they can focus on any learning target—macro or micro.

4.6.2 Example Self-assessment Checklist

The following checklist in Figure 4.15 has been built over the course of a semester, criterion by criterion, by the teacher and students in a beginning college-level ESL class (Zaki and Porter-Szucs 2016). In the course of the semester, students learn about more and more concepts of paragraph

Content (Development and Organization) (# of points)	Maximum Score	My Score
• Does my paragraph fit the assignment?		
• Does my paragraph have a topic sentence?		
• Does the topic sentence have a topic and a controlling (main) idea?		
• Does my paragraph contain 3 major supporting details?		
• Do I have minor details supporting the 3 major supporting details?		
• Do I have a concluding sentence?		
• Does the concluding sentence have a similar meaning as my topic sentence?		
Total		
Comments:		
Punctuation & Mechanics (# of points)		
• Do I have a centered title that is capitalized and underlined?		
• Did I indent the first line of the paragraph?		
• Did I capitalize the first letter of the first word in every sentence?		
• Did I put a period at the end of every sentence?		
• Did I use capital letters correctly?		
• Did I use commas correctly?		
Total		
Comments:		
Grammar & Vocabulary (# of points)		
• Does every sentence have a subject, a verb, and a complete idea?		
• Does every sentence have subject-verb agreement (singular or plural)?		
• Are my compound sentences correctly connected?		
• Am I using correct formulaic sequences?		
Total		
Comments:		

Figure 4.15 Sample self-assessment checklist. *Source:* Adapted from Zaki and Porter-Szucs (2016).

writing. Once the class reaches a consensus that a concept has been sufficiently understood, each student adds it to his/her own rubric as an evaluation criterion. Students then self-assess their writing using this ever-growing checklist. They then submit the completed checklist with their writing to the teacher.

Example Self-Assessment of Young Learners

The self-assessment of young learners in Figure 4.16 was given in a US fifth-grade class with ESL and non-ESL children. The teacher's goal was to teach children goal setting and self-assessment in general rather than specifically language assessment. Therefore, he worded broad goal-setting questions, or as O'Malley and Pierce (1996) state "map out their path" (p. 38). Some of the responses he received from the children included, *"make friends, don't argue with the teacher, learn math, don't be late for school, spell well, tell my mom about my homework, use my planner."* The follow-up self-evaluation elicited the children's thoughts and feelings about their progress, including, *"I have many friends, my planner just confuses me, my mom helps me with spelling, I'm biking to school but I'm still late."*

In a language class, effective language-related goal elicitation and progress tracking may require more targeted phrasing of goal-setting and self-assessment questions. For an example on peer-assessment, see Figure 4.17.

Benchmark: This is a term with multiple meanings.

1. This is a standard against which language production can be measured. A benchmark performance (oral or written) captures the standard at a particular scoring level. It is usually used by teachers and students, and by raters in conjunction with the rating rubric during norming/calibration sessions.
2. In US primary and secondary education, a benchmark is a test assessing where students are in relation to standards. The process of administering such tests with the purpose of informing policy makers about strengths and weaknesses in schools, school districts, educational systems is called *benchmarking*.

4.6.3 Guidelines for Setting and Administering Self-assessment

Cultural factors come into play here. Students from some backgrounds expect the teacher to be the only expert and are hesitant to engage in self- or peer-assessment or learn from a peer because

---

Step 1: Goal Setting

Directions: What are 3 goals you have in this class?

1. _____
2. _____
3. _____

Step 2: Self-evaluation

Directions: Look at your 3 goals. Have you reached them?

1. What are you doing well? _____
2. What can you do better? How? _____

Figure 4.16 Sample self-assessment for young learners.

Example Speaking Peer-assessment for Young Learners

My name (evaluator): __Amara__		*Classmate's name (speaker):* __Camran__	
Assignment: _____Show and Tell: Favorite Game_____			*Date:* _March 2_
my classmate could ...	👍	✋	👎
say what they wanted	+		
speak clearly		+	
use the right words	+		
use the right grammar		+	
I liked this: ____He showed me a fun game._____			
My classmate should ___ Speak louder.			

Figure 4.17 Sample peer-assessment for young learners. *Source:* Adapted from Hasselgreen, A. (2003). Bergen 'Can Do' project, Council of Europe Publishing.

they doubt their peers' language proficiency. Thus, it is important to explain the benefits of such assessments, provide training, and use them alongside other methods.

1. Explain the purpose and benefits of self-assessment.
2. Collaboratively, set the evaluation criteria based on the course objectives, specific assignment, etc.
3. Show the students benchmarks (aka. anchors or exemplars) specific to the assignment and the proficiency level and analyze them together. Don't assume students know how to interpret a rubric.
4. Collaboratively, create a self-assessment checklist.
5. In addition to the selected-response checklist or rubric, encouraged students to provide brief comments: something positive and areas for improvement.
6. Practice the use of the self-assessment tool with the students.
7. Guide students on interpreting and using their self-assessment results to track their progress and motivate their progress.
8. Repeat the self-assessment again and again.

Self-assessment tools can easily be adapted for peer assessment. To this effect, the previous list of guidelines should be thus appended.

4.6.4 Guidelines for Setting and Administering Peer-assessment

1. Train students to provide gentle yet constructive feedback to their peers in the target language. Even proficient language learners can be reminded (and less proficient ones taught) how to hedge (*You may want to think about adding more support / You could add more support*), how to ask questions that raise concerns (*Have you thought about adding more support? / Would it be possible to add more support?*), taking the blame, or using "I statements" (*I may be wrong, but I would like to see more support*). Training is also important to avoid the situation where peers simply tell their peers that their work is good, or no improvements are needed.

2. Be sure to impress upon the students that feedback received from a peer should be taken with a grain of salt, especially if it is at odds with the self-assessment of the same evaluation criterion. When in doubt, students can always ask the teacher.

Did you know? The Self-Assessment Grid was developed by the Council of Europe so that learners may determine their language proficiency according to the 34 scales of the Common European Framework of Reference (CEFR) in 32 European languages https://www.coe.int/en/web/portfolio/self-assessment-grid

Did you know? LinguaFolio emerged from a collaboration between the National Council of State Supervisors for Languages (NCSSFL) and the American Council on the Teaching of Foreign Languages (ACTFL). Based on the European Language Portfolio, "LinguaFolio® is a proficiency-based, learner-directed formative assessment tool for setting and achieving language goals" (NCSSFL-ACTFL 2019). The Can-Do Statements offer self-assessment checklists for learners to evaluate their language proficiency in three modes of communication: interpersonal (oral, written, signed), presentational (speaking, writing, signing), and interpretive (listening, reading, viewing; NCSSFL-ACTFL 2024a, b). This reflective learning approach aids learners in goal setting, strategy selection, self-assessment, providing evidence, and reflection before setting new goals.

4.6.5 Portfolio Assessment

A portfolio is a collection of student work. In language assessment, it has traditionally been of written work, but recently there has been an increase in e-portfolios that allow the inclusion of visual and oral texts. There are two basic types under various names. (1) summative (for final evaluation, such as archival, summative assessment, and showcasing) and (2) formative (for interim evaluation, such as progress, process, and working). Both main types contain a purposive collection of students' work and a reflection. In summative portfolios, students highlight their accomplishments in light of the learning objectives. In formative portfolios, they document their language learning goals, accomplishments, growth areas, and a plan of action for continued growth. Specifics will vary from setting to setting, from assignment to assignment though. Portfolios may be submitted electronically (e-portfolio) or physically. Gottlieb (1995) recommends that portfolios contain six attributes, spelling the acronym CRADLE: collecting, reflecting, assessing, documenting, linking, and evaluating.

Advantages include increased validity, authenticity, positive washback, and interactiveness because of the collection of multiple data points of authentic assessment. Further crucial advantage includes that students themselves can see their own progress, and with younger learners, so can their parents. They can be motivating for students because rather than pushing students to achieve a single, unrealistic level (perfect test), portfolios are customized to demonstrate individual progress. As such, they provide documentary evidence of learning over time, which can also be useful for teaching appraisals. Disadvantages include potentially decreased reliability and practicality of scoring. Some teachers mistakenly believe that using portfolio assessment means they will have to mark all work twice. This is not the case as the focus should be on the students' ability to select work, reflect on it, and make links between pieces of work that demonstrate their progress.

4.6.6 Example Language Portfolio

At a community college in the United States, ESL students build their writing portfolios throughout the semester. Students have the option to do so electronically or in a paper folder. In it they keep three drafts each of all major writing assignments. They start it with a table of contents and their learning goals for the semester and end it with a reflection of their learning in relation to their goals.

Contents of summative, end-of-semester writing portfolio:

1. *Student's writing learning goals set collaboratively with the teacher*
2. *Drafts 1, 2, and 3 of writing assignment #1 (narrative essay) and self-assessment checklist accompanying each draft*
3. *Drafts 1, 2, and 3 of writing assignment #2 (process essay) and self-assessment checklist accompanying each draft*
4. *Drafts 1, 2, and 3 of writing assignment #3 (comparison-contrast essay) and self-assessment checklist accompanying each draft*
5. *Drafts 1, 2, and 3 of writing assignment #4 (expository essay) and self-assessment checklist accompanying each draft*
6. *Drafts 1, 2, and 3 of writing assignment #5 (argumentative-persuasive essay) and self-assessment checklist accompanying each draft*
7. *Reflection on progress toward goals, critiquing process and product of each essay*
8. *Further goal setting as writer in English*

At this college, the portfolio is approximately 35–40 pages long. It is worth 30% of the final grade. Students build it from the start of the semester. Approximately 3 weeks before the end of the semester, students peer review each other's portfolios according to the evaluation criteria that has been emphasized since the start. Two weeks before the end of the term, the portfolios are submitted to the instructor. Some ESL instructors evaluate them by themselves and provide written feedback. Others have the students present their portfolios to the instructor orally, and the oral presentation becomes part of the grade.

4.6.7 Guidelines for Setting, Administering, and Scoring Portfolios

1. **Plan** carefully. Decide on the type of portfolio (formative or summative), its contents, evaluation criteria, data collection timing, and evaluation methods.
2. **Involve** students in selecting portfolio contents.
3. **Align** portfolio contents with course objectives. For example, collect written artifacts for a writing class and spoken samples for an oral communication class. Possible contents include audio/video recordings, presentations, lecture notes, writings, drawings, charts, assessments, lists of media consumed, and participation in debates or clubs.
4. **Co-create the evaluation criteria and rubric** with students. For instance, in an oral communication class, the course objectives and the portfolio evaluation criteria might be: *Give a coherent five-minute oral presentation on a personal topic; present an oral argument with confidence; while speaking, use correct word stress placement.* In a written communication class, the following may serve as suitable evaluation criteria based on course learning objectives: *Support claims with facts and opinions; use proper citations when referencing external sources; apply spelling conventions consistently and accurately.*

5. **Co-construct** with students a self-assessment checklist that reflects the evaluation criteria. For example, see Figure 4.15.
6. **Create an analytic rubric** based on the checklist for final evaluation. See, for instance, Figure 4.10.
7. **Introduce benchmark performances** (see elsewhere in this chapter) and analyze them using the checklist and rubric.
8. Regularly **refer** to the checklist, rubric, and benchmarks throughout the course.
9. **Plan** evaluation steps. Set deadlines for submission/presentation, decide evaluation format (paper or online), frequency, and grading weight. Choose evaluators (teacher, aides, peers, self-evaluation) and ensure they are trained for consistency.
10. **Decide with students** who will view the portfolios (teacher, classmates, parents, employers, decision-makers).
11. **Stay organized** throughout the process.

Did you know? The European Language Portfolio was developed by the Council of Europe "to support the development of learner autonomy, plurilingualism, and intercultural awareness and competence; to allow users to record their language learning achievements and their experience of learning and using languages" (European Language Portfolio n.d.). Its stated goals include fostering reflective self-management and the development of autonomous language learners, with an eye toward further education and employment. European Language Portfolios have three parts: the Language Passport (overview of the student's language-learning and intercultural identity), the Language Biography (reflection on using L2 and engagement with other cultures), and the Dossier (a repository of evidence of L2 proficiency and intercultural experience).

4.6.8 Journals or Logs

Another form of authentic assessment are journals or logs. Journals are logs where reflections, feelings, thoughts, steps, events, arguments, notes, vocabulary (which can include new words, definitions, example sentences, parts of speech, translations, or collocations), etc. are captured by the individual. Journals can be for private, public, or semi-public consumption. They can be oral, written, or multimodal. They can be assessed for quality, quantity, completion, or not at all. Feedback, when provided, may vary in detail. In language classes, journals primarily serve as informal records of students' thoughts and feelings, aimed at improving fluency, expressing concerns, or questioning their own progress. Usually they are written for the teacher and are assessed for completion or quantity alone. Since this is an informal assignment whose purpose is often the development of fluency and ability to think in the target language, assessing quality and accuracy would be counterproductive.

The following example is a lesser known variation on the typical journal described above. What increases its authenticity is that students communicate with other students. And what increases the appeal of the assignment is that the students do not know who their partner is, hence the secret. With **dialog journals**, the students do all the work while the teacher monitors and keeps records. A disadvantage of dialog journals, however, may be if one of the partners stops submitting journal entries. In that case the other partner has no one to correspond with until another solution is found. Another disadvantage may be if students choose to plagiarize or otherwise copy language they did not produce themselves. Finally, if the teacher decides to respond to each student's weekly journal entry, this could considerably increase the teacher's workload, which would cause low practicality of this assignment.

4.6.9 Example Secret Dialog Journal

Instructions*: You and a student in another teacher's class will be "secret journal buddies." Your goal is to improve your ability to express your thoughts and feelings while speaking. Every Monday you will submit your journal entry to your teacher and your secret journal buddy will submit their recording to their teacher. On Tuesday you will receive your partner's entry to you. Listen to it and record your response. Submit your response by the following Monday. Say as much to your partner as you can but do not give away your secret identity!*

Topics*: You may talk about anything that interests you and you may ask polite questions to your partner. Topics may include your family, hobbies, likes, dislikes, habits, favorite foods, plans, interesting things you did in the past, your language learning, this class, etc. Remember to avoid taboo questions such as money, politics, religion, and sex.*

Be kind*: Remember that you are trying to make a friend. If you don't know how to say something politely, use the polite expressions we learned in class. If you still don't know, ask your teacher.*

Grading*: If you speak for 3 minutes in your dialog journal and you submit it on time every Monday, you will receive 100% on each journal entry.*

Remember to keep your secret identity, keep the conversation going, and have fun!

4.6.10 Guidelines for Setting, Administering, and Scoring Journals

1. Determine the type of journal your students will be keeping: monologic, dialogic; written for the self, the teacher, a fellow student at the same institution, a student at another institution (maybe another country), etc. Dialogs can take place between students or the teacher and each student. Monologic journals receive no response.
2. Determine the frequency of journaling: daily, weekly, etc.
3. Determine the purpose of the journal: development of fluency, ability to reflect, critical thinking, summary of or response to studied material, summary of or response to extracurricular activities, argumentation, persuasion, analysis, synthesis, metacognition, self-discovery, organization, acculturation, etc.
4. Decide on grading. Depending on the purpose of the journal and on practicality constraints, decide whether journal entries will be checked regularly, sporadically, or not at all. When checking, will you award points for effort, quality, quantity, or a combination of the evaluation qualities. Remember that as this is a constructed-response assignment, a rating scale will be necessary for any grading scheme more rigorous than entries meeting the minimum-length and timeliness requirements.

Journals, whether they are dialogic or not, offer numerous benefits due to their high authenticity, validity, reliability, practicality, washback, and interactiveness. Drawbacks are minimal, provided that students maintain respectful communication with each other and the teacher keeps the grading simple.

Think-Pair-Share 4.6a Application   Item-writing principles of numerous authentic assessments have been introduced on the previous pages. Think of a setting you are most familiar with. Select one of the authentic assessments described in Section 4.6 and design your own assessment for the setting of your choice. As applicable, craft the instructions, stimulus, items, visuals, rating scales, etc. Ask at least two colleagues to review.

Think-Pair-Share 4.6b Discussion   Having been introduced to a wide variety of assessment items and tasks, discuss with colleagues what challenges you anticipate when trying to apply the concepts to crafting your own items. Why? How do you propose to overcome the challenges?

Think-Pair-Share 4.6c Critiquing   Select a language assessment item/task/prompt available from an external source (online, a textbook, a test bank, etc.). Evaluate it according to the general item-writing guidelines and the item-specific guidelines presented in this chapter. If there is room for improvement, make the necessary revisions. Then discuss your rationale for these changes with a peer.

Think-Pair-Share 4.6d Critiquing   Select a rating scale available from an external source (online, a textbook, a test bank, etc.). Evaluate it according to the guidelines presented in this chapter. If there is room for improvement, make the necessary revisions. Then discuss your rationale for these changes with a peer.

4.6.11   Beyond Item Writing

Creating the intended items following the recommendations in this chapter, while essential, is just a single step within the broader assessment-development process. The assessments need to undergo further development, as described below and expounded upon in other chapters in this book. For assessments with increased consequences, it becomes even more essential to engage a team in the development, compilation, piloting, administration, and analysis of the assessments.

1. **Review the items** for appropriateness of content, form, inclusiveness, fairness, and freedom from bias (FAB) (see Chapters 3 and 12). It is best to assign different reviewers for every stage of review. A pair of fresh eyes will be able to detect problems better than the item writer alone.
2. **Put the items in order**. The order of items of the same type usually progresses from easy to difficult to easy. Generally, a confidence-boosting item or two starts off the assessment. They are followed by progressively harder items. Finally, the assessment typically closes with somewhat easier items.
3. **Compile the form**. Keeping the assessment blueprint in mind, compile an assessment form with all the desired items in the desired order.
4. **Review the entire assessment form**. Assign it to two to three reviewers. Form reviewers should take the assessment as if they were the TTs, noting any challenges, such as miskeyed items, items with multiple or no keys, items that keyed other items, and any imbalance in the items. An imbalance may arise if there are several items in a row about one gender or another or if all the items from the educational domain, for instance, are about the topic of homework instead of a variety of topics.
5. **Be your own TT and take your own assessment.** This does not just mean taking quick selected-response assessments but also constructed-response, and in particular those requiring longer productions. Test the limits and see if the instructions or the items can be misinterpreted. Make sure that plausible responses will be scored favorably. Otherwise, revise the instructions and/or the items until they unambiguously elicit the response you hope they will.
6. **Pilot the assessment**. Once the assessment form has been finalized, it should be pilot-tested on a population similar to the actual TTs. For instance, if the target TTs are 10-year-old boys and girls from Spanish, Chinese, and Arabic-speaking backgrounds, then the assessment form should be tried out on students of this make-up.

7. **Follow the guidance provided in the other chapters of this book.** Strive to maximize the qualities of test usefulness and build a sound Assessment Use Argument (see Chapter 2). Refine your assessments through statistical analyses (see Chapter 14).

4.7 Chapter Conclusion

In this chapter, our aim was to bridge the gap between theoretical assessment principles and practical application. We explored assessing valuable constructs and minimizing irrelevant factors. You practiced creating items, tasks, prompts, and rating scales, skills applicable to evaluating and enhancing existing assessments. Alternative item types expanded your assessment toolkit. Self- and peer-assessments were explored as learning tools.

As you conclude this chapter, use it as a future reference for crafting assessments, evaluating others' assessments, and incorporating insights from this chapter into those in subsequent chapters of this book.

5

Tools of the Trade

Chapter Overview

This chapter introduces valuable tools for teachers and professional test developers, building on the foundations laid in the previous two chapters on test design and item-writing principles. This chapter will cover tools essential for creating assessments, such as standards, learner language samples, corpora, and readability measures.

5.1 Learning Objectives

1. Explain the meaning and use of standards, benchmarks, and frameworks
2. Name the standards most suited to your context
3. Craft an oral interview prompt for a chosen proficiency level
4. Consult a set of applicable standards and determine the proficiency level of the learner whose oral or written language sample you located
5. Based on the written or oral language sample of a concrete student and the applicable set of standards, assess the student's learning needs
6. Conduct a frequency and a collocate search in a corpus
7. Explain what readability assessment entails and run readability calculations on a passage

Think-Pair-Share 5.2a Imagine that you have been tasked with developing a placement test for your new employer: *School of World Languages*. The learners at the school are of the age that you are most familiar with. You have taught languages for a few years, but you do not have extensive experience with learners at every proficiency level. What is more, you are only marginally familiar with all the classes at the school. What steps will you take as you develop this assessment? Discuss.

5.2 Standards (Benchmarks and Frameworks)

As introduced in Chapter 1, standards are an indispensable tool of language teachers and testers. When creating tests or crafting items for a test, the assessment and its items should be aligned with a language proficiency framework. For instance, a teacher or test developer in a setting that is aligned with the CEFR would consult with the appropriate scale when crafting items targeting a particular

A Practical Guide to Language Assessment: How Do You Know That Your Students Are Learning? First Edition.
Ildiko Porter-Szucs et al.
© 2025 John Wiley & Sons, Inc. Published 2025 by John Wiley & Sons, Inc.

skill at a particular level. When developing a speaking task where the speaker's pronunciation will be assessed at the B1 (low-intermediate) level of the CEFR, the developer may consult the CEFR Phonological Control scale (Council of Europe 2020, pp. 134–135). The evaluation criteria, as depicted in Figure 5.1, are *Overall Phonological Control, Sound Articulation*, and *Prosodic Features*. The task will then target the B1 level. It is worth becoming familiar with the levels below and above B1 to know what the TTs should comfortably and not yet have control over, respectively.

At the B1 level, the TT's pronunciation "is generally intelligible … despite regular mispronunciation of individual sounds and words they are less familiar with" and the TTs can "convey their message in an intelligible way in spite of a strong influence on stress, intonation and/or rhythm from the other language(s) they speak" (pp. 133–134). Therefore, when a task has to be designed for a B1-level speaking test, again the CEFR standards will be consulted.

Figure 5.2 depicts the salient features of spoken language of a B1-level speaker (Council of Europe 2018, pp. 163–164).

	Phonological Control		
	Overall phonological control	**Sound articulation**	**Prosodic features**
C2	Can employ the full range of phonological features in the target language with a high level of control—including prosodic features such as word and sentence stress, rhythm and intonation—so that the finer points of their message are clear and precise. Intelligibility and effective conveyance and enhancement of meaning are not affected in any way by features of accent that may be retained from other language(s).	Can articulate virtually all the sounds of the target language with clarity and precision.	Can exploit prosodic features (e.g. stress, rhythm and intonation) appropriately and effectively in order to convey finer shades of meaning (e.g. to differentiate and emphasize).
C1	Can employ the full range of phonological features in the target language with sufficient control to ensure intelligibility throughout. Can articulate virtually all the sounds of the target language; some features of accent(s) retained from other language(s) may be noticeable, but they do not affect intelligibility.	Can articulate virtually all the sounds of the target language with a high degree of control. They can usually self-correct if they noticeably mispronounce a sound.	Can produce smooth, intelligible spoken discourse with only occasional lapses in control of stress, rhythm and/or intonation, which do not affect intelligibility or effectiveness. Can vary intonation and place stress correctly in order to express precisely what they mean to say

	Phonological Control		
	Overall phonological control	**Sound articulation**	**Prosodic features**
B2	Can generally use appropriate intonation, place stress correctly and articulate individual sounds clearly; accent tends to be influenced by the other language(s) they speak, but has little or no effect on intelligibility.	Can articulate a high proportion of the sounds in the target language clearly in extended stretches of production; is intelligible throughout, despite a few systematic mispronunciations. Can generalize from their repertoire to predict the phonological features of most unfamiliar words (e.g. word stress) with reasonable accuracy (e.g. while reading).	Can employ prosodic features (e.g. stress, intonation, rhythm) to support the message they intend to convey, though with some influence from the other languages they speak.
B1	Pronunciation is generally intelligible; intonation and stress at both utterance and word levels do not prevent understanding of the message. Accent is usually influenced by the other language(s) they speak.	Is generally intelligible throughout, despite regular mispronunciation of individual sounds and words they are less familiar with.	Can convey their message in an intelligible way in spite of a strong influence on stress, intonation and/or rhythm from the other language(s) they speak.
A2	Pronunciation is generally clear enough to be understood, but conversational partners will need to ask for repetition from time to time. A strong influence from the other language(s) they speak on stress, rhythm and intonation may affect intelligibility, requiring collaboration from interlocutors. Nevertheless, pronunciation of familiar words is clear.	Pronunciation is generally intelligible when communicating in simple everyday situations, provided the interlocutor makes an effort to understand specific sounds. Systematic mispronunciation of phonemes does not hinder intelligibility, provided the interlocutor makes an effort to recognise and adjust to the influence of the speaker's language background on pronunciation.	Can use the prosodic features of everyday words and phrases intelligibly, in spite of a strong influence on stress, intonation and/or rhythm from the other language(s) they speak. Prosodic features (e.g. word stress) are adequate for familiar everyday words and simple utterances.
A1	Pronunciation of a very limited repertoire of learnt words and phrases can be understood with some effort by interlocutors used to dealing with speakers of the language group. Can reproduce correctly a limited range of sounds as well as stress for simple, familiar words and phrases.	Can reproduce sounds in the target language if carefully guided. Can articulate a limited number of sounds, so that speech is only intelligible if the interlocutor provides support (e.g. by repeating correctly and by eliciting repetition of new sounds).	Can use the prosodic features of a limited repertoire of simple words and phrases intelligibly, in spite of a very strong influence on stress, rhythm and/or intonation from the other language(s) they speak; their interlocutor needs to be collaborative.

Figure 5.1 CEFR phonological control scale.

"Level B1 reflects the Threshold Level specification for a visitor to a foreign country and is perhaps most categorised by two features. The first feature is the ability to maintain interaction and get across what you want to, in a range of contexts, for example: generally follow the main points of extended discussion around him/her, provided speech is clearly articulated in standard dialect; give or seek personal views and opinions in an informal discussion with friends; express the main point he/she wants to make comprehensibly; exploit a wide range of simple language flexibly to express much of what he or she wants to; maintain a conversation or discussion but may sometimes be difficult to follow when trying to say exactly what he/she would like to; keep going comprehensibly, even though pausing for grammatical and lexical planning and repair is very evident, especially in longer stretches of free production. The second feature is the ability to cope flexibly with problems in everyday life, for example cope with less routine situations on public transport; deal with most situations likely to arise when making travel arrangements through an agent or when actually travelling; enter unprepared into conversations on familiar topics; make a complaint; take some initiatives in an interview/consultation (e.g. to bring up a new subject) but is very dependent on interviewer in the interaction; ask someone to clarify or elaborate what they have just said" (Council of Europe 2018, p. 163).

Figure 5.2 CEFR-level B1 threshold level descriptor. *Source:* https://tinyurl.com/CERFlevelB1

Think-Pair-Share 5.2b Examine Figure 5.2. What topics can a B1-level speaker be expected to speak about? Discuss.

Based on the CEFR standard depicted in Figure 5.2, topics that a B1-level speaker can be expected to talk about include the following:

- while visiting the country where the studied language is spoken, "generally follow the main points of extended discussion around him/her, provided speech is clearly articulated in standard dialect"
- "give or seek personal views and opinions in an informal discussion with friends"
- "express the main points he/she wants to make comprehensibly"
- cope flexibly "with less routine situations on public transport"
- "deal with most situations likely to arise when making travel arrangements through an agent or when travelling"
- "enter unprepared into conversations on familiar topics"
- "make a complaint"
- "ask someone to clarify or elaborate what they just have said"

Think-Pair-Share 5.2c Given the topics that B1-level speakers of the language can talk about and given the phonological control they are capable of, write a B1-level speaking prompt for the placement test at *School of World Languages*. You may wish to revisit Sections 4.5.2 and 4.5.3 in the previous chapter, where we discuss how to craft an oral-interview prompt. Share your prompt with at least two peer reviewers and solicit their honest feedback. Remember that students'/TTs' academic futures may depend on the proper wording of the prompt, so keep revising yours until all reviews are positive. The following two prompts are examples of speaking prompts targeting B1-level language (Figure 5.3).

Think-Pair-Share 5.2d Before these tasks can be used on actual students, what steps have to be taken? Consult Chapters 3 and 4 as necessary.

| | A—*First, describe the picture. Next, talk about a possible explanation for this situation.* |
| | B—*Talk about a specific situation when you arrived late. What happened? What did you do?* |

Figure 5.3 Sample B-1 level speaking prompt. *Source:* Alvaro Matzumura / Pexels

5.3 Learner Language Samples

Teaching experience brings with it familiarity with the students and TTs. Experienced teachers can—on demand—conjure up images of students they have taught with various linguistic, national, and proficiency characteristics. Each additional student from an already familiar background adds to the composite picture of student groups that teachers create. This practical knowledge is built on whatever theoretical training the teacher may have. During test design and item writing, experienced educators can thus reach for either a composite or a specific student. Although novice teachers may start with a disadvantage, i.e. their lack of teaching experience, with the following tools, even they can design assessments with confidence. And even experienced teachers are encouraged to re-calibrate themselves regularly against the standards and not rely solely on their memories of past students.

Numerous web-based sources exist where learners' language can be accessed. YouTube is a useful source, as are the websites of some assessment organizations. In Figure 5.4, we have compiled various oral and written language samples at a variety of proficiency levels.

For additional languages, we recommend searching for the key words in the target language: *speaking exam + proficiency level + video.* Furthermore, on the websites of testing organizations, one can often find sample test forms and TT performance samples.

Spoken Language Samples	
Purdue University ELL Language Portraits	Video excerpts of K-12 grade (approximately 5–18 years old) students at various SOLOM-R oral language levels speaking and reading aloud, with assessment tools for teacher training
LearnAlberta Supporting EAL Learners (2024a)	Videos of K-12 grade (approximately 5–18 years old) ELs at proficiency levels 1-5 speaking, listening, and reading with brief on-screen commentary for teachers and assessors
Pronunciation Diagnosis & Training by Meyers and Holt (1997)	Video series of non-native English speakers speaking and pronunciation teachers diagnosing the students' speech
Minnesota Literacy Council (2020)	Short and full-length ESL adult basic education lessons: teaching, learning, and formative assessment
Michigan Language Assessment sample tests: select the desired test under Test Prep ECCE Speaking sample test (2013) ECPE Speaking sample test (2014) MET Speaking sample test GSI-OET sample test	Sample tests for each high-stakes assessment are available. This includes the speaking portion of each test.
US Department of State English Language Teaching Methods	14 full-length videos of ESL classes in various contexts, from very young learners to adults
French as a second language videos by FSL	French as a second language videos from Canada at A1-B2 CEFR levels
German speech samples A1, A2, B1 (Goethe Institut 2009a)	Goethe Institut German test speech samples

Written Language samples	
LearnAlberta writing samples (2024b)	Hand-written papers of 1-12th grade ESL students at proficiency levels 1-5 with benchmark ratings on vocabulary, grammar, linguistic competencies, and editing
Purdue University ELL Language Portraits (2024)	Video excerpts of K-12th (approximately 5–18 years old) students at various SOLOM-R oral language levels speaking and reading aloud, with assessment tools for teacher training
College Board's Accuplacer (2021)	Typed up sample college-level English learner essays at proficiency levels 1-6, with rater commentary
Flo-Joe writing class by Splendid Learning (2024)	Typed up English student papers of various genres, with teacher commentary, editing corrections, and feedback to students
European Consortium for the Certificate of Attainment in Modern Languages (ECL) (n.d.)	Example English, German, Hungarian writing samples, levels A2-C1 on the CEFR Test forms available in over a dozen languages
French as a second language writing samples by FSL (2013)	French as a second language student writing from Canada at A1-B2 CEFR levels
German writing samples with commentary (Goethe Institut 2009b)	German as a foreign language writing samples with commentary by the Goethe Institut

Figure 5.4 Sources of oral and written language samples.

When a teacher of the English language or item writer wishes to witness what a student/TT is capable of linguistically in the four skills, the videos in the Alberta proficiency benchmarks can be beneficial. The videos depict students not only speaking but also listening and reading on camera. The annotated writing samples, in turn, demonstrate students' writing. The other speaking and writing examples, respectively, provide a wide range of student performances. These language samples, along with any proficiency standards they are aligned with, can provide the teacher or item writer a complete picture of the language learner that the teaching, learning, and assessment tasks target.

Learner language errors also serve test developers as inspiration for item writing in two significant ways. First, they pinpoint target elements worth assessing. Second, they are inspirations for distractors. For instance, if in a speaking or writing sample a learner talks about being busy after school because of *making homeworks*, then the item writer can conclude that the formulaic sequence *do homework* and the fact that *homework* is a noncount noun are worth assessing more directly. In one such item then, the key would be *do homework*, while one of the distractors may be *make homework*. To teachers of the English language, we also recommend Swan & Smith's *Learner English: A Teacher's Guide to Interference and Other Problems* (2001). This reference book covers ways in which speakers of 22 languages may experience first-language interference when learning English.

Think-Pair-Share 5.3a   Select one of the student/TT speaking samples from Figure 5.4 (or from another suitable source). Select a fitting[1] set of standards from Chapter 1. Evaluate the learner's speech sample in light of the standards. What is the proficiency level of the speaker? Provide evidence from both the recording and the standards.

Think-Pair-Share 5.3b   Select one of the student/TT writing samples from Figure 5.4 (or from another suitable source). Select a fitting set of standards from Chapter 1. Evaluate the learner's writing in light of the standards. What is the proficiency level of the writer? Provide evidence from both the writing sample and the standards.

Think-Pair-Share 5.3c   Based on either the written or spoken language sample from Think-Pair-Share 5.3a or b, assess the concrete student's learning needs. Determine what target element(s) the learner needs to improve on next.

5.4   Corpus (plural: Corpora)

A *corpus* is an intentional collection of authentic texts systematically gathered, analyzed, and displayed in a searchable way. Some corpora contain only written sources, such as from books, magazines, and newspapers. Others contain spoken sources, such as transcripts of lectures, office hours, TV broadcasts, or actual recordings. Some corpora specialize in a dialect, for instance, North American or British English. Others still are restricted to language samples by children.

---

1 A fitting standard means that a learner participating in adult basic education for immigration purposes, such as in the Minnesota Literary Council videos, should be evaluated by a set of standards designed for that population and setting, such as CASAS. A writing sample on the college-level Accuplacer test should be evaluated according to standards that include college-bound or well-educated adults, such as the CEFR. And a young learner's language, such as seen on the Alberta benchmark website, should be evaluated by a standard designed for children, such as the Alberta K-12 ESL Proficiency Benchmarks or the WIDA.

Corpora are indispensable to teachers, students, researchers, assessors, material writers, and anyone interested in exploring language use. Restricting further discussion of corpora to their role in assessment, teachers and assessors consult corpora for a variety of reasons. During item writing, they serve as a source of authentic uses of words in context. Ideally, the wording of test items should sound as if taken from an authentic text, rather than written in "learnerese" specifically for language learners. For instance, when prompted to produce an example sentence containing the word *bus*, we might be tempted to write, *The man is sitting on the bus* or *The man is taking the bus to work*. However, when we look up the most common uses of *bus* in the Corpus of Contemporary American English (COCA) (Brigham Young University n.d.a), instead we read *I wanted to ride the city bus*.

In addition to serving as a source of authentic language use, corpora show which words collocate[2] with other words. This can be useful both to find natural-sounding expressions and potentially keyable distractors. For instance, the following item aims to target the preposition "in" in the formulaic sequence *wait __ line*, meaning *stand in a queue*. In a multiple-choice item, the item writer supplies the distractors, all of which must be incorrect. If simply writing the distractors without consulting a corpus, the item writer might craft the following item.

Hundreds of people are waiting _____ line for concert tickets.

a. *in**
b. *on*
c. *at*
d. *to*

COCA (Figure 5.5) informs us that while *in* is the most frequent collocate, *on* is also keyable.[3] There is one instance of *to* appearing as well, but because in a different context, it can be dismissed as a keyable option. Option b—*on*—though needs to be replaced, perhaps with *by*.

In the following subsection, we will introduce free-of-cost corpora that are particularly beneficial for assessment purposes around the world. For a more complete list of English corpora, we recommend a compilation by Justus Liebig University Giessen, Germany (2023) and by Oxford University Press (2012). For a near-complete list of language-learner corpora, visit the Centre for English Corpus Linguistics at the Université catholique de Louvain (2024).

		CONTEXT	ALL FORMS (SAMPLE): 100 200 500	FREQ	TOTAL 1,002	UNIQUE 11
1		WAITING IN LINE		464	
2		WAIT IN LINE		298	
3		WAITED IN LINE		140	
4		WAITING ON LINE		39	
5		WAITS IN LINE		29	
6		WAIT ON LINE		17	
7		WAITED ON LINE		10	
8		WAITS ON LINE		2	
9		WAITING TO LINE		1	
10		WAIT UNTIL LINE		1	
11		WAIT . LINE		1	

Figure 5.5 COCA collocate search for "wait." *Source:* https://tinyurl.com/COCAcollocate

---

2 Collocate → co+locate = appear together.
3 In some parts of the English-speaking world, people wait *on* rather than *in* line. https://www.theatlantic.com/politics/archive/2012/11/semantics-voting-you-say-line-i-say-line/321708/

Other corpora may be found by typing the following search words into a search engine: *corpus +
(the name of the language sought) + video / audio / text*

Each of the corpora referenced in Figure 5.6 presents with a different interface. While learning
to use the corpus most relevant to the reader may take some time, it is time well spent. Users of
COCA can find numerous video tutorials on YouTube. Learning to use the COCA interface will
also serve users of BYU-BNC (n.d.b), GloWbE (n.d.c), NOW (n.d.d), and the dozen or more corpora
accessible on the English Corpora website.

Contemporary English Language Corpora	Description of Corpus
Australia	
Australian National Corpus (AusNC) (2023)	AusNC encompasses several corpora, such as the Griffith Corpus of Spoken Australian English and the Australian Corpus of English.
International English	
Corpus of Global Web-Based English (GloWbE) (Brigham Young University n.d.)	/glowb/ is another written corpus available on the English Corpora website (2013-) through the same interface as COCA. It is a corpus of twenty international varieties of English, such as Australian, British, Irish, Jamaican, Malay, North American, Singaporean, South Asian, etc.
North American English	
Corpus of Contemporary American English (COCA) (Brigham Young University n.d.a)	COCA is the largest and most widely used corpus of English. It is located on the English Corpora website.
Michigan Corpus of Academic Spoken English (MICASE)	This is a collection of transcripts of spoken academic English at the University of Michigan.
Michigan Corpus of Upper Level Student Papers (MICUSP)	This is a collection of well-regarded upper level student papers at the University of Michigan.
News on the Web (NOW) (Brigham Young University n.d.d)	This is a corpus of web-based newspapers and magazines, also located on the English Corpora website.
Singapore	
NIE Corpus of Spoken Singapore English (National Institute of Education 2001)	This is a collection of recordings and transcripts of speakers of Singaporean English.
Singapore Bilingual Corpus (Yow 2015)	These are classroom recordings and transcripts of children and teachers conversing and code-switching between Mandarin Chinese and English.
South Africa	
The Corpus of Black and Coloured South African English (Ruhr Universität Bochum 2023)	This is a password-protected database of group interviews with South African English speakers. Passwords can be obtained by signing the license agreement.
United Kingdom	
British National Corpus (BNC) (Natcorp)	Various services offer access to the BNC, to textual and audio files. The services accessible here are BYU-BNC, Intellitext, Phrases in English, and Audio BNC.
BYU-BNC (Brigham Young University, BYU n.d.b)	The BNC available through the English Corpora website has the same interface as COCA.
Child Language Data Exchange System (CHILDES)	The CHILDES corpus is a repository of child first-language acquisition. All folders contain transcripts. This folder also contains audio files of children acquiring British English.

Figure 5.6 Language corpora.

(Continued)

Contemporary English Language Corpora	Description of Corpus
Spanish	
Voces de Princeton (Princeton University 2019)	Voces de Princeton from Princeton University contains around 100 video recordings of Spanish speakers.
Various Languages	
Child Language Data Exchange System (CHILDES)	The CHILDES corpus is a repository of child first-language acquisition. All folders contain transcripts. Transcripts are available of children speaking various languages:
Sketch Engine	Sketch Engine is a paid corpus (with some free trial pages) with 100+ languages.
Children with Language Disorders	
Child Language Data Exchange System (CHILDES)	This folder of the CHILDES corpus contains both audio files and transcripts of children acquiring various languages. It also contains transcripts of children with language disorders acquiring their native languages.

Figure 5.6 (Cont'd)

5.4.1 COCA Searches

In the following, we will demonstrate how to conduct a collocate and a word-frequency search in COCA. For assessment purposes, these two searches are perhaps the most common. Imagine that you are writing a grammar item about the formulaic sequence *look forward to + gerund*. This is a very commonly (mis)used construction because students think that *to* mark the infinitive and continue with the base form of the verb rather than its gerund. Thus, instead of *I'm looking forward to meeting you soon*, students say *I'm looking forward to meet you soon*.

A-Collocate Search

STOP Before continuing to the following paragraphs, create an account on the COCA website. Next, watch the latest YouTube video tutorial on how to conduct a collocate search (such as on the BYU, Corpora YouTube channel n.d.e). Consider watching additional videos to understand other functionalities of COCA. Once you can independently search for collocates, continue reading.

A collocate is a formulaic sequence, in other words a sequence of words that co-occurs with greater frequency than chance (Wray 2000). In this specific COCA collocate search, we are looking for the word that co-occurs, or collocates, with the sequence *look forward to*. This is demonstrated in Figure 5.7.

As Figure 5.7 demonstrates, since we are looking for collocates, we clicked on the *Collocates* tab. In the upper search box, we entered the words whose collocates we were looking for: *[look] forward to*. Note that *look* is in square brackets. This is because we are looking for any form of *look* such as *looks, looked, looking*. Without the square brackets, we would only search for the actual form of the word typed into the search box: *look*. Before hitting the *Find collocates* button, we also set how many words to the left and right of the search terms the sought collocate should be. In this case, zero words preceding and up to four words following the search term are marked, see the lightly shaded "1 2 3 4." In the second search box, we specified that we were looking for collocates that ended in *-ing*. This can be done by clicking on the drop-down menu and selecting *verb.ING* from the list. This automatically fills in the second white search box with the appropriate code:_v?g*. Once initiating the collocate search, we see the following results (see Figure 5.8).

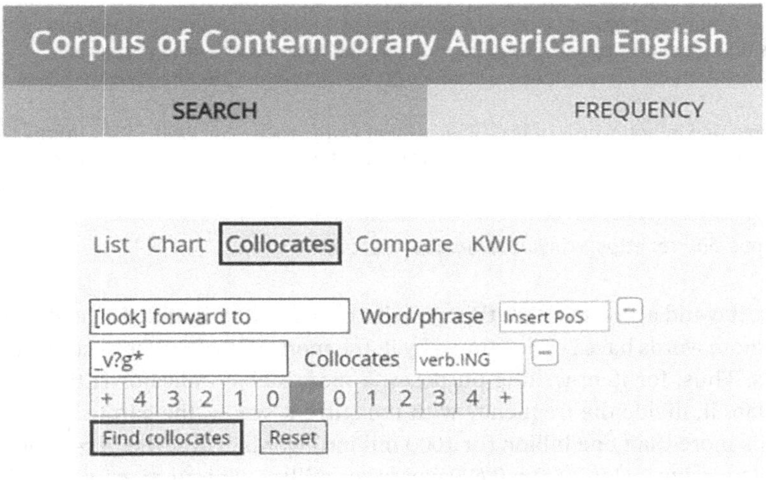

Figure 5.7 COCA collocate search "[look] forward to." *Source:* https://tinyurl.com/collocatesCOCA

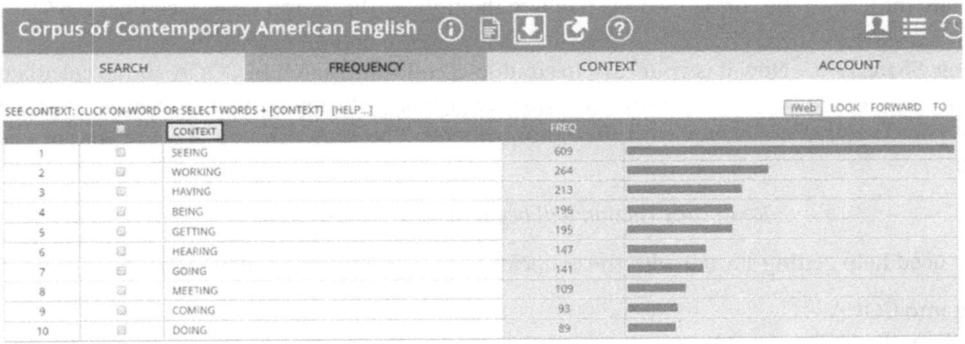

Figure 5.8 COCA collocate search frequency results. *Source:* https://tinyurl.com/collocatesCOCA

The search reveals that the most frequent word to follow *look forward to* is *seeing*. Therefore, as item writers, we will write *I'm looking forward to (see) you soon.* This way the item will sound authentic.

B-Frequency Search in COCA

STOP Before continuing to the following paragraphs, watch the latest YouTube video tutorial on how to conduct a frequency search. Once you can independently locate the word or phrase frequency, continue reading.

The frequency search indicates how frequently the search word occurs in the total corpus. In Figure 5.8, we see that *[look] forward to seeing* occurs 609 times while the sequence *[look] forward to working* appears 264 times. However, these numbers can be misleading for item-writing purposes. Because the corpora on the English Corpora website are expanded regularly, the frequency numbers are unstable indicators of actual frequency. A term's frequency might double overnight due to a sudden spike in its popularity, like "election results" during an election or "World Cup"

The Corpus of Contemporary American English (COCA) was created by Mark Davies, and it is the only large and "balanced" corpus of American English. COCA is probably the most widely-used corpus of English, and it is related to other corpora from English-Corpora.org, which offer unparalleled insight into variation in English.

The corpus contains more than one billion words of text (25+ million words each year 1990–2019) from eight genres: spoken, fiction, popular magazines, newspapers, academic texts, TV and movies subtitles, blogs, and other web pages.

Figure 5.9 COCA size of corpus. *Source:* https://tinyurl.com/collocatesCOCA

during the event. However, it could also mean that the total size of the corpus doubled. The larger the size of the corpus, the more words have been scanned by it, the more likely that the occurrence of specific terms increases. Thus, for item-writing purposes, a more stable indicator is the *per-million* quotient. To calculate it, divide the frequency with the current size of the corpus. At the moment of publication, it is more than one billion (or 1000 million) words. Thus, the per-million frequency of *[look] forward to seeing* is 609/1000 = 0.609 words per million. This number is a much more stable indicator of a term's frequency than the total frequency number is. If this number jumps, then we can be certain that the term has been occurring much more frequently in the language than before.

To locate the size of the corpus, see the panel to the right of the search fields (see Figure 5.9).

Think-Pair-Share 5.4a   Now it is your turn to conduct a collocate search in COCA and to calculate the per-million frequency of the formulaic sequence. You are writing an item and need to find a suitable adjective that collocates with the noun *summer*. The sentence you are writing goes as follows:

Road construction will begin in the _____ summer.

If you need help getting started with the collocate search, consult the following steps.

1. Log into COCA.
2. Click on the Collocates tab.
3. Enter *summer* into the Word/phrase window.
4. To the right of the second (Collocates) window, click on POS. Select *adj.ALL* since you're looking for all adjectives that collocate with *summer*.
5. From the list of numbers preceding or following the search word, select 1 or 2 to the left since adjectives in English precede their nouns.
6. Click Find collocates. The result should be a list of adjectives that most closely collocate with the noun *summer* and can complete the above sentence. They are visible in the Context column.

Should you need help with calculating the per-million frequency of the collocation you have found, see the following steps.

1. Directly to the right of the list of collocates are their frequencies in the FREQ column.
2. Looking at the most frequent word in the first row, divide the frequency number by the size of the corpus (at press time 1000). The resulting number is the per-million frequency.

The per-million word-frequency numbers can guide item writers in additional ways. They can be suggestive of the proficiency level for which the given word might be appropriate. Word frequency means that the word occurs many times in natural written and oral discourse. Leech (2001) asserts that if

> an item naturally occurs frequently in the language being taught, it is likely to be important also for the target behaviour of the learner: the learner will later often come across that item in reading and listening, and will often need to use it in communicating with others (p. 1).

Leech argues thus for the intentional teaching of high-frequency words in language classes. In addition to the intentional learning of words, their incidental, or unintentional, acquisition has also drawn researchers' attention. High-frequency words have been found repeatedly to be acquired more easily than low-frequency ones (see Hashimoto 2016; Hiebert et al. 2019; Monaghan et al. 2017). The implications of the above for assessment purposes is that, generally, the more frequent the word in the corpus, the less proficient the students who can be assessed on it. And vice versa: the less frequently the word occurs in the corpus, the more proficient the students for whom it can be appropriate.

Let us see a specific example.

[walk].[*v] (as a verb rather than a noun or adjective) appears in COCA a total of 263 409 times. At the time of printing, the size of COCA is 1000 million words. Thus, the per-million frequency of any form of "walk" as a verb (walk, walks, walked, walking) is 263 409/1000 = 263.409. This makes this a very frequent word.

Let us search for the frequency of a synonym of "walk": [amble].[*v]: 1352 and the frequency per million is 1352/1000 = 1.35. In other words, "amble" in all its verbal forms is very infrequent. Thus "walk" should be tested on beginners while "amble" on highly advanced learners or on an achievement test.

An example advanced-level vocabulary item may look like this:

Time seemed to stop while the sweethearts _____ down the riverbank at a leisurely pace.

a. *stomped [4.7/mill]*
b. *hastened [3.1/mill]*
c. *bolted [4.7/mill]*
d. *ambled* [1.35/mill] (the key is marked with an asterisk*)*

The same item at the low-beginner level would look like this:

Every Sunday, the friends slowly _____ by the river.

a. *stand [319/mill]*
b. *sit [315/mill]*
c. *walk* [263/mill]*
d. *wait [264.9/mill]*

Frequency does not clearly equate to word difficulty and vocabulary size (Hashimoto 2016). There are thus no clearly defined rules as to which frequency is appropriate for which proficiency level. The following are mere suggestions and should be adjusted according to local realities.

Proficiency level of learner on the CEFR	Possible per-million COCA frequency ranges
Low beginner	100+
High beginner	60–100

(Continued)

(*Continued*)

Proficiency level of learner on the CEFR	Possible per-million COCA frequency ranges
Low intermediate	40–60
High intermediate	20–50
Low advanced	8–20
High advanced	1–5

Any word or sequence lower than 1/mill is so infrequent that we cannot expect non-native speakers to know it unless they have had a reason to study it. Thus, assessing such infrequent words is only fair if the learner had a reasonable chance of exposure.

Predicting the difficulty level of vocabulary prior to pre-testing is very challenging. Word frequency is one potential indicator. Others are word length, number of syllables, context, cognates in the L1, recurrence of the target word in the discourse, etc. Even experienced item writers and teachers can only make educated guesses at the level of difficulty of individual words. And when a word is part of a formulaic sequence, then the difficulty may further increase, especially if the meaning of the individual word is not transparent in the formulaic sequence. Such are phrasal verbs and other idiomatic expressions. For instance, a learner may know the meaning of the individual words *look, up,* and *dictionary*, yet be baffled when faced with the sequence *look it up in the dictionary*. The frequencies of these words are as follows:

look	775.77/million
up	2332.69/million
dictionary	6.71/million
look * up in the dictionary	0.027/million

The above chart demonstrates how the frequency of individual words can differ from when used in combination. If the meaning of the word combination is easy to deduce from the meanings of the individual words, then the meaning of the word combinations may not increase its difficulty considerably. Otherwise, it may. Another consideration may be relevant in this case, however, namely the occurrence of words in the entire corpus versus in specific language contexts. The word *dictionary* occurs less frequently in everyday written and oral language; hence, it is relatively low in frequency in the entire COCA corpus. However, in a foreign-language classroom, it is one of the first words to be learned. Similarly, the formulaic sequence *look * up in the dictionary* may be rather infrequent in contemporary discourse, not so in a language classroom. Thus, we recommend that word-frequency become one of many considerations when estimating which proficiency group a particular word or word combination is appropriate for.

5.4.2 Summary of Corpus as an Assessment Tool

Testers, whether they are teachers who write classroom assessments and common assessments with their colleagues or whether they are professional item writers of standardized assessments, rely on corpora. Corpora provide information on authentic language in particular contexts. They can help identify tip-of-the-tongue keys and eliminate keyable distractors. They can also be used to calculate the frequency of words and their collocates. Since item writers make decisions about which words to use in the instructions, stimulus, and item so that TTs are assessed fairly, the information provided by corpora is essential.

5.5 Readability Assessment (Formula, Index, Score, Checker, and Test)

Another routinely used tool by item writers is a readability checker.

> **Readability:** Readability is a calculation of predicted text difficulty.

There are a variety of readability formulas in use. Each one takes into consideration a slightly different combination of factors thought to contribute to readability. Such factors include the average sentence length, average word length (calculated from the number of letters or the number of vowels per word), number or percentage of multisyllabic words, passive vs. active sentences, lexical chains, parts of speech, word tokens, word types, and other features (see Feng et al. 2010; Izgi and Seker 2012; van Oosten et al. 2010).

> **Token:** total number of words in a text
>   Every single word in a text is counted and added up

> **Type:** number of unique words in a text
>   Some words in the text are repeated, such as the, a, an, is, to, etc. Repeated words are only counted once regardless of how many times they occur.

> **Type-Token Ratio (TTR):** This is a measure of vocabulary richness in a text. It can be calculated by dividing the number of word types by the number of word tokens:
>   Type ÷ Token = TTR %
>   For instance, if a text contains 87 unique words out of 100 total words, then the TTR is 87/100 = 87%
>   Note that hyphenated and contracted words are typically counted as separate words, as if they were written with spaces between the words.

TTR is a measure of text difficulty. The higher the percentage, the lower the repetition of words, the harder the text. In other words, a paragraph where several of the words are repeated is likely to be easier to understand than the same text where synonyms are used for the previously repeated words.

Think-Pair-Share 5.5a   Calculate the TTR of the following two paragraphs. Which one would you say is easier to read? Discuss.

A: *We'll meet at the park at 5. When we meet, we can walk around the park and talk. I'll tell you about some exciting news. I want to tell you about it in person.*

B: *We'll meet at the park at 5. When we do, we can walk around the grounds and talk. I'll tell you about some exciting news. I want to share it with you in person.*

If your answer is that the TTR of passage A is 25/36 = 69.44%, then we agree.

'll × 2	I × 2	some	we × 3
about × 2	in	talk	when
and	it	tell × 2	you × 2
around	meet × 2	the × 2	5
at × 2	news	to	
can	park × 2	walk	Token = 36
exciting	person	want	Type = 25

Similarly, the TTR of passage B can be calculated as 29/36= 80.55%.

'll × 2	grounds	share	we × 3
about	I × 2	some	when
and	in	talk	with
around	it	tell	you × 2
at × 2	meet	the × 2	5
can	news	to	
do	park	walk	Token = 36
exciting	person	want	Type = 29

In other words, the higher the TTR percentage, the higher the level of difficulty: text A is easier and text B is harder to read.

There are several well-known readability indexes. Since each one is slightly differently calculated and measures slightly different features of the text, it is best to do due diligence to find the most appropriate one for the field and age group of the readers.[4] The following list displays some of the best-known readability indexes.

- Flesch-Kincaid Grade Level (FK), aka Flesch Grade Level Readability Formula—which indicates which grade level a reader would have to be at to be able to understand the text. The greater the number the harder the text. For instance, 9.5 indicates the middle of 9th grade, which would make the learner at least 14 years old.
- Flesch Reading Ease—On a scale of 0 to 100, the higher the number the easier the text is to read.
- Gunning Fog Index—The index indicates the minimum age needed to understand the text.
- Simple Measure of Gobbledygook (SMOG)—Similarly to the other grade-level calculators, this one also estimates the years of education the reader needs to be able to understand the text.
- Automated Readability Index (ARI)—This is another grade-level calculator, starting with Kindergarten and ending with college.

The aforementioned readability indexes can be calculated on numerous sites. Each website calculates any given index slightly differently, however, and produces marginally different results for the same text. The following are some of the websites where readability calculators are available:

---

4 For a comparison on readability indexes, we recommend Readability Formulas and The Readable Blog.

```
┌──────────────────────────────────────────────────────────────┐
│  Readability Statistics                         ?       ✕      │
├──────────────────────────────────────────────────────────────┤
│                                                                │
│  Counts                                                        │
│    Words                                           35          │
│    Characters                                     128          │
│    Paragraphs                                       1          │
│    Sentences                                        4          │
│                                                                │
│  Averages                                                      │
│    Sentences per Paragraph                        4.0          │
│    Words per Sentence                             8.7          │
│    Characters per Word                            3.5          │
│                                                                │
│  Readability                                                   │
│    Passive Sentences                               0%          │
│    Flesch Reading Ease                           96.4          │
│    Flesch-Kincaid Grade Level                     1.9          │
│                                                                │
│                                    ┌──────────────────┐        │
│                                    │       OK         │        │
│                                    └──────────────────┘        │
└──────────────────────────────────────────────────────────────┘
```

Figure 5.10 Flesch reading ease and Flesch-Kincaid grade level calculations in Microsoft Word. *Source:* https://tinyurl.com/readabilityMS

> Readable
> Analyze My Writing
> Readability Formulas

Most websites calculate a variety of readability indexes. Because the results across the indexes vary, it is best to use one specific index calculated by the same source consistently. For instance, text *A* above on the Readability Formulas site was calculated as second grade on FK, as third grade on the SMOG and Coleman-Liau indexes, as fourth grade according to the Linsear Write Formula, and as preschool level (for 3–5 years old) by the ARI. In contrast, on a different website—Analyze My Writing—the FK, Coleman-Liau, and Gunnin Fog indexes were nearly the same but the SMOG index was sixth grade. Microsoft Word also calculates the FK and Flesch Reading Ease scores (see Figure 5.10). Once the Spelling & Grammar check is run, the following statistics are displayed if the Readability Statistics are turned on (see BetterCloud 2016).

The TTR of a text can be automatically calculated on the text analyzer website UsingEnglish. com. The website Lexical Diversity Measurements also calculates the TTR, as well as wordlists, ngrams, and keywords (Reuneker 2017). You will note that these sites consider contractions and hyphenated words as one, rather than as two separate words, the way these constructions are treated in corpora.

Language teachers familiar with graded readers[5] will also be familiar with Lexile scores. This is another readability measure, which takes into account word count, mean sentence length, and

---

5 Graded readers are books whose language level has been simplified to match the proficiency levels of language learners. The simplification typically concerns syntax and vocabulary to make the content accessible to readers

word frequency (MetaMetrics 2024a). MetaMetrics' stated goal is to connect readers with readings that are just right for their level. Two measures are needed to achieve this: the reader's Lexile Reader Measure (LRM) and the reading's Lexile Text Measure (LTM). An estimated Lexile range of up to 250 words can be obtained freely at https://hub.lexile.com/analyzer. For instance, the Lexile readability score of this paragraph is 1210L—1400L. MetaMetrics partners with schools, governments, test developers, and materials publishers to incorporate either the Reader or the Text measure into their products (MetaMetrics 2024b). School children in 24 countries receive LRMs from an official school, state, or national assessment. Meanwhile, over 100 million books, newspapers, and other print materials have received LTMs. For the LTMs of flagship publications worldwide, see Swartz et al. 2011). As a result of a US-based study of LRMs reported from school children between 2010 and 2016, typical LRMs by grade are also available here (MetaMetrics 2024c). Thus, we learn that prodigious 11th and 12th graders in the United States could read *The Egyptian Gazette, The Financial Times, The Australian*, and *The New York Times*.

5.5.1 Summary of Readability

As should be apparent from the above discussion, readability statistics are not foolproof. They measure a variety of textual features but the scores often depend on the specific website that runs the calculations. And indexes that apparently measure similar features produce widely differing results. Another shortcoming is that they were developed for native speakers rather than non-native speakers of English. Therefore, formulaic sequences such as phrasal verbs and idioms are often considered easy, as they would be for native speakers. For instance, *run up a bill* will be considered easy because each word is frequent and one-syllable long, and the sequence is in the active rather than passive voice. However, such a formulaic sequence for non-native speakers will be a challenge to comprehend.

Still, we have no better tool at our disposal when evaluating the difficulty of a text. Thus, we recommend that test developers when writing listening or reading passages, prompt, and items for non-native speakers take the following steps:

- select a specific readability index (such as FK and Flesch Reading Ease);
- access it consistently on the same website or in Word;
- look up the word frequency of suspiciously challenging or easy words in a corpus (such as COCA); and
- use common sense when making decisions about text difficulty.

Think-Pair-Share 5.5b Imagine that you are continuing to design the B1 portion of the placement test for the *School of World Languages*. Locate a text suitable for a reading or listening passage and calculate its readability with one of the readability indexes on a particular website (or Word). Run the calculations on the same index but different websites. Are the results consistent among the websites? Now run the same text through a different readability calculator on a variety of websites. Is your text appropriate for the intended proficiency level? Discuss your findings.

(The Extensive Reading Foundation, n.d.). Graded reader scales are linked to either Lexile Reader Measures, the Graded Reader Scale by Extensive Reading Foundation, the CEFR, or the publisher's own level test (such as Macmillan's). Well-known publishers of readers include the CEFR-linked Penguin ELT, Cambridge English Readers, Scholastic, Macmillan, Helbling Readers, Burlington Books, and Black Cat. Many readers are accompanied by audio recordings as well.

Think-Pair-Share 5.5c   Graded, or leveled, readers are books written at specific reading proficiency levels. Select a passage from one such book. Calculate its readability. Next, rewrite the text for a reader at a lower reading proficiency than the level of the current text. You may vary the type or token or other features of the text to accomplish your goal.

Think-Pair-Share 5.5d   If you teach a language other than English, locate the tools mentioned in this chapter for your target language:

a. language standards, benchmarks, frameworks
b. learner language samples in all skills
c. oral and written corpora
d. word frequency and collocate searches within a corpus
e. readability measures

5.6   Chapter Conclusion

This chapter provides educators and test developers with valuable tools to improve the assessment creation process. Building on previous chapters about test design and item-writing, it includes standards, learner language samples, corpora, and readability measures. These tools will be crucial in the practical application of assessment creation in upcoming chapters. By using these tools, we can create assessments that accurately reflect learner proficiency and address individual learning needs in both assessment and teaching.

Appendix 1 – Achievement Quiz of Chapter 5

(For discussion or writing prompts, see the Think-Pair-Share tasks in this chapter.)

Directions: Select the response that best answers each question below. Each question is worth 1 point.

1. To most accurately determine a learner's proficiency level from their language sample, which method is most effective?
   a. contrasting it with language samples from other learners
   b. assessing it using a readability calculator
   c. evaluating it in comparison to a proficiency framework
   d. checking the word frequencies in a corpus

2. Based on the chapter, why are learner language errors valuable?
   a. They pinpoint target learning elements worth teaching and assessing.
   b. They indicate greater progress when compared to a final assessment.
   c. They are evidence that learners are challenged by the curriculum.
   d. They are not valuable because learners should avoid making errors.

3. Including high-frequency words in the assessment is a benefit to students at which proficiency level?
   a. beginner
   b. intermediate
   c. advanced
   d. nativelike

4. The numbers of occurrences from a frequency search are quite unstable indicators of how frequent terms actually are. To find a more stable indicator of the actual popularity of a term, you can calculate the term's _____.
   a. occurrence
   b. frequency number
   c. per million quotient
   d. collocate ratio

5. The TTR of passage (A) is 67.77 %; the TTR of passage (B) is 83.23%.
   Which passage is likely to be harder?

6

Assessing Young Learners

Chapter Overview

This chapter is intended primarily for teachers without formal education in teaching young learners (YLs). "Young learners" will refer to students aged 5–17 years. This is the first of three loosely related chapters. In this chapter, we provide information about the characteristics of these learners and suggest important assessment considerations. Chapter 7 delves into the assessment of YLs in schools from pre-kindergarten through 12th grade, primarily in the United States and Canada. Chapter 8 introduces the reader to exceptional language learners in schools and the considerations surrounding their assessment. For teachers of elementary and secondary school students in the United States and Canada, we recommend prioritizing Chapter 7 over Chapter 6. Although the current chapter is primarily focused on YLs, much of the information contained in it is applicable to students of any age.

6.1 Learning Objectives

1. Explain how YL characteristics differ from adult characteristics
2. Explain the insights from neuroscience regarding the teaching and assessment of YLs
3. Summarize the controversy surrounding YL assessment and express your position with support
4. For each age group of YLs, identify characteristics and assessment implications
5. For a specific group of YLs, optimize the washback of an assessment

Think-Pair-Share 6.1a   Look at the pictures below (Figure 6.1) and describe the YLs in them. What implications might these characteristics have for teaching, learning, and assessment of each group of students?

6.2 Introduction to Young Learners

Children should be assessed in the way they learn best. Thus, assessment professionals of YLs should be very familiar with who these learners are and how children learn best (McKay 2006).

A Practical Guide to Language Assessment: How Do You Know That Your Students Are Learning? First Edition.
Ildiko Porter-Szucs et al.
© 2025 John Wiley & Sons, Inc. Published 2025 by John Wiley & Sons, Inc.

Source: Sebastián Vargas / Pexels

Source: Safari Consoler / Pexels

Source: wr heustis / Pexels

Source: AG Z / Pexels

Source: ken19991210 / Pexels

Source: Christina Morillo / Pexels

Figure 6.1 Young learners at various activities.

> **Young Learners:** Sources define and categorize *young* differently. For McKay (2006), for instance, YLs are those who are learning a foreign or second language "during the first six or seven years of formal schooling" (p. 1). Depending on the educational system, this typically means 5–12 years old. The Cambridge Young Learners English Tests (YLE) have been designed for 7–12 years old (Barker and Shaw 2007). WIDA designs assessments for multilingual learners in grades Kindergarten–12, i.e. typically 5–18 years old.
>
> In this chapter, we will be using the British Council's definition and age categories (2021). According to this definition, young learners encompass those between the ages of 5 and 17 years. We find this categorization helpful because it generally fits into most countries' school systems and encompasses minors, who are considered vulnerable and legally speaking have not reached the age of "majority." This broad range can be broken down into three age categories: 5–8, 9–12, and 13–17 years old. Although all learners within an age group will not behave exactly in the same way, they will share enough characteristics to allow for a fruitful discussion of best assessment practices.

6.2.1 Characteristics of Young Learners

Children differ from adults in several ways. They

- are **not** autonomous agents/actors, legally speaking
- are vulnerable
- are developing their identities: adding new language and identity though previous languages and identities should never be denied (McKay 2006)
- have shorter (though growing) attention spans
- have limited life experiences
- experience intense **brain development**
- are learning about cause, effect, and consequences
- experience motor, linguistic, and conceptual development (Cameron 2001)
- undergo constant social, emotional, and physical growth (McKay 2006)[1]
- are sensitive to criticism and assess success and failure based on the reaction of significant adults and peers (McKay 2006)
- are motivated by and have a "capacity for play, fantasy, and fun" (Hasselgren 2000)
- are more instinctual, naturalistic learners
- learn best through social interaction

Did you know?   Judy Willis, a neurologist-turned-educator, summarizes the **brain development** of school-aged children and its implications on learning and assessment in the following way (Edutopia 2011). The amygdala is the brain's "switching station," whose task is to direct incoming information somewhere in the brain. If the brain is under stress, the amygdala sends the information into the lower part of the brain, which is the reactive, involuntary brain. The behavior it produces is fight, flight, or freeze. Similarly to other stressors, boredom also puts the amygdala into a hyperactive state. The higher part of the brain is in the prefrontal cortex. It is responsible for emotional–analytical thinking, problem-solving, critical analysis, and memory building. For the

---

1 For an excellent resource on the assessment of young learners, see Penny McKay (2006).

amygdala to direct incoming information here, the YLs' curious attention needs to be aroused. The YLs must feel safe to learn, think, participate, predict, and make mistakes (see Figure 6.2).

Think-Pair-Share 6.2a   What are the potential implications of Willis and Willis's (2020) summary on brain development for the language assessment of YLs? To what extent does your experience with YLs align with their ideas?

Did you know?

The field of education can derive numerous insights from video games.

a. Students can enter at the "achievable challenge level" (Edutopia 2011, 9:50 minutes), and they can level up at their own pace to maintain interest. It is not necessary for them to spend time at too high or too low a level for long.
b. Students receive feedback on their incremental progress. Receiving feedback when they can most use it provides intrinsic reinforcement because it gives the brain dopamine, a boost of pleasure.
c. Students have privacy because nobody else sees them make mistakes and the feedback they receive.
d. Once a level is conquered, the reward is more and harder work (rather than candy or high fives).

As video games excellently demonstrate, constant and regular evidence of progress increases motivation. This is what we as educators must provide our students.

For more information on how gamification—defined by Trinh (2022) as "the use of video-game elements, such as achievements, badges, avatars, adventures and customized goals, in non-game contexts" (para. 3)—can be applied to assessment, we recommend the article by Trinh (2022) and the podcast episode by Trinh and Savvides (2022).

Think-Pair-Share 6.2b   Reflect on what language teachers and assessors of YLs can learn from video games.

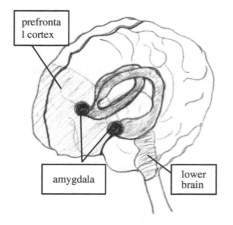

The amygdala = the brain's switching station
Source: Pixabay / Pexels

Figure 6.2   The amygdala, prefrontal cortex, and lower brain.

6.3 Debate over Testing Young Learners

Understanding the above characteristics of YLs raises a variety of questions. One of them is whether YLs should be tested, to begin with.

Think-Pair-Share 6.3a Value-clarification exercise—Part 1   Keeping in mind the difference between assessment and testing, do you believe that YLs should be *tested* in various school subjects? Why or why not?

Think-Pair-Share 6.3b Value-clarification exercise—Part 2   Recalling the various purposes and types of assessment in Chapter 1, do you believe that YLs should be *assessed* in various school subjects? Why or why not?

Having explored your beliefs about assessing and testing YLs, consider some of the public conversations on this topic.

1: One might ask first why we have to test young learners at all. This is a good question. Not everyone does it. In Norway, for example, where the learning of English appears to be highly successful, children are not formally tested on the subject. I have to confess...as someone who has spent a lot of time either testing or advising others on testing, that I feel uneasy at the thought of the damage to children's learning, and their attitude to learning that might be done by insensitive, inappropriate testing (Hughes 2003, p. 199).

2: Yet the government has so far refused to move. "We are firmly committed to national testing and performance tables," a spokeswoman for the Department for Education and Skills said. "These accountability measures are essential to maintaining and extending the improvement in standards we have already achieved," she said. "Parents need and greatly value the information they get from tables. Transparency and accountability are not negotiable." (Asthana 2007, *The Guardian*, para. 14)

3: Some Michigan lawmakers want to omit English language learners' test scores from public school districts' annual standardized test results. ... "We are not trying to back away from accountability on high educational standards, or relax the standards for anyone," Townsend said. "We just don't want to portray students or school districts as failing when they are just trying to adequately serve a different sector of the population." (Crawford 2011, *Capital News Service*, para. 1)

> **4a:** "A child whose progress is not monitored, whose results don't matter, is a child likely to fall through the cracks." (Levesque 2015, *NYT.* para. 11)

> **4b:** "The evidence shows testing has done more harm than good, with scores being pursued at the expense of deeper, broader learning" (Welner 2015, *NYT,* para. 3)

> **5:** ...the Pisa exam has also generated significant controversy over its methodology and design, leading to concerns—common to many standardised tests—that it does not adequately measure the quality of instruction. Or that it does not truly capture the diversity of contexts facing such different school systems. These concerns are reflected in the fact that fewer than half of Latin American countries currently participate.
>
> ....
>
> The [TERCE] assessment also has a broader range than Pisa, looking at children at different stages of development (at the ages of eight and 11), and evaluating the context of each school.
> What TERCE found was reason for cautious optimism - but also renewed effort. Its comparison between its last evaluation in 2006 and today showed a modest but broad improvement in test results across the majority of Latin American countries. (Sanchez Zinny 2015, *BBC,* Missing the Tests section)

> **6a:** According to US Senator Patty Murray, "we have a moral responsibility to understand how all of our students are doing, where we are falling short"..."broad annual data" offer consistency (Blad 2021, *EducationWeek*)

> **6b:** After the pandemic, "[t]he week the U.S. Department of Education told states it wouldn't issue blanket waivers from mandated annual assessments, the creators of a national guide instructing parents on how to opt their children out of the standardized tests reported a spike in web traffic to the site. 'Parents are hopping mad,' said Bob Schaeffer, the interim executive director of FairTest, an organization that promotes testing opt outs and created the guide. 'If schools don't cancel the tests, parents will.'" (Blad 2021, *EducationWeek*)

Think-Pair-Share 6.3c Synthesis—Part 1   Summarize the concerns of the various stakeholders.

a. Summarize the main arguments in the above debate. Provide textual evidence of your answer.
b. What concerns are voiced about the impact of tests on YLs? What is the potential damage?
c. What concern is raised with the scope of tests?
d. What reasons are cited in defense of large-scale standardized tests?

e. Imagine that learners of a language are tested in the target language on their knowledge of math, science, history, etc. Why might there be a concern over these YLs' test scores for the learners themselves? For their schools?

Think-Pair-Share 6.3d Synthesis and Application—Part 2   Extend your thinking.

a. In contrast to testing, what is the public conversation about assessment, such as ongoing, formative, and classroom assessment?
b. What are the laws, regulations, and practices where you live about the high-stakes standardized testing of YLs?
c. Why might some stakeholders (such as parents, educational leaders, politicians) be in favor of high-stakes standardized testing of YLs where you live?
d. Could/Should high-stakes tests currently used with YLs be completely replaced by teacher (classroom-based) assessment? Why or why not?

6.4   Considerations in Assessing Young Learners

As described before, YLs differ from adults in a variety of ways. Consequently, the assessment of YLs necessitates special considerations as well. The younger the learner, the greater the need for circumspection. The differences between children and adults have implications for assessment in terms of the

- types of tasks
- length of tasks
- skills to be assessed
- topics
- groupings
- examiner/teacher support
- examiner/teacher approval

YLs even differ from their peers. They develop at different rates: some mature early, while others bloom late. Figure 6.3 describes each of the three general age groups and the implications for their assessment. It is important to note though that the characteristics and implications below are not strictly attributable to one age group; rather, there is often an overlap among the age groups.

6.5   Recommendations for Optimizing Assessment of YLs

Although opinions are sharply divided over the soundness of *testing* YLs, few if any would dispute the benefits of *assessing* them. Ionnaou-Georgiou and Pavlou (2003) claim it is important to assess children in order to:

- monitor and aid children's progress
- provide children with evidence of their progress and enhance their motivation
- enable students to monitor their own performance and plan future work
- provide information for parents, colleagues, school authorities

Characteristics of YL Age Groups	Assessment Implications of YL Age Groups
A	
5–8 year-olds	
Characteristics of 5–8 year-olds	**Assessment implications**
• instinctual, naturalistic learners	• need frequent observational assessment of the whole child (holding pencil, social cognitive-emotional-physical skills) (McKay 2006)
• learn through discovery, direct hands-on experience, game, play, songs, rhymes, stories, fantasy with a language focus (rather than sitting, listening, reading, writing)	• topics: self, here & now, date, weather, daily routine, colors, numbers, short stories and related activities, likes and dislikes;
• still learning about the world around them	• meaning-focused and content-based (rather than form-focused) tasks
• learning to read and write in any language	• use flashcards, comic strips
• lack metalanguage or ability to explain rules of language	• ample scaffolding needed from the examiner
• enthusiastic, lively, loud, active, tire fast, recover quickly, tire more from sitting than running, may abandon task if too difficult but may complete it to please teacher	• hard time sitting but some need peace and quiet during assessment
• average attention span age +2 minutes but may not understand concept of time	• short tasks
• working on fine and gross motor skills (climbing, balancing, running, jumping, use of tools, handwriting), developing literacy skills	• hard to assess through reading/writing, keep writing to minimum, copying and word scramble OK
	• focus on speaking, word, formulaic sequence & sentence level, rather than monologuing at the paragraph level
	• beginners: Total Physical Response, moving, pointing, coloring, drawing, circling
• need "love, security, recognition and belonging" from peers (McKay 2006, p. 8), encouragement, reminder, feedback from teacher	• ample scaffolding with visuals from teacher; if assessed directly, may need warm-up, not cold start; all should "pass" and experience success

B	Characteristics of 9–12 year-olds	Assessment implications
9–12 year-olds	• development in prefrontal cortex continues; most rapid development in 8-16 year-olds, continues well into 20s (Edutopia 2011, 7:30 minutes)	• need frequent observational assessment
	• still improving hand-eye coordination	
	• growing attention span but still rather short	• short and varied tasks, quizzes in game format
		• some need peace and quiet during assessment
	• still working on hand-eye coordination	
	• in their strongest language, they are reading & writing to learn; literacy skills from L1 transfer into L2	• still enjoying speaking tasks prefer informal to formal
	• metalanguage still developing	• mostly meaning-focused and content-based (rather than form-focused) tasks (though some rule-based learning)
	• can handle more complicated topics	• continued focus on formulaic language
	• still motivated by fun, active learning, interaction with friends	• role play with friends, task with game-like elements, gamification, fantasy, humor, excitement, engagement (Hasselgren 2000), cartoons, solving mysteries, competition, technology use
		• beginners: Total Physical Response, moving, pointing, coloring, drawing, circling
	• still need "love, security, recognition and belonging" from peers (McKay 2006, p. 8)	• all should "pass" and experience success

Figure 6.3 Young-learner age groups and assessment implications.

	Characteristics of YL Age Groups	Assessment Implications of YL Age Groups
C **13–17 year-olds**	**Characteristics of 13–17 year-olds** • continued brain development, prefrontal cortex still developing into their 20s (Edutopia 2011, 7:30 minutes) • increasing interest in and understanding of the world around them • lack the same life experiences as adults • interactions with adults intimidating • longer attention span • self-conscious, distracted	**Assessment implications** • still struggle with abstract topics and formal situations • both formulaic language and rule-based learning • debates, discussions in pairs or groups, complaining about the world, likes, dislikes, opinion, exposition, short narratives, process, procedure, speech acts (greetings, requests, agreeing, disagreeing, promises, apologizing, etc.), competition, cooperation; technology use, making video, video clips, humor, creative thinking, online gamified quizzes, presentations, written assignments, projects • most familiar with school, rather than public or occupational topics • struggle with formal situations (e.g. writing a letter of complaint, job-related topics, interviews) • prefer talking to peers, peer assessment • need peace and quiet during assessment
D	**Outliers**	

The assumption behind many assessments and learning materials for young learners is that younger students are beginners while older adolescents are more proficient. As a result, finding materials and assessments for the atypical learner can be a challenge. This could include a very young learner who is already quite proficient or an older adolescent who is a beginner.

The discrepancy is further exacerbated when an older learner lacks literacy skills in their native language. Literacy education that is concurrent to language learning for older adolescents and adults (i.e. LESLLA learners) demands a teacher/ assessor with specific skills and expertise, along with age- and level-appropriate materials.

Figure 6.3 (Cont'd)

Cameron (2001) adds that:

- the power of assessment can increase awareness of neglected aspects of learning
- tests prepare children for later stresses of tests and life in general
- some innovative testing exists

To avoid negative washback, it is important not to reduce children's learning to test preparation or rush through the curriculum before the next test. Additionally, the demands of assessment can place undue stress on children, as demonstrated in the above quotations. To minimize negative and maximize positive washback, the following is recommended. Assessment should be formative and frequent. Conditions (such as procedures, teacher, surroundings) should be familiar, stress-free, and exactly understood before the assessment begins. Modes of assessment best be innovative. Language should be assessed through multiple measures and varied tasks. Tasks should be psychologically safe, short, integrated, colorful, gamified, interesting, and sequenced strategically: starting with an easy task to build self-confidence. YLs should be given multiple opportunities to demonstrate what they can do. Any inequities that are revealed through assessment should be rectified. Information about assessment results should be shared with stakeholders such as parents, colleagues, school authorities.

Did you know? In an innovative assessment task format, 11–12 years-old EFL learners in Norway are to solve a "four-episode, cartoon-picture-packed mystery" (Hasselgren 2000, p. 264) presented in a story booklet and CD about a missing elephant. The audio component simulates a radio drama. The language test assesses word recognition, spelling, and everyday expressions. The writing test asks the learners to write a diary entry and a letter about the story. The students become engaged in the adventure and genuinely wish to solve the mystery. The assessment results are interpreted alongside the YLs' self-assessment and the teachers' knowledge of their own students. Teachers receive training in administering the assessment, interpreting the results, and improving their learners' skills based on the results.

To maximize positive washback, peer-interaction components should be included. Topics should also be psychologically safe, i.e. positive, about school, home, and the learners' own stories. When assigning constructed-response topics, the teacher should steer the YLs' thinking toward something positive to avoid the students' recalling potentially traumatic experiences (e.g. from having lost a loved one or having been a refugee). Language should be level-appropriate. YLs need encouragement, frequent reminders from a teacher, or sound and visual effects from an electronic device. Multiple chances should be provided for YLs to demonstrate what they can do; scoring should not be prejudiced by the YLs' handwriting, behavior, culture, home background, religion, race, gender, socioeconomic status, etc.; and feedback should be immediate. YLs and their guardians need to be educated about assessment issues, as their support and involvement are desirable. Children can be taught to assess their own performance and that of their peers.

Did you know? In a now-famous video entitled Austin's Butterfly, educator Ron Berger demonstrates how feedback—if it is helpful, specific, and kind—gives even YLs the tools to improve their work significantly. With the help of his classmates' feedback, Austin, a first-grader at Anser Charter School in Boise, Idaho, USA, was able to revise his initial drawing in six drafts beyond all expectations (EL Education 2016).

Feedback on assessment can be beneficial to all stakeholders but most importantly, it must be beneficial to the most important of stakeholders: the YLs themselves. Spontaneous ongoing formative assessment with YL can be a challenge, especially if the YLs are afraid to make a mistake in front of their peers. Willis (Edutopia 2011) recommends having students in a face-to-face classroom use individual whiteboards to write down answers, holding them up to show the teacher, who can acknowledge the answer. The teacher can then provide immediate feedback to the whole class, and the students can erase their answers without feeling self-conscious in front of their classmates. In a synchronous online environment, the same can be achieved with literate YLs, for instance, when students chat their answers directly to the teacher only instead of everyone.

Think-Pair-Share 6.5a Application From your personal experience, recall one way to assess children aged

a. 5–8 years
b. 9–12 years
c. 13–17 years

Describe specific situations in language classes where you could employ the above ideas. Justify your answers with information from Figure 6.3.

6.6 Chapter Conclusion

This chapter guides educators without formal training in working with YLs, defined as school children aged 5–17 years. We explored traits distinguishing YLs from adults, their vulnerability, and their non-autonomous status. Examining age-specific groups (5–8, 9–12, and 13–17 years), we highlighted their sensitivity to negativity and the importance of motivation through fun, play, fantasy, social interaction, and gamification. The chapter focused on assessment implications for YLs, stressing the need to avoid stimuli that trigger fear responses and advocating for ongoing, low-stakes, formative classroom assessments by teachers, peers, and learners themselves. We also discussed the debate over mandatory high-stakes, standardized tests for YLs, promoting a balanced approach to minimize stress and maximize positive test impact.

In subsequent chapters, we will examine the assessment landscape for YLs in United States and Canadian schools (Chapter 7) and explore the assessment of exceptional language learners (Chapter 8). This journey aims to equip educators and assessment specialists with the knowledge and tools to effectively teach and assess YLs.

Appendix 1 – Achievement Quiz of Chapter 6

(For discussion or writing prompts, see the Think-Pair-Share tasks in this chapter.)

Directions Part A: Select the response that best answers each question below. Each question is worth 1 point.

1. Which of the following statements is an implication of the role the amygdala plays in the brain of a young learner? If students are _____.
   a. afraid of the teacher, the amygdala calms them down
   b. afraid, the amygdala makes them alert and prepares them to learn
   c. bored, the information goes to the lower brain and is not learned
   d. bored, they become most receptive to new information

2. Among educators, parents, politicians, and other stakeholders, there is a debate about whether
   _____.
   a. young learners should be assessed
   b. young learners should be tested
   c. language learners should be assessed
   d. language learners should be tested

3. According to the chapter, when assessing children aged 5–8 years old, the following assessment
   implications should be considered. Assessments should _____.
   a. incorporate elements of play, songs, fantasy, and discovery with a language focus
   b. involve extended periods of sitting and writing to calm the children down
   c. focus on reading and listening according to the Comprehensible Input approach
   d. prioritize abstract concepts and language rules for positive washback

Directions Part B: Select all the options that are correct. Each correct answer is worth 1 point.

4. Young learners differ from adults in all of the following ways. Young learners _____.
   a. are autonomous actors legally speaking
   b. undergo intense brain development
   c. are sensitive to the reaction of others
   d. thrive through social interaction

5. Teachers and assessors can gain all of the following insights from video games. Students can
   _____.
   a. make progress at their own pace
   b. receive candy for working quickly
   c. receive frequent and timely feedback
   d. enjoy privacy as they make mistakes

7

PK-12 in the United States and Canada: Assessment Is Not a Dirty Word

Chapter Overview

This chapter focuses on PreK-12 ELs in Canada and the United States. Readers who find this context irrelevant may skip this chapter. It covers legal and policy-related processes including identification, screening, enrollment, programming, evaluation, assessment, monitoring, and exiting. While the book primarily discusses these processes in the United States and Canada, it acknowledges their broader applicability to second or foreign-language contexts worldwide. Teacher profiles illustrate these processes within real-world contexts, emphasizing practical application beyond North America.

7.1 Learning Objectives

1. Develop an understanding of characteristics that define PreK-12 ELs in the United States and Canada
2. Synthesize the impact of laws and policies written to protect the rights of PreK-12 ELs in the United States and Canada
3. Describe how assessments are used to properly identify and appropriately service PreK-12 ELs in the United States and Canada
4. Analyze different ways of differentiating instruction and assessment for PreK-12 ELs
5. Conceptualize real-word contexts for instruction of PreK-12 ELs

> **PreK-12, also known as P-K/PK-12:** In the United States, *PreK-12* is a term that generally refers to Pre-Kindergarten (PreK) through twelfth (12th) grade. PK is typically offered in public school settings for children aged 3 to 5 years.

Did you know? Many PreK-12 teachers have negative feelings about the term "assessment." They have misconceptions about the purposes of assessment. They resent that results of assessments are used in their teacher evaluation systems. However, assessments serve many valid and important purposes, especially for ELs. The authors hope that this chapter dispels the idea that assessment is a dirty word.

A Practical Guide to Language Assessment: How Do You Know That Your Students Are Learning? First Edition.
Ildiko Porter-Szucs et al.
© 2025 John Wiley & Sons, Inc. Published 2025 by John Wiley & Sons, Inc.

7.2 PreK-12 ELs in Canada

Approximately 250 000 immigrants settle in Canada each year (Statistics Canada 2019). The Government of Canada provides a list of free newcomer services available at various locations. In Canada, education falls solely under the jurisdiction of each provincial government. As such, each province has different processes for providing instruction and assessment to ELs. School attendance is mandatory until the age of 16 in all provinces except for Manitoba, Ontario, and New Brunswick, where the required age is 18 years. Kindergarten is available to children when they turn 4 years old in Ontario and Quebec and when they turn 5 years old everywhere else. French immersion programs are offered in most places throughout the provinces as Canada is officially a bilingual country. The province of Ontario settles more immigrants than other Canadian provinces. About 43% of all immigrants to Canada settle in Ontario (Statistics Canada 2019). In response to a growing EL population, the Ontario Ministry of Education released a policy on ELs (2007a).

ELs in Canada are defined as students who are in provincially funded English language schools whose first language is a language other than English or is a **variety of English** that is significantly different from the variety used for instruction in each province's schools, and who may require focused educational supports to assist them in attaining proficiency in English. These students may be Canadian-born or recently arrived from other countries. They come from diverse backgrounds and school experiences and have a wide variety of strengths and needs. Inclusion Canada defines different types of language learners in Canada in Linguistically Responsive Education (2017). Examples of Canadian-born language learners are defined as follows:

- Aboriginal students in communities where primarily aboriginal languages are spoken
- Children from French-speaking communities
- Children from Mennonite or other cultural communities where another language is spoken
- Children from immigrant homes in which languages other than English are primarily spoken

> **Variety of English** is also referred to as *dialects of English*. Standard English is the variety of English that is used as the language of education, law, and government in English-speaking countries. Standard English is the variety of English "that is perceived to represent the accepted norms of grammatical, lexical, and phonological features that are thought to be 'correct'" (Galloway and Rose 2015). It is important to note that there is not just one "Standard English." Different English-speaking countries have slight variations in their standard. Each variety of Standard English follows specific grammar rules, such as the correct use of punctuation, spelling, verb form. Standard English varieties include Standard American English, Standard Canadian English, Standard British English, Standard South African English, and others. Some varieties are so different from standard English that many linguists consider them to be languages in their own right.

7.3 Legal Protections for ELs in Canada

The provinces of Ontario and Alberta have outlined expectations for the identification of and services offered to students identified as ELs. Each province has also developed robust resources, available online and in print, for schools and educators of ELs.

The Alberta Initiative for School Improvement (AISI) project (2009) supports the improvement of student learning and performance by encouraging teachers, parents, and the community to work collaboratively to introduce innovative and creative initiatives based on local needs and circumstances. It was developed through a partnership with the education community in 1999 and was first implemented in all Alberta school authorities in 2000.

A stated goal of Ontario's EL policy document is to implement a consistent approach to the education of ELs in Ontario, while "also affording the flexibility school boards need to meet their local needs, build capacity, and enhance program viability. The goal of Ontario's policy for ELs is to provide school boards with direction and support in meeting the needs of English language learners so that these students can develop the proficiency in English that is necessary for success in school" (Ontario Ministry of Education 2007a, p. 10).

ELs who are under the age of 18 and are otherwise entitled to be admitted to school in Ontario will be admitted to school whether or not their parent or guardian is unlawfully in Canada (Ontario Ministry of Education 2007a).

Specific directives for the orientation, registration, and initial assessment of English language proficiency (ELP) processes for K-12 ELs are outlined in the policy document. The initial screening assessment must include four components: a structured interview to assess oral communication skills, an assessment of reading comprehension, an assessment of student writing, and an assessment of mathematical knowledge and skills. The initial assessment of ELP, or **ELP screener**, is used to help identify those students who require additional instruction in English in order to succeed in school. The policy allows part of the initial assessment to be conducted in the student's first or dominant language (e.g. the language previously used for schooling) to allow a broader view of the student's linguistic development and academic background. The policy document states that the "administration and interpretation of language assessments should be linguistically appropriate" (Ontario Ministry of Education 2007a, p. 18).

> **English language proficiency (ELP) screener**, also known as a placement test or initial assessment; typically a shorter version of a summative assessment of ELP in all four domains of language; is used to determine initial eligibility for EL status.

7.4 Programming for ELs in Canada

Early childhood education in Canada is compulsory for all Canadian children, available until the age of 5 or 6. The exceptions are Ontario and Quebec, where children enter the public school system at the age of 4, continuing with grades 1 through 12. The Ontario guide for teachers, *Supporting English Language Learners in Kindergarten* (2007b), recommends informally assessing oral language use and development and through the teacher–child interaction.

In grades 1 through 12, once an EL's initial assessment is conducted, additional information (e.g. interviews with student and family, review of school documents, including transcripts, other academic assessment data) is gathered and analyzed prior to placing the student in appropriate programming. The policy document requires schools to place ELs grade appropriately. It also states that Canadian educators who coordinate ESL and **English language development (ELD)** programs and services should hold specialist qualifications, which are similar to teaching endorsements in the United States, in ESL.

Program models recommended by the Ontario EL policy document include *ESL* programs, which are for students whose first language is other than English or is a variety of English significantly different from that used for instruction in Ontario schools. Students in ESL programs have had educational opportunities to develop age-appropriate first-language literacy skills. *English literacy development (ELD)* programs are for students whose first language is other than English or is a variety of English significantly different from that used for instruction in Ontario schools. Students in these programs are most often from countries where their access to education has been limited, and they had limited opportunities to develop language and literacy skills in any language. Schooling in their countries of origin has been inconsistent, disrupted, or even completely unavailable throughout the years that these children would otherwise have been in school. As a result, they arrive in Ontario schools with significant gaps in their education. Both programs may also include courses specifically designed for **newcomer** ELs, ELs with disabilities, and **sheltered content classes**.

> **ELD** is an acronym with slightly different meanings in Canada and the United States. **ELD** in Canada stands for English *literacy* development program. In the United States, **ELD** stands for English *language* development and refers to programming for ELs in a more holistic sense, across all domains.

> **Newcomer(s)** are recently arrived students who have lived in the United States or Canada for fewer than 12 months. In some contexts, newcomer students are referred to as *beginner* or *novice* students.

> **Sheltered English instruction** (also known as **sheltered content classes**) is an instructional approach that engages ELs above the beginner level in developing grade-level content-area knowledge, academic skills, and increased English proficiency. Sheltered classes offer ELs the grade-level content instruction of their English-speaking peers, while adapting lesson delivery to suit their English proficiency level.

The AISI project manual contains a sampling of ESL/ELD projects for students across the levels of ELP and illustrates the work being done in schools across Alberta related to the development of effective ESL/ELD teaching and learning strategies. The manual is intended to inform teachers, curriculum coordinators, school administrators, central office staff, and others involved in education about successful ESL/ELD strategies to be used in Alberta schools. The variety of promising strategies outlined in the manual has been designed to provide students with meaningful ESL/ELD experiences that will strengthen their ELP and their ability to succeed in all subject areas. These strategies include smaller class sizes, pre-kindergarten English classes, short-term pull-out classes, and alternative learning opportunities or strategies. These highly student-centered programs prioritize authentic learning of integrated language skills through project-based learning and performance-based assessment.

The decision to discontinue ESL/ELD support in Canada varies by province and territory. In Ontario and Alberta, at print time, it is made by the principal in consultation with the student, the parents, and ESL/ELD and classroom teachers. No formal process for discontinuing services is provided in either policy manual.

7.5 PreK-12 ELs in the United States

ELs are a growing part of the PreK-12 student population in the United States. Between the 2009–2010 and 2014–2015 school years, the percentage of ELs increased in more than half of the states, with increases of over 40% in five states (National Center for Educational Statistics 2024). Over 4 800 000 ELs were enrolled in US schools in 2014–15, representing approximately 10% of the total K-12 student population (National Center for Educational Statistics 2024).

In the United States, an EL is defined as an individual:

A. who is aged 3 through 21;

B. who is enrolled or preparing to enroll in an elementary school or secondary school;

C. **i.** who was not born in the United States or whose native language is a language other than English;

  ii. (I) who is a Native American or Alaska Native, or a native resident of the outlying areas; and

    (II) who comes from an environment where a language other than English has had a significant impact on the individual's level of ELP; or

  iii. who is migratory, whose native language is a language other than English, and who comes from an environment where a language other than English is dominant; and

D. whose difficulties in speaking, reading, writing, or understanding the English language may be sufficient to deny the individual

  i. the ability to meet the challenging state academic standards;

  ii. the ability to successfully achieve in classrooms where the language of instruction is English; or

  iii. the opportunity to participate fully in society.

(US Department of Education 2015a, Elementary and Secondary Education Act [ESEA], Section 8101[20], p. 393)

7.6 Legal Protections for ELs in the United States

Over the last 50 years, United States federal law has established the rights of ELs and the responsibilities of educators who work with them. It is important for educators to understand the legal precedents that govern practices with ELs so that they can advocate for their students accordingly. First, Section 601 of Title VI of the Civil Rights Act of 1964 stated that "[n]o person in the United States shall, on the ground of race, color, or national origin, be excluded from participation in, be denied the benefits of, or be subjected to discrimination under any program or activity receiving federal financial assistance" (Civil Rights Act of 1964, p. 12). Title VI forbade discrimination on account of race, color, age, creed, or national origin in any federally funded activity and authorized the Department of Health, Education, and Welfare to apply compliance procedures and reviews and withhold funds. Since schools and school districts receive a per-pupil allowance of Title III (federal) funds, they must comply with these provisions, as specifically related to ELs.

The following federal cases identify additional requirements schools and districts have regarding ELs (Wright 2023):

- Lau v. Nichols (1974): School districts must take steps to help ELs overcome language barriers and to ensure that they can participate meaningfully in the district's educational programs.
- Plyler v. Doe (1982): Undocumented children and young adults have the same right to attend public primary and secondary schools as do United States citizens and permanent residents. Like other children, undocumented students are obliged under state law to attend school until they reach a mandated age. As a result of the Plyler ruling, public schools may not:
  - Deny admission to a student during initial enrollment or at any other time on the basis of undocumented status.
  - Treat a student differently to determine residency.
  - Engage in any practices to "chill" the right of access to school.

- Require students or parents to disclose or document their immigration status.
- Castañeda v. Pickard (1981): Programs for language-minority students must be (1) based on a sound educational theory, (2) implemented effectively with sufficient resources and personnel, and (3) evaluated to determine whether they are effective in helping students overcome language barriers. If found to not be effective, alternative research-based programming must be implemented.

Most recently, the ESEA was reauthorized to include the *Every Student Succeeds Act* (ESSA; US Department of Education 2015b). ESSA requires State Education Agencies to do the following:

1. Align ELP standards and assessments in speaking, listening, reading, and writing.
2. Include goals and measures for language progress and proficiency in the state accountability system.
3. Develop and allow appropriate **accommodations** for academic proficiency tests, including assessments in the language and form most likely to yield accurate information on what those students know and can do in the content area assessed.
4. Administer an ELP screener to determine eligibility for EL status within 30 school days of enrollment (or within 10 school days after the first day of school). While the Ontario, Canada policy document specifically allows the administration of the ELP screener in the child's dominant language, that is not allowable under the United States Department of Education, Office of English Language Acquisition guidance (US Department of Education 2016a). In order to determine which students may need to take an ELP screener, schools or districts refer to answers that parents write on the **Home Language Survey.**

> **Accommodations** are any changes made to classroom assignments or assessments or to the classroom environment or testing conditions that allow students to better demonstrate their knowledge and skills. Accommodations do not alter the content of assessments or assignments, give students an unfair advantage, or in the case of assessments, change what a test measures. They make it possible for all students to show what they know without being impeded by a disability, learning difference, or limited proficiency in English.

Think-Pair-Share 7.6a Brainstorming Activity   Generate a list of accommodations that might provide an EL with a better opportunity to demonstrate his/her skills on an assignment or assessment.

> The **Home Language Survey** is a questionnaire given to parents or guardians in both Canada and the United States that helps schools and districts identify which students are potential ELs and who will require assessment of their ELP to determine whether they are, in fact, eligible for language assistance services.

Think-Pair-Share 7.6b Perception Activity   Some students in the United States feel there is a stigma associated with being identified as an EL. Discuss what factors may contribute to this negative stigma. Alternatively, if you are more familiar with a context in which English is a foreign language, think of a student who does not speak the native language of the land and discuss how that student might feel about being identified as a nonspeaker.

Think-Pair-Share 7.6c Synthesize   Describe how assessments are used to identify and place ELs into appropriate services in both the United States and Canada. Re-read Sections 7.4 and 7.5 to help you identify the initial assessments required in both countries.

Think-Pair-Share 7.6d Application Exercise   Investigate the local, district, state/provincial processes for identifying potential ELs and placing them into the continuum of English language development (ELD) services offered.

Did you know?   In the United States, ELs in grades K-12 are required to participate in <u>all</u> state-mandated standardized assessments with one exception. There is a one-time exemption allowed for ELs attending school in the United States for fewer than 12 months on the English language arts (ELA) portion (only) of the state-mandated standardized assessment (e.g. PSAT, M-STEP, AzM2, and CAASPP). EL proficiency on state-mandated standardized assessments is included in the **state accountability reporting system**.

> ESSA requires all states to use a **state school accountability reporting system.** The system must report state assessment scores and other quality metrics to identify and support schools in helping students achieve state standards.
> Related to the administration of summative assessments, ESSA requires:
>
> "(A) In general.—Each State plan shall demonstrate that the State educational agency, in consultation with local educational agencies, has implemented a set of high-quality student academic assessments in mathematics, reading or language arts, and science. The State retains the right to implement such assessments in any other subject chosen by the State."
> "(B) Requirements.—The assessments under subparagraph (A) shall—"...
> "(iii) be used for purposes for which such assessments are valid and reliable, consistent with relevant, nationally recognized professional and technical testing standards, objectively measure academic achievement, knowledge, and skills, and be tests that do not evaluate or assess personal or family beliefs and attitudes, or publicly disclose personally identifiable information"

Think-Pair-Share 7.6e Application Exercise   Investigate local, district, state/provincial assessment policies. Do they include specific provisions for assessment of ELs and for accommodations on academic proficiency tests (i.e. Mathematics, Science, Social Studies, and ELA)? Discuss.

Think-Pair-Share 7.6f Application Exercise   Investigate the ELP standards and assessments used in your state or province. Discuss.

7.7   Programming for ELs in the United States

While there are no national requirements for screening, servicing, or assessing ELs in PreK programs, research asserts that preschool can play an essential role in preparing young ELs for greater success later in schooling (Ballantyne et al. 2008). Children who have an opportunity to develop basic foundational skills in language and literacy in preschool enter kindergarten ready to learn to read and write. The National Association for the Education of Young Children (2009) provides the following recommendations for assessing young ELs: using screening and assessment for appropriate purposes, choosing culturally and linguistically appropriate assessments, involving two or more professionals in making significant assessment decisions, using standardized formal assessments, increasing cultural competencies in those conducting assessments, considering the role of family in the assessment of young ELs, and making an investment in resources to developing capacity for assessment development and administration.

In grades K-12, scores from the ELP screener, along with other locally required data, are used to place qualifying ELs in the continuum of services offered by the school or district **language assistance program (LAP)**.

A **language assistance program (LAP)** provides ELs with core English language instruction, as well as instruction and support in the content areas. The LAP describes all services provided to ELs, including general education instruction and assessment, direct English instruction and assessment, progress monitoring of English language proficiency (ELP), general education and English language interventions, and all other educational opportunities funded using general education dollars.

There are four LAP models considered educationally sound under United States federal law (Pickard 1981). First, *ESL* or *ELD* are the most common programs offered to ELs throughout the United States. The programs include techniques, methodology, and a special curriculum designed to teach ELs explicitly about the English language, including the academic vocabulary needed to access content instruction and to develop their ELP in all four language domains. Typically, instruction is provided in English with little use of the ELs' primary language(s). *Structured English immersion (SEI)* programs are designed to impart English language skills so that the ELs can transition and succeed in an English-only mainstream classroom once proficient. Instruction is provided only in English. *Transitional bilingual education (TBE)*, or early-exit bilingual education programs maintain and develop skills in the primary language while introducing, maintaining, and developing skills in English. The primary purpose of a TBE program is to facilitate the ELs' transition to an all-English instructional program, while the students receive academic subject instruction in the primary language to the extent necessary. Finally, *Dual Language* or *Two-way Immersion Bilingual programs* are designed so that students develop language proficiency in two languages by receiving instruction in English and another language in a classroom that is usually composed of half primary English speakers and half primary speakers of the other language. Any of these programs may also include courses specifically designed for newcomer ELs, ELs with disabilities, and sheltered instruction in the content areas. Translanguaging is common and expected in TBE/Dual Language/and Two-way Immersion Bilingual Programs.

Many LAPs include the sheltered instruction and observation protocol (SIOP) as one approach to training, supporting, and evaluating content-area teachers working with ELs. According to the Center for Applied Linguistics (n.d.), SIOP is a research-based and validated instructional model that has proven effective in addressing the academic needs of ELs. The SIOP approach can be used within any content area. The SIOP model includes components and features, which are tools, to help teachers make content and language more accessible to students learning English. Both content and language objectives are an important element of SIOP Component 1.

Lesson preparation: When engaging with the SIOP model, teachers define and display for students both content and language objectives for every lesson.

The SIOP model consists of eight interrelated components:

- Lesson preparation
- Building background
- Comprehensible input
- Strategies
- Interaction
- Practice/application

- Lesson delivery
- Review and assessment

Using instructional strategies connected to each of these components, teachers are able to design and deliver lessons that address the academic and linguistic needs of ELs (2018).

Title VI and the Equal Opportunities Education Act independently require each school and/or district to evaluate the effectiveness of the LAP to ensure that ELs acquire English proficiency and that language programs are reasonably calculated to allow ELs to attain parity of participation in the standard instructional program within a reasonable period of time.

Many state and local educational agencies shifted from a compliance mindset to a **continuous improvement** one as a result of program evaluation requirements written into the ESSA in the ESEA (Klein 2018).

Glossary of Education Reform defines **continuous improvement** as "school- or instructional-improvement process that unfolds progressively, that does not have a fixed or predetermined endpoint, and that is sustained over extended periods. The concept also encompasses the general belief that improvement is not something that starts and stops, but it's something that requires an organizational or professional commitment to an ongoing process of learning, self-reflection, adaptation, and growth" (Continuous Improvement 2013).

Think-Pair-Share 7.7a Perception Activity   Parents have a legal right to refuse services offered by the LAP if their child is identified as an EL. How might you try to understand a parent's rationale for refusing services for their child? Might their reluctance to allow services be related to a negative stigma? Discuss.

Think-Pair-Share 7.7b Application Exercise   If you are an in-service K-12 teacher in Canada or the United States, investigate the LAP model(s) used in your school or district. Use the three-pronged test written under Castañeda v. Pickard to evaluate and determine whether your program meets federal requirements. If you are a preservice teacher, think of an English teaching setting you are familiar with and evaluate it using the three-pronged test written under Castañeda v. Pickard to evaluate and determine whether that program meets federal requirements.

In order to determine an EL's readiness to discontinue, or exit services, schools or districts must monitor and regularly assess progress toward English proficiency as well as achievement in other academic areas. This assessment of progress must include conducting an annual ELP assessment and, at least annually, measuring ELs' performance in grade-level core content areas (i.e. English Language Arts, Mathematics, Social Studies, and Science).

Forty-one US states, US territories, and other federal agencies have adopted the **WIDA** Consortium standards and instructional framework. The WIDA Consortium is a member-based organization dedicated to the research, design and implementation of a high-quality, standards-based system for PreK-12 English language learners. The WIDA Consortium offers a suite of PK-12 assessments, including a screener/placement test, a test of interim English language proficiency (ELP), and a summative assessment of ELP. The Consortium also provides resources for PreK programs in their WIDA Early Years collection.

(Continued)

(Continued)

WIDA assessments are standards-referenced tests, meaning that student performance is compared to the WIDA ELD Standards Framework (2024b). WIDA assessments are developed and refined through a rigorous four-part test development process. First, in collaboration with the Center for Applied Linguistics, the WIDA team writes test items and creates coordinating artwork. Next, WIDA coordinates numerous review activities and events, including content reviews, bias and sensitivity reviews, field tests, pilot tests, and form reviews. Then, psychometricians, who are trained experts in measuring the validity and reliability of an assessment, investigate how new test content performs during field testing. Finally, WIDA assessment experts determine which field-tested items continue as scored pieces of a WIDA assessment.

United States federal law requires potential ELs to be screened with an initial assessment of ELP, as well as annual assessment of ELP. The WIDA Screener and WIDA ACCESS assessments are approved for purposes of screening and reporting ELP. The WIDA Screener is used as a tool to determine if a student qualifies as an EL, as well as for a placement test for students who meet the entry criteria so they can be appropriately placed in the continuum of services offered by the LAP. Although not required by US federal law, the WIDA Consortium also offers the WIDA Model, an interim measure of ELP. The WIDA Model is most often used between summative assessment cycles to provide in-real-time ELP data. It provides information that informs instructional planning and other decisions related to students' education.

Finally, the WIDA ACCESS is a summative assessment, given annually to kindergarten through 12th-grade students who have been identified as ELs. It meets US federal requirements of the ESSA for monitoring and reporting ELs' progress toward ELP. The WIDA Consortium offers an Alternate ACCESS assessment of ELP for students with significant cognitive impairments.

ESSA requires state education agencies to develop standard EL exit criteria, which serves as guidance to educators on specific local requirements ELs must meet in order to exit EL status. When students exit EL status, they are considered former English learners (FEL). Also required under ESSA is a 4-year period of monitoring FELs. The US Department of Education (2016), Office of English Language Acquisition cautions that exiting EL students either too soon or too late raise civil rights concerns. EL students who are exited too soon are denied access to EL services, while EL students who are exited too late may be denied access to parts of the general curriculum. Denying or delaying access to the general curriculum can impede academic growth and contribute to a higher risk of dropping out of school.

Did you know?   Students worry about exiting EL services. They do not want to lose the help provided by the EL department. At first, this may appear to be an assessment issue. Educators may wonder whether the assessment might be too easy if the student passes but continues to return for services. ELs may return to EL services for a variety of reasons, including feeling comfortable with the ESL teacher and for camaraderie with other ELs. Some ELs even purposefully fail the content area and/or ELP tests because they believe it is the only way to continue to receive EL services. However, this illuminates an issue with the service-delivery model. When students exit EL services, they should still be able to participate in whatever appropriate intervention services exist. It is important to prepare students for what happens after they exit EL status. Educators should consider meeting individually with each student qualifying for exit to discuss scheduling and available support. To avoid misuse of assessment, it is important to help students understand the purpose of the assessment. Understanding the purpose of the assessment also helps students feel more comfortable and decreases test anxiety.

Think-Pair-Share 7.7c Application Exercise   Investigate the exit protocol used in your state or province. How are students monitored after they exit EL services?

Think-Pair-Share 7.7d Compare   You have learned about laws and processes regarding the education of ELs in both Canada and the United States. Discuss the similarities and differences.

7.8   K-12 Cognitive Benefits of Bilingualism

Did you know?   There are many cognitive benefits of bilingualism. It is important for PreK-12 teachers of ELs to become familiar with the benefits of bilingualism so that they can maximize opportunities to build on the assets that ELs bring to the classroom.

The cognitive benefits of bilingualism, such as working memory, abstract thinking skills, and multitasking, are well documented. According to Marian and Shook (2012), speaking a second language can mean that one has a better attention span and can multitask better than monolinguals. Bilinguals experience health benefits, including a reduced risk of having a stroke and there is a growing research body of evidence that bilingualism can delay the onset of dementia and Alzheimer's disease (Fratiglioni et al. 2004). Research from the Millennium Cohort Study found that even though bilingual children who are educated in their second language may initially lag behind around 3, 4, and 5 years old, they soon catch up and outperform their peers by the age 7 (Bennett 2011).

7.9   K-12 EL Teacher Profiles

Below are three profiles of K-12 teachers of ELs. Each profile is situated in a different geographical context, representing different grade levels/spans. There is considerable variance in K-12 teaching situations; the requirements for curriculum, instruction, and assessment differ across states/provinces. However, the need to plan for and intentionally support the development of **academic language** is evident in each scenario. In each teacher profile, note how the teacher connects content and language instruction. Neither is taught or assessed in isolation.

> **Academic language** is formal and complex language that is used in content area classrooms and other academic settings. Academic language is often more abstract, less contextualized, and more nuanced than the language used in social settings.

Effective teachers use the unique assets their students bring to the classroom to provide scaffolds to aid in new learning. In each of the teacher profiles, you will look for and make a list of examples when and how the teacher provides scaffolds. In the application exercise, you will choose three of the scaffolds demonstrated in the teacher profiles and describe how you might use these scaffolds with students.

> A **scaffold** is an instructional technique or strategy used to move students progressively toward stronger understanding and, ultimately, greater independence in the learning process. Like physical scaffolding, the supportive strategies are temporary and incrementally removed when they are no longer needed, and the teacher gradually shifts more responsibility over the learning process to the student.

Think-Pair-Share 7.9a Compare   Following each profile, you will Think-Pair-Share and discuss the following:

a. Describe the characteristics of the teacher's ELs.
b. What makes the teacher's teaching context unique?
c. How does the teacher differentiate instruction and assessment to meet the needs of the students?

Andy

Andy teaches a kindergarten/first-grade split class in an inner-city school in Michigan. Arabic is the first language of Andy's predominantly refugee-status students. There is a large Arabic-speaking community residing in Andy's district and the parents are often involved in the school. Although Andy is not bilingual himself, he is fortunate to have an Arabic-speaking paraprofessional scheduled in his class for the greater part of every school day. Additionally, Andy's school uses both bilingual text messaging and phone interpretation services to communicate to parents in a language they understand. Since Michigan participates in the WIDA Consortium, Andy and his colleagues use WIDA assessments, WIDA standards, and the WIDA instructional framework. As a kindergarten/first-grade split teacher, Andy uses the kindergarten WIDA ACCESS Placement Test for new kindergarten students and the WIDA Screener for his new first-grade students. Andy's school also has a center-based program for students with cognitive impairments and two of Andy's ELs also have cognitive impairments. Those students take the WIDA Alternate assessment during the annual WIDA assessment window when Andy's other students take the annual summative assessments of ELP, WIDA ACCESS or WIDA ACCESS Kindergarten. Because Andy's students have not yet reached third grade, they are not required to take Michigan's Student Test of Educational Progress (M-STEP). Andy constructs WIDA Language Expectations for each unit so that he can set realistic language learning targets for his students, based on their levels of ELP. A Language Expectation is important when assessing language and content concurrently. Language Expectations include a direct connection to an academic content standard. They describe the language necessary for meeting the grade-level academic content standard. In a recent Mathematics unit, Andy wrote the following language Expectation: **ELD-MA.K.Inform.Expressive: Construct mathematical information texts (with prompting and support) that describe a concept or entity through sequential signals (first, second, etc.) to describe patterns**. Because Andy knows that in order to meet the grade-level academic content standard related to describing mathematical patterns, students need to have a command of using sequential words. He connects these two skills, one mathematical and one writing, as he constructs this language learning goal.

Andy scaffolds his instruction to meet the unique needs of his students by using the following strategies:

- **Patterned oral language,** which uses a similar sentence structure and vocabulary within the context of a familiar classroom activity to help learners comprehend classroom routines.

Andy uses patterned oral language with all of his young learners as one strategy to help them construct new language, either when speaking, or in writing. For example, when Andy reads anything to his students, he always uses the same language pattern; he says, "Today we are going to read about _____." (Andy points to the title.) "Let's read the title together" (Levine et al. 2013).

- **Teacher read-alouds,** which scaffold the text content and provide an excellent model of reading in English. Andy reads aloud with his students daily to promote reading comprehension skills and to build a trusting community of learners.

To monitor his students' progress toward proficiency in English and other content skills, Andy uses a variety of age-appropriate formative assessment techniques, with a high degree of interactiveness, such as the following:

- **Total physical response (TPR),** which requires students to take action based on oral instruction and is used to increase comprehension of oral language input. Andy uses TPR to quickly gauge his students' understanding.
- **Exit tickets** are one type of formative assessment that students complete as they transition from one activity to another or as they leave the room. Exit tickets can require students to write or draw to explain their understanding or to ask questions. Andy uses the responses on the exit tickets to adjust his instruction and to determine what concepts might need reteaching.

Think-Pair-Share 7.9b Teacher Profile Reflection—Part 1   Describe the characteristics of Andy's ELs. What makes Andy's teaching context unique? How does Andy differentiate instruction and assessment to meet the needs of his students?

Marguerite

Marguerite is a Mathematics teacher of students in Grades 9 and 10 Mathematics in an intermediate school (any combination of grades 6 through 9; ages 11 through 15 years) in Toronto, Ontario, Canada. Many of Marguerite's students live in immigrant homes in which languages other than English are primarily spoken. Marguerite's school has a large number of families immigrating from South Asia (e.g. Afghanistan, Bangladesh, Bhutan, Maldives, Nepal, India, Pakistan, and Sri Lanka) and China. Growing up in a bilingual English/French-speaking home has helped Marguerite both empathize and communicate with her multilingual students. When they first arrive in Ontario and enroll in school, Marguerite's students visit a Newcomer Reception Center, where they participate in an interactive, day-long assessment of their proficiency in English and Mathematics before attending school. Marguerite's students will also take assessments given by the education quality and accountability office (EQAO), in Grade 9 (Mathematics) and Grade 10 (literacy skills). In order to graduate from high school, students must pass the Grade 10 literacy test, also known as the Ontario Secondary School Literacy Test (OSSLT). The Ontario Ministry of Education policy on ELs affords an exception for ELs and the OSSLT. It states that students should only participate in the tests "when they have acquired the level of proficiency in English required for success." This allows newcomer ELs to defer participation in the test until they have improved their English proficiency. Alternatively, ELs may meet the literacy graduation requirement by taking the Ontario Secondary School Literacy Course (OSSLC), which is offered at all high schools. Students are eligible to take the OSSLC if they have deferred the Grade 10 literacy test two times. Many of Marguerite's ELs have taken and passed the OSSLC.

In doing so, they have earned credit and met the literacy requirement for their secondary school graduation diploma.

Marguerite scaffolds her instruction to meet the unique needs of her students by using the following strategies:

- **Text to graphics and back again**, using a graphic organizer, Marguerite uses this strategy to teach text organization formats. Students learn how text is organized and how to identify main ideas and major concepts.
- **Extended wait time** of 8–10 seconds, which provides the time needed for ELs to comprehend the teacher's question or statement. The linguistic complexity of the high school curriculum is challenging in every course. Marguerite has extended her wait time for all students and believes this strategy helps all students develop more sophisticated responses and a deeper understanding of content.

To monitor her students' progress toward proficiency in English and other content skills, Marguerite uses a variety of age-appropriate formative assessment techniques such as the following:

- **K-W-L charts** (Ogle 1986), which are used to activate prior knowledge and then confirm learning. The student writes what they already **k**now, **w**ant to know, and **l**earn about a targeted concept or topic. Marguerite can monitor the K-W-L charts throughout the lesson cycle and adjust her instruction or pull small groups of students together to provide additional instruction.
- **Rubrics**, which are used in each of Marguerite's classes. Rubrics explicitly state the criteria that will be used to score/grade the assignment or assessment. Sometimes, her students receive the rubric in advance of the assignment or assessment to better understand the expectations for processing and producing language. Other times, Marguerite co-constructs standards-based rubrics with her students using the content standards from the unit.

Think-Pair-Share 7.9c Teacher Profile Reflection—Part 2 Describe the characteristics of Marguerite's ELs. What makes Marguerite's teaching context unique? How does Marguerite differentiate instruction and assessment to meet the needs of her students?

Gus

Gustavo (Gus) is a middle school Social Studies teacher in an urban city in California. Gus is in his 25th year of teaching and is teaching in the same district in which he was a student. Throughout his career, Gus has seen many changes in requirements for and approaches to instruction and assessment of ELs. Although he is bilingual and holds a bilingual teacher certification, he has not been teaching in a bilingual classroom since he was a very young teacher. He is hopeful to return to teaching in a bilingual classroom once his school district enacts changes allowed under California's Multilingual Education Act of 2016 (Proposition 58, 2016), which repealed earlier **"English only"** legislation.

Many of Gus's students are labeled **"Experienced,"** or **"Long term English learners (LTELs)"** because they have been classified as ELs since elementary school. Gus often has to explain to his colleagues that although his students sound proficient, or have demonstrated mastery of **basic** interpersonal communication skills (BICS), they lack **cognitive academic language proficiency (CALP**; Cummins 1979), or the language skills required for success in the rigorous high-school content-area classes. He spends his planning time mentoring colleagues in providing appropriate scaffolds and accommodations that help LTELs both process and produce academic language in content-area classes. Gus has been piloting a new "evidence-based" reading intervention program designed to help LTELs accelerate their reading skills and is hopeful about the initial results (Hougen 2014).

Experienced/LTEL is a formal educational classification given to students who have been enrolled in schools in the United States for more than 6 years, who are not progressing toward English proficiency, and who are struggling academically due to their limited English skills.

Basic interpersonal communication skills (BICS) – Researcher Jim Cummins theorizes two types of language skills: social and academic. BICS are the language skills children use in social situations. BICS begin to develop within 6 months to 2 years after arrival in the United States (Cummins 1979).

Cognitive academic language proficiency (CALP) refers to the formal language of school and academia. CALP typically takes from 5 to 7 years. If a child has no prior schooling or has limited development in L1, it may take 7–10 years for ELs to reach near-native proficiency.

All students at Gus's school must take the summative California Assessment of Student Performance and Progress (CAASPP) in ELA, Mathematics, and Science. Additionally, Gus's ELs take the grade-specific English Language Proficiency Assessments for California (ELPAC). When potential ELs arrive, they are given the ELPAC Initial Assessment (IA), which is an initial identification of students as ELs. Once classified as ELs, his students take the ELPAC summative assessment, which is an annual assessment to measure an EL's progress in learning English and to identify the student's ELP level. Depending on their arrival, some of his students must take the two assessments in a close timeframe, while others may have a few months between assessments.

Gus scaffolds his instruction to meet the unique needs of his students by using the following strategies:

- **Comprehension checking** is one strategy Gus uses with his whole class but finds it most beneficial for his newcomer students. Gus uses a variety of comprehension checks, throughout instruction, including signal responses (e.g. thumbs up/down), individual whiteboards, short written responses, and multiple questions on the same topic.
- **Contextualized language** is another strategy that Gus uses to provide newcomer students with increased comprehension of oral language input. In order to contextualize language, Gus provides visuals, gestures, facial expressions, body language, illustrations, realia (real objects), maps, graphs, timelines, diagrams, and **manipulatives**.

Manipulatives are physical tools of teaching, engaging students visually and physically with objects such as counters, blocks, coins, sand, etc.

To monitor his students' progress toward proficiency in English and other content skills, Gus uses a variety of age-appropriate formative assessment techniques such as the following:

- **4–1**, which helps students analyze a topic for critical concepts. Students are grouped into small groups of four. Students share one word/phrase (1) that captures important aspects of the reading, lecture, or discussion. Gus listens and takes anecdotal records as his student groups discuss a content-area concept during the 4–1 activity. He is then able to gauge whether to move on or reteach (Levine et al. 2013).
- **Anticipation guides** require students to assess their level of content understanding prior to reading a text. Gus generates a list of true–false statements about a content area concept or idea. Students work individually to complete the statements with their conjectures. Then, students work in pairs or small groups to discuss the concept and conjectures. Gus monitors individual and small group work to determine which students need additional instruction prior to or during the lesson.

Think-Pair-Share 7.9d Teacher Profile Reflection—Part 3   Describe the characteristics of Gus's ELs. What makes Gus's teaching context unique? How does Gus differentiate instruction and assessment to meet the needs of his students?

Think-Pair-Share 7.9e Application Exercise   Review the list of scaffolds you created as you read the teacher profiles. Choose three and describe how you might use these scaffolds with students.

Think-Pair-Share 7.9f Application Exercise   Interview a PreK-12 teacher of ELs. Gather the following information:

- Describe the characteristics of the ELs in the teacher's school and classroom.
- Describe the teacher (e.g. how long has she/he been teaching? Is the teacher bilingual? Does the teacher have ESL certification? How comfortable is the teacher in working with ELs? and so on)
- What makes this teacher's teaching context unique?
- How does this teacher differentiate instruction to meet the needs of his/her students? How does this teacher differentiate assessment to meet the needs of his/her students?

Finally, write a teacher profile that summarizes the teacher interviewed.

7.10   Chapter Conclusion

PreK-12 ELs are vital members of school communities. The United States and Canadian governments have laws and policies to protect and support these learners (see Summary Chart). With thoughtful planning and explicit instruction, teachers can help ELs achieve proficiency in English and success in content areas. Effective use of formative and summative assessments is crucial in this process.

7.11   Summary Chart: PreK-12 language learners in the United States and Canada

	United States	**Canada**

Definition of English learner	An individual:
	
	(A) who is aged 3 through 21;
	
	(B) who is enrolled or preparing to enroll in an elementary school or secondary school;
	
	(C) (i) who was not born in the United States or whose native language is a language other than English;
	     (ii) (I) who is a Native American or Alaska Native, or a native resident of the outlying areas; and (II) who comes from an environment where a language other than English has had a significant impact on the individual's level of English language proficiency (ELP); or
	     (iii) who is migratory, whose native language is a language other than English, and who comes from an environment where a language other than English is dominant; and
	
	(D) whose difficulties in speaking, reading, writing, or understanding the English language may be sufficient to deny the individual
	     (i) the ability to meet the challenging state academic standards;
	     (ii) the ability to successfully achieve in classrooms where the language of instruction is English; or
	     (iii) the opportunity to participate fully in society.
	
	(US Department of Education 2015a ESEA Act, Section 8101[20], p. 393)
		Students who are in provincially funded English language schools whose first language is a language other than English, or is a variety of English that is significantly different from the variety used for instruction in Ontario's schools, and who may require focused educational support to assist them in attaining proficiency in English. These students may be Canadian-born or recently arrived from other countries (Inclusion Canada 2017).

Legal protections	Over the last 50 years, US federal law has established the rights of ELs and the responsibilities of educators who work with them. They include the following: Section 601 of Title VI of the Civil Rights Act of 1964, Nichols (1974), Doe (1982), Pickard (1981), and Every Student Succeeds Act (ESSA) (2015).	The provinces of Ontario and Alberta have outlined expectations for the identification of and services offered to students identified as ELs. Each province has also developed robust resources, available online and in print, for schools and educators of ELs.
Programming	Scores from the ELP screener, along with other locally required data, are used to place qualifying ELs in the continuum of services offered by the school or district language assistance program (LAP). There are four LAP models considered educationally sound under US federal law: ESL/ELD, Structured English immersion (SEI), transitional bilingual education, and two-way bilingual.	Once an EL's initial assessment is conducted, additional information (e.g. interviews with student and family, review of school documents, including transcripts, and other academic assessment data) is gathered and analyzed prior to placing the student in appropriate programming.

Appendix 1 – Achievement Quiz of Chapter 7

(For discussion or writing prompts, see the Think-Pair-Share tasks in this chapter.)

Directions: For questions 1–4, select the response that best answers each question below. Questions 1–4 are worth 1 point each. For question 5, pair the options that correspond to each other. Question 5 is worth 3 points if entirely correct or 1 point partial credit for each correct match.

1. Which country's or countries' definition of an English Learner includes native-born children whose English dialect differs greatly from Standard English?
   a. only Canada
   b. only the United States
   c. both Canada and the United States
   d. neither Canada nor the United States

2. An English language screener _____.
   a. determines, in the United States and Canada, if students qualify for ESL at school
   b. is a survey completed by parents at home about eligibility for ESL services
   c. changes the classroom environment so ELs can better demonstrate their skills
   d. is a questionnaire conducted in the student's first language, in both the United States and Canada

3. Between exiting ELs from ESL services too soon or too late, which of them presents a problem?
   a. only too soon
   b. only too late
   c. both too soon and too late
   d. neither too soon nor too late

4. You teach in a secondary school in an ESL environment. There are several non-native English students at your school who arrived from their native countries 3 years ago. When they speak to their native English friends, they do so without a foreign accent. You overhear colleagues of yours who know little about second-/foreign-language development commenting that these students should not be receiving ESL services anymore since they are as fluent as native speakers. How might you respond to your colleagues?
   a. You expect that the results of their upcoming language proficiency test will show that they are proficient enough to be exited from the ESL system.
   b. We cannot tell how advanced their cognitive academic language proficiency is by simply listening to their basic interpersonal communication with their friends.
   c. The students are probably failing the language proficiency test on purpose so that they continue to be eligible for ESL services.
   d. These are so-called long-term English learners; in the ESL program, they are allowed to use their native language, which slows down their English language development.

5. Match each United States law/policy with its central concept. One law/policy will have no match.

Laws/Policies	Central concepts
a. Section 601 of Title VI of the Civil Rights Act of 1964	A. Programs for ELs must be based on educational theory, implemented effectively, and evaluated for their effectiveness in helping ELs
b. Lau v. Nichols (1974)	
c. Castañeda v. Pickard (1981)	B. Undocumented students have the same right to attend public primary and secondary schools as do United States citizens and permanent residents
d. Plyler v. Doe (1982)	C. Prohibits discrimination based on race, color, or national origin in any federally funded program or activity

8

Assessing Exceptional Language Learners

Chapter Overview

In this chapter, "exceptional language learners" refers to students identified with disabilities, those demonstrating special gifts and talents, and those affected by trauma. Despite their distinct characteristics, these groups share common educational needs and legal protections in the United States and globally. The chapter will offer context, examples, and explore relevant laws and protections for each group of exceptional language learners. Special assessment considerations for these learners will also be examined.

> **Individualized Education Program (IEP):** an IEP must be designed for one student and must be a truly individualized document. The IEP creates an opportunity for teachers, parents, school administrators, related services personnel, and students (when appropriate) to work together to improve educational results for children with disabilities.

8.1 Learning Objectives

1. Develop an understanding of the unique characteristics of three types of exceptional language learners and interpret how these characteristics impact student participation in assessment
2. Synthesize the impacts of precedents, laws, and policies written to protect the rights of students with disabilities in the United States, Canada, Japan, South Korea, and Brazil
3. Describe the implications of providing accommodations and modifications to language learners during assessment
4. Advocate for inclusionary pathways for language learners within Gifted and Talented programs
5. Adopt trauma-informed approaches and practices within your teaching context

8.2 Legal Precedents and Protections for Language Learners with Suspected or Identified Disabilities in the United States

Did you know?   United States Federal law protects ELs (and all students) with disabilities.

A Practical Guide to Language Assessment: How Do You Know That Your Students Are Learning? First Edition.
Ildiko Porter-Szucs et al.
© 2025 John Wiley & Sons, Inc. Published 2025 by John Wiley & Sons, Inc.

> **Individuals with Disabilities Education Act (IDEA):** In the United States, the IDEA is a law that makes available free appropriate public education to eligible children with disabilities throughout the nation and ensures special education and related services to those children.
>
> The IDEA governs how states and public agencies provide early intervention, special education, and related services to more than 7.5 million (as of school year 2018–2019) eligible infants, toddlers, children, and youth with disabilities.

In earlier chapters, the differences between the concepts of evaluation and assessment were outlined. It is important to revisit that distinction in this chapter as it relates directly to students with suspected or identified disabilities. It is also important to note that while limited English proficiency may present learning challenges for a student, limited English proficiency **is not** considered a disability. Multilingual learners may appear to "be behind" their peers; however, they are managing a greater cognitive load than their monolingual peers, as they are processing in two or more languages. While many of the protections outlined are specific to students learning English in the United States, the same concepts can be applied more broadly to any child learning content and language in English or any additional language.

In the United States, the initial evaluation of a child is required by federal law before any special education and related services can be provided to that child. According to Section 300.301 of IDEA law, an initial evaluation "consists of procedures to determine whether a child is a child with a disability within 60 days of receiving parental consent for the evaluations, or, if the State establishes a timeframe within which the evaluation must be conducted, within such time frame; and to determine the educational needs of such child" (US Department of Education, About IDEA 2024). It is important to note that some states shorten the length of the requirement for an initial evaluation. In Michigan the requirement states that "within 30 school days, the IEP Team is convened to determine initial eligibility or ineligibility and provide an initial offer of a free appropriate public education (FAPE)" (MDE Guidance for Timeline for Initial Evaluations). An initial evaluation must be completed within 45 school days of receiving parent consent for evaluation in Utah (Utah Parent Center). Students at the community college and postsecondary levels may have an IEP from their PK-12 experience. The IEP outlines requirements for educators at all levels, K-postsecondary. Educators providing instruction to students with IEPs can use them to set realistic goals and provide appropriate tools and resources that match the specific needs of the student.

The purposes of conducting initial evaluations include:

- to see if the student is a "child with a disability," as defined by IDEA;
- to gather information that will help determine the child's educational needs;
- to guide decision-making about appropriate educational programming for the child (US Department of Education, About IDEA).

Assessing language learners who are suspected of having disabilities is complex. Students with disabilities may need accommodations and/or modifications to access the curriculum, actively participate during instruction, and engage in assessment. Common **accommodations** provided during the assessment of a language learner with an IEP include extended time on test, use of native language dictionaries, tests written with simplified text and/or visuals, allowing the student to test in a location other than the classroom, and testing with an educator other than the teacher, who is familiar to the student. It is important to note that for the purposes of language assessment, some accommodations, such as linguistic simplification may be inappropriate for determining the level of language proficiency. On the contrary, linguistic simplification is necessary and appropriate when testing subject content ability, which ensures that we are testing content knowledge, not language proficiency. In contrast, assessment **modifications** might include reading aloud of text, scribing, reduced number of questions, reduced requirement for written responses, and/or entirely different assessment questions or format.

> **Modifications** refer to changes in the expectation for student completion of grade-level standards, curriculum, instruction, and/or assessment. Modifications may alter the content of assessments, which may change what a test measures. As a result, modifications are not universally available and should only be used when they are explicitly named in a student's IEP. Examples of modifications on assessments include: being assigned a completely different assessment that is less complex or does not cover the same standards, allowing outlining instead of writing an essay, use of alternate books or materials on the topic being studied, changing the workload or length of the assessment.

Think-Pair-Share 8.2a Perception Activity   There may be concerns of "fairness" among students regarding accommodations and modifications provided on assessments. While any student may benefit from receiving an accommodation, they should be used only as needed and individualized accordingly. Modifications are reserved for use with students with documented disabilities. How might you address the concern of "fairness" with students in terms of who receives accommodations and modifications and who does not?

Think-Pair-Share 8.2b Application Exercise   What are the implications of providing accommodations to ELs during assessment?

Did you know?   The incidence of disability occurs at the same rate among ELs and non-ELs.

Approximately 10% of all K-12 students in the United States are ELs. ELs also make up approximately 10% of students with disabilities. Additionally, 14% of all ELs are students with disabilities, compared to 13% of the overall student population (US Department of Education 2017).

There are numerous classifications of disabilities in the United States. They include specific learning disability, speech or language impairment, intellectual disability, autism, emotional disturbance, etc. Multilingual learners are represented within and across every disability category. The following chart (see Figure 8.1) breaks down the percentage of non-ELs and ELs in the United States with identified disabilities (US Department of Education 2017).

Approximately 14% of all ELs in the United States have identified disabilities. The chart above displays the distribution of that 14% of ELs across seven different disability categories. It **should not** be interpreted that nearly 45% of all ELs have a diagnosed specific learning disability. Rather, 45% of ELs with IEPs have been diagnosed with specific learning disabilities.

Did you know?   "Other disabilities" may include visual and/or hearing impairments as well as "other" health impairments.

Assessment of visually and hearing impaired language learners as well as language learners with "other" health impairments presents unique challenges. Traditional assessments of ELP include testing skills in all four domains of language (listening, speaking, reading, and writing). For hearing-impaired students, assessment of listening and speaking skills is inherently problematic. Students with visual impairments may have difficulty demonstrating proficiency in reading and writing domains without appropriate accommodations.

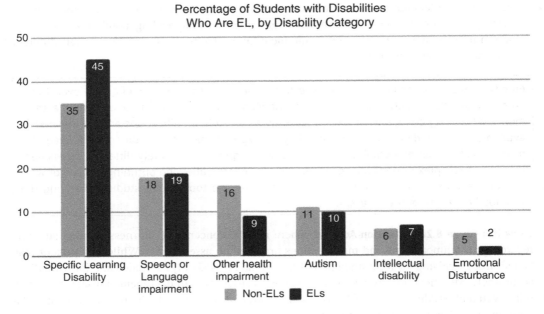

Figure 8.1 Percentage of students with disabilities who are ELs, by disability category.

According to IDEA, **visual impairment**, including blindness, means an impairment in vision that, even with correction, adversely affects a child's educational performance. The term includes both partial sight and blindness (2024).

Hearing impairment is defined by IDEA as "an impairment in hearing, whether permanent or fluctuating, that adversely affects a child's educational performance." **Deafness** is defined as "a hearing impairment that is so severe that the child is impaired in processing linguistic information through hearing, with or without amplification" (2024 §300.8(c)(5)).

Thus, deafness is viewed as a condition that prevents an individual from receiving sound in all or most of its forms. In contrast, a child with a hearing loss can generally respond to auditory stimuli, including speech.

Other Health Impairment, according to IDEA, means having limited strength, vitality, or alertness, including a heightened alertness to environmental stimuli, that results in limited alertness with respect to the educational environment, that—

i. Is due to chronic or acute health problems such as asthma, attention deficit disorder or attention deficit hyperactivity disorder, diabetes, epilepsy, a heart condition, hemophilia, lead poisoning, leukemia, nephritis, rheumatic fever, sickle cell anemia, and Tourette syndrome; and

ii. Adversely affects a child's educational performance (§300.8(c)(9)).

What's immediately clear from this definition is that there are quite a few disabilities and disorders that fall under the umbrella of "other health impairment." And those disabilities are very different from one another.

The US Department of Education requires K-12 English Learners to score proficient in all four domains of language (listening, speaking, reading, and writing) in order to exit EL status (US Department of Education 2016a). This requirement prevents ELs in the United States from exiting EL status if they are unable to participate in, therefore unable to demonstrate proficiency in, specific domains. This issue is in contrast with the United States' federal requirement that ELs not be unnecessarily segregated. Unnecessary segregation might happen if an EL is kept in pull-out classes for ELD when the student's needs would be better served in the general education or special education classroom. If an EL with a hearing impairment cannot take the listening section of the ELP assessment but would otherwise qualify to exit the EL program and the student is not removed from EL services, this might also be considered "unnecessary" segregation. The OELA EL Tool Kit states Local Education Agencies "should not keep EL students in EL programs for periods that are longer or shorter than necessary to achieve the program's educational goals" (US Department of Education 2016b, chapter 5, p. 1)." Doing so may constitute "unnecessary" segregation. The degree of segregation, or placement in EL services, should be "necessary to achieve the stated goals of the program and required by each student's level of ELP and his or her time and progress in the EL program" (US Department of Education 2016b, chapter 5, pp. 1–2)."

In order to meet this legal requirement, the multidisciplinary team should collaborate to ensure that language learners with visual and/or hearing impairments are not unnecessarily participating in classes or services for English language development if they are able to demonstrate proficiency in the relevant language domains. This requires teams to carefully monitor language development and remove English language services as they are no longer needed since traditional testing of ELP cannot be used as criteria for exiting "official" EL status. Unfortunately, until US Federal Law allows exemptions from specific domains, as appropriately documented in the IEP, these students must still be "officially" identified as ELs even if they demonstrate proficiency sufficient to remove services.

Bochner and Walter (2005) investigated alternative methods for evaluating deaf students' readiness to meet the English language and literacy demands of postsecondary educational programs. They concluded that neither the ACT Assessment nor COMPASS/ESL taken in isolation are appropriate for the full range of deaf students seeking admission to postsecondary educational programs. However, taken together, the combination of the ACT Assessment and COMPASS/ESL appears able to provide a valid, reliable, and coherent approach to admissions screening assessment for the full range of deaf students seeking admission to postsecondary programs. Language learners with visual impairments do not benefit from one of the most common strategies used by language teachers, the use of visuals to scaffold instruction. Visual materials such as images, videos, flashcards, and body language/gesturing, are not accessible to many visually impaired learners. Hands-on materials and realia may be suitable alternatives.

Accommodations on assignments and assessments for language learners with visual and/or hearing impairments will help students better and more fully demonstrate their knowledge and skills. Common accommodations for visually impaired language learners include being provided the assessment in Braille or large print, having the directions or questions read aloud by a human or screen reader/text-to-speech application, using Braille to provide written responses, and using technology such as magnification equipment. For language learners with hearing impairments, accommodations may include the use of assistive listening devices or captions, being given extended time on assignments and/or assessments, and having access to real-time sign language interpreters and scribes.

In order to get a complete profile of academic and social-emotional strengths and areas of need, it is important to go beyond traditional assessment of ELP for hearing and/or visually impaired language learners. Informal measures can be used to ascertain their developmental, cultural, and linguistic needs. English language teachers should consult with experts such as a special educator or school psychologist to take a team approach to meeting the language learning needs of hearing-impaired students. A communication plan should be collaboratively created by the team and with the student/family. It should clearly articulate the communication needs (e.g. Braille version, audio recording of messages, etc.) of the student and/or family members and outline a plan for effectively and consistently communicating between the student, family, and educational team. Hernandez (2024) recommends creating a sample communication plan for students who are blind or visually impaired.

Think-Pair-Share 8.2c Synthesis   ELs appear over-identified and under-identified in certain disability categories. Discuss what factors or considerations may be at play with these discrepancies.

Did you know?   The impacts of acculturation and culture shock can mirror disabilities.

Educators should note that cultural differences and typical characteristics of acculturation can mirror those of Attention Deficit Disorder as well as other categories of disability (Collier 2011). For example, a teacher may attribute defensive behavior such as when a student wastes class time or consistently arrives to class late to an underlying issue. However, concepts of time vary considerably from culture to culture. A student who does not respond when spoken to may not have a disability; he or she may be in a normal and predictable stage of language acquisition. Seemingly aggressive behaviors such as talking out in class, talking back to the teacher, and fighting, maybe culturally appropriate in the native culture and not at all indicative of a behavioral disability. Again, the identification of a language learner with a disability is an extremely complex process. In order to determine if behaviors are significant enough to warrant outside expertise and consideration, it is important for educators to become familiar with the cultural norms of their students as well as the patterns of typical language development.

Did you know?   PK-12 schools in the United States cannot wait to evaluate an EL if there is suspicion of a disability.

The Individuals with Disabilities Education Act (IDEA) and Section 504 of the Rehabilitation Act of 1973 (Section 504) address the rights of students with disabilities in K-12 schools in the United States. If an EL is suspected of having one or more disabilities, the school or district must evaluate the EL promptly to determine if the EL has a disability or disabilities and whether the EL needs disability-related services (which are special education and related services under IDEA or regular or special education and related aids and services under Section 504). Special education evaluations may not be delayed because of a student's limited ELP or because the student participates in EL programming.

Did you know?   Postsecondary students with disabilities must advocate within their institution of higher education for their own services and accommodations.

The IDEA covers all children with disabilities residing in states that receive financial assistance under the act. It does not extend, however, to students with disabilities in college or other postsecondary education and training programs. But, Section 504 does and the US Department of Education has issued separate regulations specifically elaborating that provision's application to preschool, elementary, and secondary education, as well as to postsecondary education. The Americans with Disabilities Act (ADA) also does not directly address the provisions of educational services; it instead prohibits discrimination against individuals with disabilities across many contexts, including by a "public entity" such as a public school, college, or university.

In the United States, postsecondary-level educational institutions have no legal responsibility for evaluating students for a disability. However, if a student requests modifications, accommodations, or auxiliary aids or services because of a disability, institutions of higher education are allowed, though not required, to request that the student provide "reasonable" documentation of his or her disability and need for the requested accommodations or services. At the postsecondary level, students must self-identify as having a disability, provide appropriate documentation of their disability, and arrange with campus disability support services for any accommodations and services for which they may be entitled. To receive accommodations or services under the ADA or Section 504 at the postsecondary level, students with disabilities must seek out the person or office at their institution who is responsible for arranging accommodations for students with disabilities, request the accommodations they need, and provide the documentation and/or personal history necessary to support their request.

Did you know?   In districts where articulated protocols for separating difference from disability do not exist, ELs are often over- and under-identified as having disabilities.

Think-Pair-Share 8.2d Prediction   What challenges might exist when evaluating an EL for potential disabilities? Discuss.

It is important for educators to accurately determine whether ELs are eligible for disability-related services. Special education identification practices vary greatly among PK-12 educational institutions. There are instances where districts over-identify and others where they under-identify ELs as eligible for special education services when compared to their non-EL peers (Artiles et al. 2005; Zehler et al. 2003).

Researchers identified four potential factors that may contribute to the misidentification of special education needs among ELs:

1. the evaluating professional's lack of knowledge of second language development and disabilities
2. poor instructional practices
3. weak intervention strategies and
4. inappropriate assessment tools (Sánchez et al. 2010)

To avoid misidentification of special education needs among ELs, educational teams should familiarize themselves with the research articulating evidence-based, appropriate processes for disability identification. One promising practice in the evaluation of ELs for purposes of disability determination is the use of **Dynamic Assessment**. The American Speech-Language-Hearing Association defines Dynamic Assessment as "an evaluation method used to identify an individual's skills as well as their learning potential (ASHA, What is Dynamic Assessment? 2024)." Dynamic Assessment is interactive and uses a test-teach-test model based on Vygotsky's *Zone of Proximal Development*. In Dynamic Assessment, the focus is on determining difference from disorder in multilingual children; it helps educators set realistic learning goals for individual students. Appropriate disability identification processes evaluate a student's disability-related educational needs and take into account various other factors, including the student's ELP when determining if the student exhibits learning differences or if a true disability is present (Collier 2011; Gutierrez-Clellen and Peña 2001). Practitioners seeking to properly and fairly evaluate an

EL with suspected disabilities are encouraged to utilize the processes and tools described in Katakowski et al. (2018).

When an EL student is determined to have one or more disabilities an IEP is written. The IEP should outline services to meet all educational needs. ELs with disabilities should participate in any and all programs to meet their English language acquisition, general learning, and specialized learning needs. Parents have the right to refuse services provided by the district LAP and/or disability-related services under IDEA and Section 504. If parents decline one program and not the other, the district shall provide services under the program acceptable to the parents. Ultimately, the district must comply with providing services at the discretion of the parents.

Think-Pair-Share 8.2e Application Exercise   Investigate your school or district protocol for servicing and assessing ELs with suspected or identified disabilities.

8.3   Legal Precedents and Protections for Language Learners with Suspected or Identified Disabilities in Canada

Did you know?   Canadian law outlines specific protections for students with disabilities.

In Canada, education is recognized and legislated as a fundamental social good. A publicly funded education system, accessible to all, is recognized as a core responsibility of the government.

The Ontario *Human Rights Code* (1962) prevents discrimination based on disability status. It defines "disability" as:

1. any degree of physical disability, infirmity, malformation or disfigurement that is caused by bodily injury, birth defect or illness and, without limiting the generality of the foregoing, includes diabetes mellitus, epilepsy, a brain injury, any degree of paralysis, amputation, lack of physical coordination, blindness or visual impediment, deafness or hearing impairment, muteness or speech impediment, or physical reliance on a guide dog or other animal or on a wheelchair or other remedial appliance or device,
2. a condition of mental impairment or a developmental disability,
3. a learning disability, or a dysfunction in one or more of the processes involved in understanding or using symbols or spoken language,
4. a mental disorder, or
5. an injury or disability for which benefits were claimed or received under the insurance plan established under the *Workplace Safety and Insurance Act, 1997*.

Under the *Education Act*, the Ministry of Education is responsible for setting out a process for identifying and accommodating disability-related needs in the publicly-funded elementary and secondary school systems. The Ministry of Education must ensure that students with disabilities can access special education programs and services without payment of fees. The Ministry of Education is responsible for funding levels and structures, legislating procedures, and creating appeal and monitoring mechanisms.

The Ministry of Training, Colleges and Universities is responsible for providing similar educational services at the postsecondary level. Both ministries are also required, under the Ontarians with Disabilities Act, to complete an annual accessibility plan that addresses the identification, removal, and prevention of barriers to students/people with disabilities.

Under the *Education Act*, Elementary and Secondary school principals are responsible for referring students with suspected disabilities to a committee for identification and placement, for preparing an individual education plan for each exceptional student, and for communicating board policies and procedures to staff, students, and parents. Teachers are responsible for providing appropriate accommodations during instruction and assessment, assessing students' progress in English and core subject areas, and communicating with parents. Canadian schools report similar issues to schools in the United States in regards to over-identification of minority students with disabilities (Ontario Human Rights Commission report 2002; Barshay 2019). Additionally, the Ontario Human Rights Commission named the concern that language learners are being misdiagnosed as having learning disabilities and that in areas where programming for English language development is not accessible nor fully developed, language learners are disproportionately identified with disabilities.

Postsecondary institutions must ensure that their facilities and services are accessible, that appropriate, effective and dignified accommodation processes are in place, and that students who require accommodations because of their disabilities are accommodated to the point of undue hardship. Under the Ontarians with Disabilities Act, postsecondary institutions are also required to complete an accessibility plan. Educators at the postsecondary level are responsible for participating in the accommodation process (including the provision of specific accommodations), being knowledgeable about and sensitive to disability issues, and maintaining student confidentiality. Similar to the required process in the United States, in Canada, a postsecondary student with a disability is required to advise the education provider of the need for accommodation.

8.4 International Legal Precedents and Protections for Language Learners with Suspected or Identified Disabilities

At the international level, various United Nations conventions (2024) recognize the importance of education to persons with disabilities, including the *Covenant on Economic, Social and Cultural Rights, the Convention on the Rights of the Child, and the Declaration of the Rights of Disabled Persons* and *Convention on the Rights of Persons with Disabilities,* which includes eight guiding principles:

1. Respect for inherent dignity, individual autonomy including the freedom to make one's own choices, and independence of persons;
2. Non-discrimination;
3. Full and effective participation and inclusion in society;
4. Respect for difference and acceptance of persons with disabilities as part of human diversity and humanity;
5. Equality of opportunity;
6. Accessibility;
7. Equality between men and women;
8. Respect for the evolving capacities of children with disabilities and respect for the right of children with disabilities to preserve their identities.

Did you know?   There are many taboos and misconceptions about disabilities across cultures.

It is important to note that the concept of "disability" varies greatly from country to country and culture to culture. Some cultures do not recognize the concept of "disability" at all. Responsibilities of educational institutions to students with disabilities vary in international law as well. The following are brief summaries of laws protecting the rights of students with disabilities, across three countries.

8.4.1 Japan

Japan has several policies related to persons with disabilities. "Special Needs Education is education for students with disabilities, in consideration of their individual educational needs, which aims at full development of their capabilities and their independence and school participation" (Ministry of Education, Culture, Sports, Science and Technology n.d., para. 1). It also requires the development of individualized teaching plans, similar to the Individualized Education Program in the United States.

In Japan, most students with disabilities are integrated into local school systems. However, Japan does have specialized educational settings such as Special Schools for the Blind, Special Schools for the Deaf, Disabled Schools, and Special Education Classes, according to the types and degrees of their disabilities.

8.4.2 Brazil

Two foundational laws outline protections for students with disabilities. Public Law 7853 established a national policy for integration and a universal right to education, while Public Law 13146 mandates the consideration of universal design in program conceptualization and promotes social inclusion and integration.

Unlike Japan, which has a stated priority of integration of students with disabilities into regular education, Brazil has a parallel education system, one for students with special education needs and another for students without special education needs. In this segregated system, students with special education needs are marginalized and isolated from peers, reinforcing negative perceptions of this student population. Additionally, students with special needs from low-income families are further marginalized by the lack of access to services (Kiru and Cooc 2018).

8.4.3 South Korea

All students in South Korea have the right to an education and should receive an equal opportunity to learn under the Education Law of 1949. Free, mandatory public education services for students with disabilities is required under the Special Education Promotion Act (SEPA). Similar to the IDEA of the United States, SEPA has defined disability categories as follows:

- Visual impaired
- Hearing impaired
- Mentally retarded
- Physically impaired
- Emotionally disturbed (including autism)
- Speech impaired
- Learning disabilities
- Otherwise physically and psychologically impaired

Discrimination of students with disabilities is a violation of the Education Law. It states "When children with disabilities want to enter schools at any level, the principal should not take any actions that would put these students at a disadvantage. Such actions include refusing to receive applications, denial of acceptance to those who passed entrance examinations, and other disciplinary actions due to disabled conditions. Special school principals at all school levels should take appropriate measures to provide appropriate convenience for entrance examination and schooling for children with disabilities based on types and degree of disability" (Special Education Promotion Law, Screening and Enrollment section, Article 13, 1994).

Think-Pair-Share 8.4a Synthesis   What similarities and differences exist between legal precedents and protections for students with suspected or identified disabilities in the United States, Canada, Japan, South Korea, and Brazil? Discuss.

Think-Pair-Share 8.4b Synthesis   Investigate the laws of the country in which you are teaching. How are the precedents and protections for students with suspected or identified disabilities similar or different to those described in this chapter? Discuss.

8.5   Language Learners with Special Gifts and Talents

Did you know?   Language learners are underrepresented in programs for gifted and talented students in PK-12 education.

The Civil Rights Data Collection defines gifted and talented programs as those conducted during regular school hours that provide specialized educational opportunities, including accelerated promotion and an enriched curriculum, for students who demonstrate a high degree of mental ability and/or exceptional physical coordination, creativity, interest, or talent (OELA 2021).

ELs represent about 10% of students in the United States. However, fewer than 3% of students in talented and gifted programs nationwide are identified as ELs. Research indicates nomination and assessment practices may be some of the key barriers to identification. Harris et al. identified several notable barriers that prevented language learners from being identified for participation in gifted and talented programs, including (2009):

1. a lack of clear guidance on identifying students from underrepresented populations who may be gifted;
2. the frequent mobility among some ELs;
3. some teachers' belief that attaining ELP should occur before identifying ELs as gifted and talented;
4. **assessment instruments that are not culturally appropriate;**
5. a lack of professional development for general education teachers about the cultural backgrounds and histories of ELs; and
6. a lack of effective communication with EL parents.

There are numerous reasons that might render an assessment culturally inappropriate. Two common reasons include **construct-validity bias** and **content-related bias**.

> **Construct-validity bias** refers to the extent to which an assessment fails to measure what it is intending to measure.

For language learners, construct-validity bias might be evident if the assessment includes vocabulary and terms they have not yet learned. Thus, the assessment instrument may measure the language learners' vocabulary knowledge rather than the intended construct.

> **Content-related validity bias** is evident when the content of the assessment is more difficult for one group of students than another.

Language learners are often not of the majority culture. Linguistic and cultural differences may make certain questions inaccessible to language learners. If questions are more well-suited to the language and culture of the majority group, the questions contain content-related, or item-selection bias. If an assessment favors responses appropriate to the majority culture perspective, then it may have evidence of content-related bias.

Additionally, the diversity of assessment developers, the process of norming, and even the assessment format may impact the cultural appropriateness of a specific assessment. To ensure that ELs have the opportunity to participate in programs for gifted and talented students, schools should evaluate them using multiple assessment tools, methods (e.g. nonverbal assessments, such as drawing, matching, portfolios, performances, etc.), and contexts (e.g. in-school and out-of-school), so that ELs can demonstrate their knowledge without relying primarily on their ability to use English (Harris et al. 2007). Authentic assessments with a high degree of interactiveness may elicit the most accurate results for ELs with potential gifts or talents.

The National Association of Gifted and Talented Children recommends that schools develop culturally responsive and sensitive protocols for identifying students for participation in programming for gifted and talented students. They recommend that states and school districts critically examine policies and practices related to identification to determine where and how diverse students are excluded from gifted programs. Additionally, they recommend a holistic approach to developing a full profile for every student. They encourage the collection of qualitative data points, such as checklists and interviews, in addition to traditional quantitative assessment data.

Serrano and Scardina (2018) emphasize the power of professional learning to help educators challenge their own biases about giftedness and ELs. During professional development, they recommend three critical steps: first, examining biases about giftedness in ELs; second, challenging the strong value placed on ELP as a characteristic of giftedness: and, finally, considering the tendency to favor behaviors that reflect the dominant culture.

If a gifted language learner finishes an assignment or assessment before the rest of the group should they be given more work? The answer is complicated. Sometimes providing additional work might be appropriate. However, there are many other research-informed strategies for meeting the needs of gifted language learners. Here are a few:

- Offering a choice of modalities
  - Gifted language learners might be encouraged to explore a more personally challenging modality or practice with an additional modality when finishing early.

> **Learning modalities** generally refer to the different ways students process and produce information. The four most common learning modalities include visual, auditory, kinesthetic, and tactile.

- Providing open-ended, extended, and independent assessment options
  - The challenge of these types of assignments is determined by the student; gifted language learners who work more quickly than traditional students might expand their performance in a direction that exceeds the expectations of the original assignment.
- Creating learning centers that provide differentiated opportunities for students across varying levels of English proficiency
  - Gifted language learners may have the opportunity to explore multiple learning stations at the same time it takes traditional students to complete only one station. Consider adding a "challenge" station and allowing students to try out more challenging content there.

- Utilizing inquiry, design-thinking, and project-based learning opportunities
  - Like open-ended, extended, and independent assessment options, inquiry, design-thinking, and project-based learning opportunities, allow students to determine their own pathways to demonstrate understanding and mastery. These opportunities afford gifted language learners to make connections to their passions and deeply explore their creativity.

These strategies enable gifted and traditional language learners alike the support needed to excel. All students need access to rigorous instruction and should be provided assignments and assessments that are engaging and allow them to reach their fullest potential as learners.

Think-Pair-Share 8.5a Application Exercise   Investigate your school or district protocol or process for identifying students for participation in gifted and talented programs. Analyze the protocol or process to determine whether or not it provides inclusionary pathways for language learners. If your school or district does not have an articulated process, further investigate recommendations from the National Association of Gifted and Talented Children and share appropriate recommendations with your principal, curriculum director, or supervisor.

8.6 Impacts of Trauma Can Mirror Disabilities: What Does This Mean for Assessment?

Did you know?   Children who have experienced trauma may experience long-term negative impacts on their cognitive and emotional development.

Students come to school and university with a multitude of personal life experiences. While these experiences develop unique skills such as perseverance and resilience, some students may need additional support to help them manage their academic and social skills within the school setting.

Trauma-induced changes to the brain can result in varying degrees of cognitive impairment and emotional dysregulation that can lead to a host of problems, including difficulty with attention and focus, learning disabilities, low self-esteem, impaired social skills, and sleep disturbances (Nemeroff 2016). As a result, specialized, **wraparound** services are critically important for students who have experienced trauma. Wraparound services may include additional social work and school psychology services, connections to community resources, peer interaction groups, after-school programs, and parent/family engagement.

> **Wraparound** services in schools are comprehensive in nature, designed to give a child the support he or she needs throughout the school day, whether the support is academic, social, or behavioral.

According to Cook et al. (2005), exposure to chronic, prolonged traumatic experiences has the potential to alter children's brains, which may cause longer-term effects in areas such as

- Attachment: Trouble with relationships, boundaries, empathy, and social isolation
- Physical Health: Impaired sensorimotor development, coordination problems, increased medical problems, and somatic symptoms
- Emotional Regulation: Difficulty identifying or labeling feelings and communicating needs
- Dissociation: Altered states of consciousness, amnesia, impaired memory
- Cognitive Ability: Problems with focus, learning, processing new information, language development, planning, and orientation to time and space

- Self-Concept: Lack of consistent sense of self, body image issues, low self-esteem, shame and guilt
- Behavioral Control: Difficulty controlling impulses, oppositional behavior, aggression, disrupted sleep and eating patterns, trauma re-enactment.

These longer-term effects can significantly impact a student's ability to be successful in school. For students who have experienced trauma, creating a safe and secure environment in school is paramount.

To help mitigate the impacts of trauma, educators should engage in trauma-informed approaches and practices. According to the Jim Casey Youth Opportunities Initiative (2011), impactful practices, include explicitly teaching and fostering:

- Goal setting skills
- Decision-making skills
- Stress-management techniques
- Well-being practices

> **Trauma-informed approaches** represent a holistic approach to shaping organizational culture, practices, and policies to be sensitive to the experiences and needs of traumatized individuals (McInerney and McKlindon 2014).

There is emerging research that supports the positive impacts of practicing mindfulness on helping students be calm, gain clarity, and become focused. Mindfulness can be practiced in the classroom through meditation and yoga.

So, what does this have to do with assessment? Educators can be better prepared to support students during assessment if they are well versed in trauma-informed approaches. Students will respond to feelings of safety and security created by the trauma-informed educator. Using mindfulness techniques can help teachers create a sense of calm and peace in the classroom environment, making it most suitable for student success.

Think-Pair-Share 8.6a Reflection   How might you incorporate mindfulness practices into your classroom routines? Discuss.

Think-Pair-Share 8.6b Application Exercise   Visit the following resources, which address the needs of children and youth who have experienced trauma, and consider how these might help you better support your students who have experienced trauma. Identify three action steps you might take to advocate for students with trauma within your school or educational setting.

- **Child Trauma Academy** http://childtrauma.org, nonprofit organization dedicated to helping high-risk children in therapeutic, child protection, and educational settings through direct service, research, and education
- **National Child Traumatic Stress Network** http://www.nctsnet.org, the database of empirically supported treatments and promising practices for responding to trauma and tools for assessing children's exposure to trauma and related mental health issues

8.7 Chapter Conclusion

This chapter covered three types of exceptional language learners: those with an IEP or disabilities, those with special gifts and talents, and those affected by trauma. It examined relevant laws and protections and explored special considerations for assessing each group.

Appendix 1 – Achievement Quiz of Chapter 8

(For discussion or writing prompts, see the Think-Pair-Share tasks in this chapter.)

Directions: For question 1, decide if the statement is true or false. For questions 2–3, select the response that best answers each question below. Questions 1–3 are worth 1 point each. For question 4, select all the answers that are correct. Question 4 is worth 2 points if entirely correct or 1 point partial credit regardless of the number of correct answers. For question 5, pair the options that correspond to each other. Question 5 is worth 3 points if entirely correct or 1 point partial credit for each correct match.

1. True or False? Under the Individuals with Disabilities Education Act (IDEA) in the United States, limited English proficiency is considered a disability.

2. Maria had lived in a happy family in her home country for the first 5 years of her life. When she lost her parents in the war, she was adopted by her uncle living abroad, whom she did not know. At her new school, she often becomes frustrated and throws her pencils, and disrupts class during writing workshop time. Her teachers suspect that she might be an exceptional learner. The category that might fit her is a student who _____.
   a. exhibits special gifts and talents
   b. has a documented disability
   c. is an advanced writer for her age
   d. has been impacted by trauma

3. How can educators mitigate content-related bias in assessments for language learners?
   a. develop culturally responsive protocols for identifying gifted and talented students
   b. include vocabulary and terms that are beyond the students' current learning level
   c. design questions that align with the language and culture of the majority group
   d. use a standardized assessment format for students of all language backgrounds

4. Select all that apply. The long-term effects of trauma can impact a student's ability to be successful in school. In what ways can educators create a safe and supportive learning environment? Educators can _____.
   a. model stress-management techniques
   b. teach students well-being practices
   c. foster decision-making skills
   d. develop goal-setting skills

5. Match each term with its examples. There will be at least one example for each term.

Terms	Examples
a. accommodation	A. in a reading class, reading a text out loud
	B. reducing the number of test questions
	C. assessment taken in an alternate setting
	D. a Braille test for a visually impaired student
b. modification	E. changing the content of the assessment

9

Assessing Listening, Viewing, Representing, Speaking, and Pronunciation

Chapter Overview

The chapter begins with a discussion of skills and subskills as well as an assessment of isolated vs. integrated skills. It continues with the assessment of oral–aural skills: listening, viewing, representing, speaking, and pronunciation formatively, summatively, and through the CEFR's categorization (as one-way, two-way, interactional, transactional, evaluative, and interpersonal). Guidance is provided on the evaluation criteria to be included in the rating scale, or rubric, for assessing speaking skills.

9.1 Learning Objectives

1. Evaluate the complexities of assessing listening and speaking as isolated vs. integrated skills
2. Discuss different ways to assess listening formatively and summatively
3. After selecting two lesser-known reasons why listeners listen, design an assessment task for a specific setting
4. Recognize the features influencing the difficulty of the listening stimulus
5. Discuss different ways to assess speaking formatively and summatively

Think-Pair-Share 9.2a   Recall what you learned about the assessment of oral–aural skills in previous chapters, in particular Chapter 4: Crafting Assessments. Discuss.

9.2 The Skills: Isolated vs. Integrated

The ability to use a language has long been carved up into teachable chunks, called skills. These include listening, speaking, reading, and writing. Additionally, three subskills—grammar, vocabulary, and pronunciation—transcend skill boundaries. Traditionally, many language programs have taught these skills and subskills in isolation. In such a model, students would study speaking in one class, reading in another, and grammar in yet another one. Most programs have now transitioned to teaching at least some skills in an integrated fashion. Speaking is often taught with listening, pronunciation, or both. Vocabulary is integrated into reading or writing or both. Grammar, when integrated with other skills, is usually taught with writing. In PK-12 and adult education

A Practical Guide to Language Assessment: How Do You Know That Your Students Are Learning? First Edition.
Ildiko Porter-Szucs et al.
© 2025 John Wiley & Sons, Inc. Published 2025 by John Wiley & Sons, Inc.

settings, the skills—to the extent that they are covered—are usually taught in an integrated fashion.

Language assessments have followed a similar model. Many have traditionally assessed the various skills and subskills in isolation. For instance, the now-discontinued paper-based TOEFL test arguably assessed listening, reading, and grammar as separate sections (ETS 2007). We say arguably because the targeted skills and subskills were inevitably mediated by another skill. A grammar item was presented using vocabulary, so demonstrating grammar knowledge hinged on reading the item and understanding the words. Similarly, listening comprehension could only be demonstrated by selecting from written answer choices. Speaking and writing, while necessarily separate, integrated grammar and vocabulary and hinged on understanding a prompt.

Think-Pair-Share 9.2b Based on information from Chapter 4, how do you think item writers can minimize construct-irrelevant variance in single-skill assessments? For instance, how can they ensure that in a listening-comprehension test, it is truly listening comprehension that is measured and no other skill? And how can they ensure that a speaking test measures speaking rather than other skills? Discuss.

Steps can be taken to reduce, though not eliminate, the influence of unintended skills in assessments. These include keeping the vocabulary simple in a grammar item and conversely, keeping the grammar simple in a vocabulary item. Another way is to use pictorial input or response modes. For instance, answer choices on a listening test are pictures rather than words or the stimulus for the speaking or writing test can be a picture. Additionally, designing rating scales for productive skills to minimize the influence of other skills is helpful. Thus, depending on the construct definition of speaking, the rating scale may primarily assess fluency and comprehensible pronunciation, while describing a picture and minimally consider accurate grammar and precise word choice. In settings where TTs share a native language (for instance, in a French class in Vietnam, where all the students speak Vietnamese), directions and prompts for a speaking test can be given in the native language.

However, as should be evident by now, truly separating skills and subskills in assessments is impossible. Speaking involves words, grammar, or pronunciation, so speaking cannot be separated from these subskills. In fact, separating skills is not only impossible but also inauthentic and undesirable (Aryadoust 2018). Instead, assessment organizations should aim for *communicative authenticity*. Examples of this can already be found. The TOEFL iBT intentionally integrates all four skills (ETS 2019). The speaking section, for instance, challenges TTs to speak after reading and listening to stimulus passages. The writing section requires responses to listening and reading tasks. These integrated tasks increase authenticity but also raise questions about their suitability for TTs with uneven skill profiles, as is the case with learners with emergent literacy skills (for a discussion of assessing the speaking of LESLLA, SLIFE, and community college students, see Porter-Szucs 2014).

Further steps toward communicative authenticity are reflected in the updated CEFR standards, in the so-called Companion Volume, which moves beyond the traditional four-skill model to focus on modes of communication: reception, production, interaction, and **mediation** (2020). Reception includes the receptive skills of listening (oral comprehension), reading (reading comprehension), and viewing (audio-visual comprehension). Production includes the productive skills of speaking and writing (and representing, although the latter is not explicitly addressed in the CEFR). Interaction can be oral or written two-way communication.

The CEFR (2020) defines **mediation** as the process of "making meaning and facilitating communication beyond linguistic and cultural barriers" (Council of Europe 2020 Mediation video 00:30). This collaborative endeavor encompasses and extends beyond interaction, or

> the social use of language, and focuses on making meaning and/or enabling communication beyond linguistic or cultural barriers (COE n.d.).
>
> Within the CEFR, there are rating scales that extend to both mediation activities and strategies. The former can be further categorized into the mediation of text, concepts, and communication, while the latter can be subdivided into strategies such as explaining new concepts or simplifying texts (Council of Europe 2020b).
>
> Examples of text mediation include note-taking, translation, analysis, and criticism of creative texts. Concept mediation involves collaboration in groups and leading group work. Communication mediation, on the other hand, covers acting as an intermediary or facilitating communication in delicate situations. Moreover, mediation strategies encompass those aimed at explaining new concepts or simplifying a text.

In Chapters 9 and 10, we will be relying heavily on the CEFR Companion Volume's approach. In today's ever-evolving educational landscape, we recognize the interconnectedness of skills and the need for an integrated approach. Simultaneously, examining the building blocks separately affords us the opportunity for a more nuanced exploration of each skill, which continues to be practiced in numerous teaching, learning, and assessment contexts.

9.3 Listening Comprehension

In first-language acquisition, listening develops first. In second-language acquisition, it is either listening or reading, depending on whether the language input is aural or written. In a second-language learning context, the target language surrounds the learner. It is the spoken and written language of society: the street, schools, shops, and offices. In a foreign-language learning context, learners often need to actively seek out opportunities to be exposed to the target language. For English, even in countries where it is not an official or commonly used language, learners increasingly have access through the internet, airwaves, and a growing number of proficient speakers. Access to other languages might be more limited, but is also becoming more available online.

Let us break down the process of listening into its components. **Listening includes the listener's ability to**

a. construct meaning from a rapid stream of sounds (segmental and suprasegmental features of the language) considering the dialect and rate of speech

b. construct meaning from lexical (vocabulary, formulaic sequences, idiomatic usage), syntactic, semantic, and pragmatic features of the language even if they are presented through incomplete sentences (bottom-up processes)

c. access, in the brain, relevant sociocultural, contextual, background schemata (top-down processes)

d. identify speakers' attitude, mood, and sociocultural implications of discussion at natural speed (CEFR 2018)

e. follow talks, lines of argument (CEFR 2018)

f. incorporate new content into existing content knowledge

g. identify inferences

h. evaluate the role of pauses, disfluencies, hesitations, speech fillers, false starts, and nonverbal clues, distortions in audio (ignore them or derive meaning from them)

i. process language automatically as spoken language is "fast and fleeting" (Buck 2000)

j. employ listening strategies and automatically coordinate top-down and bottom-up processes (Vandergrift and Goh 2012)

k. exploit visual clues, as a receptive strategy (CEFR 2018)

Top-down processing relies on higher cognitive processes and background knowledge to understand the specifics. It is characterized by situating the task at hand within a larger cultural, historical, contextual, and pragmatic context.

Bottom-up processing constructs the whole from the parts. It relies on the decoding of language systems such as phonemes, morphemes, lexis, syntax, from which it builds meaning.

The aforementioned are demands that the process of listening makes on the listener. The listening task itself can be categorized in a variety of ways, such as one-way (e.g. announcements, academic lectures, media broadcasts, podcasts, etc.) or two-way (e.g. formal or informal conversations, discussions; transactional (message-oriented) or interactional (for maintaining social relationships).

The CEFR Companion Volume (2018) not only categorizes and describes the various receptive speech events but also provides can-do rubrics for each type of event. These rubrics can be used for teaching, learning, and assessment purposes.

9.4 Assessing Listening

"Listening (similarly to reading) is a receptive skill, and unlike productive skills (such as speaking and writing) listening takes place entirely inside the listener's brain" (Porter-Szucs 2018). Both the result of listening, i.e. comprehension, and the process are hidden, presenting a challenge for assessment. Listening comprehension cannot be directly observed or assessed; it must be inferred from the TTs' response to tasks. Another challenge for assessment involves two-way listening tasks, which are common in real life, as demonstrated above. Most two-way tasks primarily assess speaking, while listening is almost exclusively assessed in a one-way manner. Assessing listening can be more cumbersome than assessing reading if technological requirements are involved. Buck recommends assessing general receptive language through reading, limiting listening assessments to aspects that can only be tested aurally, i.e. "fast automatic processing of realistic spoken texts" (2000, Testing Listening video 05:36).

9.4.1 Assessing Listening in the Classroom

In a language classroom, students are usually surrounded by housekeeping and content-specific instructional language. The former includes routines and comprehension checks (*Open your books. Do you have any questions?*). The latter includes any concepts being taught (*"Māori were the first to arrive in New Zealand, journeying in canoes from Hawaiki about 1,000 years ago"*) (100% Pure New Zealand n.d.). Listening comprehension assessment of either type of language can be formative or summative, low stakes or high stakes.

Think-Pair-Share 9.4a Revisit Chapter 4 and make a list of formative, low-stakes ways in which listening can be assessed in the classroom. Discuss.

Because speaking in the target language is a primary information source in both second- and foreign-language classrooms, ongoing formative assessment of comprehension is essential. When the focus is on overall class understanding rather than individual comprehension, the following **ongoing formative comprehension checks** can be performed (a–g):

   a. Look for signs of comprehension or incomprehension on the students' faces: There may be a cultural component to the way students feel comfortable expressing incomprehension though. In some East Asian cultures, students may nod in response to the question "Do you understand?" even when they do not understand, for fear of implying that the teacher's explanation was unclear. Thus, while nods may indicate comprehension, they should be interpreted in context.

   b. Look for body language indicating action in accordance with the instructions: This may mean that students turn to the appropriate page in their textbooks or turn to a partner for partner work.

   c. Ask students to indicate comprehension of the instructions or explanations nonverbally by modeling the desired behavior: In front of your body, hold your thumb up for total comprehension, hold your thumb down for total lack of comprehension, and hold your thumb sideways for partial comprehension. Many students feel uncomfortable admitting to a lack of comprehension, so they are unlikely to turn their thumbs down, but they tend to feel comfortable turning their thumbs sideways to indicate slight confusion. Holding the thumb close to the body provides the students with some privacy. The teacher can see it but the other students cannot, so it is easier for students to save face in front of their peers.

   d. Ask for a verbal indication of comprehension: The verbal equivalent of the previous point is Yes/No/Maybe. After the teacher gives the instructions or explanation, she asks, "Yes, no, maybe?" To which the class responds orally and chorally with one of the words. Again, few will admit to "no" but "maybe" can be a sign that more explanation is needed.

   e. Ask for a show of hands of "Who understands?": We recommend this question instead of the typical "Do you understand?" or "Who doesn't understand?" The recommended "Who understands?" encourages those students to self-identify who do understand rather than those who do not. In response, some of the students will respond that they do understand and whoever does not can be assumed to benefit from further explanation.

   f. Ask student volunteers to explain and/or demonstrate: Students sometimes benefit from explanations and directions or demonstrations from their peers rather than the teacher. For the teacher, hearing a student's paraphrase can be informative.

   g. Ask all students to explain to a partner: All students pair up and explain to their partners what they understood. Next, they pair up with a different partner and explain their understanding. Any discrepancies in comprehension can then be resolved as a class.

   No teaching is complete without ongoing formative assessment. The aforementioned strategies allow the teacher to assess the class's comprehension of instructions and explanations quickly and efficiently. The teacher receives instantaneous feedback and can take immediate action, depending on the results of the assessment.

If the teacher's goal is the **assessment of individual students' listening comprehension** rather than that of the class as a whole, then the following strategies can be employed (h–o). They are best used in ongoing, low-stakes, formative situations although they could become part of summative assessment as well:

   h. Ask specific content questions for which responses demonstrate comprehension.

   i. No-tech non-verbal response: It is possible to create a multiple-choice listening-comprehension quiz on the spot. After the class listens to some content (about literature or any other subject), the teacher can quickly ask several MC or T/F questions. The questions can be written on the board or asked verbally one at a time. The answers are indicated by holding up fingers. For instance, if on the board the question is *Who is the author of Don Quixote?* and the answer choices are *1-Lope de Vega, 2-Ana de Jesús, 3-Miguel de Cervantes*, then the students can hold up one, two, or three fingers to indicate their answers. Again, the students should hold their hands directly in front of their bodies so that only the teacher can see their answers. Depending on the number of students in the class, the teacher can right away make a note of which students were able to answer the question correctly.

j. Variation on no-tech response: Instead of holding up fingers, the students can hold up small flashcards with the numbers or letters of the answer choices printed on them. For instance, at the beginning of the school year, each student writes on a piece of paper the letters from A to D or numbers 1, 2, 3, 4, one per piece of paper. When it is time to respond, the students hold up the appropriate paper directly in front of them, for the teacher to see.

k. Total Physical Response (TPR): It is a form of assessment, whereby one speaker (the teacher or a student) gives the class verbal instructions to be followed. For instance, one such command could be to *touch your nose*. In order to avoid groupthink, the speaker could personalize the instructions. In this version, the command could be, *If you were born in January, sit down; if you were born in February, turn around; everyone else, keep standing.*

l. Low-tech response: In many classrooms, students do not or cannot have internet-connected devices such as cell phones, tablets, computers, or other student response tools. However, if the teacher has a cell phone or tablet, *Plickers* can still be used (plickers.com). Only the teacher needs to create a free account, enter the names of the students (up to 20), download and print out the response cards (QR codes), download the app onto the teacher's cell phone or tablet, and get started. Each student receives their own response card, which—depending on how it is rotated—indicates answer choice A, B, C, or D. Using a phone or tablet with the app, the teacher scans each student's card by pointing the phone at the card for a split second, and the students' scores are registered on the app.

m. High-tech response: In some classrooms, every student has an internet-connected mobile device (such as a smartphone or tablet) or the school provides computers or student response devices such as iClickers (iClicker.com). In such classrooms, numerous websites and applications that gather student responses can be utilized.

n. Written response: Keeping in mind the above discussion about mixing skills, listening comprehension can be assessed in writing. Students may be asked to summarize the main idea. Their exit ticket could be the most important takeaway, the muddiest point (Mosteller, 1989), or the K-W-L chart (see Chapter 7). Unlike the previous methods of assessment, for practicality reasons, feedback on these written responses is typically given in subsequent class periods rather than immediately.

o. Information transfer: In this variation on a written response, students demonstrate their listening comprehension by transferring aural information to a chart, graph, diagram, or picture. For instance, the speaker may describe the overlapping area of a Venn diagram and the students draw a Venn diagram and in the intersection of the two circles write the correct information.

In the above points (a–o), we presented a number of common listening comprehension tasks that are appropriate in both low-stakes formative and summative classroom situations. Because of their suitability to inform teaching and learning, they should be implemented on an ongoing basis. Whether or not they require any advance preparation, they have positive washback and provide students and teachers with prompt feedback.

Think-Pair-Share 9.4b Application   Choose at least three formative listening assessment tasks, at least one from *a-g* and *h-o* each. Apply them to the language teaching setting you are most familiar with. Discuss a concrete topic you would assess in such a way. Can you think of additional ways of assessing listening comprehension formatively?

9.4.2   Assessing Listening Formally

Think-Pair-Share 9.4c   Revisit Chapter 4 and make a list of summative, low- or high-stakes ways in which listening can be assessed in the classroom or standardized testing. Discuss.

Due to their formal nature, many summative classroom assessments resemble standardized assessments. The iconic listening comprehension test includes an audio or video recording playing the stimulus after which TTs respond to a series of multiple-choice comprehension questions. Chapter 4 introduced item types, such as multiple-choice, which can be used to assess listening comprehension. In this section, we introduce listening events and how they can be turned into both traditional and authentic forms of assessment.

9.4.3   Listening Events

One-way listening situations can be placed on a continuum from short to extended. While there is no clear line between short and extended events, we will draw it at approximately two to three sentences. That is the approximate length of monologue to which the listener could (if given the chance) respond with a single sentence or action.

While listening, the listener's attention may focus on different aspects of the spoken language. Similarly to how readers read with different purposes in mind, good listeners listen for various reasons and are able to vary their **reasons for listening** in mid-stream, including

a. scanning for specific information, for example at what time the show starts, from which platform the train leaves, or which student is supposed to answer the teacher's question
b. listening to identify the main topic
c. summarizing the main idea, takeaway, conclusion, moral of the story
d. identifying significant details, supporting arguments, important stages of development, steps in cooking a recipe, parts of narrative
e. inferring undertones, unstated arguments, backgrounds
f. anticipating logical next steps and consequences
g. identifying the speaker's attitude, stance, emotion
h. coming up with examples to illustrate a larger point
i. generalizing from examples mentioned to a larger point
j. synthesizing the information mentioned with the listener's knowledge
k. evaluating the usefulness or veracity of the information heard

l. seeking to be affected emotionally, for instance, to be inspired, calmed, riled up, and entertained

m. making a personal connection, establishing rapport, making small talk, etc.

As listeners enter into authentic listening situations, they use their knowledge of the situation to anticipate one or more of the reasons for listening. Their purpose determines whether they attend more to the tone of the speaker, specific words, the beauty of the language, the complexity of ideas, or how the new information integrates into existing knowledge the listener holds. Their purpose shifts depending on what they hear.

Compared to the breadth of authentic listening situations, assessments of listening fall short of authenticity. Most listening tests—in the classroom or on standardized assessments—include brief conversations and longer lectures, where the TT identifies the main idea, significant details, and occasionally inferences. This is hardly surprising as there are some obvious limitations to assessing listening when there are stakes. The listening situation has to be sufficiently standardized for the scores to be fair, valid, and reliable. This is easiest to achieve with a carefully scripted stimulus passage, recorded by a voice actor, delivered from a recording, and tested with selected response items. Which brings us back to the present-day situation with most classrooms and standardized assessments...

Think-Pair-Share 9.4d Consider an authentic listening situation and purpose for listening (e.g. a phone message with specific meeting information). Revisit Chapter 4. Describe two different listening tasks for the language setting you are most familiar with. Try to be as creative as you can be. Be sure to consider the proficiency level of your students as you design the tasks. Balance authenticity, practicality, reliability, and validity. Discuss with at least two colleagues.

Going beyond the listening item and task types introduced in Chapter 4, here we will introduce listening assessments that target various purposes in authentic situations (Figures 9.1–9.3).

9.4.4 Beginner-level Listening Task

I. Directions: Listen to the conversation. Choose the correct picture (a, b, c).

The stimulus that the students hear:

W2[1]: Wow! What a great museum!
M2: Yeah, I really like a lot of the pictures. *[slight pause[2]]* I think that one is my favorite.
W2: Which one? The pear? It looks delicious.
M2: *[Laughing]* No, *[slight pause]* the bell!

Narrator: What does the man like?

---

1 M2 = young man, M1 = older man, W2 = young woman, W1 = older woman
  Item writers leave such notes for the production crew about the participants in the dialog.
2 These notes are also left by item writers for the production crew so they will know how the item writer intended for the dialog to sound on the recording.

[Students see in their test booklet.]

a.

Figure 9.1   Baby bear. *Source:* Robert Anthony Carbone / Pexels

b.

Figure 9.2   Bell. *Source:* dimitrisvetsikas1969 / Pixabay

c.

Figure 9.3   Pear reflected. *Source:* Vika_Glitter / Pixabay

Rationale: This is designed as a beginner-level item because it uses simple, high-frequency vocabulary, fairly simple sentence structure, and discusses a concrete (as opposed to abstract) topic. The situation is authentic because friends can go to a museum to see a photography exhibit and discuss which picture they like the most.

This listening item assesses not only the main idea but also phonemic discrimination. The main idea is assessed because, from the conversation, the TT has to understand which of the words the man likes. The male speaker (M2) says "I like" in his first turn. Later he paraphrases it as "is my favorite" and finally he says that it's the one depicting the "bell" that he likes. So the TT has to piece together the relevant words from the dialog to understand the main idea. An added difficulty for the TT may be that in his final turn, the man says "no," then pauses before correcting the woman with the correct answer: "bell" (or option *b*). A student who does not fully understand the exchange may think that it is *not the bell* that the man likes. This item also assesses listening for minimal pairs: /p/ vs./ b/, as in *pear* vs. *bear*, and /r/ vs. /l/, as in *bear* vs. *bell*.

The pictorial response format is appropriate for two reasons. One reason is that beginner-level TTs may have excellent listening comprehension skills but find reading the answer choices a challenge. In this task design, listening is less confounded with other skills than it would be otherwise. Another is the desire for authenticity. In the stimulus, the friends are at a museum, pointing at the pictures they are looking at. This response format lends itself well for the TT to point at (check off/click) the correct answer. The level of authenticity of the task could be further increased if the TT could actually point at the correct picture by, for example, touching the screen of a touch-screen electronic device.

Communicative authenticity could be introduced into this task if, after listening to the stimulus, the TTs were invited to participate in the conversation as a third friend. At the highest level of authenticity, the TT would participate in a conversation with either an oral examiner or another TT about the topic in this stimulus. Then while one participant would take the role of the speaker, the other that of the listener. Disambiguating speaking from listening though raises task-design and scoring challenges for assessment.

9.4.5   Intermediate-level Listening Task

II. Directions: Listen to the conversation. Then answer the question you hear.

The stimulus that the students hear:

W2:   Thank you for calling the Blue Sky Hotel. How may I help you?

M1:   Hello, I'll be staying with you next week from Thursday to Saturday. *[rising intonation, as if needing encouragement to talk]* For a conference at the convention center?

W2:   Yes, Sir. Do you have a question about your reservation?

M1:   Actually, my question is about transportation. How far is your hotel from the convention center? Is it within walking distance?

W2:   *[doubtful]* Well, it's a 30-minute walk, *[encouraging]* but we can call you a taxi.

M1:   What about public transportation?

W2:   The system here is excellent. Buses run every 10 minutes.

M1:   Sounds good. I'll get the schedule from you when I check in.

Narrator: What was the purpose of the man's call?

a. *to make a reservation at the Blue Sky Hotel*
b. *to learn how he can get to his conference**
c. *to ask about public transportation options*

Rationale: This is designed as an intermediate-level main-idea item. The language is somewhat more complex than in the beginning stimulus. For instance, the future progressive tense is used ("*I'll be staying*"), and high-frequency idiomatic language occurs ("*thank you for calling, how may I help you, do you have a question about, how far is, what about, sounds good*"). Occasionally lower frequency idiomatic language and incomplete sentences occur but they are also glossed; in other words, redundancy is built in so TTs have a few chances to catch on ("*within walking distance*"–"*a 30-minute walk,*" "*what about public transportation*"–"*the system*"–"*buses run*"–"*I'll get a schedule*").

The main idea is also intermediate. What makes it slightly more challenging than the beginning stimulus is that the main idea is mentioned in the middle (rather than at the beginning or end) of the stimulus. However, what keeps the difficulty level moderate is that a lot of time is spent talking about the main idea and that the main idea is explored from several angles (*transportation, how far, walking distance, walk, taxi, public transportation, system, buses*).

Similar to variations above on increasing the authenticity of the task, this intermediate-level task could also become more authentic if the listener TT became an active participant. Specifically, the TT could be invited to incorporate the heard dialog into their own opinion about the topic of how to get to the convention center. The TT could then respond, for example, that "because the hotel is far from the convention center, the guest prefers to take the bus, but I like to walk and I would prefer to walk 30 minutes." Such a response would demonstrate the listening comprehension of the stimulus in a more authentic and communicative manner.

9.4.6 Advanced-level Listening Task

III. Directions: Listen to the conversation. Then answer the question you hear.

The stimulus that the students hear:

M1: *[with longing]* Let's get out of town one of these days. I can't stand the city in this heat.
W1: What do you have in mind? Hiking in the mountains? Swimming in the sea?
M1: Wherever there are good last-minute deals. Surprise me.
W1: Alright! When can you get away?
M1: I've got a project due this Monday but I'm free the weekend after.
W1: Same here. Don't make any other plans.

Narrator: What will the woman probably do next?

[Students read in their test booklet.]

a. *wait for the man to make travel plans*
b. *leave on Monday for a holiday by the sea*
c. *research discounted vacation destinations**

Rationale: This is an advanced-level dialogic item for several reasons. It contains idiomatic language, such as "*get out of town, one of these days, can't stand, have in mind, last-minute deals, surprise me, get away, same here.*" Also, there is no redundancy of information or explicit cohesive devices. In fact, there are numerous incomplete thoughts and sentences, which is a common characteristic of spontaneous conversations. For example, the cause–effect in the man's first turn is implied rather than explicitly stated: "*Let's get out of town <u>because</u> I can't stand the city.*" In her response, the woman leaves out the explicit context and connection among the ideas, such as "<u>*when we get out of town, would you like to go*</u> *hiking in the mountains <u>or</u> swimming in the sea.*" In his second turn, the man responds with an incomplete sentence: "<u>*I would like to go*</u> *wherever there are good last-minute deals.*" His response "*surprise me*" implies that he expects the woman to research the last-minute deals and make all the travel arrangements for their trip. He would like the decision to be a surprise. The rest of the stimulus contains further examples of this. All the implied, rather than stated, information increases the challenge for the TT.

The question asked of the TT is also rather challenging to predict the logical next step. The answer choices are written in words, and no longer presented as pictures. This is appropriate for a literate, advanced-level TT.

The exchange in the stimulus and the comprehension question about it are authentic. Friends/family members can plan mini-vacations together out of a desire to escape their everyday surroundings. When they do, it could happen in such an informal manner. Yet, sufficient context is given in the dialog early on that someone overhearing the conversation can follow it. The first turn establishes the desire to get out of the city due to the heat and that the speakers should do it together. The next turn introduces some options. The following turn adds two new pieces of information: that the destination should depend on the price and that the man expects the woman to make the decision. In the following turn she agrees and inquires about the best time to go on vacation and in her last turn she confirms the date. The listener cannot miss any information because each turn contributes to the main idea. This again is a sign of an advanced-level stimulus. The question the TT is to answer is also authentic. We can imagine that if someone overheard this conversation and relayed it to a third party, that person could ask, "So what's going to happen next?"

The level of communicative authenticity of this task could be further increased if, after having heard the stimulus, the TTs were invited to comment. For instance, the TT could be tasked with comparing–contrasting how a conversation on a similar topic would have transpired between the TT and a friend. A sample response could be, "Sometimes I, too, feel that I want to get away, get out of town; but the difference for me is that I would not go where the deals are but rather choose the seaside; I can always go to the mountains in the winter; and another difference would be that I would not expect that my friend makes all the arrangements but I would help plan the trip." In such a way, the TT could demonstrate comprehension of the stimulus while incorporating the interactiveness of dialogic listening situations.

In the above-mentioned three listening-comprehension tasks, we have emphasized how to increase the communicative authenticity of the tasks. Such tasks exist already.

Did you know? The graduate student instructor oral English test (GSI OET),[3] an oral proficiency test of international teaching assistants' English at the University of Michigan, does

---

3 The GSI OET was developed and is administered by Michigan Language Assessment, formerly the University of Michigan English Language Institute Testing Division.

evaluate listening in a way that is communicative, authentic, and reliable. In one task, the TT views videotaped questions or statements from university students and has to respond to the students in the recording. The trained evaluators listen specifically for signs of comprehension in the way the TT responds to the students in the video. In another task, while the TT gives an extended one-way speech on a topic, the oral examiner poses questions to the TT. In listening to the TT's response, the examiner marks on the evaluation sheet the extent to which the TT understood the examiner's questions.

9.4.7 Item Types and Placement in Listening Comprehension Tests

Of the three listening comprehension tasks above, the beginner and intermediate ones asked questions about the main idea of the stimulus passage. This is the most common item type. Other typical item types include significant details, vocabulary, and—as demonstrated in the advanced-level task—inference. When multiple questions are asked about a listening stimulus, the coverage of the stimulus should be even: some items should assess the beginning, some the middle, and some the end. The sequence of the questions generally follows the order in which the answers appear in the stimulus. One noteworthy exception to this practice is the placement of the main-idea question. It is rare for the main idea question to be placed in the order corresponding to the location of the answer within the listening passage. Most commonly, it is either first or last, irrespective of where it actually keys within the passage. This deliberate practice is rooted in the rationale that maintaining a consistent placement of the main-idea question, either first or last, prevents TTs from gaining additional clues as to what the main idea of the passage is.

9.4.8 Factors Influencing Difficulty

Earlier we named the processes involved in listening and, in the three example assessments described above, we demonstrated several factors that may influence the difficulty of listening passages and items. Below, we present these and additional features concisely:

- topic (top-down processing: TTs' knowledge of it, conventionality of perspective, cognitive complexity of arguments, pragmatic knowledge)
- vocabulary (TTs' familiarity with it, frequency in isolation and context, cognates, technical terminology)
- sentence structure (complexity, length, order of acquisition of structures)
- speech (bottom-up processing: TTs' familiarity with accent, rate of speech, pauses in stream of speech, volume, automaticity of processing, speech fillers, phonological features, prosody, suprasegmentals, stress, rhythm, intonation)
- discourse features (organization, development, coherence, cohesive devices, type-token ratio, redundancy of information, "propositional complexity, that is, the degree of nonlinearity in the presentation of ideas" (Aryadoust 2018)
- listening strategies (familiar to TT, used by TT, automatic coordination of top-down and bottom-up processes) (Shockey and Cavar 2013)
- modality (audio, video, audio accompanied by visual support)
- working memory
- number of opportunities to listen (recordings can be played again for increased comprehension)

There is extensive literature on every one of the above factors, and for further reading, we recommend the listening assessment section of the TESOL Encyclopedia (2018).

9.4.9 Speech Rate

Relying heavily on Chang (2018), we present the gist of speech-rate studies because of their implications for recording stimuli for assessment purposes. In general, slower speeds are more comprehensible to nonnative speakers than faster speeds, and even highly proficient nonnative speakers prefer slower speeds than do native speakers (East and King 2012; McBride 2011). Pauses in the delivery further increase comprehension (Blau 1990). There are no firmly established definitions of *fast* and *slow* because listening speed is both subjective and contextual. In one study (Zhao 1997), learners were allowed to adjust the speed of the recording themselves during a task. Most (83%) slowed it down and more than half (53%) adjusted the speed multiple times while listening, suggesting that the optimal speed depended on the participant and on the exact nature of the listening they were engaged in.

The most oft-cited speech-rate guidelines by Tauroza and Allison (1990) set the following speeds:

Speech event	Average speed rate (words/minute)
Conversations	190–230
Interviews	160–210
Radio monologues	150–170
Lectures	125–160

Speeds slower than the lower boundary can be considered slow and speeds faster than the upper boundary can be considered fast. However, it is important to keep in mind that much more research needs to be done before these or any numbers can become firm recommendations.

9.4.10 Summary of Assessing Listening

Listening is difficult for learners to learn, teachers to teach, and assessors to assess. Both product and process are invisible and fleeting. Unlike the written word, which is stable and consistent in its presentation, the spoken word changes depending on the speaker who utters it and the context it occurs in. The listener must engage in concurrent top-down and bottom-up processing, moving automatically between the two, depending on the demands of the listening task. This process is aided and hindered by a long list of factors. Assessing listening comprehension poses a challenge because at tension are authenticity and reliability.

Think-Pair-Share 9.4e Following the example of the three dialogic items at three levels, design a listening task for three different proficiency levels. This could be a single utterance to which the listener has to respond, a short dialog, a short monologue, an extended monologue, a dictation, an information transfer, or any other type of listening task. Keep the task the same and adjust the level of the task depending on the proficiency it is intended for. Provide a rationale for each. Share with at least two colleagues.

9.5 Assessing Speaking

In first-language acquisition, speaking develops second after listening. In second-language acquisition, speaking development varies. Young learners in second-language contexts frequently develop speaking proficiency that is indistinguishable from their native-speaking peers. Foreign-language learners and older learners in both second and foreign-language settings, in contrast, may find that speaking is the last skill they master if they lack practice opportunities and face other challenges.

Do you speak Slovak? Do you speak Japanese? Do you speak Swahili? This is how we commonly word the question aimed at determining whether someone knows a language. It is as if speaking a language equaled knowing the language (Ur 1996). Although "knowing" comprises much more than the ability to speak, let us examine what a **language speaker must do** to answer this question in the affirmative (based on Thornbury 2005 and the CEFR 2018).

- produce speech comprehensibly (segmental and suprasegmental)
- construct meaning and express it lexically (with words and formulaic sequences), syntactically, semantically, and pragmatically
- in real time, conceptualize and formulate discourse type, genre, topic, purpose (interpersonal, transactional, evaluative), organization, and coherence
- attend to accuracy
- use suprasegmentals and pauses to underscore the intended message
- produce language with fluency and automaticity (with little planning time: the planning of one utterance overlaps with the production of another)
- hold the floor with deliberate use of pauses, speech fillers, hesitancy, vagueness; minimal false starts; and steady and appropriate speed
- self-monitor and repair in real time
- manage talk (cooperate with an interlocutor, take turns, respond spontaneously, use paralinguistic signals)
- provide detailed descriptions on complex subjects, integrating sub-themes, concluding appropriately
- employ production strategies such as *planning* (mental preparation, rehearsal, considering listener's reaction), *compensating* (using different tactics, self-correcting surreptitiously, gesturing, circumlocuting, paraphrasing to cover lapses in vocabulary and structure, using a similar but wrong word and qualifying it), *monitoring and repair* (to further smooth speech, changing approach, self-correcting slips, backtracking, restructuring)

Many of the concepts introduced about listening also apply to speaking. Knowing about the factors involved in successful speaking as well as listening or factors contributing to the difficulty of the task can help the teacher and student diagnose aspects of language proficiency in need of attention. For instance, if a learner continues to have listening comprehension problems despite understanding each word they hear, such a list of factors can direct the teacher's attention to problems with sentence structure or top-down factors. Similarly, if a learner speaks fluently but is not understood by others, the above list could direct their attention to potential deficiencies in pronunciation, vocabulary, or grammar.

Think-Pair-Share 9.5a Recall and Apply   Recall what the following terms mean and apply them to speaking. Discuss.

- isolated vs. integrated skills
- top-down vs. bottom-up processing
- one-way vs. two-way
- transactional vs. interactional
- ongoing formative assessment
- summative assessment

Did you know? The WIDA English Language Development Standards Framework, 2020 Edition (WIDA 2024b) consolidates communication into interpretive (encompassing listening, reading, and viewing) and expressive (speaking, writing, and representing) modes of communication. The new terms acknowledge that people communicate not only through the traditional four skills (formerly called *domains* by WIDA) but rather multimodally: through gestures, facial expressions, images, equations, maps, timelines, symbols, acting, and more (WIDA 2020: Overview of WIDA 2020 Standards; WIDA 2024b: ELD Standards).

The CEFR (2018) **categorizes spoken production** as **interpersonal, transactional,** and **evaluative**. In the following speech events, we see examples of each:

- **sustained monologue—describing experience (one-way transactional):** such as about plans, routines, and past experiences
- **sustained monologue—giving information (one-way transactional):** professional and academic lectures and procedures
- **sustained monologue—making a case (one- or two-way transactional)**: debate and argumentation
- **public announcement (one-way transactional)**: toast, flight attendant's announcement, and retirement speech
- **addressing audiences (one-way** and **two-way transactional)**: public talk, class lecture, and professional presentation
- **understanding interlocutor (two-way spoken interactional)**: speaker must understand and accommodate the interlocutor, negotiate meaning, and adjust their speech
- **conversation (two-way spoken interactional interpersonal)**: personal or public topics, employing language functions (greetings, offers, permissions, etc.)
- **informal discussion** (with friends) **(two-way spoken interactional with interpersonal and evaluative elements)**: leading and following the discussion, employing colloquial language, using varied language functions, responding to criticism
- **formal discussion** (in meetings) **(two-way spoken interactional event with evaluative and transactional elements)**: following a discussion, asking for clarification and repetition, and participating in a debate
- **goal-oriented cooperation (two-way spoken interactional event with evaluative elements)**: cooking, studying, planning, and organizing
- **obtaining goods and services (two-way spoken interactional event with transactional elements)**: doing business in restaurants, shops, banks; disputing traffic tickets, accidents, and financial blame
- **information exchange (two-way spoken interactional transactional)**: personal details, dates, prices, habits, routines, advice, etc., and using technical terminology when talking to a specialist
- **participating in an interview (two-way spoken interactional transactional)**: participating in or leading an interaction, developing points, responding to interruptions or interrupting in a fluent, clear, and well-structured way
- **using telecommunication devices (two-way spoken interactional event with transactional, interpersonal, and evaluative elements)**: using the telephone and video app to participate in casual or formal conversations confidently and effectively, despite potentially unfamiliar accents

9.5.1   Assessing Speaking in the Classroom

Speaking assessment in a classroom immediately sparks concerns over practicality. Listening comprehension can be assessed with one person speaking and everyone else listening. The practicality of listening assessment is high. The converse is not. The larger the class size, the less practical direct speaking assessment becomes. Yet, students must be given the chance to learn to speak in the target language. And if you—as the teacher—teach speaking, how do you know if your students are learning? You must assess their speaking.

Think-Pair-Share 9.5b   Revisit Chapter 4 and make a list of formative, low-stakes ways in which speaking can be assessed in the classroom. Discuss their practicality implications in a teaching environment you are most familiar with.

Speaking is a productive skill; in other words, speakers produce language. Reliable assessment of language of anything more than a few words requires an appropriate rating scale or rubric. For formative purposes, we recommend a series of primary-trait rubrics and the rewarding of effort. In the following paragraphs, we describe various **ongoing formative speaking assessments in the classroom** and ways to balance practicality with reliability and validity.

A. **Self-assessment of pronunciation** (or accuracy-focused speaking) may target the following:
   - The pronunciation of a sound, cluster, stressed syllable, reduced syllable, etc. in a low-tech way: Students' single-trait rubric defines the target performance; each student assesses the achievement of their own production of the target element and marks it on the rubric.
      a. For instance, if the target element is the voiceless "th" sound /θ/, the rubric may contain a picture of the mouth, with the tongue sticking out from between the teeth, with the lower lip not touching the upper teeth. The picture is accompanied by a description to the same effect. Each student, holding a mirror, pronounces a list of words with /θ/ in initial, medial, and final positions. Students check off each word where the target element is mastered.
      b. For another example, the aspiration of /p/, /t/, /k/ in English can be self-assessed with a single-trait rubric explaining that a sheet of tissue paper flutters due to the puff of air resulting from the correctly pronounced plosives.
      c. Similarly, the lengthening of stressed vowel sounds lasts as long as a rubber band stretches.
      d. The shortening of reduced vowels happens when the rubber band snaps back.
      e. Syllable- and stressed-timed rhythm can be self-assessed to a metronome or the tapping of a finger.
      f. Pitch and intonation can be self-assessed with the help of a kazoo or humming. Each of the target performances is described in a single-trait rubric with words and pictures, if possible. In this way, any practice exercise can be turned into an assessment.
   - The above tasks, self-assessed with the help of audio- or video-recording devices: if students have access to recording devices in the classroom, they can record themselves, replay their recordings, and evaluate themselves using the single-trait rubric. Such devices include computers, tablets, phones, and video or tape recorders.

- The above tasks in a high-tech setting: speech-recognition software is becoming increasingly precise. Students can dictate into applications for smartphones and tablets as well as online programs, while the program recognizes the speech and types it up. Students can compare the original with the computer-generated text and award themselves points accordingly. Some programs even have playback capability, so students can play the written text back at various speeds in various languages and dialects and practice pronouncing the text. At the time of publication, free online programs with excellent voice recognition include the following:

    a. Dictation https://dictation.io/

    b. SpeechTexter https://www.speechtexter.com/

    c. VoiceNotebook https://voicenotebook.com/

    d. TalkTyper https://talktyper.com/

- Grammar or vocabulary: paired speaking practice is often focused on the use of correct vocabulary or grammar, starting with basic introductions (*What's your name? My name's...*), continuing with modals expressing what someone can/can't do (*Can you swim? Yes, I can. Can you fly a plane? No, I can't.*), and past-tense Wh-questions and answers (*Where did you go last week? I went to... When did you get there? I got there...*), etc. In this activity, students practice common structures, phrases, and formulaic sequences. If they have easy access to both the exercise and the answer key, they can check their own responses and self-assess.

B. Self-assessment of fluency-focused tasks may entail

- facilitating the production of words with increased automaticity, reducing unwanted pauses (searching for words), and pushing more words out in less time while maintaining thought group boundaries. These goals can be self-assessed with a single-trait rubric describing the above qualities of fluency. Activities conducive to this assessment include:

    a. 4/3/2, wherein the speaker says the same thing in a decreasing amount of time (for example, first in 4 minutes, next in 3 minutes, next in 2 minutes);

    b. pyramid, in which the speaker gives the same presentation to an increasing number of listeners, filling the same amount of time with more and better-organized details;

    c. onion, where students pair up in two concentric circles, one circle only speaks for a specified amount of time and one only listens; after each round of speaking, the listener peer-evaluates and the speaker self-evaluates and plans to improve the speech in the next round; then the outside circle rotates one seat clockwise; now with new partners, the same circle speaks and the same one listens to the improved speech; this continues for three to four rounds, after which the speakers and listeners switch roles; the same can be performed in two lines facing each other if circles are impractical;

    d. ping-pong: in pairs, students take turns monologuing on the same topic; turn-taking is signaled by the teacher at unpredictable intervals: sometimes 5 seconds (to encourage a quick start), sometimes 1 minute (to encourage elaboration); two rules are followed: while speakers speak, listeners listen and don't comment or interrupt and speakers cannot repeat themselves but can repeat their partner's statements; topics may include anything universal, e.g. sun, chocolate, and music; self-assessment takes place immediately following several rounds of a ping-pong topic, but before switching partners;

e. role plays or simulations: in pairs or small groups, students prepare the script for a given situation and enact it in front of the class; topics may include shopping, hotel guest and employee, classmates, teacher and student, family members, etc. Students can self-evaluate their performance either with a single-trait rubric or a checklist.

C. Self-assessment of meaning-focused tasks may entail

- focusing not on the accuracy of language or on the automaticity of production but on the meaning of what is said (i.e. topic, content, information). Here, speakers of a second language may set various goals for themselves. They may focus on conveying factual and logical information. They may also focus on developing the ability to express their thoughts in the TL, whatever the quality of those thoughts may be. The former may include knowing that climate change is a concern worldwide while the latter entails knowing that this thought is communicated in this way: *Climate change is a concern worldwide.* However, even if someone is factually incorrect and says that *climate change is a hoax*, if they communicate their meaning idiomatically and clearly, then the second (though not the first) goal has been accomplished. However, saying that *climate change worldwide also gives reason to concern* achieves the factual goal but not the second goal of communicating meaning clearly and idiomatically. Importantly, the single-trait rubric should reflect the meaning-focused goal of the speaker;

- the following meaning-focused tasks: a) information gap; b) paraphrasing; c) summarizing; d) debate; e) desert island (if you could only take five objects with you to a desert island, what would your and your group's consensus be); f) jigsaw reading or listening and then reporting back to the group; g) spot the difference;

- task-, scenario- project-, and performance-based activities: These are authentic and highly engaging models of teaching, learning, and assessment. In all three types, the learner engages in an activity that is meaningful and could be performed just as well outside of the classroom, in the real world. Speaking-intensive activities include creating a podcast, creating a movie, preparing an oral presentation for the school leadership team, preparing for a job interview, cooking in class, and preparing a multimedia project (such as about one's country for the local library or for prospective students about the school). These activities are multi-stage and complex and often result in the presentation of project results beyond the classroom. When students self-assess their participation in the project, they could focus on any single aspect (even accuracy or fluency) though focusing on meaning makes the most sense. The student can self-assess with the help of a single-trait rubric or a checklist.

D. Peer assessment of accuracy-, fluency-, and meaning-focused tasks:

- The pronunciation activities in a), instead of being self-assessed, can be peer-assessed. Using the same single-trait rubric and focusing on one target element at a time (the pronunciation of particular segmentals or suprasegmentals; the use of specific grammar, vocabulary, formulaic language, etc.), students can assess each other's performance.

- Dictation: There are numerous variations on dictation activities. In the most basic one, student A dictates a text to student B, who writes it down. Student A can read the text multiple times or just once, as specified in the rating scale. Then either A or B can compare the original text to the one written by B. In another version—called running dictation—the text is several steps away from student B, the scribe. Student A, the runner, goes back and forth between the text and the scribe. A may not bring the text closer to the scribe or dictate from a distance; thus, A has to keep chunks of the text in their short-term memory and then dictate it clearly enough for B to write it down. One important consideration when using dictation for self- or peer-assessment is that students can sometimes understand each other even when the speaker does not speak correctly, while at other times they fail to understand each other even when the speaker does speak correctly. Thus, the negotiation of meaning resulting from the exercise may be more valuable than the assessment, so little weight should be attached to the evaluation.

- The grammar and vocabulary accuracy-focused activities can also be peer-assessed either directly after the interaction or from an audio- or video-recording.
- Fluency-focused tasks can be peer-assessed as well as self-assessed. The listener should be very familiar with the single-trait rubric to be used for assessment in any given task. During the task, the listener should listen and make eye contact with the speaker. After the speaker is finished, the listener can peer-evaluate. This way, the listener can fully attend to the speaker and the speaker is not distracted by their peer's furious scribbling. Even trained oral examiners find it a challenge to multitask: pay attention to the TT and take notes on a rating sheet. Classmates evaluating each other's performance should be discouraged from attempting to rate while listening.
- Meaning-focused classroom speaking tasks can be assessed by peers as well as by the speakers themselves. It is perhaps even more essential in meaning-focused activities than in others for the listener-evaluator's attention to be focused on the speaker because during such activities the listener engages in the negotiation of meaning. Meaning-focused tasks require that the roles of listener and speaker alternate. In particular, in a debate, opponents try to convince each other of the soundness of their viewpoints over another's arguments. This requires the listener's (peer-evaluator's) full attention. Thus, the evaluation should be left for after the activity.

E. **Teacher assessment of accuracy-, fluency-, and meaning-focused tasks**:
- Teacher's helper: If the teacher has access to proficient speakers of the TL, then classroom volunteers, conversation partners, teachers' aids, assistant teachers, etc. can be recruited. These helpers can maximize the students' speaking time. Such helpers can also be trained in the use of evaluation rubrics for increased reliability.
- Language teachers evaluate their students formatively on an ongoing basis. In fact, many students resist other forms of evaluation arguing that if they or their classmates knew what was wrong with their language, then they would not need teachers. They liken peer-assessment to the proverbial blind leading the blind. In the face of such arguments, the teacher would do best to point out to the students the advantages of self- and peer-assessment. However, the classroom teacher's assessment of the students does carry special significance for the students. Thus, it is essential that the teacher engage in it systematically.

A peer-assessed meaning-focused speaking activity recommended by Yule and Tarone (1997) asks learners to describe objects whose names they do not know. Suitable objects might include a *tape dispenser* (Figure 9.4), the so-called *bottomless portafilter*, i.e. the inner metal basket of a coffee maker (Figure 9.5).

Figure 9.4 Tape dispenser. *Source:* Wikimedial mages / Pixabay

Figure 9.5 Bottomless portafilter. *Source:* Miftah R. Baristarasa / Pexels

In pairs, students can take turns describing such objects. The listener can either draw what they hear or select from among pictures on their worksheet.

Think-Pair-Share 9.5c Recall and Application   Revisit Chapter 1, where we discussed various ways of categorizing assessment. Which methods apply to teachers informally and formatively assessing their classes? Discuss.

There are numerous ways in which teachers can assess their students' language development formatively. Above we discussed the use of single-trait rubrics with a range of tasks. In Chapter 1, we demonstrated on-the-run and checklist assessment. Below we highlight a few others that lend themselves particularly well to **authentic speaking assessment by the teacher**.

- One-on-one conferences or interviews: Though time-consuming and low in practicality for larger classes, these can occasionally be integrated into the instructional cycle. Teachers can hold them in-class, while other students work on projects or out-of-class to avoid taking up class time. Conferences or interviews can be accuracy-, fluency-, or meaning-focused. They can simply be friendly chats in the target language. For assessments, use a rubric, checklist, or narrative according to some predetermined evaluation criteria for consistency of rating and feedback. While out-of-class conferences or interviews add to both the teacher's and the students' workload, they offer a private alternative for self-conscious students.

F. Formative assessment of very young learner's speaking and pronunciation: preliterate and early literate learners cannot be given a single-trait rubric or checklist and expected to complete it for themselves or their peers. However, they can still participate in self- and peer-assessment. They can award themselves or their classmates a smiley face or thumb up if they think the performance was excellent, a straight face (😐) or thumb sideways if they think the performance was alright but could be improved, or a sad face or thumb down if they think the performance was not very good and could be improved a lot. They can also be asked to provide verbal feedback. Since young children are rather fragile emotionally, we are not advocating for providing them with critical feedback. In fact, they can be taught to give each other and themselves encouraging feedback for effort. At the earliest age, they can simply be accustomed to trying their best. And as they grow, they can be taught to attend to actual evaluation criteria.

9.5.2 On Feedback

On the preceding pages, we presented numerous formative speaking assessments, from informal to slightly more formal. Readers, however, may wonder about feedback provision. Nearly all tasks and exercises should include corrective feedback from peers or the teacher. Such feedback may occur during the speaking event through **negotiation of meaning** (an exchange when speakers try to understand each other clearly), **recasting** (when the listener naturally and casually repeats the error back to the speaker but correctly), **direct error correction** (when the listener draws the speaker's attention to the correctness of the correct form instead of the incorrect form), or **nonverbally** (with a questioning glance, tilt of the head, movement of the eyebrows). Feedback can also follow the speaking event, with individualized or group feedback. For instance, if multiple students struggle with the same target element, the teacher can review the theory, correct errors on the board, and provide focused practice for the class. For more on feedback, see Chapter 11. Ultimately, one of the aspects that distinguishes formative assessment from just practice on the one hand and summative assessment on the other is that the goal is to improve teaching and learning. Closing the feedback loop, i.e. receiving feedback, allows for learners to reflect on their proficiency and improve.

9.5.3 Summary of Assessing Speaking in the Classroom

In order for students to learn to speak, they need the opportunity to produce comprehensible output (Swain 1985). Yet providing every single student regular opportunities to speak in class is time-consuming, especially in large classes. Sometimes, this need also clashes with the curricular requirements or cultural norms prevailing in the teaching context. In the aforementioned speaking tasks, we have tried to balance the conflict between the need to produce output and practicality as well as the need for tracking students' learning in a variety of practical ways. For more on this topic, including an extended example of how to assess the speaking of beginners in the classroom, see Boas (2018).

Think-Pair-Share 9.5d Application Choose at least three formative listening assessment tasks, at least one from *a-g* and *h-o* each. Apply them to the language teaching setting you are most familiar with. Discuss a concrete topic you would assess in such a way. Can you think of additional ways of assessing listening comprehension formatively?

Think-Pair-Share 9.5e Application Rewatch one of the videos of speaking performances recommended in Figure 5.4. Pretend that that is your student speaking and making mistakes. Select one target element to focus on:

a. Keeping in mind the student's age and educational setting, assess the student's speaking formatively using a single-trait rubric you create for this purpose.
b. Provide concurrent feedback to the student where appropriate. You may pause the video while you do so.

c. Provide subsequent feedback to the student either verbally or in writing. View the opportunity to assess formatively and to provide feedback as an extension of the teaching–learning process.

9.5.4 Assessing Speaking Formally

Think-Pair-Share 9.5f   Revisit the list of speaking events in Section 9.5 above. How could you turn some of them into formal and authentic speaking assessment?

Think-Pair-Share 9.5g   Revisit Chapter 4 and make a list of summative, low- or high-stakes ways in which speaking can be assessed in the classroom or in standardized testing. Discuss.

As in the case of listening comprehension, summative classroom assessments of speaking pattern themselves after standardized assessments. The quintessential speaking test in both—classroom and standardized—settings is the oral proficiency interview. The examiner asks the TT a series of level-appropriate questions on a wide range of topics. The TT's responses are assessed based on a holistic or analytic rubric. The ACTFL oral proficiency interview (OPI) (2024a) is one of the best-known examples of this. Such oral interviews rarely occur in real life though. As Ockey (2018) argues, authentic oral proficiency test tasks are better gauges of oral proficiency than other tasks because they simulate real-world tasks. Having presented the spoken-language taxonomy developed by the CEFR (2018), we will instead introduce formal speaking assessments following this approach and suggest ways to increase the authenticity of the tasks.

9.5.5 Beginner-level Speaking Task—One-way

I. Directions: You are a guest on a radio show. You will speak about your country (or the place where you live). Explain what is interesting in your country and why people should visit it. (planning time: 2 minutes, speaking time: 2 minutes) (Figures 9.6 and 9.7)

Figure 9.6   Headphone and microphone. *Source:* Barthy Bonhomme / Pexels

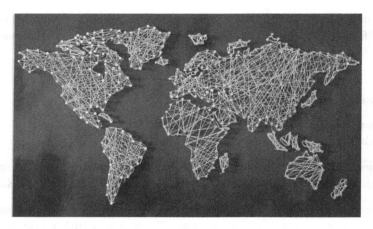

Figure 9.7 World map. *Source:* Barthy Bonhomme / Pexels

Rationale: This is a beginner-level sustained monologue designed to give information. A TT either interacts with a live examiner, who delivers the prompt and rates the performance, or a computer, which plays a recorded prompt and records the response for later evaluation.

This task is beginner-friendly (a microphone and world map) to activate the learners' background schema. The topic and task are concrete (rather than abstract) and relatable: their own place of residence. In a foreign-language setting for low-proficiency learners, the prompt can be given in their native language.

The 2-minute planning time is motivated more by face-validity considerations than a conviction that it leads to improved performance (Wigglesworth and Elder 2010).

The task is considered authentic, as people often describe their home countries to others. This task requires that they provide a simple description, include factual information, provide details, and connect ideas and concepts with simple conjunctions such as "and, but, so."

The rating scale can be holistic or analytic but should cover all the relevant evaluation criteria: task accomplishment (describing and recommending details about a place), pronunciation (segmentals, suprasegmentals), and language use (grammar, vocabulary, formulaic language). Organization (sequence, coherence, cohesion) can also be assessed. Since this is a monologue, other skills do not interfere with evaluating the TT's speaking proficiency, especially if the prompt is given in the TT's native language.

To increase the authenticity of the task, the monologue may be preceded by a one-on-one conversation with the examiner about the TT's background, further contextualizing the prompt. Alternatively, a reading or listening stimulus passage about traveling or planning a school trip could precede the speaking, providing context and language support. The evaluation of speaking may also be hindered if the influence of the stimulus cannot be separated from its effect on the speaking.

9.5.6 Beginner-level Speaking Task—Two-way

II. Directions: You and your partner are new classmates. You don't know each other well. You want to do something together on the weekend. First, ask each other about two hobbies. Second, talk about what you both like to do. Third, decide what you will do this weekend. Talk about the cost, time, and location. (planning time: 2 minutes, speaking time: 3 minutes) (Figure 9.8)

Figure 9.8 Classmates. *Source:* Tima Miroshnichenko / Pexels

Rationale: This is a two-way interpersonal interactional task or a conversation. Two TTs partici-pate either face-to-face with a live examiner or with a computer, whose roles are similar to the previous transactional task.

The task is beginner-friendly for several reasons. The picture of two students activates the TTs' background schema on school and friendships. The topic is personal and concrete: getting to know each other and making plans. The language needed for this task is taught early in language classes. In a foreign-language setting with low-proficiency learners, the prompt can be given in their native language.

Again, the 2-minute planning time is designed to put the TTs at ease.

The task is authentic, as classmates often try to get to know each other's likes and dislikes and make plans together. The speakers focus on both personal relationships and accomplish-ing the task. They practice politeness, ask about likes and dislikes, make and respond to invita-tions, greet, and take leave.

Similarly to the other beginner-level tasks, the rating scale can be holistic or analytic as long as it considers all the relevant evaluation criteria: task accomplishment (discussing hob-bies, making concrete plans to do something together), pronunciation, and language use. Since this is a paired task (two TTs are assessed at the same time), it must be designed to prevent personality and talkativeness from affecting the assessment. A live examiner can intervene if one TT dominates the conversation. Without a live examiner, the task should include specific questions directed at each TT to ensure balanced participation.

Another rating-related consideration of a paired speaking task is the two TTs' differing pro-ficiency levels. For instance, if one TT struggles to understand the other TT or the task, it may hinder the task's completion and the more proficient TT's performance. Paired speaking tasks are, therefore, best suited for certificate, proficiency, and achievement tests, where TTs are preselected for their level (e.g. they all sit for a B2, high-intermediate test). Paired tasks should be avoided in placement tests, where proficiency is yet to be determined and accidentally a beginner could be paired with an advanced learner.

Did you know? The speaking portion of the Examination for the Certificate of Proficiency in English by Michigan Language Assessment is a paired exam. Notice the way the design of the task facilitates a display of each TT's language proficiency. There are questions and task cards for each of the TTs. Even though one TT—"Stefanos"—is more fluent and proficient than the other—"David"—both students can accomplish the task and display their proficiency. During Stage 1, for instance, the examiner, Diane, asks an open question and waits for each TT to respond. One readily does so while the other waits for the examiner's prompting: "How about you, David?" Once he is invited to speak, he does so willingly and ably.

9.5.7 Intermediate-level Speaking Task—One-way

III. Directions: You have just started a new school in a new town. Your new teacher would like to hear about your best day at your old school. Describe in detail what happened and explain why this was your best day. Explain to the new teacher whether such a good day could be repeated at the new school. Why or why not? (planning time: 1 minute, speaking time: 3 minutes)

Rationale: In this sustained monologue, the speaker describes an experience in a one-way transactional task at the intermediate level. One TT participates with either a live examiner or a computer, similarly to the beginner-level one-way task.

This is an intermediate task for several reasons. At this level, a picture is unnecessary unless the task is complex. The topic, a personal experience, is not inherently difficult. However, sustaining a past-tense narrative is challenging in English, as many TTs slip into the present or mix tenses inappropriately. Also, providing ample details for 3 minutes can be a challenge while maintaining fluency and accuracy.

The holistic or analytic rating scale should cover task accomplishment (focusing on the past-tense narrative), pronunciation, and language use. Intermediate speakers should also deliver their narrative with some fluency and automaticity, which can be included under *pronunciation* or as a separate category, like *delivery*. Organization may also be assessed. At this level, the prompt need not be delivered in the students' native language, though doing so would isolate speaking skills from listening, and prevent TTs from relying on prompt language in their response.

To increase communicative authenticity, TT could read or listen to a stimulus related to the prompt, such as a topic on change, transitions, new beginnings, or a psychological concept related to memory. Again, disambiguating speaking from the other skills may present a scoring challenge if the TT does not fully understand the stimulus.

9.5.8 Intermediate-level Speaking Task—Two-way

IV. Directions: You and your partner work for a museum in your city. The museum has money for one new exhibit of your choice. Each of you should suggest two new exhibit ideas. Briefly discuss all four. Then select one of them and explain why that is your group's recommendation for the museum. (planning time: 1 minute, speaking time: 4 minutes)

Rationale: This is a formal discussion in a meeting. In this two-way spoken interaction, the TTs will use both evaluative and transactional language elements. Two TTs participate with either a face-to-face examiner or a computer, similarly to the intermediate-level one-way task.

This is designed as an intermediate task for a variety of reasons. A picture prompt is no longer necessary to activate the TTs' background schemata. The task is set in a professional, workplace setting, where the TTs are employees. This introduces the possible use of a more formal register if the TTs are capable of it. Despite the more challenging setting, the task itself should not be too difficult. Most students are familiar with museums and exhibits. Even if they are not familiar with the full range of exhibits a museum can hold, they can think of two painters, two photographers, or two ancient artifacts that can be exhibited. Evaluating ideas and then seeking consensus are also somewhat challenging tasks.

The authenticity of this scenario is very high. Such decision-seeking discussions take place at jobs worldwide; only the topic varies depending on the exact nature of the job.

The rating scale at this level should incorporate task accomplishment, pronunciation, language use, and perhaps delivery. The TTs can be expected to make their points clearly and relate to the points made by their interlocutor. This aspect can be included in task accomplishment or even a separate evaluation criterion.

The concerns voiced in the last paragraph of the rationale of the beginning two-way task are also valid here. In paired speaking, the task design, examiner, and rater must all consider how to assess each TT's speaking proficiency separately from the other TT's performance and from any other skill's influence, unless the way the speaking construct is defined acknowledges that speaking ability includes the ability to respond to stimuli.

9.5.9 Advanced-level Speaking Task—One-way

V. Directions: A company would like to build a large automotive factory in your neighborhood. The city government is unsure whether to allow it or not. Some of your neighbors support the idea because the factory may create new jobs, while others oppose it because of increased traffic and pollution. You represent your neighborhood. Make a formal speech to the city government summarizing both sides of the issue. Then, while incorporating the complex perspectives of your neighbors, support one of the sides with additional persuasive arguments. Be sure to hypothesize about the negative consequences if your argument is ignored. (planning time: 1 minute, speaking time: 5 minutes)

Rationale: This is a sustained monologue while addressing an audience. It is designed as a one-way, evaluative, and transactional, advanced-level task. One TT speaks to either a live examiner-rater or a computer.

This is an advanced task for several reasons. It requires not only an examination of multiple viewpoints but also a persuasive presentation based on them. This goes beyond the linguistic demands of descriptively comparing options and selecting an option, as in the intermediate museum task. Here the speaker must incorporate multiple perspectives into their persuasive speech. This is to be done in the formal register. There is no pictorial support and the TT is to speak for 5 minutes.

The task is authentic. The scenario that people would speak up formally for or against a proposal is common in many countries. This may occur on the job, at a university, or in the public sphere. When doing so, they acknowledge both sides and take a firm stance on one side of the issue. Hypothesizing and speculating in order to build an argument is an advanced-level task according to the CEFR (2018).

(Continued)

> *(Continued)*
>
> The evaluation criteria on the rating scale will take into consideration task accomplishment (effectively building an argument), pronunciation (use of stress, pauses, and intonation to make a point), language use (well-chosen vocabulary, grammar, formulaic sequences in the right register), and organization (logical sequencing of ideas, use of cohesive devices).
>
> To increase task authenticity, the live examiner will pose a somewhat hostile question for the TT to respond effectively. If this is included, the rating scale should be expanded to evaluate the TT's ability to handle challenging questions.

9.5.10 Advanced-level Speaking Task—Two-way

VI. Directions:[4] *You and your partner are teachers at a school and on the hiring committee for a new teacher. There are three applicants: a teacher of health, a teacher of business, and a teacher of English. Your school needs all three, but there is only money for one. Look at the task cards you have received. Each one of you knows one of the teachers best. You have heard rumors that some of the teachers prefer the third applicant.*

  a. *Get to know each teacher by discussing the contents of your cards with each other (do not show your cards to each other).*
  b. *Select your top two applicants and ask each one at least one more question to the Director of Human Resources of all schools in your city (the examiner).*
  c. *After you receive your answers, decide which one to hire and why.*
  d. *Share with the Director of Human Resources your recommendation for hire. Give at least three specific reasons for your recommendation.*

(planning time: 1 minute, speaking time: 10 minutes)
  Task card 1 (to be given to one of the TTs):

> Ms. Samantha Ali—27 years old, health teacher
> Educational background:
> *certified to teach 5–18-year-old children
> Professional background:
> *teacher of relaxation
> *owner of health-food business
> Personal background:
> *last year ran a 42 km (26 mile) race
> You may want to know about her previous jobs:
> *why she left
> *how long she stayed
> *her relationship with teacher colleagues

---

4 Michigan Language Assessment's ECPE served as an inspiration for this task format.

Task card 2 (to be given to the other TT):

Mr. Benjamin Chen—38 years old, business teacher
Educational background:
*certified to teach 10–18-year-old children
Professional background:
*owner of three businesses
*many former students now own businesses
You may want to know about his background:
*what businesses he owns
*his relationship to current students
*his relationship with teacher colleagues

Task card 3 (to be shown to both TTs):

Ms. Angela Gonzalez—31 years old, English teacher
Educational background:
*certified to teach 5–18-year-old children and adults
Professional background:
*poet and writer
*volunteer English teacher
What test takers may want to know about her background:
*her beliefs about English
*topic of her writing
*her relationship with teacher colleagues

Examiner sheet: [contains all three task cards and possible answers to information questions]

Ms. Samantha Ali—27 years old, health teacher
Educational background:
*certified to teach 5–18-year-old children
Professional background:
*teacher of relaxation
*owner of health-food business
Personal background:
*last year ran a 42 km (26 mile) race
What test takers may want to know about her previous jobs:
*why she left—everyone is afraid to say
*how long she stayed—one school year each at each of the last three jobs
*her relationship with teacher colleagues—she made negative comments about coworkers' appearance

Mr. Benjamin Chen—38 years old, business teacher
Educational background:
*certified to teach 10–18-year-old children
Professional background:
*owner of three businesses
*many former students now own businesses
What test takers may want to know about his background:
*what businesses he owns—an alcohol store, a 24-hour bar, a website about beer
*his relationship to current students—he hires them
*his relationship with teacher colleagues—organizes parties for them

Ms. Angela Gonzalez—31 years old, English teacher
Educational background:
*certified to teach 5–18-year-old children and adults
Professional background:
*poet and writer
*volunteer ESL teacher
What test takers may want to know about her background:
*her beliefs about English—is superior to all other languages
*topic of her writing—nightmares and horror stories
*her relationship with teacher colleagues—corrects their grammar

Rationale: This is a goal-oriented, cooperative, two-way task with evaluative and transactional elements. Two TTs participate with a live examiner, who delivers the prompt, answers questions, and rates performances in real time.

This is designed as an advanced-level task. The linguistic and cognitive demands are substantial. TTs must analyze, evaluate, and synthesize positive and negative information about three applicants to recommend one for hire. They can use informal language between themselves but must switch to a formal register with the Director of Human Resources. Each TT must actively contribute to the work, request information, provide data, weigh facts, summarize what they heard and read, and advocate for or against applicants. Furthermore, the discussion must be sustained for 10 minutes, switching between evaluative and transactional elements.

The task is authentic as it mirrors the complexity of a hiring committee's discussion. The rating scale should include evaluation criteria about task accomplishment (whether all the criteria in the directions are met), pronunciation (segmentals; suprasegmentals; use of pauses, stress, and intonation to further opinion), language use (grammar, vocabulary, formulaic language, skillful choice of language to argue for and against a stance), organization (building a case, sequencing, comparison, contrast, coherence, cohesion). Concerns about uneven contribution from TTs are also valid here. Since this task is only possible with a live examiner, she can step in if a TT monopolizes talk time and does not allow the other TT to demonstrate their language proficiency. The speaking construct of this test must allow for the fact that here reading comprehension and listening comprehension are closely intertwined with the speaking task.

9.5.11 Summary of Assessing Speaking Formally

Formal, summative, high-stakes tests of speaking should be less frequent than informal formative assessments. Nevertheless, such tests serve as useful signposts in the language learner's growth. Learners also have common external motivations for sitting for such tests: college admission, job advancement, and professional certification.

Think-Pair-Share 9.5h   Following the example of the six speaking items at three levels, design one speaking task for three different proficiency levels. Keep the nature of the task the same (monologic vs. dialogic) and adjust the level of the task depending on the proficiency it is intended for. Provide a rationale for each. Share with at least two colleagues.

Think-Pair-Share 9.5i   Revisit Chapter 4 and both the listening and speaking sections of this chapter, focusing on their relevance to the assessment of pronunciation.

   a. Considering the usual way of dividing pronunciation into segmental (vowels, consonants) and suprasegmentals (clusters, stress, rhythm, intonation, pausing, thought grouping), which aspects of listening comprehension may apply to pronunciation?

   b. Considering the above, which aspects of speaking may apply to pronunciation?

   c. Examine items or tasks within the chapters that are specifically designed to assess pronunciation in isolation.

   d. Look for instances where the assessment of pronunciation is integrated with other skills.

   e. Examine a speaking rating scale to understand how it evaluates pronunciation.

9.6 Chapter Conclusion

Oral skills are challenging for learners to master, teachers to teach, and testers to assess. These skills are often intertwined, making separation difficult. Testers, including classroom teachers and professional test developers, must clearly define the construct they aim to assess. They must decide whether they intend to assess isolated or integrated skills and ensure that the task design and rating scale align with this approach.

Appendix 1 – Achievement Quiz of Chapter 9

(For discussion or writing prompts, see the Think-Pair-Share tasks in this chapter.)

Directions: Select the response that best answers each question below. Question 1 is worth 2 points if entirely correct or 1 point partial credit. Questions 2–5 are worth 1 point each.

   1. Select all that apply. To assess the listening comprehension of your advanced learners, you design an assessment with all of the following qualities:

      a. idiomatic language on unfamiliar topics

      b. incomplete thoughts and sentences

      c. information that is not stated directly

      d. inclusion of redundant wording

2. In your language class, you show your students a video of speakers discussing a concert. As your students aim to comprehend the video, which aspect involves top-down processing?
   a. decoding formulaic language to build meaning from the spoken words
   b. accessing relevant contextual and socio-cultural schemata in the brain
   c. recognizing phonemes and morphemes in the speakers' pronunciation
   d. focusing on the grammatical structure of the sentences in the video clip

3. Peer assessment can be beneficial when assessing speaking because _____.
   a. it is impractical for teachers to do frequent formal speaking assessments
   b. peers are often better at assessing each other's problems in pronunciation
   c. it is a valid and reliable method of assessing speaking as an integrated skill
   d. students of all ages prefer to be assessed by their peers rather than their teacher

4. You teach an oral communication class of 42 students. Which meaning-focused assessment technique is practical in your classroom on a daily basis?
   a. reading aloud into speech-recognition software
   b. peer-assessment of paired practice of segmentals
   c. having pairs of students play spot the difference
   d. proficiency interviews with individual students

5. At the language school, you teach pronunciation. You would like to administer to each student a direct authentic assessment of their pronunciation of a difficult sound. What will you do?
   a. listen to how the students pronounce the target sound as they teach the class to cook a recipe
   b. have the students silently read a text and underline all letters that are pronounced as this sound
   c. do a minimal-pair task with each student where you listen to their pronunciation of this sound
   d. ask the students to raise their hands whenever they hear you say the target sound in a story

10

Assessing Reading, Vocabulary, Grammar, and Writing

Chapter Overview

This chapter extends the discussion from the previous one, which covered the assessment of oral–aural skills (listening, speaking, and pronunciation), as well as viewing and representing. It introduces literacy and contrasts it with multiliteracies and then explores the assessment of written skills (reading and writing) and supporting subskills like vocabulary and grammar. Emphasis is placed on communicative assessment of grammar within a communicative language classroom. The chapter also introduces assessment considerations for LESLLA and SLIFE learners, concluding with a discussion on plagiarism.

10.1 Learning Objectives

1. Apply to a specific setting the teaching and assessment of reading as a process
2. Explain the importance of teaching and assessing formulaic sequences
3. Summarize the dilemma over assessing the construct of vocabulary
4. Describe what is involved in assessing reading, vocabulary, grammar, and writing
5. Calculate the lexical density of two pieces of writing written by students
6. Give one example each for assessing form, meaning, and use
7. Devise a plan for handling plagiarism in a culturally sensitive manner

Think-Pair-Share 10.1a Recall what you learned about the assessment of written skills (reading, writing, grammar, vocabulary) in previous chapters, in particular Chapter 4. Discuss.

Think-Pair-Share 10.1b Recall what you learned in the previous chapter about assessing oral communication skills in an isolated or integrated way. Discuss how this might apply to the assessment of literacy skills.

10.2 Literacy, Multiliteracies

Think-Pair-Share 10.2a Recall what you learned in Chapter 1 about multiliteracies.

Traditionally, literacy has been defined as the ability to read and write. More recently, though, literacy has encompassed a much broader meaning. The Government of Alberta defines literacy as

A Practical Guide to Language Assessment: How Do You Know That Your Students Are Learning? First Edition.
Ildiko Porter-Szucs et al.

"the ability, confidence, and willingness to engage with language to acquire, construct, and communicate meaning in all aspects of daily living" (2019, p. 1). This view of literacy bears the hallmarks of the conceptualization of **multiliteracies** by the New London Group (1996).

To summarize, in the 21st century, literacy means much more than the ability to read and write. There are additional elements that a literate person must master, including linguistic, audio, spatial, gestural, and visual design elements. Thus, our discussion of assessments will include multiliteracies, though chapters are organized by the more familiar skills of reading and writing.

Unlike listening and speaking, which—in a conducive environment—emerge automatically in neuro-typically developing individuals, reading and writing require effort in both the L1 and the L2. In one's L2, written skills may even be learned before oral skills. One reason for this is that in many foreign-language contexts, subsequent opportunities to produce and practice the target language orally for authentic communicative purposes may be scarce both in and out of the classroom. Reading materials, however, tend to be abundant. Another reason is that many language learners study another language solely to develop reading proficiency.

Did you know?   Some users of foreign languages, such as graduate students and researchers, may simply need to develop reading knowledge of the target language for their work. Classes that meet their needs are offered at various universities. For instance, see Reading Spanish for Research Purposes at the University of Chicago, French for Reading Proficiency at the University of Hawaii, and various languages for reading and translation at the University of Wisconsin.

10.3   Reading Comprehension

Reading is a complex, interactive, active, receptive, interpretive process that involves the reader, the reader's background knowledge, and the text. Let us break down the process of reading into its components. **Reading includes the reader's ability to**

- decode the written message through an unobservable mental process
- convert "written symbols (alphabet) to sounds" and subsequently "combine the sounds to meaningful units as words" (Sadeghi 2018, n.p.)
- access, in the brain, relevant sociocultural, contextual (both when and where the text was produced and where it is read), textual, background schemata, design elements, awareness of linguistic diversity, critical thinking, creativity, and digital technology (top-down processes)
- construct meaning from lexical (vocabulary, formulaic sequences, idiomatic usage), syntactic, semantic, pragmatic features, spelling, visual presentation of the text, and design elements (bottom-up processes)
- employ reading strategies and automatically coordinate top-down and bottom-up processes, use "contextual, grammatical, and lexical cues to infer attitude, mood, and intentions and anticipate what will come next" (CEFR 2018, p. 67)
- construct meaning: interpret, and connect ideas
- interpret cohesive devices (connectors, pronoun-antecedent reference, repetition, synonym use)
- understand explicit meanings (main idea, significant details, vocabulary in context) and implicit meanings (infer, predict)
- activate textual knowledge (of "text types, text structure, organization, coherence, cohesion, reference, and inference") (Sadeghi 2018, n.p.)
- activate the reader's personal characteristics ("alertness, motivation, selectivity, interest, and purposiveness") (Sadeghi 2018, n.p.)

- recognize reading purpose (such as for correspondence, orientation, information and argument, instructions, leisure) (CEFR 2018)
- understand abstract, structurally complex, colloquial, or nonliterary writings (CEFR 2018)
- "adapt style and speed of reading to different texts and purposes" (CEFR 2018, p. 60)
- incorporate new content into existing content knowledge
- exploit visual clues, as a receptive strategy (CEFR 2018)

The above serves not simply as a list of the various components of reading but also as a list of abilities that the learner may potentially struggle with and target elements that can be assessed in a reading assessment.

Think-Pair-Share 10.3a Recall what you learned in the previous chapter about top-down and bottom-up processes. Discuss how this might apply to the assessment of reading.

Think-Pair-Share 10.3b Think of a language learner you know well, as you complete this task. Reflect on the learner's reading processes in light of the above list. Apply as many of the aforementioned skills and abilities to this learner's situation as you can. Discuss your evidence for the presence or lack of each. Alternatively, complete this exercise by considering your own foreign- or second-language learning.

10.3.1 Assessing Reading in the Classroom

Think-Pair-Share 10.3.1a Revisit Chapter 4 and make a list of formative, low-stakes ways in which reading can be assessed in the classroom. Discuss.

In language classrooms, students are often surrounded by the written word. They usually have a textbook and receive handouts from the teacher. Tests are often presented on paper or displayed in written form on computer screens. The classroom walls are often decorated with posters, maps, rules, key vocabulary, student work, etc. as depicted in Figure 10.1. Students nowadays are exposed to and must learn the impact of more than just print, i.e. visual modes encompassing color, font, size of font, placement, white space, as well as accompanying images, and symbols.

Figure 10.1 Literacy on classroom walls. *Source:* shannonmatthew / Pixabay

Essential multiliteracy skills need to be taught to help students understand and effectively integrate these modes to communicate meaning in ways that enhance rather than detract from the intended message.

Reading in the target language is a crucial source of information in both second- and foreign-language classrooms. This is particularly true of students who are no longer learning to read but are rather reading to learn. Such is the case in classrooms where **English** is **the medium of instruction**.

Did you know?   Increasingly, English is a medium of instruction (EMI) to teach subjects other than English (e.g. geography or science) in countries where the majority of the population does not use English most of the time. This trend is increasing in primary, secondary, and tertiary institutions. In continental Europe alone in 2007, over 2400 programs were taught entirely in English in over 400 higher educational institutions (Doiz et al. 2012). It is widely believed that in today's globalized environment, such programs can provide a competitive advantage. In EMI programs, typically the textbooks and other materials are in English, as are the assessments, but the actual language of instruction varies greatly depending on the English-language proficiency of the students and their teachers (Kan et al. 2011; Marsh et al. 2009).

Reading is arguably the **most convenient skill to assess**. The authenticity of passages, if not item types, can be high when they are taken directly from authentic sources. The assessment of reading can be done with high practicality, in that large numbers of students/TTs can be assessed concurrently and without any technology. If the reading passages do not need to be developed by the test designer/teacher, then creating the items alone is not nearly as time-consuming as when original passages must be written. While, typically, multiple-choice comprehension questions do need to be crafted, reading test forms are often reused year after year. Reading assessments can easily be automated, leading to a quick turnaround time for results.

Reading comprehension questions comprise a few typical **types**:

1. vocabulary in context
2. explicitly stated main idea
3. explicitly stated significant details and
4. inferencing (implied but not explicitly stated)

On a reading comprehension test, students/TTs are presented with at least one stimulus passage and asked several questions about it. The items are usually arranged in the order in which the information is presented in the passage. Main-idea items, however, are ordinarily placed either first or last regardless of where they appear in the passage. This way the location of the main idea item does not provide the students/TTs an unintentional clue as to the location of the main idea in the reading passage. On the following pages, we will demonstrate each of the reading comprehension question types. For more information, see Chapter 4.

When it matters less which individual student comprehends and more that the class as a whole understands, the following **ongoing formative whole-class reading comprehension checks** can be performed.

a. Look for signs of incomprehension during read-alouds: when students read aloud, sometimes they stumble over words, read without emotion, ignore punctuation marks and thought-group boundaries, break up formulaic sequences, pace themselves incorrectly, emphasize the wrong words or syllables, use incorrect pitch, etc. These symptoms may indicate decoding and comprehension struggles with letters, word parts, words, formulaic sequences, grammatical categories, and other fundamental elements of the reading process (Kuzborska 2018). This frequently happens to young learners and beginner readers but also to students who do not understand the text, signaling the need for the teacher to investigate the students' comprehension further.

b. Look for signs of (in)comprehension on the students' faces: students who avoid the teacher's eye contact, look down, look away, appear to be busy doing something else may be confused or may not understand, However, cultural differences can also influence these behaviors; in some cultures, averting one's eyes is a sign of respect for an authority figure. Thus, all nonverbal signals should be interpreted in context to avoid jumping to conclusions.

c. Read aloud and translate into the L1: while the grammar-translation method is largely a thing of the past, it remains beneficial in beginner language classes where the students and teacher share a common language. This is also a favorite of students who prefer traditional methods of instruction or of those who have a great need to understand fully, lest they should feel anxious.

d. Have students perform a comprehension check in pairs: after reading a passage, students discuss or answer comprehension questions with a partner. The teacher can assess the class's overall comprehension by listening to their discussion and/or reviewing their written responses. This procedure focuses on the **product of comprehension** as opposed to the **process**.

> Receptive skills, i.e. listening and reading, take place in the language user's brain in their entirety. Both the process and product of comprehension are internal. The **product approach** to teaching receptive skills focuses on the final product, which is comprehension: i.e. the correct answer. The **process approach**, on the other hand, focuses on the process. The process is broken down into strategies, skills, and mental processes that apply broadly, beyond the text under review (Porter-Szucs 2018). These processes consist of "decoding" and "meaning-building" processes (Field 2008, p. 125). Under the process approach, the student learns to predict, verify predictions, reconcile inaccuracies in predictions, connect new and old information, evaluate, etc. (Porter-Szucs 2018). For a more complete list of processes that learners can be taught in both listening and reading, see Field (2008).

e. Assess the process of reading: In keeping with the process approach to teaching reading, the assessment of reading can focus on the process rather than the product. The instructor can stop the class's reading of the passage, elicit predictions about the upcoming section, ask the students to justify their predictions, have them continue the reading and verify their predictions, elicit reflections on any discrepancies between their prediction and the actual information in the passage, encourage the students to revise their approach in light of any discrepancies, and continue the process-oriented cycle. The instructor has a great opportunity to observe the students' thinking and assess the accuracy and soundness of their predictions given textual evidence.

f. Have students complete a graphic organizer (e.g. T-chart, Venn diagram, concept map) either individually or in pairs/groups. As students read, their reading comprehension can be guided and supported by a graphic organizer, tailored to the structure of the reading. In some cases, only the structure of the reading passage is depicted in the graphic organizer but no part of it is completed in advance by the teacher; it is the students' task to fill it in completely while reading. In other cases, some parts of the organizer are prefilled and the students complete the missing information. The graphic organizer can be completed at home or in class; individually, in pairs, or in groups; on paper or electronically; to be displayed in the classroom, put on a poster, kept in a portfolio, or saved in a notebook. Each student's work can be assessed individually summatively or formatively, but the graphic organizer lends itself to a quick assessment of the whole classroom's comprehension as well. Figure 10.2 depicts a graphic organizer that we have created to accompany a reading on the history of Australia.[1] The main headings in the graphic organizer are provided for the students, who will complete the rest of the organizer as they read.

Assessment can take place in a variety of ways. The teacher can elicit students' answers verbally individually, in groups, or as a whole class. Students can be invited to complete one whole-class graphic organizer displayed on the wall. Students can peer-assess with a partner or self-assess against an answer key. Or the teacher can collect the homework and check it himself.

History of Australia	**Aboriginal peoples**
	-years:
	-origins:
	-way of life:
	European explorers
	-years:
	-origins:
	-way of life:
	Federation
	-years:
	-origins:
	-way of life:

Figure 10.2 Sample graphic organizer.

Figure 10.3 depicts a different type of graphic organizer. It is a completed flowchart of the life cycle of a butterfly. The students receive a version where only the white circle (the title) is filled in; the other circles only contain the numbers 1 through 4. As they read, they write in the missing (here underlined) stages of the life cycle. Each arrow connects the previous circle (stage) to the next one, visually depicting the chronological relationship of the stages.

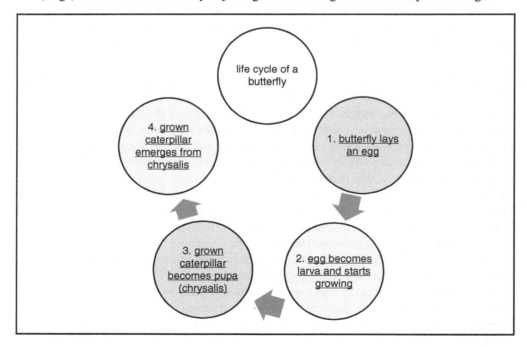

Figure 10.3 Flowchart of the life cycle of the butterfly.

---

1 The two readings are Tonkinson, R., and Brendt, R.M. (2024) and Encyclopedia Britannica (n.d.).

Students can easily self-assess the accuracy of their reading comprehension by comparing their graphic organizers either against an answer key provided by the teacher or against each other's answers.

If the classroom teacher's purpose is to **assess each individual student's reading comprehension**, then the following (g–l) techniques can be successfully implemented in classrooms both on an ongoing, formative, low-stakes basis and as intermittent, summative, higher-stakes assessments.

g. Low-tech or high-tech comprehension questions: similarly to the ideas mentioned in the previous chapter on assessing individual students' listening comprehension, a variety of comprehension questions can be asked of the whole class, to which students respond individually. The questions may focus on the four aforementioned types: (1) vocabulary in context, (2) explicitly stated main idea, (3) explicitly stated significant details, and (4) inferencing. In a low-tech environment, the teacher may write each question on the board with numbered answer choices and the students hold up the corresponding number of fingers. In a setting where students can record their responses on paper, they can provide written answers (selected- or constructed response). In a high-tech setting, students indicate their comprehension of the reading on an electronic device, such as a computer, tablet, or telephone app.

h. Reenactment: many reading genres can be reenacted by students. Narratives, processes, historical descriptions, and plays naturally lend themselves to this. For instance, after students have read and analyzed one of the Harry Potter books, they can select a scene and act it out. Their classmates and/or the teacher can assess the accuracy of the recreation with the help of a rubric.

i. Information transfer: this is similar to but broader than *reenactment*. In *transfer*, the reader transfers the written word into some other type of output, such as a poem, song, limerick, painting, drawing, computerized image, collage, sculpture, human sculpture, dance, and pantomime. The students' and teachers' imagination is the limit to how aspects of reading can be given a new form of life. Assessment can, again, be conducted by peers, the teacher, or the creators themselves. Peers and the teacher may wish to use a rubric while the students who created the transfer product may self-assess narratively so as to be able to reflect on both the process and the product.

j. Self-/peer-assessment rubric: students, even in the earliest grades, can be taught to reflect on their own and their classmates' performance. An example self-assessment reading questionnaire (Victoria State Government n.d.) is used in Australia in older grades.

k. Book report or reading log: if the class is engaged in extensive reading, such as of a novel or biography, each student can keep a reading log on paper or electronically. The students can be provided guiding questions by the teacher about the plot, main characters, any foils, themes, questions the student may wish to ask the author or characters, etc. A book report also presents an opportunity to focus on new and important vocabulary. The students identify words, copy them in context, define them, look up formulaic sequences, depict them visually, write down synonyms and antonyms, and sometimes even write original sentences with them. Assessment of reading comprehension can focus on the four aforementioned types of reading comprehension questions (as demonstrated on the following pages): (1) vocabulary in context, (2) explicitly stated main idea, (3) explicitly stated significant details and (4) inferencing. Accordingly, in class students can share details from their reading logs; they can self-assess and peer-assess. The teacher can also assess individual students' progress either in class or out of class.

l. Written response: similarly to listening comprehension, reading comprehension can also be assessed in writing. Students may summarize, paraphrase, analyze, and synthesize a reading.

For instance, they may research a product, nonprofit, or concept and then write an advertisement to promote it to others in their community.

In the above points (a–l), we presented a number of common reading comprehension tasks that are appropriate in low-stakes, formative, and summative classroom situations in broad-ranging settings. For suggestions on crafting reading-comprehension items and tasks, see Chapter 4.

Think-Pair-Share 10.3.1b Application   Choose at least three formative reading assessment tasks, at least one from a–g and h–l each. Apply them to the language teaching setting you are most familiar with. Discuss a concrete topic you would assess in such a way. Can you think of additional ways of assessing reading comprehension formatively?

Common Reading Comprehension Questions

> **Main idea:** Arguably the most important comprehension question pertains to the main idea of the reading. The main idea may be stated in one (thesis) statement or synthesized from the entire reading. Questions about the main idea may take various forms.
>
> *What is the main idea of the passage?*
> *What is the passage mainly about?*
> *What would be a good title for the passage?*
>
> The following is an example of a main idea item about the beginning of Jane Austen's classic novel *Pride and Prejudice* (1813, pp. 5–6).
>
> | line 3 | "My dear Mr. Bennet," said his lady to him one day, |
> | line 4 | "have you heard that Netherfield Park is let at last?" |
> | line 5 | Mr. Bennet replied that he had not. |
> | line 6 | "But it is," returned she; "for Mrs. Long has just been there, and she told me all about it." |
> | line 7 | Mr. Bennet made no answer. |
> | line 8 | "Do not you want to know who has taken it?" cried his wife impatiently. |
> | line 9 | "You want to tell me, and I have no objection to hearing it." |
> | line 10 | This was invitation enough. |
>
> *Question 1: What would be a good title for the passage?*
> **a.** *A New Neighbor's Arrival**
> **b.** *A Disagreement of Husband and Wife*
> **c.** *Mr. Bennett's Invitation*
> **d.** *Mrs. Long's Visit to Netherfield Park*

In this excerpt, Mr. and Mrs. Bennett are discussing that someone has finally rented Netherfield Park ("let at last"). Since Mrs. Long has just been there and the Bennetts are familiar with the property in question, it is likely that Netherfield Park is in their neighborhood; thus, the new arrival will be a new neighbor. Option B is not entirely accurate. Mrs. Bennett is excited to share the news while Mr. Bennett shows indifference. Still, he agrees to hear more about it, so while their levels of excitement are different, they do not disagree. Further, the topic of conversation is the arrival of the new neighbor and not the Bennetts' differing degrees of interest. Option C focuses on the last line in the passage "This was invitation enough." Main idea sentences are frequently the first or the last of the passage and a casual reader who does not understand what the passage is really about may be distracted by their exact recognition of a word. Finally, option D is a minor, insignificant detail because the conversation is about the news of a new tenant of Netherfield Park and not Mrs. Long, who visited the place.

Vocabulary in context: Reading comprehension assessments frequently target vocabulary in context. This is in contrast to a vocabulary item that is not connected to a reading passage and the word assessed is decontextualized, as is the case on single-skill vocabulary assessments.

The following is an example of a contextualized vocabulary item about the same Jane Austen passage.

> *Question 2: In line 6, which of the following words is closest in meaning to **returned**?*
>   **a.** *replaced*
>   **b.** *reentered*
>   **c.** *recovered*
>   **d.** *responded**

The verb "return" has multiple meanings. The context of the passage is necessary for the reader to narrow the meanings down to the correct one. (For more information on context-dependent items, see elsewhere in this chapter).

Significant detail: Questions about significant details typically predominate. If eight items follow a reading passage, then one is about the main idea, perhaps two about vocabulary, one about something not fully stated, and the rest are about details. Detail questions assess a close, verbatim reading of an important part of the passage. Frequently, there is at least one question about each paragraph. Detail questions can be about any fact in the passage that is important enough.

The following is an example of a detail item about the same Austen passage.

> *Question 3: What invitation is mentioned in line 10?*
>   **a.** *Mr. Bennett letting someone purchase Netherfield Park*
>   **b.** *Mr. Bennett's lack of objection to his wife's talking**
>   **c.** *Mrs. Long's visit to the owner of Netherfield Park*
>   **d.** *Mrs. Bennett encouraging her husband to talk*

Option B best paraphrases the meaning of "This was invitation enough." In the previous sentence, Mr. Bennett acknowledges that his wife is eager to tell her who had moved into Netherfield Park. He also states that he has no objection to her talking. This is not exactly a warm invitation for his wife to talk but because she is impatient to do so, even a lack of objection sounds like an invitation. The other options simply combine logical possibilities with factual information from the passage, which when put together is no longer accurate.

Other detail items about this passage may be about

- *what was true of Netherfield Park until recently* → that it had been empty for a long time
- *who first found out about the renting of Netherfield Park* → Mrs. Long
- *at the end of line 6, what does "it" refer to* → the fact that Netherfield Park has a new tenant

(Continued)

(Continued)

Inferencing: This is a very broad category of items about anything that is not explicitly mentioned in the text but can logically be guessed. Such questions may include

- *Which of the following statements would the author most likely agree with?*
- *Which of the following statements would the author most likely disagree with?*
- *What would the next paragraph probably be about?*
- *What is the previous paragraph probably about?*
- *From this story we may conclude that _____.*
- *The author suggests that _____.*

The following is an example of an inferential item about the same Austen passage.

> *Question 4: What is probably going to happen in the paragraph following this passage?*
> **a.** *The Bennetts will visit Mrs. Long at Netherfield Park.*
> **b.** *Mrs. Bennett will tell her husband what she heard.**
> **c.** *The Bennetts will continue to have an argument.*
> **d.** *Mr. Bennett will invite the neighbor to his house.*

We do not know for sure because we do not see the lines following line 10 but based on the previous lines, we can make an educated guess that Mrs. Bennett will tell her husband what she heard from Mrs. Long. In Line 6, Mrs. Bennett says that Mrs. Long has been there and told her about it (*it* being the fact that Netherfield Park is finally rented). Then she is eager to tell her husband, who makes no answer until prompted directly. And then he says that he does not object to hearing what his wife wants to say. Since his wife takes this sentence in line 9 as an invitation to speak, we can logically conclude that in line 11 she will begin to tell him what she knows. Options a. and c. are factually incorrect: Mrs. Long is not at Netherfield Park; she does not live there; she was just a visitor there herself, so the Bennetts could not visit her there. The Bennetts were not having an argument, so they could not continue it. As for option d., while it is possible that at some point Mr. Bennett will, in fact, invite the new neighbor over, since he does not yet know him, it is unlikely that this will happen right away, in the next paragraph, before he even finds out from his wife who he is.

10.3.2 Assessing Reading Formally

Think-Pair-Share 10.3.2a Revisit Chapter 4 and make a list of summative, low- or high-stakes ways in which reading can be assessed in the classroom or in standardized testing. Discuss.

Summative classroom assessments of reading often resemble standardized assessments. Therefore, in this section, we present reading events and ways to assess them formally, through both traditional and authentic assessments.

A. Reading Purposes and Genres:

Reading can be categorized by purpose and genre (CEFR 2018), as enumerated below:

1. reading correspondence for personal and professional purposes
2. reading for orientation: skimming (to gain a quick overview and evaluate whether the text is worth closer reading) and scanning (to locate specific information)
3. reading for detailed information and argument: close reading of personal or professional texts
4. reading for pleasure: fiction and nonfiction

Think-Pair-Share 10.3.2b   Revisit the section on Assessing Listening Formally at the end of Section 9.4.2. and recall the strategies good listeners use. Compare this list to the Common Reading Comprehension Questions in this chapter in the Jane Austen passage above. What strategies might good readers use? How can these strategies be assessed? Discuss.

Good readers employ various strategies, many of which are assessed through the four most common reading comprehension question types (see the Austen passage above). These include

a. scanning for specific information, such as what time the train arrives; but also skimming a text, such as which of the many articles on a topic is worth reading more carefully
b. reading to identify the main topic or idea
c. summarizing the main idea, takeaway, conclusion, and moral of the story
d. identifying significant details, supporting arguments, important stages of development, steps in cooking a recipe, parts of a narrative, points of comparison or contrast
e. inferring undertones, unstated arguments, backgrounds; intentionality behind design elements
f. anticipating logical next steps and consequences
g. identifying the writer's attitude, stance, and emotion
h. thinking of examples to illustrate a larger point mentioned in the reading
i. thinking of generalizations to larger points from examples mentioned in the reading
j. synthesizing the information mentioned in the reading
k. evaluating the usefulness or veracity of the information written
l. seeking to be affected emotionally, for instance, to be inspired, calmed, riled up, and entertained
m. making a personal connection, establishing rapport

Readers enter into reading situations considering the earlier mentioned purposes and genres (1–4) and employing the above strategies (a–m). The purpose and genre help to focus the reader's attention on a strategy. For instance, a cook reading a recipe approaches the instructions in the cookbook with the intention of identifying significant details (i.e. steps in the recipe). The original purpose, however, may shift during the reading. For example, although the recipe may not call for the washing of the vegetables, the reader may infer the background that before chopping the vegetables, they should be washed. The purpose may then shift again as the reader encounters an unknown word in the recipe and tries to understand it from context or looks it up in a dictionary. The purposes and strategies used by good readers in authentic situations are often fluid.

Assessment of reading comprehension in summative classroom and high-stakes standardized situations tends to employ the same highly practical but rather unimaginative item types: TT reads a passage and then answers a series of multiple-choice comprehension questions on the main idea, significant details, vocabulary in context, and inferencing.

Did you know?   The connection among ideas in/between reading passages can be assessed in a variety of ways. On the TOEFL, TTs are tasked with inserting an additional sentence into one of four slots in the reading passage, depending on where it fits most logically (ETS 2024c). On the MET, TTs read three separate reading passages, then answer a question that can only be understood if two or all of the passages are understood, as the item refers to ideas in multiple passages (Michigan Language Assessment 2024).

Think-Pair-Share 10.3.2c   Consider the wide array of authentic reading situations and purposes for reading. Revisit Chapter 4 and the different item types. Describe two different reading tasks for the language setting you are most familiar with. Try to be as creative as you can be. Be sure to consider the proficiency level of your students as you design the tasks. Balance authenticity, practicality, reliability, and validity. Discuss with at least two colleagues.

On the following pages, we will demonstrate reading comprehension assessments that go beyond the traditional, inauthentic item types.

Beginner-level reading task

I. Directions: Read the menus. Choose the correct answer.

The students read:

a.

b.

You would like to eat something sweet. Where will you go: a* or b?

Figure 10.4 Menus for beginning reading. *Sources:* Brigitte Tohm / Pexels, catalinserban / Pixabay

---

Rationale: This is a beginning-level reading item- for a variety of reasons. Both the stimulus and the item options contain pictures. The grammar contained in the stem is very simple. While the stimulus (the two menus Figure 10.4) contains both high- and low-frequency vocabulary, the item asks about two very high-frequency words (*eat* and *sweet*).

This reading item assesses a significant detail. The purpose is to read for orientation and scan the menus for the words "*eat*" and "*sweet.*" The reader sorts through irrelevant pieces of information, much of it probably too challenging for beginners—as is often the case in authentic texts—looking for the detail in question. The word "*eat*" is not displayed but "*sweets*" is and it is followed by examples of well-known sweets: *cookie, cake.*

The situation is authentic because people frequently decide where to go based on which restaurant offers what they feel like eating or drinking. Often authenticity and practicality are at odds with each other but less so in this item. The practicality of development depends on whether real menus can be used for the stimulus or whether they need to be created by the teacher/item writer. Since this is a multiple-choice item though scoring will be quick and easy.

This assessment is appropriate for TTs who are likely to be familiar with the practices of eating out, looking at restaurant menus, and making decisions based on what the menu contains. The genre and text structure of menus differ significantly enough from others that the TTs would need to have been introduced to them prior to encountering them in an assessment context.

Intermediate-level reading task

II. Directions: Read the passage. Choose the correct answer.

The students read:

Star-nosed mole *Source:* Liliya / Adobe Stock

The star-nosed mole can be seen in wet, low-lying areas in North America. Its name comes from the 22 pink fleshy appendages around its nose. These appendages are covered with more than 25 000 sensory receptors. The star-nosed mole can use them like eyes. The appendages can decide in 8 milliseconds if something is edible, which is so fast that it is a Guinness world record!

According to the passage, the word appendage is closest in meaning to _____.
a. organ*   b. eye   c. nose   d. receptor

Rationale: This is an intermediate-level item. The language in the passage is more complex than in the beginning stimulus. It contains low-frequency words and formulaic expressions, such as *mole, fleshy, appendage, and sensory receptor*. However, all these words are contextualized, and the picture accompanying the passage depicts the animal. This makes the passage accessible to intermediate-level TTs. The sentence structure is also more complex than in the beginning passages. There is passive voice (*are covered with*) and subordinate clauses (*if something is edible; which is so fast; that it is a Guinness world record*). The length of sentences varies from 8 words to 22.

The item assesses the TT's ability to understand vocabulary in context. The word *appendage* is very-low frequency (1.54 occurrences/million in COCA) and ordinarily would not be appropriate for intermediate-level learners who are not specializing in biology. However, since it is arguably the most important word in the entire passage, appears multiple times, and is described by the majority of the passage—most crucially occurs with the description that it is something that is around the nose, is pink, and consists of 22 something—, it can be deduced from context and is probably a fair item. In fact, if this passage were displayed in an authentic setting, the expectation would be that the reader would perhaps have to work out the meaning but that they would be able to do so. The selection of the options presented a challenge. Words that are mentioned in the text in conjunction with *appendages* are *star* (189.6/mill), *receptor* (5.7/mill), and *sensor* (14.8).

A word that describes what this appendage looks like includes *nose* (54.5/mill). The word *eye* (365.86/mill) may also be an attractive distractor because it, too, is a sensory organ. The best synonym of *appendage* that is high enough frequency for an intermediate TT to be likely to be familiar with is *organ* (22.98/mill). We balanced the competing needs of frequency and attractiveness in context in the present way.

The passage itself is based on authentic texts. We have simplified them to lower the reading complexity and to make it more accessible to intermediate students. On online-utility.org, the following readability indexes have been calculated: Flesch Kincaid Grade level (7.45), Flesch Reading Ease (64.79), SMOG (10.35), ARI (6.23), and Gunning Fog index (9.51). Although readability calculators remain an inexact science, based on our experience this passage would be appropriate for a B1-level TT.

On authenticity, the passage is adapted from authentic texts and could easily be encountered by a reader in a zoo, museum, primary-school biology textbook, or a website on animal curiosities. In reality, no multiple-choice questions would follow the passage; readers would figure out the meaning from context or ask someone. To enhance the authenticity of the assessment task—albeit at the cost of practicality—the TT could be prompted to speak or write about the star-nosed mole based on the passage.

Advanced-level reading task

III. Directions: Read the passage. Choose the correct answer.

The students read:

> *A great deal of emphasis has been placed on the importance of the well-rounded man. It is a label which is generally regarded as desirable, but too often we mistake participation in a variety of activities as the sign of a well-rounded man. Too many of us overlook completely the real meaning of the words—the development of a whole person. We keep ourselves so busy with the external manifestations of well-founded interests that we neglect to fill our minds to any significant depth.*
>
> *We end up a whiz on a golf course—but with no personal philosophy to sustain us in time of reversal or trouble. We are full of social conversation at a party—but devoid of thoughts to occupy our minds when we are left alone. We work hard in business—but with no well-defined principles to give us a sturdy, inflexible integrity. We busy ourselves dutifully in civic activities— but with no real understanding of a dedication to service. We are often hollow men. To meet this growing need for intellectual depth, the Private Library Edition of the 'Great Books' was published. A new "Syntopicon" published with it is designed to guide the reader through the great ideas by which man has survived and progressed—to make them meaningful to readers and their life. In their quest for well roundedness, it will be of interest and perhaps of value to the public to read this description of the "Great Books."*

The main idea of the passage is that _____.

- **a.** *the "Great Books" analyze the concept of the well-rounded man*
- **b.** *a well-rounded man can never be a hollow man**
- **c.** *the "Syntopicon" disagrees with the need for well-roundedness*
- **d.** *a well-rounded man has narrow, focused interests*

> **Rationale:** This is an advanced-level item. The language in the passage is even more complex than in the intermediate stimulus. This is demonstrated by the following readability calculations in Online Utility: Flesch Kincaid Grade Level: 10.93, Gunning Fog index 13.75, Flesch Reading Ease: 53.50, ARI 10.14, SMOG 13.49, and Coleman Liau index 9.30. In other words, a secondary-school education would be required to comprehend it. The passage contains low-frequency vocabulary, such as *well-rounded* (spelled with the hyphen, without it, and as one word, altogether 1.22 occurrences/million), *manifestation* (7.77/million), *whiz* (2.07/million), *devoid of* (3.74/million), *sturdy* (7.35/million). It also contains numerous mid-frequency words and formulaic sequences (*place emphasis on, overlook* as a verb, *external, neglect, sustain, hollow, quest*). The sentence structure includes passives (*has been placed*), subordination (*which is generally regarded*), long phrases (*with no personal philosophy to sustain us in time of reversal or trouble*). The topic requires abstract thinking. All these features of the text place a high demand on the TT's reading ability.
>
> The passage has been adapted from an authentic text, one someone might read in a monthly magazine. While the authenticity of the passage could not be increased, that of the task could if the TTs were asked to write, speak, or represent the topic.

In the three passages and items above, we have demonstrated reading comprehension tasks at various proficiency levels (one beginner, one intermediate, and one advanced) with three of the most common types of questions: main idea, significant detail, and vocabulary in context. In the passage about Austen's Pride and Prejudice, we also demonstrated an inferencing question. For item types other than multiple-choice, please see Chapter 4.

10.3.3 Lexical Density

This statistic calculates the percentage of content words in a text (the number of content words divided by the number of total words multiplied by 100). Ure (1971) found that the majority of written text is characterized by a relatively high percentage (over 40%) of lexical (or content) words, as compared to grammatical (or function[2]) words. Thus, a higher lexical-density score suggests a text that contains a higher percentage of content words and is more informative and less conversational. Spoken text, in particular the interactive kind, is characterized by the opposite.

The following sentence contains **high lexical density**. Content words are underlined.

Glass Onion, a movie written and directed by Rian Johnson, takes place on a tech-billionaire's private island in Greece.

Rationale: Of the 20 total words, 14 are content words while 6 are function words. The lexical density score is 14/20 = 70%.

The following sentence contains **low lexical density**. Content words are underlined although it is arguable whether the repetitious use of the verb BE should even be counted repeatedly as content words.

There's this movie by Rian Johnson, it's called the Glass Onion, and they're in Greece, they're on the island of this tech-billionaire.

Rationale: Of the total 27 words, 13 are content words while 14 are function words. The lexical density score is 13/27 = 48%. Although this score is above the 40% cut-off calculated by Ure, its

---

2 Words can be subdivided into **content** and **function words**. The former tends to carry the meaning of the utterance (e.g. nouns, verbs, adjectives, and adverbs) while the latter contains grammatical or structural information (e.g. articles, pronouns, prepositions, auxiliary verbs, and conjunctions).

lower score is a true reflection of how much more conversational and less dense it is than the first sentence although they both communicate the same message.

10.3.4 Reading Fluency

> **Reading fluency,** according to the International Literacy Association, can be defined as having three "observable and measurable components: accuracy, rate, and expression (sometimes referred to as prosody)" (2018, p. 2). The desirable outcome of fluent reading is "accurate and deep comprehension and motivation to read" (Hasbrouck and Glaser 2012, p. 13 in ILA p. 2).

The word-per-minute rate of fluent reading, as defined by reading specialists, ranges from 200 to 300 (Zwick 2018). For adult second-language readers, fluency can be defined at "200 words per minute with 70% comprehension" (Anderson 2008, in Zwick 2018, Framing the Issue section, para. 4). Fluent readers can recognize, process, and comprehend printed information automatically. Research on reading fluency has implications for language assessment. First, reading fluency can be assessed directly. Students/TTs can, for instance, read a paragraph of specified length (for example, 100 words) as quickly as they can while maintaining comprehension. Their reading speed can be measured by having the students/TTs stop a timer once they complete the reading. Their comprehension can be measured through a reading comprehension task, such as the ones presented in Section 10.3.2. A second way in which reading fluency has implications for assessment is the amount of time allotted for reading a passage and answering the comprehension questions that follow it. The exact amount of time per item depends on numerous factors, including the length and complexity of the reading passage, the task the TT is to complete, and the age and proficiency of the TT.

10.3.5 Summary of Assessing Reading

Unlike listening comprehension, where the source, the process, and the product are invisible and fleeting, in reading comprehension at least the source—the reading passage—is stable. The process of comprehending itself is invisible, as is the result: comprehension. Therefore, reading can only be assessed indirectly. The assessor observes the student's/TT's behavior and from the result infers the extent to which comprehension has taken place. The assessment of reading comprehension in both formative and summative situations is widespread. The task/item types utilized are quite extensive. Yet the challenge for assessment designers remains to broaden the assessment of the various strategies employed by good readers that are mentioned earlier in the chapter.

Think-Pair-Share 10.3.3a Following the example of the three reading comprehension passages at three levels, design a reading task for three different proficiency levels. You may choose to go beyond multiple-choice when designing the task following the passage. Be sure to consult Chapter 4. Keep the task the same and adjust the level of the task depending on the proficiency it is intended for. Provide a rationale for each. Share with at least two colleagues.

10.4 Vocabulary

"Words are the basic building blocks of language, the units of meaning from which larger structures such as sentences, paragraphs, and whole texts are formed" (Read 2000, p. 1).

10.4.1 Knowing a Word

What does it mean to know a word? Numerous categorizations exist. The one we have found most helpful is **Nation's Components of Word Knowledge** (1990, as cited in Read 2000, p. 26). This classification highlights the multifaceted nature of vocabulary knowledge. Figure 10.5 provides examples of items and tasks assessing the various facets of vocabulary knowledge, based on Nation's categorization.[3] We present it through the example of the content word *"snake,"* a word that might occur in a primary-school science unit.

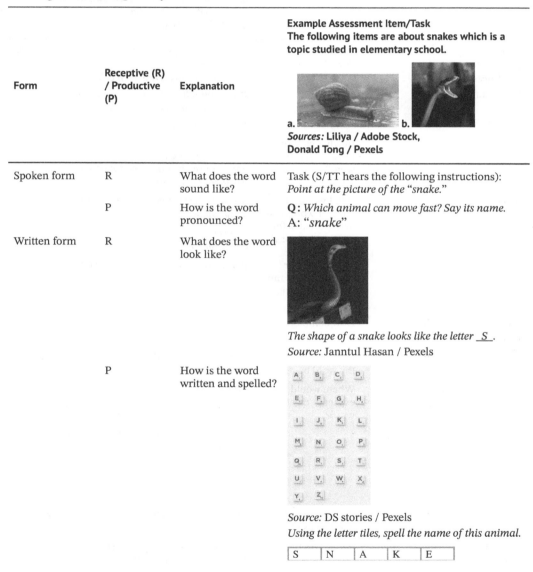

Form	Receptive (R) / Productive (P)	Explanation	Example Assessment Item/Task The following items are about snakes which is a topic studied in elementary school.
Spoken form	R	What does the word sound like?	Task (S/TT hears the following instructions): *Point at the picture of the "snake."*
	P	How is the word pronounced?	**Q:** *Which animal can move fast? Say its name.* A: *"snake"*
Written form	R	What does the word look like?	*The shape of a snake looks like the letter _S_.* *Source:* Janntul Hasan / Pexels
	P	How is the word written and spelled?	*Using the letter tiles, spell the name of this animal.* S N A K E *Source:* DS stories / Pexels

Figure 10.5 Examples and items based on Nation's Components of Word Knowledge: Snake.

(Continued)

---

3 The first three columns of the table are nearly identical to Nation's Components of Word Knowledge (1990), p. 31. We have added the fourth column to demonstrate each component in concrete terms.

Form	Receptive (R) / Productive (P)	Explanation	Example Assessment Item/Task The following items are about snakes which is a topic studied in elementary school.
			a. b. *Sources:* **Liliya / Adobe Stock, Donald Tong / Pexels**
Position: Formulaic sequences: a. Grammatical	R	In what patterns does the word occur?	*In the following sentence, what part of speech is the word snakes?* "*Venomous snakes are often colorful.*" *It is a noun. It is the subject of the sentence.* *Is it a count or non-count noun?* *It is a count noun.*
	P	In what patterns must we use the word?	*In 3–5 sentences, compare snakes and snails based on what we have learned. Describe their appearance, their diet, their movement, and whether they are dangerous.*
b. Lexical	R	What words or types of words can be expected before or after the word?	*Select the two words that can describe snakes.* a. *poisonous** b. *toxic* c. *venomous**
	P	What words or types of words must we use with this word?	*If a snake's bite is dangerous, then the snake is* <u>*venomous*</u>.
Function: Frequency	R	How common is the word?	*snake occurs 19.7/million times in COCA*
	P	How often should the word be used?	(When describing the animal, it can be used as often as necessary.)
Appropriateness	R	Where would we expect to meet this word?	*True or False?* 1. *Using the word snake for a person is appropriate.* 2. *Using the word snake for the animal is appropriate.* 1. *False* 2. *True*
	P	Where can this word be used?	(When describing the animal, it can be used in any context.)
Meaning: Concept	R	What does the word mean?	*According to the Merriam-Webster Dictionary, snakes are "limbless scaled reptiles."*
	P	What word should be used to express this meaning?	**Q:** *Which animal am I describing? It is a limbless, scaled reptile.* **A:** *snake*

Figure 10.5 (Cont'd)

Form	Receptive (R) / Productive (P)	Explanation	**Example Assessment Item/Task** **The following items are about snakes which is a topic studied in elementary school.**
			a. b. *Sources:* **Liliya / Adobe Stock, Donald Tong / Pexels**
Associations	R	What other words does this word make us think of?	plumbing Adam & Eve traitor snake serpent Harry Potter
	P	What other words could we use instead of this one?	*Based on what we have read, name at least four types of snakes: pythons, boas, vipers, cobras.*

Figure 10.5 (Cont'd)

10.4.2 Assessing Vocabulary

The CEFR Companion Volume (2018) assesses vocabulary **range** and **control**. Vocabulary range is defined as breadth and variety while control is defined as the selection of the appropriate words. Regarding the balance between the two, the authors of the CEFR caution that, as learners experiment with more complex linguistic forms and expand their range, their control over them naturally declines. "Learners will tend to have less control over more difficult, more recently learnt morphology and syntax than when they stay within their linguistic comfort zone and this needs to be taken into consideration when viewing (lack of) accuracy" (p. 131).

As learners' proficiency increases, they express themselves more idiomatically through **formulaic language or formulaic sequences**. In Chapter 5 we introduced formulaic language, or sequences as "a sequence, continuous or discontinuous, of words or other elements, which is, or appears to be, prefabricated: that is, stored and retrieved whole from memory at the time of use, rather than being subject to generation or analysis by the language grammar" (Wray 2002, p. 9). Because they are stored and retrieved from the brain as one unit, they aid receptive and productive fluency. They also contribute to idiomatic language use.

Formulaic sequences can be **contiguous** or **non-contiguous, lexical** or **grammatical** in nature. Examples include *a venomous snake and a poisonous snake*—the words "venomous" and "poisonous" tend to co-occur with the word "snake." However, "toxic," which has a synonymous meaning to "venomous" and "poisonous" is not used to describe a snake. Thus, the former adjective phrases are formulaic sequences but the latter is not.

These formulaic sequences are **lexical** (because the words have connections to each other) and **contiguous** (words directly next to each other).

(Continued)

> *(Continued)*
>
> Conversely, *I am looking forward to (gerund, noun, pronoun, noun phrase, etc.)* is a **grammatical** formulaic sequence. The expression typically co-occurs with the words *seeing* and *meeting* but, more importantly, it is followed by a grammatical category that can act as a noun, such as a gerund, regardless of the actual word because *to* is a preposition rather than the infinitive particle.
>
> An example of a **non-contiguous** formulaic sequence is *the man who...is a friend of mine* (grammatical), *on (the) one hand...on the other hand* (lexical), and *as many...as possible* (lexical).

Think-Pair-Share 10.4.2a   **Corpora** Look through Chapters 4 and 5 for information about COCA and other corpora. Recall how calculating word frequencies can help improve item writing. Recall how to conduct a collocate search and how this can be helpful in writing vocabulary items.

A. Dimensions of Vocabulary Assessment

Another helpful categorization of vocabulary assessment is presented by Read (2000). Read's three pairs of categories include *discrete/embedded, selective/comprehensive,* and *context-independent/ context-dependent*.

1. discrete vs. embedded (vocabulary knowledge or use being the sole independent construct that is assessed vs. vocabulary being just one evaluation criterion as part of a larger construct)
2. selective vs. comprehensive (specific vocabulary items as the focus vs. all the vocabulary in the stimulus material or students' spoken or written response)
3. context-independent vs. context-dependent (learners' response does not rely on context vs. need for contextual information)

In previous chapters, we have demonstrated 1. and 2. extensively (see Figure 4.1 for a discrete item, see Figure 4.9 for vocabulary embedded in a rating scale of writing, see the word lists in Chapter 10 as examples of selective measures of vocabulary to be tested, and see Figure 4.10 for a rubric that assesses the student's or TT's vocabulary comprehensively). The third pair of dimensions, however, deserves further exemplification. A context-independent item is keyable because the distractors are wrong under any circumstances, as in the item below.

When playing hide and seek, the boy hid behind the tree _____.

  a. *trunk**
  b. *wood*
  c. *plant*
  d. *bush*

Rationale: Regardless of the context, only "tree trunk" is a possible word combination. The other word combinations, while related to trees, do not exist.

Now consider the following item.
What does the underlined word mean in this sentence?
Is there enough room in the <u>trunk</u> for three large suitcases and the golf bags?

  a. *the main part of the tree*
  b. *an old-fashioned travel box*

c. *the storage area of a car**

d. *an elephant's nose*

Rationale: The word "trunk" has multiple meanings. The correct meaning depends on the context within the sentence. Because the sentence mentions room for three large suitcases and the golf bags, the closest meaning is the storage area of a car or *boot* in British English.

B. Word Lists

Word lists are useful for teaching, learning, and assessment. Two commonly used lists are:

1. Tier 1, 2, and 3 vocabulary lists for schools:
   - Tier 1: high-frequency words used for daily communication
   - Tier 2: academic words encountered across multiple classes
   - Tier 3: low-frequency subject-specific words. For an example, see the list from Wagner High School (n.d.)
2. The Academic Word List (AWL) (Coxhead 2000) contains 570 word families beyond the most frequent 2000 words. It prepares students for university study. For ready-made AWL games, quizzes, and crossword puzzles, see RMIT University's AWL resources (n.d.).

C. Vocabulary Size Tests

These tests estimate the number of words in a learner's mental lexicon. The assessment of vocabulary size has been an elusive quest for decades. Read (2000) discusses studies that estimate the vocabulary size of US university students to range from 15 000 to 200 000 (Anderson and Freebody 1981, p. 96). This wide discrepancy is mainly due to differing definitions of what constitutes a word. Is each form of a word counted separately or are word families counted as one because each inflected and derived form of the word within a family can be reached with word-formation rules? For example, should the following list of words be counted as 1 (word family) or 15 (individual word forms) or something in between?[4]

> intent, intent's, intents, intend, intends, intended, intending, intention, intention's, intentions, intentional, intentionally, unintended, unintentional, unintentionally

---

4 The example demonstrates how a word can consist of a base form and its inflectional and/or derivational forms. **Inflectional morphemes** do not change the part of speech of the word and in the mental lexicon are considered the same word (ex. *play, plays, playing, played*). They include

- the plural -s of nouns (table+s)
- the third-person singular -s of Simple Present verbs (she play+s)
- possessive -s of nouns (the dog's tail)
- the past-tense -ed (played)
- the present participle -ing (playing)
- the past participle -ed/-en (play+ed, eat+en)
- suffix of comparative adjectives (calm+er)
- suffix of superlative adjectives (calm+est)

Derivational morphemes, on the other hand, usually change the part of speech and create new words in our mental lexicon (Denham and Loebeck, 2012). They include

- suffixes: -able, -ity, -ment, -ness, -ize, -ly
- prefixes: un-, dis-, semi-, ex-, anti-, in-, de-
- word families

Did you know?   A lesser-known method for measuring vocabulary size includes the self-assessment checklist. In one checklist designed by researchers Anderson and Freebody (1983, cited by Read 2000, p. 88), in the list of words to be assessed, the researchers included approximately 40% of nonsense words. These words were either slightly misspelled versions of real words (such as *porfame* from *perfume*) or pseudowords, which are nonexistent combinations of parts of existing words (such as *observement*). To correct for potential overestimation of vocabulary size by TTs, Anderson and Freebody applied a correction formula. If the TTs indicated knowledge of nonsense words, the researchers adjusted for them using the formula. The corrected results were more consistent with in-depth interview findings about some of these words than with the multiple-choice measurement.

Think-Pair-Share 10.4.2b   **Measuring vocabulary size**

   a. Critique the Anderson-Freebody assessment described in the Did you know? above. What is your opinion about a "bad speller" checking off misspelled words such as *porfame* as ones they recognize and as a result their score being adjusted down? Discuss.
   b. Investigate measures of vocabulary size. Select one that can be used in a teaching/assessment context you are familiar with. Discuss the strengths and weaknesses of this measurement.

D. What Are We Really Assessing?

Knowledge of vocabulary is closely intertwined with reading comprehension and conceptual understanding, and is essential for literacy and content proficiency, argued Anderson and Freebody (1985). Read (2000), in his seminal book on vocabulary assessment, reports on studies attempting to show the construct validity of vocabulary studies. Researchers have failed to show that vocabulary is a trait that is something separate from other aspects of reading. Instead, what studies did show is that test items of the same type (for instance, multiple-choice vs. blank fill) have more in common with each other than items of the same skill (for instance, vocabulary vs. grammar). As Read states while describing a construct-validation study by Corrigan and Upshur, "Vocabulary did not emerge from their test results as a distinct trait, because the type of item used had a greater influence on the learners' performance than whether it was a vocabulary test or not" (p. 97).

   Thus, on the question whether vocabulary should be assessed in isolation or in context, Read (2000) concludes that even if individual words are assessed in isolation, it is doubtful that vocabulary is actually being assessed distinctly from other aspects of linguistic knowledge. On the other hand, research into cloze tests suggests that "the more we contextualise the assessment of vocabulary, the less clear it may be to what extent it is vocabulary knowledge that is influencing the test-takers' performance" (p. 116). No single vocabulary test can measure all the purposes of knowledge (i.e. depth, breadth, Nation's components of word knowledge, see Figure 10.5).

Think-Pair-Share 10.4.2c

   a. Peruse Chapter 4 for item types that lend themselves to assessing vocabulary. Select two or three and analyze what other constructs (in addition to vocabulary knowledge) they may assess in light of the discussion above.
   b. Examine Figure 10.5 based on Nation's Components of Word Knowledge and the items designed to assess each component in it. Select two or three and analyze what other constructs (in addition to vocabulary knowledge) they may assess in light of the discussion above.

Think-Pair-Share 10.4.2d   Make a case for assessing vocabulary in isolation and/or in context. Support your view with information from this chapter.

E. Other Item Types That Are Commonly Designed to Assess Vocabulary

Chapter 4 presents dozens of item types that can be used to assess vocabulary both in isolation and in context. Below we present three additional item types.

1. *Fill in the blank with the first letter supplied*: It can be used on an achievement assessment to trigger the students' memory of which of the studied words is being elicited by the sentence. For example, after the students have been studying the northern lights, they complete the following sentence.
   The northern lights happen when energized p_____ from the sun meet the Earth's m_____ field. (particles, magnetic) (Waldek and Dobrijevic 2024)

2. *Sentence-writing task*: Students/TTs are provided with words and are directed to use them in sentences that clearly demonstrate their meaning. For example, after studying the northern lights, the directions are as follows.
   Write a sentence with each one of the words below. Show that you know each word's meaning. Do not change the word form or part of speech.
   particles   _____
   magnetic   _____

3. *Sentence completion* is a task that can be employed to assess various constructs; here it demonstrates how to assess vocabulary depth along with formulaic language.
   a. *If your goal is definitely not to do something, then you have no inten_____ to do it.*
   b. *Did you do it accidentally or inten_____?*
   c. *The company apologized for the uninten_____ consequences of its actions.*

4. *Word associations* intend to measure vocabulary richness. The following item demonstrates the three types of relationships between the headword (here *conduct*) and the options (following the headword), as categorized by Read (2000). The types of relationships are (1) synonyms, (2) collocates, and (3) definitions.[5]

   conduct

baggage	behavior	control	described	disorderly	ethical
equipment	handling	manner	rough	transport	trouble

The words that are associated with the headword "conduct" (with their category in parentheses) are: control (1), transport (1), handling (1), disorderly (2), ethical (2), behavior (3), manner (3). The remaining words are not associated with the headword.

10.4.3 Summary of Assessing Vocabulary

In this section of the chapter on assessing literacy, we have introduced a definition of vocabulary, provided examples for each of Nation's Components of Word Knowledge (1990), presented the CEFR's approach to assessing vocabulary range and control, categorized and exemplified formulaic sequences, demonstrated Read's (2000) dimensions of vocabulary assessment, introduced common word lists and vocabulary size tests, and raised the question what we are really assessing when we claim to be assessing vocabulary. Given the inextricability of vocabulary from other constructs in research studies, our intention in devoting a separate section to it is more to underscore its importance in language acquisition than to urge the reader to assess it in isolation.

---

5 John Read calls the three types *paradigmatic, syntagmatic,* and *analytic,* respectively (2000, p. 181).

10.5   Grammar

Think-Pair-Share 10.5a   Schema activation: Grammar   What is grammar? How would you define it?

Think-Pair-Share 10.5b   Schema activation: Assessing Grammar

a. Look through Chapter 4 and make a list of all item types that can be used to assess grammar.
b. Given your definition of grammar above, what is your experience (as a student or teacher of languages) with assessing all of grammar's dimensions?

10.5.1   Defining Grammar

"Grammar is a meaning-making resource. It is made up of lexicogrammatical form, meaning, and use constructions that are appropriate to the context and that operate at the word, phrase, sentence, and textual levels" (Larsen-Freeman and Celce-Murcia 2016, p. 2).

In the aforementioned definition, **form** refers to accuracy, or how the grammatical structure is formed; **meaning** refers to meaningfulness, or what the grammatical structure means; and **use** refers to appropriateness, or when or why the form is used. Although these categories at times overlap, keeping these dimensions in mind allows us to consider the assessment (as well as teaching and learning) of grammar more broadly than would we if we focused simply on form.

Think-Pair-Share 10.5.1 Application   Below we present three items on the same target element: "hang on," which can be a figurative phrasal verb or a literal single-word verb and a preposition. See how each item taps into the form, meaning, or use of the target grammatical structure. Do you agree with the rationale we provide after each item? Why or why not?

Form-focused grammar item

I'll be ready in 5 minutes; just hang_____!
it on
on it
on*

This item assesses the form of the phrasal verb "hang on." One question is whether the phrasal verb is transitive or intransitive (this one is intransitive) and separable or inseparable (this one is inseparable). In other words, the accurate form of this phrasal verb is just the main verb and its particle, without a direct object or another preposition.

Meaning-focused grammar

What is a good synonym for the underlined words?
How many pictures would you like to <u>hang on</u> the wall?
wait for
put on*
hold on to

The item is meaning-focused because "hang on" can have both figurative and literal meanings. In the stem, the literal meaning is assessed. However, one could also assess the meaning of the phrasal verb.

Use-focused grammar item

Your Honor, I would ask most respectfully, that you _____.
hang on
hold on
*wait**

This item assesses the pragmatic appropriateness, or use, of the phrasal verb. In general, phrasal verbs are used in informal situations while the single-word verbs that share their meaning are used in formal situations. The courtroom is a very formal setting, in which the phrasal verb would be inappropriate.

10.5.2 The Alignment of Teaching and Assessment Practices

Few would disagree that the main purpose of language use is communication. Many teachers even profess to be using the method of communicative language teaching. In terms of assessment though, most grammar, even in a communicative classroom, is assessed syntactically. If gaining information about the students'/TTs' grammatical performance in communicative situations is a goal, then selected-response assessment should be sidelined in favor of constructed response. Constructed response needs to be assessed with an analytic rating scale (rather than a holistic one) to be able to highlight grammar as an evaluation criterion. Otherwise, we fail to get a clear picture how the single holistic score came about and to what extent it was influenced by grammar.

The CEFR Companion Volume (Council of Europe 2018) assesses the criteria of **grammatical accuracy, general linguistic range** (aka morpho-syntactic range), **sociolinguistic competence**, and **pragmatic use** in separate rating scales. **Accuracy** encompasses the use of formulaic sequences and "the capacity to focus on grammatical forms whilst articulating thought" (p. 133). **Range** entails the amount of language the learner can exploit to formulate thoughts clearly, appropriately, and flexibly. As learners attempt linguistically more demanding tasks, more of their mental processing capacity is being used, and less is available to attend to accuracy. "[R]esearch in English, French and German suggests that inaccuracy increases at around B1 as the learner is beginning to use language more independently and creatively" (p. 133). **Sociolinguistic** competence means that the learner can use the language appropriately in social situations (politeness, register, style). Finally, **pragmatic** use pertains to actual language use in terms of development, coherence, cohesion, turn-taking, flexibility, speaker meaning, or propositional precision.

To illustrate the alignment between communicative teaching and assessment, we present a rating scale where within a writing task grammar is assessed (see Figure 10.6). Before use, the descriptors for the remaining evaluation criteria would be filled in.

Examining the two approaches to grammar presented so far, it becomes clear that both define grammar beyond the traditional accuracy of forms. Something else strikes the reader, however: that the different skills and subskills are intertwined. It is almost impossible to discuss grammar without discussing vocabulary, writing, speaking, representing, reading, and listening. Yet, defining grammar is essential, for it influences how the grammatical construct is assessed. Below we suggest ways to assess form, meaning, and use.[6]

Did you know? Building on Larsen-Freeman's (1997) "form, meaning, and use" model of grammatical knowledge, "Purpura (2004, p. 91) conceptualized the components of grammatical and

---

6 The rubric has not been validated. It has been designed to demonstrate a point and should not be used as is.

	Approaches Target	Meets Target	Exceeds Target
Task Accomplishment			
Organization, Coherence, Cohesion			
Grammar Form, Meaning, Use	*limited range of structures present *inaccuracies present in simple structures *meaning at times unclear	*both more and less frequent structures present *frequent structures mostly under control *meaning at time may be imprecise but not unclear	*more and less frequent structures present and used with reasonable accuracy *meaning is clear and precise *selection of structures is often appropriate for the context and register
Vocabulary, Formulaic Language			
Mechanics			

Figure 10.6 A sample analytic rubric[7] to assess grammar in context.

pragmatic knowledge to synthesize the three aspects to two: grammatical (form and meaning) and pragmatic (use) knowledge." He identified grammar points that could be used for assessment at the sentential and discourse levels, across various linguistics systems (e.g. phonological, graphological, lexical, morphosyntactic, sociolinguistic, sociocultural, etc.).

Based on McTighe and Ferrara (1998), we present the following chart for assessing grammar through various item and task types (see Figure 10.7). Most of the assessment types in this chart have been introduced elsewhere in this volume. Following the chart, we discuss one of the lesser-known task types in greater detail.

The **product-approach** and the **process-approach** to teaching are analogous to the **product-focused assessment** and the **process-focused assessment**. In the former, it is the product of learning or assessment that takes center stage. For instance, when writing an essay, typically what counts is each interim draft and ultimately the final product. In process-focused teaching and assessment, however, how students reach the end product is equally important. Each draft is accompanied by a reflective checklist of target areas that the whole class and/or the individual student is working on. For instance, in an essay about what students did on the weekend, one student may wish to narrate the events of the weekend by managing the Simple Past and the Past Progressive verb tenses. The student then demonstrates how they ensured that they used the appropriate verb forms to tell the past-tense story. Thus, how the student reached the goal of writing the paper is at least as important as the fact that they did so.

The **think-aloud** protocol is an excellent example of process-focused assessment. It has been described as "eavesdropping on someone's thinking" (Reading Rockets 2024, para 1.). It is not only an effective teaching strategy, whereby the teachers narrate out loud their thinking process about solving a problem or writing an introduction, but it is also an effective assessment technique when students do the same. For instance, as the above student is writing the narrative essay on last weekend's events, they say their words out loud while writing them. When they reach a decision point,

---

7 For an in-depth discussion of defining grammar, we recommend Purpura's monograph *Assessing Grammar* (2004).

Selected-Response (SR) Format	Constructed-Response (CR) Format			
	brief CR	extended CR / performance-based		
		product-focused	performance-focused	process-focused
multiple-choice	fill-in-the blank/gap fill	essay	oral presentation about - research topic - art exhibit - science project - collage, model	interview
true/ false/ not stated	short answer	research paper	science lab demonstration	conference
matching	labeling without a word bank	story/play	debate	process description
odd word out	mind web	poem	teaching demonstration	process portfolio
find the error	concept map	product portfolio	role play	learning log
dialogic item	flow chart	video/audio recording		reflective journal
pictures as options	graph/ table	spreadsheet		think-aloud
select cloze	illustration	lab report		dictogloss
labeling with a word bank	supply cloze	dialog journals		noticing
sequencing		information gap		oral questioning
unscrambling				writing with mentor text

Figure 10.7 Assessing grammar through item and task types, based on a framework by McTighe and Ferrara (1998).

about a word or a verb tense, they may backtrack, correct themselves, slow down, recall a rule that applies, and eventually write what they have settled on. Hearing this thinking process aloud is informative for both the student engaging in the think-aloud and the teacher or fellow students who are listening to it. For a demonstration of the technique, we recommend a video by Citizens Academy (CitizensAcademyCleve 2011).

"**Dictogloss** is a type of supported dictation" (The Bell Foundation 2024, What is Dictogloss section), where the teacher reads the story multiple times without pausing for writing. In dictogloss, students focus on both meaning and language, improving linguistic analysis, meaning focus, and strategic notetaking. For example, watch the following video on Dictogloss—Present Perfect Simple (Learn English with KT 2017). **Dictocomp** is similar to dictogloss but students reconstruct the text from memory, without taking notes, after the teacher reads it several times. Both techniques lend themselves to assessment when learners compare their answers for accuracy. Errors—such as missing, misheard, or substituted words—can be indicative of the learners' interlanguage. For continuous improvement, learners can regularly self- or peer-assess their dictation and reflect on their performance in a journal.

Writing with Mentor Text is a technique that teachers of young writers use to demonstrate how good writing and reading go together. Mentor texts help students observe and understand authors' techniques (called crafts), such as writing style, structure, sentence formation, tone, voice, and vocabulary choice.

1. Noticing the craft: where have they seen it before?
2. Thinking about the craft.
3. Considering why the author made that craft choice and what effect they were trying to have on their reader.
4. Applying what they learned to their own writing: how can they use the craft themselves?
5. Trying it out.

This is a great example of teaching young learners and assessing their ability to look more at the process over the product. During a writing assessment, students might analyze one or more mentor texts to see how an author created a specific effect on the reader. For example, if students are writing a narrative essay, they might identify how the author starts the story, builds suspense, uses dialogue, and treats the passage of time. Students can use these observations to help shape their own writing decisions on their writing assessment.

Ellis draws our attention to the benefits of **noticing tasks** for language acquisition (1997, in Purpura 2014). Attention to the form facilitates the acquisition of the target element. Students indicate their noticing by identifying (such as circling, underlining, clicking, dragging, highlighting, or otherwise manipulating) all examples of a specific form in a text. This learning task is also an assessment task. The learners can then check their answers with an answer key or a peer. To enhance the process-focus in this task, learners can then be asked to write or talk about the process of noticing and thereby raise their consciousness of the process.

The final process-focused assessment technique we will highlight is **oral questioning**. Here the teacher calls on the learner to justify choices they have made in the creation of an assignment, such as the essay narrating a weekend's activities. The teacher may ask why the student used a particular word or grammar or why they gave the story a particular title. The teacher can direct the questions on any aspect of the creative or thinking process that is desired.

10.5.3 Summary of Assessing Grammar

Grammar assessment is a staple of language tests, be they classroom or large-scale, formal or informal. Often, however, grammar assessment is narrowly focused on the accuracy of form and multiple-choice items. In this section, we tried to expand the realm of possibility to other dimensions (meaning and use) as well as numerous item types beyond multiple-choice. We also argued that in a communicative language classroom, the teaching and assessment practices can and should be aligned.

10.6 Writing

Think-Pair-Share 10.6a   Schema Activation

a. How old were you when you learned to write? Was it considered early, average, late?
b. Think about all the ways in which you write during the day. Has this changed in the last 15+ years at all?
c. For what kind of writing do today's children need to be prepared?

Think-Pair-Share 10.6b Review

Recall what you learned about the assessment of writing in previous chapters, in particular in Chapter 4. Discuss.

Within the **multiliteracies** framework, students actively generate knowledge through digital projects. Using a multimodal approach, they not only communicate through traditional writing but also visually by incorporating various multimedia elements into their digital artifacts. When assessing such projects, the rating scale should include evaluation criteria for each of the design elements mentioned earlier in the chapter. For instance, if the project is to create a multimedia welcome packet for recent arrivals to your neighborhood or school, the evaluation criteria (based on the project description) will include traditional linguistic elements (vocabulary, grammar, fluency, pronunciation, coherence, delivery, etc.) and may also include multiliteracies design elements like audio (music, sound effects), visual (colors, perspective, foregrounding), and gestural (gestures, feelings, proxemics). (For more information on how the affordances of new technology can be incorporated into learning objectives and assessment rating scales, see Chapter 13.)

10.6.1 Considerations for Assessing Writing

Think-Pair-Share 10.6c Review

a. In Chapter 2, the term "construct" is introduced. Review what it means.
b. In Chapter 4, following Think-Pair-Share 4.2a, two example construct definitions of "composition" are given. What implications do differences in construct definitions have for assessing the writing of two different groups of students that you are familiar with?

The criteria for evaluating writing depend on the construct definition. This means that the number and nature of writing tasks should match the information needed about the students/TTs. To assess students'/TTs' overall writing ability, a variety of writing tasks is necessary. The British Council (2016) cautions against assigning too few or too many assignments to assess overall writing ability. A single writing assignment may not provide enough information to judge the students'/TTs' writing proficiency. Assigning multiple pieces of writing within the same genre could limit the scope of the assessment to a narrow aspect of the students'/TTs' writing abilities. On the other hand, overwhelming students/TTs with too many assignments can take excessive time and cause fatigue. Therefore, programs should follow the Goldilocks principle: not too few, not too many, but just right.

Think-Pair-Share 10.6d Review   In our discussion about test design (see Chapter 3), we highlight the importance of understanding the students/TTs (who they are, how old they are, for what purposes their language proficiency needs to be assessed, what type of language they need to produce, etc.). Review what information the teacher/examiner needs to have to make sound assessment decisions. What implications does this have for the assessment of writing?

Think-Pair-Share 10.6e Application   What authentic writing tasks could you assign in your classroom if you were teaching the following three groups of learners?

a. Young learners,
b. College/university language learners,
c. Adult learners in your community.

In concrete terms, a 12-year-old young learner who would like to demonstrate that they can write at the A2 level in the target language may be presented with the following writing task.

> *Some teachers give their students homework every day. Other teachers do not believe that homework is helpful and they do not give homework. What is your opinion about homework for students? Is it a good idea? Give reasons and examples.*

Note that the above prompt contains simple and compound sentences with high-frequency vocabulary. Instead of "homework is beneficial," the prompt contains "homework is helpful." And instead of "assign homework," the prompt uses the less advanced "give homework" construction.

A 12-year-old is unlikely to have knowledge about the world of work (occupational domain) or public debates about social phenomena (public domain). However, they are likely to know about school and homework (educational domain) as well as home and personal life (personal domain). The type of writing a 12-year-old is likely to engage with successfully will ask for an opinion, description, narrative, personal preference, reasons, and examples. On the other hand, it is unlikely that a student of this age could produce definition, argumentation, persuasion, process description, and cause and effect analysis extemporaneously, on in-class writing, without prior study. It should not be assumed that just because a learner successfully writes a personal narrative or opinion piece that they can also produce a different type of writing, in a different domain.

Writing tasks need to keep up with the times. They need to be relevant to the lives of the TTs/students and be as meaningful and authentic as possible. Authenticity depends on the situation. Composing a job application letter may be authentic for students who are seeking a job, but it may not be suitable for those who, due to their age, circumstances, and personal goals, are not on the job market. The ideal authentic writing assessment requires the TT to write the same kind of task as they would be required to do outside of the assessment situation. The task should be related to the assessment use, in other words to the decisions that stakeholders would like to make about the TT's writing ability. Writing is often the mode of production in authentic or content-, task-, or performance-based assessment. In other words, the main goal is not necessarily to assess writing but to assess *through* writing.

Did you know? The IELTS Academic test has TTs describe visual information, such as a graph, table, chart, or diagram. They have 20 minutes to write at least 150 words in complete sentences. TTs are assessed on their ability to: "give a well-organised overview of the visual information using language that is appropriate in its register and style...organise, present and possibly compare data, describe stages of a process or procedure, describe an object, event or sequence of events, explain how something works." https://www.cambridgeenglish.org/exams-and-tests/ielts/test-format/ (Academic Writing Task 1).

10.6.2 Assessing the Writing of LESLLA and SLIFE Students

LESLLA stands for Literacy Education and Second Language Learning for Adults. These learners with emergent literacy are 15 years or older and "are learning to read and write for the first time in their lives in a new language" (LESLLA n.d., Vision section, para. 1). These learners of a second language have had limited or interrupted formal education in their first language.

A related term is **SLIFE**, which stands for Students with Limited or Interrupted Formal Education. These students—who might be refugees, migrants—received limited schooling in their native country, "have limited backgrounds in reading and writing in their native language(s) and are below grade level in most academic skills" (WIDA 2015, Who Are Students with Limited or Interrupted Formal Education? section, para. 1).

10.6.3   LESLLA Learner Profile

At the age of 16, Berezira was resettled from Afghanistan to the United States with her family. Not having had any formal education, she has been enrolled in the local high school as a newcomer freshman.[8] Berezira has been acclimating not only to her new country, city, home, and school culture but also to the concept of schooling. Four months into school the EL teachers noticed that Berezira's attendance was becoming very irregular. A Pashto-speaking interpreter was hired for a family meeting where the attendance expectations in the United States and in the state were explained. Berezira and her parents also had the opportunity to share their feelings and thoughts on school and ask questions. The family was unaware of the attendance laws and agreed that Berezira would be in school. She has not missed a day since. The parents also shared they were very thankful for all the support their daughter was receiving. When at school, Berezira is learning to hold a pencil, turn on a computer, and locate Afghanistan and the United States on a map. She is learning to form letters in English, can already write her name, and knows several numbers. She is enrolled in sheltered English, Art, Media Studies, and Algebra I. While in her co-taught math class, she learns using the platform ST Math. Her ESL teacher summarizes the lesson contents for her, uses an automatic translator to render the text in Pashto, then has text-to-speech software read the text out loud in Pashto. This is how Berezira learns the content of the lessons. Concurrently, she learns English from the beginning with a one-on-one tutor through the GrapeSEED program (2024). The assessment of her writing focuses on the fundamentals: letters, script, key words. In class, she reads brief stories, such as ones about the current season. To demonstrate reading comprehension, she orders pictures that depict the story. Next, she writes a summary using a sentence stem like, "In the spring, I see _____." It will be a long road to full literacy for Berezira, but she is exhibiting remarkable positivity, curiosity, and grit, which bode well for her ultimate success.

Think-Pair-Share 10.6f Review   In Chapter 1, we introduce the terms "direct" and "indirect" assessment. Review what they mean and what implications this concept has for assessing writing.

10.6.4   Direct vs. Indirect Assessment

Assessment of writing should be direct for all learners. In other words, writing should be assessed by asking the student/TT to write something. The writing tasks, however, should be tailored to the student's/TT's qualities and the decision to be made about them.

---

8 In the United States, first-year students in high school (also called ninth grade) are referred to as *freshmen*. They are usually 14 years old and have completed 9 years of formal education, from Kindergarten to eighth grade.

A. Prompt Language

It is important that prompts not contain idiomatic cultural language that might be unclear to L2 learners (e.g. "tell about a time" being interpreted as talking about the clock). Pilot-testing prompts, even higher-stakes classroom prompts, can reduce the likelihood of students being assessed with problematic wording.

B. Prompt Options

The question whether writers should be given prompt options is a complex one. On the one hand, studies show that students/TTs prefer to have prompt options (Polio and Glew 1996), and they tend to select prompts on topics they are more familiar with (Weigle et al. 2000). This may reduce the effect of task-, topic-familiarity, and anxiety. On the other hand, students/TTs do not always make the best decision for themselves. In our experience, sometimes their enthusiasm for or against a topic may result in responses that are not explained clearly. Another concern is that topics may not be of equal difficulty and may elicit unequal responses. Thus, as Weigle urges, care needs to be taken to ensure that prompts place equal "cognitive demands [and] complexity of instructions" on the students/TTs (2002, p. 104).

C. Resources During In-class Writing

Assessment designers also need to consider what kind of help writers should be allowed access to before or during writing. Help may include dictionaries (monolingual, bilingual, paper, electronic, collocation, synonym-antonym; and student-generated ones), word banks, word walls, notes taken earlier, electronic translators, discussion about the topic (whole class, in pairs/groups, in the L1, in the L2), etc. These decisions should be taken after careful consideration of the test blueprint and in particular of the construct being assessed.

10.6.5 Plagiarism vs. Fair Source Use

It is not uncommon for instructors of writing or content areas to accuse language learners of academic dishonesty, or **plagiarism**, in other words of using someone else's ideas or words without proper attribution. The consequences can range from grade penalty through failing the course to expulsion from the institution. Examples of select responses from universities in the United Kingdom can be read in George (2021).

Although some writers may plagiarize intentionally, a large number of them do so because they may

- not be aware of the concept of plagiarism
- come from cultures where reciting the words of great thinkers verbatim is a sign of a good education
- be unaware of what precisely constitutes plagiarism
- not fully understand the source material and thus be unable to capture its meaning in their own words
- lack the linguistic resources to paraphrase or summarize
- not have learned expected citation techniques, etc.

Tomaš and Shapiro (2021) raise awareness about the complexity of the topic. They provide "rhetorical framing and pedagogical strategies that can guide [...] conversations with colleagues, in addition to informing [...] teaching practice" (p. 1104). Mott-Smith, Tomaš, and Kostka (2017) describe how intentional course design, teaching effective source use, and training students to provide peer feedback, among other strategies, can prevent problematic *textual reuse* in the first place.

Think-Pair-Share 10.6g Reflect on your experiences as a teacher, student, or assessor. Have you ever encountered academic dishonesty or plagiarism as defined above? What were the consequences? Would this incident have been considered academic dishonesty in another setting? In light of the authors cited above, how could the incident have been handled in a culturally sensitive manner?

10.6.6 Time Allotment for a Writing Task

How much time to allot for writing? Considerations in this decision include

- how old are the students/TTs
- how proficient are the students/TTs
- how many pieces of writing are the students/TTs to produce
- are the pieces of writing supposed to be polished final drafts or rough first drafts
- how long is the expected writing supposed to be
- how complex or involved is the writing task

Offering a precise recommendation for the optimal time allotment for in-class writing proves challenging. Regardless, it is recommended that the entire assessment (including the time limit) be pilot-tested prior to the initial administration. For classroom assessments, at the very least, a suggested approach involves instructors personally completing the test. Then, depending on the circumstances, the instructor should allocate double or even triple the amount of time it took them to produce the writing; it is this extended duration that students should be allotted for their own writing tasks.

10.6.7 High-Stakes Writing Characteristics

Hamp-Lyons (1991) includes the following characteristics of high-stakes writing tasks:

- TTs must write at least one "piece of continuous text of 100 words or longer" (p. 5) within a time limit.
- TTs address an unknown prompt.
- Evaluation takes place by trained judges using rating scales.
- Judgments are quantified (not just expressed in verbal descriptions).
- Test scores can be reviewed by a supervising authority, as desired.

10.6.8 Considerations

Considerations in the rating process are crucial for any constructed-response assessment. Well-established rating procedures are essential to avoid potential issues. For one, Weigle (2002) warns that various construct-irrelevant factors, such as handwriting versus word processing, raters' knowledge about the students/TTs, rater familiarity with the students' native language or culture, raters' native language, the presence of other raters, time of day of the rating session, etc. may influence scores.

Further insights from a study by Linnarud (1986) emphasize the importance of understanding which evaluation criteria raters prioritize: results have shown that raters attend to grammatical errors more than to vocabulary errors while Read (2000) has found that the role of lexical ability in writing remains inconclusive.

In integrated-skills assessments, where reading and writing are intertwined, clarity is paramount. The construct, rating scale, and raters must explicitly define whether the assessment aims to evaluate reading, writing, or both.

Standardizing the rating process and training raters thoroughly are essential in the assessment of productive, or expressive language skills. These guidelines should also be incorporated into the test blueprint for effective implementation.

10.6.9 Summary of Assessing Writing

In this section, we examined various aspects of what it means to write and determined that, unlike speech, writing does not emerge by itself. We named the most common fiction and non-fiction genres in school settings. We introduced the terms LESLLA and SLIFE. We examined the complexities of plagiarism among language learners. Finally, we discussed numerous special considerations of writing assessment.

10.7 Chapter Conclusion

Chapter 10 explores literacy; multiliteracies; assessing reading, vocabulary, grammar, and writing; calculating readability; and creating culturally sensitive plans for addressing plagiarism. Building on the previous chapter on oral-aural skills, it provides specific assessment techniques and strategies, equipping readers to evaluate language proficiency effectively.

Appendix 1 – Achievement Quiz of Chapter 10

(For discussion or writing prompts, see the Think-Pair-Share tasks in this chapter.)

Directions: Select the response that best answers each question below. Each question is worth 1 point.

1. Which of the following tools can help teachers determine which words to teach?
   a. word lists
   b. readability measures
   c. lexical density calculators
   d. type-token ratio calculators

2. What does the following item intend to assess?

   > *Yo, Man!* _____
   >
   > **a.** *What's up?*
   > **b.** *How do you do?*
   > **c.** *I trust you are well?*

   a. accuracy
   b. meaning
   c. use
   d. form

3. The assessment of content knowledge of LESLLA learners in content-based settings needs to take place _____.
   a. on test forms with reduced questions and answer choices
   b. after they have learned to read and write in the target language
   c. after they have learned to read and write in their native language
   d. with creativity, such as through pictures, an interpreter or translator

4. In which approach to teaching and assessment is the focus of reading (or another skill) not only on the end result (the correct answer) but also on the strategies, skills, and mental processes that lead to the end result?
   a. process
   b. product
   c. communicative
   d. multiliteracies

5. True or False? When an international learner plagiarizes, the instructor can assume that the learner cheated knowingly.

11

Grading, Evaluation, and Feedback

Chapter Overview

This chapter reframes grading, evaluation, and feedback as opportunities for celebrating students' achievements, reflecting on teaching practices, and identifying areas for improvement. It emphasizes the importance of helping students appreciate the benefits of evaluation and feedback. The chapter starts with an overview of grading systems and related issues, then delves into creating and using grading rubrics, and the significance of providing clear, detailed feedback. It concludes with an examination of self- and peer-assessment.

11.1 Learning Objectives

1. Articulate a philosophy of grading that is contextualized to your institution and context
2. Communicate to students grading criteria that are both clear and an appropriate fit in your institutional context
3. Calculate grades based on a reliable system of scoring that is consistent with your institutional context and personal philosophy
4. Resolve any cross-cultural dilemmas that might otherwise cause a mismatch between a teacher's and student's understanding of what a specific grade means in your context
5. Employ various types of written and oral feedback that will empower students and help them use the feedback for further development

11.2 Grading, Evaluation, and Feedback

Think-Pair-Share 11.2a Activating Background Schema

a. Think back to your schooling, as far back as you can remember. What various methods of grading were used in your classes?
b. Which ones did you consider fair and which ones unfair? Give specific reasons in support of your memories.
c. From the perspective of the student that you were at the time, what would have made the grading more fair?

A Practical Guide to Language Assessment: How Do You Know That Your Students Are Learning? First Edition.
Ildiko Porter-Szucs et al.
© 2025 John Wiley & Sons, Inc. Published 2025 by John Wiley & Sons, Inc.

Think-Pair-Share 11.2b Activating Background Schema

a. In terms of language teaching and learning, what aspects of work or performance warrant feedback?

b. What kind of feedback do you think is most useful?

Think-Pair-Share 11.2c Activating Background Schema Think of a time you may have felt either really proud or really disappointed in yourself because of a grade you received from a teacher.

11.2.1 The Meaning of a Grade

Often **all** the work done by students is awarded a letter or number. Generally, letters range from A to E or F, where A is the best score and E or F is the worst, and numbers may be percentages or grade points where one is the worst or best grade. Grade points can range from one to four (Russia and Romania) or to twelve or more (Ukraine, Chile, and some universities in Bangladesh). Reducing student work to letters or numbers risks affecting a person's sense of academic self-esteem.

Notice that we often label ourselves based on numbers or letter grades:

- A—"Wow, I'm brilliant!"
- C—"Ouch, not so good, I messed up big time. I'll never be an A student."
- F—"Oh, no, a complete, utter disaster; I'm a failure."

Grades can be awarded for assignments or tests throughout a course, and at the end of a course. A final assignment or test is known as an **"assessment *of* learning"** or a **summative assessment** because it sums up what the student has learned with no subsequent opportunity to improve the grade (see Chapter 1 for more discussion on types of assessment). Typically, summative assessments and results determine achievement and whether a student can move on to another course or level. Beyond affecting self-esteem, final grades can also have considerable consequences for students who have to achieve high grades to maintain a scholarship or for students whose families had to make deep sacrifices (financial, emotional) to enable them to pursue their studies. Imagine the pressure, for example, on a student from rural India, whose family had to sell their farm and borrow from neighbors to raise enough money to send their child overseas to study.

Grades can also have an effect on how the students are defined by teachers and educational systems, who may categorize them as:

- Honors students
- High achievers
- Marginal or "at-risk" students
- College-/university-bound students
- Exceptional students (on either end of the scale)
- Failing students
- Average students

Think about that. Students in these categories are defined by numbers and grades—not so much by the quality of their performance and not necessarily by demonstrated skills that have been observed. Depending on the individual and the context, grades can motivate students or de-motivate them. For some students, an A grade might give a sense of security so that they may feel they don't need to study so hard in the future. Students who receive a C, D, or F grade may be challenged to work harder, or they may give up entirely, feeling that they will never succeed.

To complicate matters more, standards for assigning grades are extraordinarily variable depending on the teacher, subject matter/discipline, culture, and across courses, programs, institutions, education systems. In our own schooling experience, for example, we have all probably heard of a teacher who was considered "easy" and another that was considered "tough." This occurs because teachers use different grading standards or because in their individual beliefs, they give more weightage to particular aspects of work or performance that they value more than others. In standards-based programs, this should not occur because a student who meets the criteria for a particular standard should be credited by all teachers in the same way.

Another way that grades can vary at the local level occurs when some foundational university courses are graded more strictly in order to "weed out" students who are predicted not to be able to meet future challenges. These are sometimes known as "gateway courses" in a program of study. Different programs may grade easier or harder according to the discipline and level of subjectivity involved in scoring assignments. A multiple-choice test or math paper based on formulas will be graded very differently than an English essay.

At a broader level, grading systems differ in different systems of education: compare, for instance, the following grading scales at various international universities (see Figures 11.1–11.3).

Canada's McGill University, Grading Scale (2024) (except engineering and law)

Grades	Grade points	Numerical scale of grades (%)
A	4.0	85–100
A−	3.7	80–84
B+	3.3	75–79
B	3.0	70–74
B−	2.7	65–69
C+	2.3	60–64
C	2.0	55–59
D	1.0	50–54
F (Fail)	0	0–49

Figure 11.1 Canada's McGill University grading scale.

USA's Virginia International University, Grading Scale (2019)

Percentage (%)	Letter grade	Grade points	CGPA[1]	Academic standing
94.00–100.00	A	4.00	4.00	
90.00–93.99	A−	3.70		
87.00–89.99	B+	3.30		

Figure 11.2 USA's Virginia International University grading scale.

(Continued)

---

1 CGPA = Cumulative Grade Point Average: it is the average (arithmetic mean) of all grade points the student has earned in all classes at that school divided by all the credits the student has taken.

Percentage (%)	Letter grade	Grade points	CGPA[1]	Academic standing
83.00–86.99	B	3.00	3.00	Satisfactory grade for graduate-level programs
80.00–82.99	B–	2.70		
77.00–79.99	C+	2.30		
73.00–76.99	C	2.00	2.00	Lowest passing grade for graduate-level courses, and satisfactory grade for undergraduate-level programs

Figure 11.2 (Cont'd)

Norway's University of Oslo, Grading Scale

Some disciplines use a pass/fail system of assessment; others use a letter grade system based on written descriptors. Dentistry uses this scale for assessing exams:

A	92–100%	Fremragende (distinguished)
B	84–91%	Meget god (very good)
C	72–83%	God (good)
D	66–71%	Nokså god (fairly good)
E	60–65%	Tilstrekkelig (adequate)
F	0–59%	Ikke bestått (not passing)

Figure 11.3   Norway's University of Oslo grading scale.

Notice how a "B" is valued at 74 in one country and 91 in another, or labeled as "meget god" (very good) in one country and "satisfactory" in another. Moreover, many US institutions use letter grades or grade point averages (on a 4-, 5-, or 9-point system), while other institutions may refuse to use a letter or numerical system and instead use narrative evaluations of their students. For institutions outside the United States, it is common to use point systems (using 100 points or percentages).

Another factor that affects grading is that in some education systems and institutions, grading is done using **a curve**, where quotas for the number of students awarded each grade are set in advance. The goal is to ensure a desired distribution of grades in order to clearly distinguish individuals for particular academic or career paths that align with numbers of openings available. In other systems, grades are inflated. Possible reasons for **grade inflation** include efforts to maintain the reputations of institutions, contributing to positive appraisals of teachers, enabling institutions or students to qualify for funding, showing empathy to students for particular circumstances, or supporting views that education is a business where high fees (tuition) entitle customers (students) to the best products (high grades).

It is useful for teachers to understand grading differences in other education systems because it may help explain some of the confusion that international students experience in their classes. Language educators can also help raise pre-service teachers' awareness of the differences, in order to prepare those who may teach abroad in a different system of education. If grading policies are not made explicit at their institution, it is advisable for teachers to seek them out.

Did you know?   In an increasing number of schools in the United States **standards-based grading** is being implemented. The primary purpose of such a system is for each student to "meet standards," in other words, to be able to master each standard of the curriculum (O'Conner 2011, p. 2, in Lehman et al. 2018). Instruction can be differentiated through accommodations or modifications for each standard (Marzano Resources n.d.). Standards are often written in student-friendly language and learners are taught to self-assess (Otus 2022). Grading is frequent, formative, and focused on the progress each student makes toward the end goal of mastery. It is designed to avoid some of the criticisms of traditional grading practices, where evaluation criteria extraneous to the achievement of learning objectives are incorporated into the final course grade. Such criteria might include effort, attendance, behavior, extra credit, participation, bonus points, grading on a curve, timeliness. Indeed, such indirect measures are prohibited on achievement reports by some accrediting agencies like CEA (Commission on English Language Program Accreditation in the United States). In traditional grading practices, there might be great variability in the meaning of a C among teachers of the same subject. On the other hand, in a standards-based grading system, student learning is standards-based, evaluation is criterion-referenced, the mastery of each academic standard is tracked separately, and nonacademic criteria are evaluated separately as well (Lehman et al. 2018). A standards-based report card provides detailed, analytic, information about the students' strengths, weaknesses, and how well they have mastered each standard. It is akin to a checklist a car mechanic might use when looking a car over thoroughly: do the brakes meet the standard, are the wheels aligned, do all the lights work properly, and so on, rather than giving the car a vague, holistic, grade of C.

Think-Pair-Share 11.2d Discussion Questions

a. What can a letter grade tell you about a person's knowledge, abilities, skills, talents, and potential?
b. What can a GPA spanning 4 years tell you about a person's knowledge, abilities, skills, talents, and potential?

Think-Pair-Share 11.2e Discussion Questions

a. What issues might arise when work is graded on a curve?
b. Conversely, what issues might arise with grade inflation?

Think-Pair-Share 11.2f Discussion Questions What problems can you envision for people who want to attend university or find a job in another country?

Think-Pair-Share 11.2g Discussion Questions How would you respond to someone who believes that it doesn't matter if a grading system is unfair because life is not always fair and we need to help students prepare for life?

All teachers, but those working with learners from other countries in particular, need to be aware of different cultural expectations regarding grading. We have already shown that in some countries and institutions a "B" can be considered an excellent grade, while in others it is not. In some cultures, a single final exam dictates the student's results in the course or program. In some cultures, students do not question their grades. In some cultures, self- and peer-assessment are not used. In some cultures, there is no such thing as a perfect score because that would indicate that the assessment was not difficult enough or it would challenge the expertise of the teacher.

11.2.2 Determining Test Difficulty

Unfortunately, there is no simple answer to the question of how one can determine the difficulty of a test. Brown and Abeywickrama (2010) offer the following factors to determine test difficulty. The instructor should

- use their teaching experience and intuition
- design feasible tasks, clear and relevant items
- mirror in-class tasks that students have mastered
- refer to prior tests in the same course
- prepare students for the test
- know the students' collective abilities and
- have luck

We would add the following practical advice, whereby the instructor should

- utilize the Tools of the Trade discussed in Chapter 5, specifically word frequency and readability information
- analyze previous tests and the students' success at them; analyze every part of the test: instructions, stimulus, graphic information, audio/video recording, prompt wording, stem, key, distractors, idiomatic language, etc.
- examine the review questions included in the language coursebook and use them as a starting point
- pilot test the test with available students with similar characteristics or if unavailable, then on fellow teachers
- take their own test and double, triple, or quadruple the time, depending on how much more proficient the instructor is than the students (for example, primary-school children vs. doctoral students)

We can try to develop the perfect test for our context (and maybe succeed), but when we have tests that turn out either too easy or too challenging, we should learn from it, revise our test questions, prepare our students better, and/or predict our students' performance better. It can be frustrating to navigate through the many issues that arise around grades. Consequently, it is important for teachers to remember why grading matters, what is being graded, and how to follow trusted principles and practices of good grading.

11.2.3 On the Importance of Grading

Letter or numerical grades and their descriptors are overgeneralizations of a student's abilities, yet they play a huge part when it comes to gate-keeping in admissions decisions and employment. For these high-stakes reasons, it is important for teachers to grade in a principled way using carefully constructed grading procedures and assign grades on the basis of clear criteria that reflect course objectives or the assessment system. Teachers and administrators should also keep in mind that letter grades and numerical evaluations do not fully represent a student's ability or potential.

11.2.4 What is being assessed?

Think-Pair-Share 11.2.4a   Consider the following poem (see Figure 11.4). Then answer the questions that follow.

a. What was the teacher grading in the poems?
b. How do the two versions of the boy's poem differ?
c. How did the grades affect the boy? Why?
d. Do you think it is possible to align assessment and creativity?
e. (How) do you think a poem created by learners should be graded?

A Boy Wrote a Poem by Nicholas Chapman A boy wrote a poem, It was homework from class, He wrote about cliff-tops, And how the winds pass. He just let it flow From his head to his pen, But his spelling was bad, "C, do this again!"	A boy wrote a poem And thought of his mark And this time he checked it And wrote of the dark. He changed and corrected, Gave it in the next day, He got "B+ Good effort" And threw it away.
Times Higher Educational Supplement 16/08/85	

Figure 11.4 Poem by Nicholas Chapman.

It is important to design assignments with a clear purpose and try to make them as valid as possible. As suggested in the poem, it is also important to make grading expectations clear to students. We need to be transparent about what we want to assess.

Typically when we think about grading in language courses (or in general), we think about tests and assignments. Where does creativity come in? Have you ever been assessed on class participation? attendance? effort? other factors? A question of validity arises when language performance is not the sole indicator of final grades. Consider the following questions.

Think-Pair-Share 11.2.4b How can punctuality affect a students' language grade? How can effort be observed? How can participation be measured? Should grades be restricted to performance on tests and assignments in order to maintain validity, or can other indirect measures be included? Might students or stakeholders have an inaccurate perception of their language abilities if indirect measures are used? If a student arrives late for a test or misses a test, should they receive 0? Discuss.

You may believe that a student's overall competence cannot be demonstrated on tests or assignments alone and that observations of classroom behaviors can also help indicate ability, even if measuring these observations is subjective. To be fair, indirect measures, like attendance and participation—if allowed—should carry a lower weightage than direct measures, like tests or assignments because they are not valid measures of the target construct. Teachers and stakeholders who use indirect measures, like attendance or punctuality, must remember that the students' true abilities in the target skill may not be reflected. Of course, it is nice to have the freedom to align our beliefs with our practice, but this is not always possible. If your institution or education system requires specific grading procedures, then you must follow them, particularly if you are a guest working in another country.

Regardless, you need to make the grading procedures clear to students at the beginning of the course. This means being transparent about what will be assessed and how it will be assessed. This may include giving students details (including weightages) of formal tests and assignments, as well as any indirect measures of assessment. In addition, copies of any grading rubrics should be shared, as well as policies regarding grading penalties (e.g. deductions for unexcused absences) or extra credits (additional points for extra work). Teachers need to be able to account for the grades they award, so making grading procedures clear and transparent and documenting all grading decisions is important.

11.2.5 Absolute Grading

When you grade based on standards of performance described on a predetermined numerical point system, you are using absolute grading. The key to making absolute grading systems work is to be very clear on objectives, competencies, tests, tasks, and other assignments that will be counted in the grade. Unclear definitions of grading criteria result in grades that are relatively meaningless. Teachers who are new to grading and are still trying to calibrate the appropriate test difficulty should be particularly careful about potentially using absolute grading without being absolutely certain about the difficulty of the test.

11.2.6 Relative Grading

When you grade on a curve with predetermined percentages of grades allowed at each level, you are using relative grading. Relative grading can also be applied if test results need to be adjusted, e.g. if a test ends up being easier or more difficult for your students than expected, you can rank students in order of performance (percentile ranks) and assign cut-off points for grades. A word of caution, however: teachers should not allow themselves to be swayed by the temptation to follow their intuition and "bend" a student's grade based on anything other than their performance. Teachers are human (and often tired and overworked), but they need to be aware of various grading traps they may fall into:

- The **halo effect** occurs when knowledge of a student's classroom performance influences the grader's perceptions of the student on a formal assessment. For example, if Ali consistently performs well in class, but his test responses are weak, the teacher might give him the benefit of the doubt by grading more leniently. If so, the teacher is experiencing a halo effect.
- Another form of the **halo effect** occurs when a previous student's performance overshadows the following one. This could take two directions. (1) After several mediocre responses a *slightly better* response may appear *much better* than the previous ones and receive an unfairly high grade. (2) After several excellent responses, a *slightly weaker* response may appear *much weaker* than the previous ones and receive an unfairly low grade. The halo of the previous responses could be cast over the subsequent ones. A way to avoid it with constructed responses (such as essays and oral presentations) is with proper rater training and adherence to the rating scale.
- Teachers may inflate grades due to their nurturing nature and empathy for their students or due to external pressures (e.g. scholarship or award requirements, promotion or placement consequences, etc.).

Teachers may assign grades that are higher than their institution's expectations due to their own beliefs about grading.

11.2.7 Recording Grades

It is important to record and organize grades in a practical and coherent way, whether on an electronic or paper-based "gradebook." Gradebooks vary on how grades and related information are arranged, organized, and displayed. Often a course management software, like Blackboard or Canvas, used by the institution provides a "gradebook" for this purpose. Alternatively, new teachers may want to check out a few online resources like www.classmategrading.com, or www.teach-nology.com/downloads/grading, or consult classroom assessment textbooks for ways to organize a gradebook.

11.3 Alternatives to Grades

11.3.1 "Ungrading"

We have already mentioned some of the issues that arise with grading, such as different interpretations of grades, cultural expectations, grade inflation, teacher fatigue, cheating, anxiety, unfair labeling of individuals, unfair use of grades, etc. Blum (2020), Kohn (1999), and others point out that fixation with grades causes other problems as well. While grades may motivate some students, this motivation is only for the short term, and more often, grades de-motivate students. Stommel (2020) points out that grades incentivize product over process; they reduce the complexity of learning to an overly simplistic numerical result; they often reflect an individual's ability to follow instructions rather than reflecting their learning; they emphasize competition rather than collaboration; and they are unfair. Kohn explains that grades reduce students' interest in learning and in taking on challenging tasks, and grades reduce quality thinking, among other things. Feldman (2019) takes this further to assert that grading practices are inequitable due to flawed methods of calculating grades and wildly varying methods of awarding grades. For example, a student with a strong and supportive home environment may arrive in and leave a course with an A, while another student, possibly from an underprivileged background, might arrive with a C and leave with B, which demonstrates greater achievement; yet averaging the grades yields a result that doesn't reflect this progress in learning. To address the issues, and focus more on learning, and developing curiosity and intrinsic motivation rather than grades, many educators and institutions implement "ungrading," which is an approach that emphasizes the learning process and replaces grades with meaningful comments on achievement. "Ungrading" may include:

- self-reflections, self-assessments, and peer-assessments, which build metacognition
- contract grading or individualized learning plans, whereby expectations for each potential grade are explained or negotiated in advance and individuals work towards the grade they want to achieve
- student-created rubrics, which involve learning during the process of their creation
- minimal scales: 1–3 or pass/fail/distinction to eliminate the problem of performance not fitting into designated boxes or the often unfair and subjective minutiae of trying to distinguish narrow bands, e.g. 93% from 94%
- progress portfolios for which students select pieces of work that demonstrate evidence of their learning and include a written justification of their selections. The benefit is that students work to improve their own language abilities in relevant ways rather than respond to a limited number of questions on a test, which ranks students against each other.

"Ungrading" is not suitable for every context and it has its challenges. Moreover, there are still a lot of questions about the approach; however, research continues to progress on its implementation and benefits, and perhaps one day it will become more common.

11.3.2   Formative Assessment

While grades are still a more common form of evaluation, very limited information is conveyed through them. Often just a total score or overall letter grade is given. Even if sub-scores are provided for different abilities or skills (e.g. reading, writing, listening, and speaking), a student who receives a B on writing may have no idea what she did well and what she needs to improve in her writing. Other forms of evaluation can give more formative information that can help learners to identify their strengths and weaknesses, plan where they need to make improvements, and monitor their progress. **Formative assessment** including **assessment for learning** and **assessment as learning** (see Chapter 1 for more information) can encourage metacognition and reflection on learning that has been proven to benefit language learning (Anderson 2012; Goh, 2018; Haukås et al. 2018; Oxford 2016; Renandya and Widodo 2016).

That said, we spend considerable time writing detailed feedback on tests and assignments to help students see where and how they could have improved their responses so that they would do better next time.

Think-Pair-Share 11.3.2   Consider the following true story and discuss the questions that follow.

One day, after quickly seeing his score on a language test, a student stood up and made a show of crumpling his test paper, striding to the garbage bin, and throwing his test in.

a. Why do you think the student did this?
b. How do you think the teacher felt?

Positive washback occurs when assessment becomes a learning experience for students, which begs the question: what can we do to make assessments a positive learning experience? We have learned that our own attitude affects our students. When we convey the perception that an assessment is a high-stakes, "do or die" exercise, rather than an opportunity to showcase knowledge and celebrate learning, students become anxious and frustrated and may display rebellious behavior, like the boy above, to save face when results are disappointing.

To combat this, we continuously provide formative feedback and help students view assessments as opportunities. We vary the forms of formative evaluation we use, so that different learning preferences are accommodated. Positive washback is achieved not only when students' different learning preferences are accommodated but also when students are allowed to **translanguage**—use any language they wish to demonstrate their knowledge, skills, and understanding. This practice gives teachers the best representation of what a student knows and can do.

> **Translanguaging** is seamlessly switching between languages and is an educational method where teachers encourage this practice; students think in several languages at once and utilize their native language to aid in learning academic English.

Traditionally, languages are tested separately but as the legitimacy of translanguaging increases, more holistic approaches to **multilingual assessment** are being implemented. Gorter and Cenoz (2017) identify three approaches to multilingual assessment. The first is using the mother tongue for assessment (particularly for content comprehension). The second is multilingual scoring, which uses two scores: one normed for comparison within the age group and another normed for comparison to peers who share the same L1. The European Language Portfolio uses self-assessment for this scoring (Council of Europe 2024a, 2024b). The third is a translanguaging approach, which is based on bilingual tasks, and can be assessed using a bilingual rubric, such as that of Escamilla et al. (2013). Although multilingual assessment is still evolving, these efforts acknowledge the complexities and realities of authentic language today. When students translanguage as part of the formative assessment process, they engage in use of new and complex language practices that enhance their learning experience.

11.3.3   Forms of formative assessment include:

- a teacher's targeted comments written in the margin, near the "error" or omission they refer to
- a teacher's summary comments written at the end of an assignment
- a teacher's written response or reaction to a student's self-assessment of performance
- a teacher's checklist
- a teacher's oral review of the test in the next class period
- a teacher's conference with the student
- a teacher's oral feedback during a lesson
- self-assessment of performance
- peer-assessment of performance

For more on specific formative assessment of oral or written skills, see Chapters 9 and 10, respectively.

11.4   Rubrics

Before we discuss formative evaluation in detail, let us look at rubrics. A rubric is a set of descriptors or criteria indicating the expected level of performance at particular points on a scale. In fact, some refer to a rating scale, rather than a rubric. For various types of scales see Chapters 3 and 4. When well-designed, rubrics can be very useful for both the students and the teacher. A detailed rubric makes expectations transparent for students and it lessens any subjectivity for teachers when grading. For example, look at the rubric below designed for grading a written academic argument at the university level (Figure 11.5):

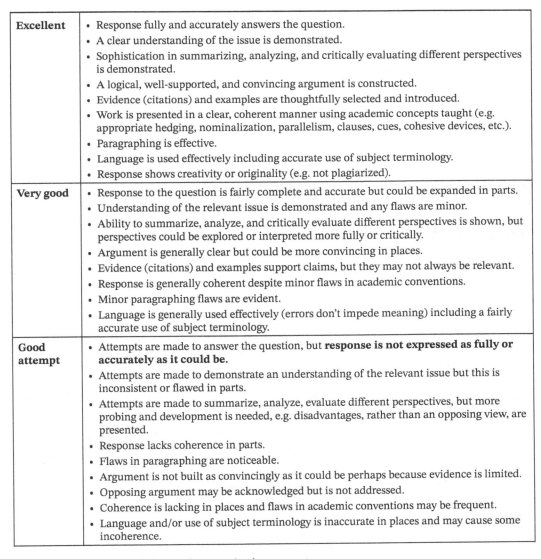

Excellent	• Response fully and accurately answers the question. • A clear understanding of the issue is demonstrated. • Sophistication in summarizing, analyzing, and critically evaluating different perspectives is demonstrated. • A logical, well-supported, and convincing argument is constructed. • Evidence (citations) and examples are thoughtfully selected and introduced. • Work is presented in a clear, coherent manner using academic concepts taught (e.g. appropriate hedging, nominalization, parallelism, clauses, cues, cohesive devices, etc.). • Paragraphing is effective. • Language is used effectively including accurate use of subject terminology. • Response shows creativity or originality (e.g. not plagiarized).
Very good	• Response to the question is fairly complete and accurate but could be expanded in parts. • Understanding of the relevant issue is demonstrated and any flaws are minor. • Ability to summarize, analyze, and critically evaluate different perspectives is shown, but perspectives could be explored or interpreted more fully or critically. • Argument is generally clear but could be more convincing in places. • Evidence (citations) and examples support claims, but they may not always be relevant. • Response is generally coherent despite minor flaws in academic conventions. • Minor paragraphing flaws are evident. • Language is generally used effectively (errors don't impede meaning) including a fairly accurate use of subject terminology.
Good attempt	• Attempts are made to answer the question, but **response is not expressed as fully or accurately as it could be.** • Attempts are made to demonstrate an understanding of the relevant issue but this is inconsistent or flawed in parts. • Attempts are made to summarize, analyze, evaluate different perspectives, but more probing and development is needed, e.g. disadvantages, rather than an opposing view, are presented. • Response lacks coherence in parts. • Flaws in paragraphing are noticeable. • Argument is not built as convincingly as it could be perhaps because evidence is limited. • Opposing argument may be acknowledged but is not addressed. • Coherence is lacking in places and flaws in academic conventions may be frequent. • Language and/or use of subject terminology is inaccurate in places and may cause some incoherence.

Figure 11.5   Sample rubric for a written academic argument.

(Continued)

Acceptable	• Response does not answer the question as expected, perhaps due to a misunderstanding of the instructions or digression from the topic.
	• **Only one perspective (side of the argument) is presented** or a misunderstanding of the issue is evident.
	• Irrelevancy, inappropriacy, omissions, etc. weaken the response; or an overuse of sources with limited original work, or possible plagiarism in some parts weakens the response.
	• Ability to summarize, analyze, and evaluate is not demonstrated satisfactorily.
	• Response lacks organization and clarity.
	• An attempt is made to build an argument but it is unconvincing due to misguided claims, flaws in logic, and weak justification.
	• A lack of coherence negatively affects the response and academic writing conventions are not followed consistently.
	• Paragraphing is seriously flawed.
	• Language and/or use of subject terminology is **frequently inaccurate**.
Not acceptable	• Response fails to answer the questions due to a complete misunderstanding of the subject or question; or response is incomprehensible due to a lack of coherence or copious grammatical or content errors.
	OR
	• Much or all of the paper is plagiarized.

Figure 11.5 (Cont'd)

A student who carefully examines this rubric would see that if he does not cite relevant evidence, he would not receive a rating of "excellent." Similarly, the teacher would know that a paper that lacked relevant citations would be limited to a rating of "very good" or below.

Think-Pair-Share 11.4a Discussion Questions   What does this rubric tell you about the aspects of the writing that are valued, in other words the construct of writing in this context? Why do you think the rubric highlights certain descriptors in bold? How easy or difficult do you think it would be to distinguish the bands using this rubric to grade an argumentative essay? What happens when a paper straddles bands?

Think-Pair-Share 11.4b Discussion Questions   What do you think about how language errors are described? (e.g. Why doesn't the rating of "excellent" require flawless grammar?) Why is it not usually a good idea to quantify the language errors on a rubric?

Think-Pair-Share 11.4c Discussion Questions   How would you modify this rubric if you were to use it? What would be the benefit of having students create the assignment rubric with the teacher? How can teachers work with their students to understand and use rubrics effectively?

You may have to use rubrics set by your institution or governing body. If you need to provide your own, an internet search will point to various generic ones online that could be modified for your purposes. Alternatively, you may prefer to design your own and customize it to the assignment. Online there are rubric generators or you can just create your own. **When creating rubrics, it helps to keep certain guidelines in mind:**

1. Always start with the purpose of the assessment and align the rubric with that purpose and the assignment requirements.

2. As much as possible, write positive descriptors, e.g. focus on what you want the student to do (i.e. "can-do statements"), not errors and omissions.
3. Try to identify one or two essential requirements for each band that will distinguish papers at that level. Then add other requirements by degree.
4. Be as detailed as possible.
5. Try to avoid vague terminology, e.g. it is very difficult to objectively distinguish the difference between "some" and "a few," or "sometimes" and "occasionally."
6. Avoid quantifying errors for the practical reason that it takes too long to count them. Moreover, there is an issue of equating minor errors (such as making non-countable noun plural, e.g. "researches" and "homeworks") with serious errors (those that affect meaning, e.g. "proofs provide in examples for object").

Think-Pair-Share 11.4d Application   What else might help you to create an effective rubric?

11.5   Formative Evaluation

As noted, assessment should be a learning experience. Most teachers give some sort of formative feedback to their students following the belief that it benefits students to know what errors they are making and how they can improve. Similarly, most students expect feedback. There has been much research and discussion on the effectiveness of feedback in second- and foreign-language teaching, particularly corrective feedback on written work. Evidence from an analysis of studies on this topic (Bitchener and Ferris 2012) suggests that short-term improvements can be made, but long-term learning from feedback is still being explored. Indeed, in an earlier analysis of research on the subject, Truscott (1996) made the claim that feedback is not effective and may even be harmful to students' progress. The debate continues, but it is generally accepted that feedback can be beneficial as long as it is appropriate for the context.

Think-Pair-Share 11.5a Activation of Background Knowledge   Let us begin by considering the types of errors that language learners make. What different kinds of errors do language learners make? How could you categorize errors? How do you distinguish minor errors from serious errors, and how should we assess them?

Think-Pair-Share 11.5b Pre-reflection   What are the issues/questions surrounding providing corrective feedback (error correction) on student writing and speaking? What are best practices for corrective feedback? What are ways to move students towards autonomy and independence as self-editors of their own work?

11.5.1   Mistakes and Errors

In our field an important distinction to make here is between mistakes and errors. **Mistakes** are non-systematic; i.e. they don't always occur. They may be due to problems with performing, or demonstrating, what the learner may know. They are "slips" that may be made due to lack of time, attention, or even because a learner doesn't have good strategies to use to avoid those mistakes. On the other hand, **errors** are systematic problems that may be made because a learner has not learned a structure or rule. They can be morphological, syntactic, and lexical forms that violate the rules or expectations of the target language users. Errors may occur when there is L1 interference, i.e. a learner's first language affects the errors he or she makes in their L2. For example, in Chinese, conjunctions appear in pairs, so in English a Mandarin speaker may say: ***Although** she prefers business, **but** she studies engineering.* Errors may also occur from L2 interlanguage in which a learner may apply a "rule" incorrectly. For example, *The bird flyed in the sky.*

Second language acquisition research shows that:

- Errors can fossilize. In other words, certain errors remain and learners may fail to progress over time with certain structures (Selinker 1972).
- Also, for adult learners, feedback (correction) and attention (noticing language features) are necessary for continued improvement (Ellis et al. 2006).
- And in many academic and professional/workplace settings, non-native-like errors in writing may be harshly judged by readers—so attention to written error definitely has practical importance (Wolfe et al. 2016).

11.5.2 Categorizing Errors

Language errors can vary in terms of their severity, impact, and frequency.

The severity of errors is usually broken down into global vs. local categories. **Global errors** are more severe because they interfere with communication, e.g. structural errors, such as *I home go.* **Local errors** are noticeable (and maybe distracting), e.g. errors of tense, number, etc., but they do not interfere with the readers' comprehension of the message, for instance, *I've never wrote that.*

Some errors may have a stigmatizing impact. They signal that the speaker or writer may have a foreign status, and, unfortunately, this may distract or annoy some people. **Stigmatizing errors** are subjective, based on stereotypes, and depend on what irritates the interlocutor about the "error" or mistake, e.g. a low-proficiency speaker might say *I go store* for *I am going to the store*, or a high-proficiency speaker might repeatedly misuse gender pronouns. Such errors could result in an interlocutor perceiving the individuals negatively as "foreigners" or "uneducated" or "non-inclusive."

Frequent errors, or **patterns of error** suggest a learner's lack of understanding or awareness of rules. As teachers, if we notice a frequent error in a learner's writing, we should address it, especially in frequently occurring structures in English. To balance the feedback, teachers should also make a point of noting how many times the writer used the structure correctly.

In summary, teachers need to analyze an error to decide how or whether to treat it. To do this, they should determine if the error is serious or minor, whether it is stigmatizing, and how frequently it occurs. So what does all this information about errors tell us? It is important to think about when and how to give feedback. The goal should not be to have students achieve perfection. It should be progress and increasing student autonomy.

Think-Pair-Share 11.5.2a Comprehension Check With this in mind, how would you answer the following questions: When should errors be corrected? Which errors should be addressed? How should errors be corrected?

Think-Pair-Share 11.5.2b Application How do we help students understand and apply feedback? How can teachers use time wisely and avoid burnout?

11.6 Feedback

In order to help students improve, **formative feedback** needs to be given at the drafting stage. But, imagine spending hours poring over a student's draft pointing out all the grammatical errors, as well as content and structural problems in their writing. Seeing marks all over the paper (often in red) can make the student feel defeated and overwhelmed. She may spend considerable time correcting the grammar errors, but when she revises the content and organization of the paper, many of the parts she corrected may no longer be included in the paper! This could be such a waste of time for her, not to mention demotivating! Therefore, early in the writing process, it is important to focus on the **macro issues**—those major structural (organization) and content problems. Once those are addressed, the teacher can focus on the **micro issues**, such as use of grammar, vocabulary, and mechanics in subsequent drafts. **Summative feedback** can be given on the final submission.

As indicated earlier, we typically focus first on global errors—those that affect meaning—, stigmatizing errors, and frequently occurring errors. Subsequently, more local errors can be addressed. That said, context is important. Feedback should be given selectively according to the purpose of the assignment, the learning objectives, and the learner. For example, feedback on an assignment to assess the use of a target grammar feature will be more focused on that structure than a more general writing assignment would be. Teachers should also consider student expectations and needs. A reticent learner might feel frustrated or overwhelmed by too much feedback, while another student might request feedback on every error. If a student who habitually makes a common error, suddenly gets it right, it may seem appropriate to give **positive feedback** on this. Similarly, positive feedback should be given on a response that is above expectations.

11.6.1 Ways to Provide Feedback

There are several ways to give feedback. When teachers give **direct feedback**, they provide the corrections for the student. When teachers give **indirect feedback**, they point out errors or indicate that errors exist, and it is up to the student to correct them. Sometimes teachers use a **marking, or error-correction, code**. This needs to be shared and explained to students. See examples of types of feedback below. To decide which type of feedback to give, consider the learner's needs and preferences. If appropriate, you may decide to just ask the students what they think would be most beneficial for them.

Think-Pair-Share 11. 61.a Background Activation Examine Figure 11.6, where a writing teacher responded to a low-intermediate (B1) secondary school's student's writing. Then, answer the questions that follow.

Original writing by EFL student	Teacher's sample feedback	Correction guide
This is new invention help man lives longer.	This is new invention <u>help man lives</u> longer. **agr WC VF**	agr = agreement WC = word choice VF = verb form

Figure 11.6 Sample feedback on student writing.

What is your opinion about the teacher's feedback? What are its strengths? What are its weaknesses? How do you think the student may have felt upon receiving this feedback? How do you think the student may have been able to use the feedback to improve his writing?

Back in 1985, Vivian Zamel wrote a paper published in *TESOL Quarterly* about responding to student writing. Although it is decades later, many of the issues she raised may still persist today. She observed that ESL writing teachers view themselves as language teachers, rather than writing teachers, focusing on surface-level errors (local errors), rather than content. She also observed that they often:

- misread student text, e.g. teachers incorrectly interpret what they think the student is trying to say
- are inconsistent in their reactions, which has implications for reliability
- make arbitrary corrections, e.g. identify surface errors in a sentence that has bigger structural problems, or address some grammar errors and not others
- write contradictory comments
- provide vague prescriptions, like "wrong word," or "too general." Ironically, we often ask students to be more precise, yet our own feedback is imprecise
- impose abstract rules and standards; feedback like this tends to be overly prescriptive
- respond to text as fixed and final products; this is a problem when our goal is to provide formative feedback
- rarely make content-specific comments or offer specific strategies for revising text; these specific comments and strategies are probably what makes feedback most useful

Given these issues, it may not be surprising that students often fail to follow up on feedback.

Another issue that may arise is that in our role as nurturing teachers, we may be too indirect in our feedback causing language learners to misinterpret the intended instruction. For example, using modals of possibility might be interpreted by students as a suggestion only (*You could add an example here*) and students may choose to dismiss it.

Think-Pair-Share 11. 6.1b Application   Consider how language learners would feel receiving the feedback that you give. How would you modify the following feedback comments to make them more helpful to students? For example, instead of "good," be specific about what is good, e.g. "Good example to illustrate your claim," or "Good use of the present perfect." (Figure 11.7)

Original comment	Improved comment
Example:	Example*:* *A relevant example to illustrate your claim.* *Accurate use of the present perfect.*
Good	
Wrong word	
This needs work.	
What do you mean here?	
????	
You could add an example here.	
Incoherent	
See me!	

Figure 11.7   Feedback comments.

Think-Pair-Share 11. 6.1c Application Now, find a sample of student writing in your context.

1. Identify one to two possible feedback points. How do you prioritize what needs correction?
2. What comments would you give to the student writer?
3. Prepare a short activity that would help the whole class learn the points you are addressing.

If you do not currently have access to student writing, select a writing sample from Chapter 5.

11.6.2 Feedback Guidelines

The type of feedback to give depends on the assignment, the context, and the learner, but there are some general guidelines (modified from Macknish 2010):

- It is advisable to provide feedback immediately for oral responses (if appropriate) and as soon as possible for written work.
- Remember the purpose of the comments—you are praising the students for work well done and encouraging them to improve their work. Start and end with positive comments. Comments that scold or denigrate students are generally counterproductive. This has also been referred to as the "hamburger or sandwich principle" (see Figure 11.8).
- Try to make comments as detailed as possible.
- Be specific and clear, not ambiguous–what <u>exactly</u> is good?, what <u>exactly</u> needs improvement?, etc.
- Make comments constructive by including specific guidance for improvement, e.g. *Add an example here.*
- Rather than over-using "good," employ a variety of words and expressions that praise good work, e.g. *thorough, creative, neat, insightful, original, innovative, perceptive, imaginative, thoughtful, artistic, inventive, resourceful, detailed, comprehensive, unique, unusual, etc.*
- Use words and expressions that guide students to exactly what needs improvement, e.g. *you can improve this part by xyz..., you need to add an example to support this claim, please give a definition of this technical word, this verb needs to be in the past, this sentence needs to start with a cohesive device to link it to the previous one,* etc.
- Use variety. Rather than *This work **is**...,* try: *This work expresses..., demonstrates..., shows...,* etc.
- Comment on the work or the effort (things that can be changed), not on the student. Instead of: **You** *didn't do xyz,* try: *Xyz is needed to improve your answer.*
- Don't use offensive labels or names e.g. *stupid, lazy, slow, troublesome, etc.*

	Start with a positive comment (top bun/bread)
	Provide the meat of the feedback: sandwich the constructive feedback between the two slices of bread (positive comments)
	End with a positive comment (bottom bun/bread)

Figure 11.8 The "hamburger or sandwich principle" for feedback comments. *Source:* Shameel mukkath / Pexels

- Use modals and passive constructions to be less accusatory. Instead of, *You didn't develop this idea completely*, write, *This idea could be developed more fully with….* However, make sure that learners understand that your feedback requires follow-up.
- Check the spelling and grammar as well as the content of your comments.
- Remember that the target reader is the student, but possibly parents and others, like the principal and/or other teachers may read your comments too.
- Too often, teachers focus on the areas needing improvement and only contact parents to inform them of their child's negative performance or behavior. Parents (and students themselves) would probably like to know that the teacher has noticed a strong performance or behavior in class. Why not send occasional informal reports to parents to present positive comments?

Ferris (2007) explains that error feedback is most effective when it is limited/narrow in scope, when some instruction/metalinguistic explanation is provided, and when student follow-up after feedback is required. She also suggests using color-coding to draw attention to the different types of errors and holding conferences with students to discuss them.

One useful technique, first developed at Brigham Young University is **Dynamic Written Corrective Feedback (DWCF)** (Kurzer 2018).

DWCF involves:

- short (e.g.10-minute), frequent (daily or regular) writing samples
- teacher marking all errors immediately (by next class) using standard error codes
- students immediately correcting all marked errors and returning for credit
- students charting their ongoing progress

DWCF is beneficial because it is individualized as each student attends to his/her own error patterns. It is consistent (not just every few weeks when a paper is due), manageable because texts are short, measurable and student progress can be tracked, and motivating as student awareness is raised and progress can be observed.

Think-Pair-Share 11.6.2 Synthesis and Application   Examine Figure 11.6 again, where a writing teacher responded to a low-intermediate (B1) student's sentence. Incorporating the above principles for giving feedback (from Ferris 2007 and Macknish 2010), how would you provide feedback to the same student? What advice would you give to the teacher on providing feedback?

11.7   Avoiding Burnout

Ferris (2014) provides a list of best practices for giving feedback on writing. Providing detailed corrective feedback, though, can be tiring, and avoiding burnout is important. The following suggestions may help in some contexts:

- Set realistic goals for error feedback. You don't have to identify/comment on every error.
- Do not feel that you must give written error feedback on every paper students write.
- When relevant, implement conferencing with verbal feedback that promotes self-correction.
- Over time, require students to take increasing responsibility for their own progress.

Additionally, one method of avoiding burnout we have used with some success in our college ESL classes is bringing the students into the decision-making process. On the final papers of the semester, when students are not expected to revise their papers, we ask them what kind of feedback they would like. We explain that students tend not to look at and learn from the feedback if they do not need to incorporate it into another draft, yet the provision of feedback is extremely time-consuming for the teacher. If the student is truly going to learn from our detailed feedback, then we will provide it gladly. Otherwise, we will simply make summative comments, which will save us hours upon hours. We assure the students that their honest answer will have no negative consequences for them. Over the years we have found that 30–50% of the students in any given class opt out of detailed feedback and simply wish us a pleasant semester break!

11.8 Self- and Peer-Assessment

Another way to lessen the teacher's load a little and to improve students' metacognitive skills is to implement self- and peer-assessments, also known as "assessment *as* learning." A teacher's ultimate goal should be to move students towards autonomous learning and self- and peer-assessment helps move students toward autonomy. In assessment as learning, students engage their metacognition and are able to identify their own strengths and weaknesses, revise their work, monitor their own progress over time, set goals for improvement, and reflect on their learning. Students, however, cannot be expected to engage in self-assessment without training and practice. To demonstrate their metacognition, students can write journals or essays reflecting on their progress. Finally, teachers can foster self-assessment through conferencing. Teachers can start by providing less or less-explicit feedback as the course progresses and explicitly teach students how to edit their own or their peers' work. Modeling the use of tools like rubrics and checklists is helpful, as is sharing model reflections and role playing a conference session. Then opportunities should be provided to practice self-editing strategies. While this training is time consuming, it is crucial for the effectiveness of the assessment. Time can be saved later by having students complete the self- and peer-assessments outside of class.

When introducing self- and peer-assessment, be aware that there may be students from cultures where expectations of student and teacher roles are more traditional and where self- or peer-assessment is not used. There may also be students who believe that peers lack the proficiency or expertise needed to give language advice. There may be others who view peer-assessment as an exercise in humiliation. It is crucial, therefore, to first discuss with students the benefits of and provide training in self- and peer-assessment, and then train them in how to do it effectively.

Liang (2014) suggests a three-stage pedagogy for helping students with peer- and self-assessment:

Stage 1: Teacher modeling—diagnosing needs, sharing models of weak writing, providing extensive feedback based on scoring rubric, explaining criteria, demonstrating revisions, engaging students in analysis, providing explicit grammar instruction on target issues, strategizing error feedback.

Stage 2: Teacher assessment and guided peer-assessment—providing multiple opportunities for practice with use of rubrics or checklists, continued feedback, targeting one paragraph at a time, focusing on common errors first, scaffolding whole class/small group/pair work.

Stage 3: Independent self-assessment—sharing models of strong writing, reviewing guidelines, implementing targeted independent assessment.

To reiterate, we cannot assume that students are familiar with peer- and self-assessment so the importance of training students, modeling, and giving multiple opportunities to practice cannot be stressed enough. It is suggested to look for both strengths and weaknesses when assessing. For some students, it might be helpful to provide sentence starters or sentence frames for written feedback, for example:

> *Overall your paragraph _____ (is clear, is comprehensible, is cohesive, presents interesting ideas, etc.).*
>
> *Your use of verbs _____ (needs checking for tense/subject-verb agreement/placement, is accurate).*
>
> *Your use of cohesive devices _____ (needs checking for meaning/form/placement, is appropriate)*

You might also consider using role-plays of oral peer-feedback sessions to model expectations.

11.9 Co-Construction of Success Criteria

While not developed specifically for language learning, another technique for self-assessment that has many benefits for learning is the co-construction of success criteria (Sackstein 2021). Typically, the teacher designs the assignment, but by getting students involved in identifying criteria depicting excellent work, they develop skills in discernment, critical thinking, and metacognition. Moreover, expectations are clarified, which can reduce anxiety. On the *Cult of Pedagogy* website, Gonzales (2021) outlines some ideas on how this could work in a classroom, starting with the guiding standards.

1. Analyze the standards: The teacher has students underline verbs (often representing skills), and circle nouns (often representing concepts) in specific target standards. Then, in groups, they discuss meanings and suggest evidence that would demonstrate achievement of the standards.
2. Study the assessment guidelines: The assignment instructions are studied and annotated by students. Informed by the standards, descriptors for the assignment that reflect relevant learning in student-friendly language can be developed together. A full rubric may or may not be developed.
3. Share models: Models or exemplars of completed assignments are shared and analyzed individually or with a partner. A whole class discussion follows to highlight examples of where and how specific criteria are demonstrated.
4. Identify needs: Once expectations are clear, students can identify what instructional support they will need, including what they need to learn themselves and what scaffolding the teacher can provide. One suggestion would be to create a K-W-L chart for this. From here the teacher can plan lessons and resources needed.

11.10 Checklist Assessment

One tool that teachers can use or students can use for self- or peer-assessment is a checklist. Using a checklist can minimize time and ensure that uniform measures are applied. This increases practicality and reliability and can result in positive washback because students can learn from both completing the assessment for their peer and from reading and following up on the completed

Sample Checklist

✓	**Proofreading Checklist**
	Is the main idea/argument coherent (easy to follow)?
	Is each paragraph limited to one idea?
	Are the sentences within each paragraph logically linked together?
	Are the conjunctions/connectors used correctly?
	Is there a mix of simple and complex sentences?
	Do all the clauses have a subject and verb?
	Does the verb agree in number with the subject?
	Do the verb tenses match the intended time?
	Are there any words missing/repeated?
	Are the articles (*the, a, an*) used correctly?
	Are the singulars and plurals formed correctly?
	Are the prepositions necessary/correct?
	Are the adverbs and adjectives in the right place?
	Do the pronouns refer back to an identifiable antecedent?
	Is the spelling correct?
	Is the punctuation correct?

Figure 11.9 Sample checklist.

checklist they receive. Moreover, they may be more likely to process checked boxes easier than to read lengthy comments.

Think-Pair-Share 11.10 Application   Examine the sample checklist above (see Figure 11.9). At what point in the writing process should such a checklist be used (if at all)? How easy or difficult would it be for your students to use? How could it be modified to be more suitable for your context?

11.11   Journals and Reflection Essays

Journals or reflection essays allow for individualization as students can set goals relevant to their needs and reflect on their own progress. Depending on the context, teachers can provide a set template with prompt questions or allow free writing. This form of assessment allows students to evaluate multiple objectives and results in increased face validity, and positive washback potential. However, narratives are not as practical as checklists because they take more time for students to write and for teachers to evaluate.

Think-Pair-Share 11.11 Application   Read the sample reflection prompts (a–e), which are written for students to use for self-reflection. Which ones might you, as a language teacher, use in your practice? What other prompts could you add to this list?
   Sample Reflection Prompts

   a. Read your assignment feedback and set one or two goals that you will focus on in your future writing.
   b. What do you feel confident about in your writing? Why?

    c. What parts of your assignment are you less confident about? Why?

    d. What questions do you have about your writing?

    e. What is your biggest strength: Grammar? Vocabulary? Organization? Development of ideas? Creativity? Other? Why do you say that?

Remember how even very young learners can be taught to review their peers' work, as demonstrated in the EL Education (2016) video about Austin's Butterfly (see Chapter 6 for more information).

11.12   Student-Teacher Conferences

Conferences enable teachers to get insight into their students' metacognitive processes. As mentioned earlier, it is important to make students feel comfortable so that they will share their thoughts. Asking open-ended questions, like the reflection prompts above, and asking students to give reasons and specific examples can lead to more useful reflections that compel metacognition.

Individual conferences of 5–10 minutes or more can be conducted in class, while the rest of the students are working on individual work, or they can be scheduled outside of class. To save time, group consultations can be conducted, where students with similar needs can be grouped together. This may help some reticent students who can learn from the others or gain confidence and support with the presence of peers. Be aware, however, that some students may feel shy talking about their academic problems in front of others, or they may prefer more individual attention from the teacher. Teachers need to get to know their students' needs and preferences and do what is best in their context.

11.12.1   Suggestions for Student-Teacher Conferencing

Create a friendly, non-threatening environment for conferencing by engaging in some small talk. You want the student to feel comfortable sharing. Then ask the student to reflect on their writing progress and identify specific challenges they may face. Discuss these with the student. Next, have the student read their paper aloud to you. Often, they may stumble over problem areas, which may cause them to identify an error and self-correct. Next, you read the paper to the student stopping at any other errors you want the student to notice and correct. The errors can be underlined in different colors to distinguish between local and global errors, and/or errors that were identified by the student vs. those identified by the teacher. The teacher can give grammatical explanations where appropriate and specific suggestions can be made for any further revisions or applications.

Think-Pair-Share 11.12.1 Application

1. Select an assignment that you are thinking of using. Consider the purpose and objectives of the assessment and create a rubric to best represent five or more ability levels.

2. Based on the assignment selected, create some prompt questions that would encourage students to reflect on their learning, thereby engaging their metacognition.

3. Write some feedback comments that you might use for a student who achieved weak results on the assignment selected, or who did not reflect very deeply on their learning. For this hypothetical situation, you will have to make some assumptions.

4. What strategies would you use in a teacher-student conference to help the student?

11.13   Chapter Conclusion

This chapter distinguishes between summative and formative assessment, including self-assessment and "assessment *of/for/as* learning." It provides an overview of local and international grading systems, emphasizing the importance of understanding how grades are assigned and used. The chapter discusses designing robust rubrics to enhance the validity and reliability of graded assignments. Since grades provide limited information about ability and competence, teachers should focus on formative assessment, including error analysis and the provision of effective feedback. Tips for giving feedback and discussions on self- and peer-assessment are also presented.

Appendix 1 – Achievement Quiz of Chapter 11

(For discussion or writing prompts, see the Think-Pair-Share tasks in this chapter.)

Directions: For questions 1–3, select the response that best answers the questions below. Questions 1–3 are worth 1 point each. For question 4, select all the answers that are correct. Question 4 is worth 2 points if entirely correct or 1 point partial credit regardless of the number of correct answers. For question 5, pair the options that correspond to each other. Question 5 is worth 3 points if entirely correct or 1 point partial credit for each correct match.

1. Ms. Lee is grading David's oral presentation based on a rubric. Before finalizing the grade of 8/13, she remembers how well David usually performs in class. Ms. Lee then bends David's grade to 10/13.
   This is an example of _____.
   a. relative grading
   b. positive washback
   c. the halo effect
   d. absolute grading

2. Why is it best to avoid quantifying errors on a rubric?
   a. It hinders transparency for students.
   b. It hinders the subjectivity of grading.
   c. It leads to overemphasis on total scores.
   d. It is time-consuming and impractical.

3. When giving feedback in the initial stages of drafting an essay, what issues should be commented on first?
   a. macro
   b. micro
   c. direct
   d. indirect

4. Select all that apply. How can a teacher provide effective feedback while avoiding burnout?
   a. summatively comment on the finished product only
   b. offer feedback only on the highest priority errors
   c. provide corrective feedback on a subset of papers
   d. gradually train students for self- and peer-assessment

5. Match each term with the correct definition. One term will have no match.

Terms	Definitions
a. stigmatizing errors	A. incorrect forms that are more severe because they interfere with communication
b. mistakes	
c. local errors	B. incorrect forms that have an impact and signal that the writer may be a non-native speaker of the language
d. global errors	
	C. incorrect forms that are non-systematic and occur due to lapses in performance

12

Ethics, Fairness, and Security

Chapter Overview

This chapter explores the ethical considerations surrounding assessment. As discussed in earlier chapters, assessment often evokes strong emotions such as anxiety, frustration, and claims of unfairness or inequality, particularly in high-stakes settings, but also in low-stakes assessments. These concerns can be mitigated by designing and implementing assessments that are valid, transparent, and ethically used for their intended purposes. The chapter defines ethics, discusses ethical issues, and provides examples of assessments that raise ethical concerns.

12.1 Learning Objectives

1. Form and express beliefs about the importance of ethical assessment
2. Explain important ethical considerations in assessment
3. Evaluate assessment tools and materials according to ethical principles

It should be understood that there are important reasons for conducting various forms of assessment. For example, testing has been shown to be "demonstrably effective at improving learning and memory in younger students" (Meyer 2011). Additionally, "[s]tudents who receive formative assessment perform better on a variety of achievement indicators than their peers do" (Hanover Research 2014, p. 5). This is on top of the many uses we have for knowing the results of language assessments:

- measuring and tracking progress in language learning
- providing evidence for placing students in appropriate course levels
- providing evidence for promoting students to subsequent levels
- diagnosing language strengths and weaknesses
- meeting entry requirements for higher education
- meeting entry requirements for immigration, etc.

The benefits and uses, however, are only valid if the assessment is fair and ethical.

STOP View this video on "what you should know about exams and scoring" by Dr. Aryadoust: https://www.youtube.com/watch?v=JFZQcn8ijr0. As you watch, confirm your understanding of the concepts that make a test and test scoring fair.

A Practical Guide to Language Assessment: How Do You Know That Your Students Are Learning? First Edition.
Ildiko Porter-Szucs et al.
© 2025 John Wiley & Sons, Inc. Published 2025 by John Wiley & Sons, Inc.

STOP Before reading further, we need to understand what we mean by *ethical*. Write down your interpretation of ethics and include some examples of what you think are characteristics of an ethical assessment. With a partner, compare your interpretations and discuss examples.

12.2 Defining "Ethics"

The term *ethics* is commonly heard but not always understood as the meaning can be interpreted differently in different disciplines and cultures. In the context of language assessment, our interpretation of ethics is:

> **Ethics in language testing** is a set of guiding principles that ensures a standard of behavior that brings accountability andwe legitimacy to the field of language testing.

When referring to ethical testing or assessment, we often refer to such concepts as validity, transparency, fairness, professional conduct, accepted norms, elimination of bias, and doing no harm. Chapter 2 delved into the notion of validity, as well as the *Assessment Use Argument*, which serves as a justification for the ethical development and use of assessments to benefit all involved parties. However, what exactly do the other concepts mean in the context of language assessment?

Transparency means that information should be clear and accessible. In language assessment, transparency typically refers to clarity of purpose, format, instructions, content, scoring criteria, and how the results will be used and shared. Note that not all information should be transparent. For example, sharing test results with unauthorized individuals or entities is unethical, as is sharing test questions with TTs in advance of the test is unethical—unless it is a take-home test, etc.

Fairness means that assessments should strive to be equitable and meet the needs of the students or TTs and the context so that the results are as valid and reliable as possible. It is important to note the distinction between equitable and equal. Some language learners may need special accommodations, such as additional time to complete assessments or access to a dictionary or glossary. Sometimes, "native-speaking" peers complain that this is unfair because they see that resources or attention are not equally distributed, and they are jealous or have a fear of missing out (*FOMO*), known in Singapore as *kiasu*. These peers need to understand that the playing field is not level to begin with. For example, some students see better than others, so we give glasses to some, but not all students; therefore, glasses are not used equally in the class, but there is equity, or a more even playing field, because everyone can see clearly. In the same way, teachers and test administrators work to make assessments more equitable for students who are learning additional languages. For more details on how to characterize fairness in classroom-based language tests, see Wallace and Qin (2021), who break fairness down into three dimensions: "distributive fairness (how fairly test scores represent performance), procedural fairness (how equally test procedures are applied), and interactional fairness (how respectful communication is between students and teachers during a test)" (p. 492).

Kunnan (2004, 2008) developed a model for test fairness, which identifies five aspects of fairness in language assessment: validity, absence of bias, access, administration, and social consequences. **Validity** is discussed in Chapter 2, and **bias** is discussed in the following. **Access** refers to financial, geographic, and personal access (e.g. transportation, wheelchair ramps), as well as access to equipment and conditions necessary for test implementation. To be fair, resources should be provided to TTs who face challenges in accessing assessments. These resources might include financial aid, transportation, elevators, and customized test adaptations for visual, hearing, or cognitive impairments. Conditions should be evaluated to ensure that there is no noise pollution, etc., in the testing venue. This relates to test **administration**, which involves ensuring appropriate physical conditions, such as lighting, temperature, equipment, and facilities. Administration also involves ensuring the provision of proper test forms, administration manuals, rules and instructions for registering TTs, invigilating tests, training and norming exercises for examiners and raters, as well as procedures for collecting papers, reporting, storing, and using results. **Social consequences** include positive and negative washback. Positive consequences are desired outcomes, such as selection or eligibility for further studies. Negative washback refers to harm caused by assessment, such as severe illness or denial of access to desired outcomes. If a lack of fairness is a suspected cause, there should be opportunities for appeal and investigation. For more on washback, see Chapter 2.

Another type of assessment that sometimes elicits cries of unfairness is the **group project**, where all the members of the group receive the same grade, regardless of whether the workload was divided equally or not. Typically, complaints arise when one member of the group contributed little or no work, while another or others contributed more than a fair share. In what ways can teachers address this issue of unfairness? Group projects are valuable learning experiences that can teach teamwork skills that are needed in many careers. If group assessments are viewed as unfair, teachers may allow students to choose their own partners, and/or they may include an individual component in the project, such as a paper reflecting on learning or a report on individual contributions to the project. Sometimes, group projects include self- and peer-assessments that help inform decisions about whether individual grades, rather than a group grade, should be awarded.

Professional conduct refers to the need for ethical action at all stages of assessment—design, implementation, scoring, and use. Unethical professional conduct might include designing tests that are deliberately too difficult or too easy for candidates to pass in order to deny or ensure entry to an institution or country; sharing confidential information (e.g. test questions or test results) with unauthorized individuals or groups; enabling cheating or providing inappropriate assistance during a test; and using assessment results for unintended purposes, such as teacher promotion or funding. In terms of classroom assessment, teachers should be aware of the halo effect, which can intentionally or unintentionally result in unethical conduct. For more information on the halo effect, see Chapter 11.

Accepted norms refers to standard procedures for designing, implementing, scoring, storing, and using assessments and results. These procedures are assumed to be understood for most assessments. For high-stakes tests, additional norms are required in terms of examiner training and security measures. Explicit rules for test administration, even scripted instructions, etc. are written down and monitored to ensure compliance.

A questionable issue that falls under norms is the reliance on traditional paper-and-pencil tests, despite the use of multimodalities and emphasis on multiliteracies in educational approaches. Validity may be compromised when there is a misalignment between the pedagogy and the assessment, and a lack of validity can raise ethical questions.

Elimination of bias is striven for, though it may never be completely possible. Every effort should be made to check and pilot assessment content and language for bias related to race, ethnicity, first language, gender, age, religion, sexual orientation, socio-economic status, etc. For high-stakes tests, committees of experts are set up to review test items for bias. Bias can also be a factor in the administration and scoring of tests. TTs should not be penalized based on appearance, manner or handwriting during a test, or any cultural indicators, such as name. Another important aspect of bias to be aware of in language assessment is that ideas should not be judged.

For example, a TT who claims that women should not work outside the home should not be penalized, even if the examiner's views are different.

Doing no harm should always be the goal. Harm can occur if candidates or TTs are not treated equitably or feel offended by assessment questions or administration procedures. For example, candidates may feel that they are unjustly penalized for misunderstanding test registration procedures, or test formats, or instructions, or for not knowing an item that is culturally biased. In addition, tests that cause unnecessary anxiety can do harm, resulting in a lack of validity. This can happen when severe anxiety prevents TTs from responding to items in a way that reflects their true proficiency. Test administrators and examiners should do everything they can to make TTs feel comfortable and at ease, ensuring that responses are an accurate and valid representation of a TT's capabilities.

In their interpretation of ethics, De Costa et al. (2021) include three core principles:

1. respect for persons
2. yielding optimal benefits while minimizing harm
3. preserving justice

While they primarily refer to ethics in applied linguistics research, these principles can also be applied to assessment. The inclusion of justice is important in English-language studies, where emergent bi- and multilingual learners are often marginalized.

Think-Pair-Share 12.2a   List some specific instances that you know of in which an assessment might be considered unethical. In what way was the assessment unethical?

Did you know?   The International Language Testing Association (ILTA) prepared a Code of Ethics for language testers in 2000 and made minor revisions in 2018. The full Code of Ethics is available on the ILTA website at https://www.iltaonline.com/page/CodeofEthics.

Think-Pair-Share 12.2b   Go to the ILTA website, https://www.iltaonline.com/page/CodeofEthics, and read the details in the annotated notes for nine principles. Explain your interpretation and/or experience of each to your partner.

Did you know?   Using verbal reports in a study of Cambridge raters, Orr (2002) found that "many raters show difficulty in adhering to the assessment criteria. There is also evidence that raters do not understand the model of communicative language ability on which the rating scales are based" (p. 153).

12.3   Importance of Ethical Testing

Ethical testing is particularly important given the commercialization of the testing industry and the high-stakes nature of some assessments. It is precisely due to the high-stakes nature of some tests that some people resort to unethical practices. For example, conduct an Internet search for *buying* IELTS or TOEFL certificates and you will find multiple hits. Consider, too, how often news stories report on unfair English testing practices or corruption.

- ***Student visa system fraud exposed in BBC investigation***: Secret filming of government-approved exams needed for a visa shows candidates having tests faked for them (Watson 2014)

- *College Board tightens SAT exam security, but key risk remains* (Stecklow and Dudley 2017)
- *German students protest unfair English exam* (Lynn 2018)
- *Italian police investigate claims Luis Suárez's citizenship exam was rigged* (Giuffrida 2020)
- *English test scandal*: *Home Office accused of "shocking miscarriage of justice"* (Gentleman 2022)

Think-Pair-Share 12.3a Why do you think so many instances of unethical assessment practices are reported in the media?

12.4 More on Consequences

Assessment results are often used to make high-stakes decisions, such as eligibility for immigration, citizenship, further studies, professional qualifications, and selection for placement, promotion, and awards. The consequence of using tests for such gatekeeping is an increase in the risk of unethical practices because, sadly, some people resort to unethical behavior when they are desperate. Notably, it is sometimes the test providers or stakeholders who conduct unfair practices. Consider the 2014 scandal in the United Kingdom in which thousands of international students were wrongly accused of cheating on an ETS test by the Home Office and subsequently detained and had their visas canceled. Ten years on, they were still in legal proceedings over unlawful detention and loss of earnings (Gentleman 2020, 2022, 2024a, 2024b). Moreover, testing has become a multimillion-dollar industry and the costs of a test can be a financial burden for individuals and families. For this reason, TTs have both a vested interest and a financial investment in getting fair treatment and results. Perhaps the reason these unethical practices are often reported in the media is that they violate readers' sense of justice and fairness, when a news item incites a reaction, readership increases.

Menken et al. (2014) discuss other consequences. They claim that "[q]uestionable ELP [English-language proficiency] tests have serious consequences, including provision of inappropriate educational services, poor predictions of English-classroom success or ability to take English-administered content assessments, and unfair school penalties under current accountability practices" (p. 603)... "What is clear is that emergent bilinguals consistently underperform in comparison to monolingual peers, making these students, their teachers, and schools serving them disproportionately likely to be penalized" (p. 604). These are serious consequences indeed and language educators should be doing everything possible to advocate for these learners.

De Costa et al. (2021) challenge interpretations of test scores and cite critiques of the way cut scores are used. For example, the B2 level in CEFR, often used as a cut score for many European universities, is criticized for its arbitrary use of proficiency criteria in language assessment without accounting for empirical data or performing a needs analysis. In another example, they cite Deygers et al. (2018), who suggest researching the profiles of international students who score just above and just below the cut scores on in-house university English entrance tests. The concern is that students who are denied direct admission may be unfairly required to enroll in in-house ESL courses, thus incurring more tuition fees.

German students cite excerpts from the English portion of the Abitur test, which is an exam for students who are completing high school and preparing to enter college (Lynn 2018). The excerpts are too difficult for the Abitur, and the Technische Universität Dresden (Rennert 2023) indicates that approximately a CEFR B2 level is needed to pass the language portion of the Abitur. Eisenmann (Baden-Württemberg's minister of culture) is cited saying, "I have full confidence in the teachers that they will use their discretion to make responsible and balanced corrections" (Lynn 2018, final para). In other words, it seems that it is up to the teachers to make corrections rather than test developers or a psychometrician equating this test form with previous years' test forms to ensure that the levels are equivalent.

Sometimes, the negative consequences and the strong reactions in the press and elsewhere have resulted in decisions being reversed. For example, the Michigan Student Test of Education Progress (M-STEP) had a recommended score of 1300 as a potential cut-off for determining which third graders would be promoted to fourth grade. Research addressing this by Winke and Zhang (2019) showed that "if the 1300 cut-off point is used, few English-language learners would pass. In addition, they found that other factors unrelated to language skills, such as economic status, contributed to the students failing the exam" (p. 63). Subsequently, M-STEP policy makers scrapped this as a requirement for promotion to fourth grade. In another example, the 2020 *revisions* to the US naturalization test by the Trump administration were more challenging and lengthier than before, according to the US Citizenship and Immigration Services (USCIS), and, in 2021, reverted to the *earlier version*.

Did you know? There has been some discussion about the fragmentation of international high-stakes tests, partly due to lack of trust over the reported misuse of tests and partly due to highly contextualized local needs (O'Sullivan 2012). The big international language tests, like IELTS and TOEFL, involve significant amounts of research, validation, and security procedures, and they continue to be trusted and valued by most people and institutions; however, as local assessment literacy is increasing and local needs become more contextualized, local tests may, in future, become more dominant.

12.5 Language Test Security

Test security is another aspect that may involve ethics. Some security breaches may be accidental, such as forgetting to lock a door or cabinet where tests or test results are stored. This is a serious issue that needs to be addressed, but if it was not an intentional breach of security, it is probably not an ethical issue. In contrast, deliberate test security breaches are unethical. For example, teachers or school administrators might give away answers to students on a school test to ensure high-test scores. Reasons for doing this may include a desire to nurture the students, or ensure a high score that would increase chances of promotion or reward. If it is done on a wide scale, it may be to ensure positive teacher evaluations or school funding. Regardless of the reason, such test security breaches are unethical.

Breaches of security on international language tests, such as IELTS or TOEFL, are extremely serious, whether intentional or accidental because the whole purpose is to have a reliable, trustworthy product that institutions and countries can depend on for making high-stakes decisions such as admission to a university or granting visas for immigration. If that trust is lost, the testing service will lose credibility and cease to be used. Consequently, if a test is leaked before the test date, hundreds or even thousands of tests must be replaced globally or tests must be canceled. Other security issues involve test candidates falsifying identification documents during the registration process, or bribing examiners to falsify scores. If such security breaches occur repeatedly at a specific test center, that test center will be shut down. Some colleges and universities that have lost trust in the testing system in some countries, go to great effort to send their own personnel to conduct the tests. This undoubtedly would increase the cost of testing. During the COVID-19 pandemic, when some testing centers closed down, some universities provisionally accepted the results of Duolingo and other home tests and, upon arrival, the students were required to take the institutional language test to verify the results.

Going forward, as remote and computerized tests become more popular, issues of test security need to be addressed. Some companies offer monitoring services. There are also cameras and browser locks, such as Respondus, to monitor candidates during testing. Michigan Language Assessment, for instance, has Zoom administrations of their Graduate Student Instructor Oral English Test, where the TT must do a 360 pan of their entire workspace area, aim the camera down on the desk and the floor, and have to power down their phone(s) right in front of the examiners' eyes. While such measures may increase test security, there are corresponding costs, both financial and in terms of accessibility. If TTs do not have the required equipment, they may be denied access to the test.

Think-Pair-Share 12.5 Investigate   In 2014, the United Kingdom experienced a now infamous security breach in the administration of the Test of English for International Communication (TOEIC). In the years since the scandal broke, the narrative has changed multiple times.

  a. Watch a report (Watson 2014) of the initial investigation by Panorama and make a list of test security breaches: https://www.bbc.com/news/uk-26024375 (for a more in-depth look at the fraud uncovered in the UK student visa program, see https://www.dailymotion.com/video/x1bx5uj) (BBC Panorama 2014a).
  b. Watch a video https://www.youtube.com/watch?v=cvotuj3wBsk (BBC Panorama 2014b) and read an article https://www.theguardian.com/uk-news/2022/feb/09/english-test-scandal-home-office-accused-of-shocking-miscarriage-of-justice providing updates on how the fraud investigation has unfolded.
  c. What lessons can stakeholders in language assessment draw from this international incident? Discuss.

12.6   Sample Language Assessment Items and Scenarios

Study the following language assessment items and scenarios and determine what might make them unethical. See suggested responses in Appendix 1 in the following.

12.6.1 Items from the Naturalization Civics Test for American citizenship:
  Who lived in America before the Europeans arrived?
  a. Canadians
  b. American Indians
  c. No one
  d. Floridians

12.6.2 Item on a general knowledge test:
  "The _____ of Oz" is a story that children love to read.
  a. Land
  b. Wizard
  c. Garden
  d. Magician

12.6.3 Item on a test for 8-year-old ESL students:
You need a _____ to enter that military establishment.
a. permit
b. precaution
c. proposition
d. permutation

12.6.4 Item on a reading comprehension test:
Eskimos use ice and earth to build their houses because these materials _____.
a. keep them cool
b. can be easily found
c. can last for a long time
d. are available and affordable

12.6.5 Item on a multiple-choice test:
Your family wants to go to Paris on vacation to _____.
a. visit the Leaning Tower of Pisa
b. meet French-speaking people
c. sunbathe on the beach
d. ski in the mountains

12.6.6 A TT's claim on a written language test states that men are more intelligent than women. The examiner penalizes the response for sexist content.

12.6.7 Instructions for examiners for scoring responses on a multiple-choice test:
Full credit is awarded for correct answers, no credit is awarded for items not attempted, and a penalty is given for items answered incorrectly.

12.6.8 You teach a "language for academic purposes" course. On the final exam, a highly proficient student makes some careless errors. You know her work in-class is of high quality so you decide to ignore the errors on the test.

12.6.9 An institution conducts an English entrance test that only takes 10 minutes to administer.

12.6.10 The space on a test where TTs are required to write their name is very small.

12.6.11 During a high-stakes test, a TT tells the invigilator that they need to use the toilet. The invigilator tells the TT they must wait until the test is over.

12.7 A Word on the Importance of Quality Assessment

Some language education institutions borrow from industry and adopt a "Quality Management Cycle" in an effort to demonstrate effective practices according to the purpose and relevant principles. This includes checking for ethical practice and enables accountability and standardization. However, defining *quality* can be very subjective and problematic given the highly contextualized nature of language education and assessment. Determining "client" satisfaction can be difficult, particularly long-term satisfaction, since values specific to assessment may often be conflated with values of education overall. For example, a student may not benefit from the assessment at the time, but later—perhaps even after the course is completed—the concepts become clear. Alternatively, a student may be fine with an assessment tool, but not the overall course or program, and, thus, give negative feedback on the assessment tool. Moreover, an assessment that is successful for one individual may not be for another. That said, it is important to continue to strive for quality assessments, which go hand-in-hand with improving programs and teaching and learning. We advocate ongoing review of language education and assessment practices, which involves checking that tools and practices are fair and align with ethical policies, documenting what works and what doesn't work in a given context, reviewing progress and assessment results clearly with students, professional development for educators, and taking action for improvement based on informed decisions and discussions with those involved.

12.8 Chapter Conclusion

To ensure ethical language assessments, we must examine our assessments and procedures for unethical content and practices. Educators, examiners, and administrators are accountable at all stages, from design to administration, scoring, and result use, especially for both high-stakes and low-stakes assessments. Following the ILTA Code of Ethics and creating assessments that are valid, transparent, fair, unbiased, just, and harmless will help make language assessments ethical.

Appendix 1 – Suggested Answers for 12.6 Sample Language Assessment Items and Scenarios

12.6.1 *American Indian* is a misnomer. *Native people* or *indigenous people* are preferred (McDowell-Wahpekeche 2021).

12.6.2 While "The Wizard of Oz" may be a well-known story in English-speaking countries, it may not be a story that children in other parts of the world "love to read." Moreover, this is the title of the movie. The book title is *The Wonderful Wizard of Oz* by L. Frank Baum.

12.6.3 The stem and options in this item are too advanced for the target TT.

12.6.4 The term Eskimo may be considered racist, as it was applied by colonizers and replaced by Inuit (Kaplan n.d.). Moreover, ice and earth are not used to build houses today.

12.6.5 This item suggests an elitist lifestyle that the TT's family may not follow.

12.6.6 Penalizing an idea or opinion on a language test makes the item invalid.

12.6.7 In a world where risk takers are often rewarded, it does not seem fair to penalize TTs for guessing. There is also a risk that TTs are not familiar with this format of test and the instructions may cause confusion.

12.6.8 This is an example of the halo effect, where the teacher is not scoring the assessment based on the responses given, but rather using their familiarity with the student's past performance to bias their judgment.

12.6.9 A 10-minute test would not present enough items to allow the TT to demonstrate a full range of language ability. This makes the test invalid, hence, unfair.

12.6.10 Not providing enough space for TTs to write their name shows bias against cultures with long names.

12.6.11 This does not comply with the first principle of the ILTA Code of Ethics—respect for humanity and dignity of TTs.

Appendix 2 – Achievement Quiz of Chapter 12

(For discussion or writing prompts, see the Think-Pair-Share tasks in this chapter.)

Directions: For questions 1–3, select all the answers that are correct. Questions 1–3 are worth 2 points each if entirely correct or 1 point each partial credit regardless of the number of correct answers per question. For questions 4–5, select the response that best answers the question below. Questions 4–5 are worth 1 point each.

1. Select all that apply. Which of the following are mentioned as a purpose for conducting language assessments?
   a. measuring and tracking progress in language learning
   b. offering proof for appropriate student placement
   c. assessing the effectiveness of teaching methods
   d. meeting entry requirements for education and immigration

2. Select all that apply. According to De Costa et al. (2021), what are the core principles of ethics?
   a. yielding optimal benefits while minimizing harm
   b. maximizing the washback of assessments
   c. maintaining respect for persons
   d. preserving justice

3. Select all that apply. In the case of an in-class oral presentation, which of the following aspects of the assessment would need to be clear and accessible to test takers for optimal transparency?
   a. assessment purpose
   b. assessment instructions
   c. scoring criteria
   d. sample responses

4. What additional factor should the teacher consider when assigning a group project?
   a. interrater reliability and access
   b. bias and lack of fairness
   c. high interactiveness
   d. low authenticity

5. Which of the following assessment situations features a teacher/test administrator behaving **un**ethically?
   a. permitting an immigrant language learner to use a bilingual dictionary during a science quiz
   b. granting extra time on a reading test with short answers to a student with diagnosed dyslexia
   c. penalizing a student for writing critically about the government's foreign policy
   d. confiscating a test taker's phone when they leave the test to use the restroom

13

Technology for Language Assessment

Chapter Overview

This chapter explores the role of technology in assessment, emphasizing the knowledge necessary for classroom teachers and language assessors. Given the rapid evolution of technology, it is important to note that specific examples and websites mentioned here may become outdated quickly. Instead of focusing on specific product names and links to the latest advances, the chapter provides concepts, categories, and search terms to help readers find current developments.

13.1 Learning Objectives

1. Explain the differences between fixed-path and flexible-path (computer-adaptive) assessment
2. Describe the features of text-to-speech technology and explain how it could be used to assess a specific group of language learners
3. Describe the features of automatic speech recognition and explain how it could be used to assess a specific group of language learners
4. Discuss/demonstrate which technology-aided strategies can be used to assess a specific group of language learners' multiliteracy skills
5. Explain the use the following terms in language assessment: artificial intelligence (AI), machine learning, and natural language processing (NLP)
6. Explain the impact of technology on the following overarching themes: timing, flexibility, feedback/scoring, item types, accessibility, security, and job loss

Think-Pair-Share 13.1 Schema Activation Which of the following words do you associate with technology? Mark them. Explain your choices.

Cassette players	Videos	Voicemail	Computers
E-mail	CD players	Smart phones	QR code readers
LP record players	Dictionaries	VR headsets	Calculators
Internet	Voice recorders	Films on TV	Video cameras
PowerPoint	Prezi	Clocks	Tablets
Audio-lingual labs	Smartboards	Classroom projectors	Augmented reality

A Practical Guide to Language Assessment: How Do You Know That Your Students Are Learning? First Edition.
Ildiko Porter-Szucs et al.
© 2025 John Wiley & Sons, Inc. Published 2025 by John Wiley & Sons, Inc.

13.2 Definitions

> **Technology:** "a practical application of knowledge especially in a particular area" (Merriam-Webster Dictionary 2024).
> **Educational technology, or ed tech:** "IT tools (hardware, software, internet) and educational practices aimed at enhancing and facilitating learning" (Daley 2022, Ed Tech 101 Section). It "is meant to boost student learning outcomes" (Tophat Glossary n.d., Educational technology section).
> **Technology in assessment:** The use of educational technology for assessment purposes.

Think-Pair-Share 13.2   Complete a quest in all chapters in this book for examples of technology. Search broadly. List at least five examples from various chapters. How do these technological tools serve purposes of assessment?

Think-Pair-Share 13.3a   What other examples of technology are you aware of that can be used for assessment? As you describe their uses, use assessment terminology you already know, such as formative, summative, no-/low-/high-stakes, and selected/constructed response, which part of the teaching-learning-assessment cycle it belongs to, where in the blueprint it belongs, etc.

13.3 No Tech or Low(er) Tech

Although the majority of the chapter discusses technology that is highly complex, we begin at the less complex end of the spectrum (see Figure 13.1). In some teaching settings, there is a scarcity of resources. Teachers may have little more available to them than themselves and their students. In such cases, the teacher can still implement on-the-run assessment, pair and group work, and other techniques that do not rely on any tools. If there is no electricity or battery, then wind-up clocks, chalkboards, pencils, and paper can be sustainable in the long run for timed assessments. If there is electricity or battery, simple devices such as stopwatches and cassette players are practicable. If the teacher has a smartphone—even if the students do not—Plicker quizzes (Plickers 2022) or ZipGrade (ZipGrade 2024) can offer instant selected-response assessment. A Scantron machine and an overhead projector are true and tried tools of teaching and assessment. In settings when young learners can benefit from receiving auditory feedback directly from their own reading, so-called whisper phones are low-tech tools for self-assessment. It is worth keeping such lower tech tools in mind, especially when teaching in settings where fewer resources are available.

Think-Pair-Share 13.3b   What other examples of no- or low(er)-tech are you aware of that can be used for assessment? In what settings and for what assessment purposes are they beneficial?

13.4 Skill by Skill

Listening, reading, grammar, vocabulary, formulaic language, etc. are traditionally assessed by selected-response items. Because of this high-practicality component, they can be easily administered and scored in a variety of settings. Placement decisions at institutions are commonly based on institutional placement tests that focus solely on the assessment of those skills that can be

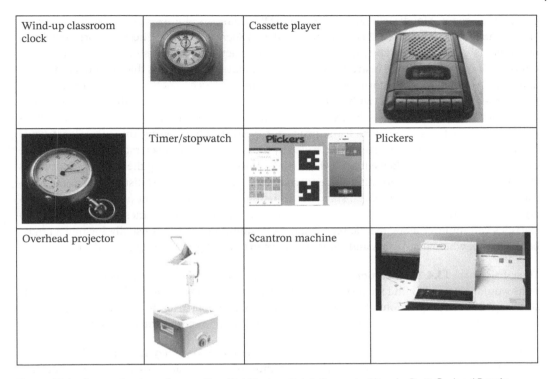

Wind-up classroom clock		Cassette player	
	Timer/stopwatch	Plickers	Plickers
Overhead projector		Scantron machine	

Figure 13.1 Low technology. *Sources:* Barni1 / Pixabay, Caleb Oquendo / Pexels, Brett Sayles / Pexels, PLICKERS / http://baharyurgu.blogspot.com/2015/06/plickers.html/ / last accessed on August 22, 2024, chungking / Adobe Stock, Lisa Giles / flickr / Public domain

administered quickly to a large number of prospective students. The assessment of productive skills, in contrast, typically lacks practicality. The assessment of speaking, pronunciation, and fluency often involves a private interview with a teacher/rater, who rates the speech sample in real time or later from a recording. The assessment of writing can be administered to a group of TTs, but requires that a teacher or rater then score each writing sample individually. Thus, for reasons of practicality, institutions often make their placement decisions solely based on the assessment of receptive skills through selected-response tests.

13.4.1 Receptive Skills

On the lower tech end of the spectrum, traditional paper-and-pencil tests are typed into a computer or website. Search terms such as "[insert language] quizzes," "online [insert language] quizzes," and "test your [insert language]" produce numerous results. These websites abound with multiple-choice grammar and vocabulary tests, with occasional listening and reading assessments. They are freely available to teachers and learners alike and provide instant scoring. It is important to note though that their quality can vary. The designers of these assessments are rarely trained in assessment principles, so users should approach them critically.

Learning management systems (LMSs) and other quiz-creation websites allow teachers to create their own quizzes. Examples of LMSs include Blackboard, Educator, Schoology by Power School,

Google Classroom, Moodle, Canvas, and Talent LMS. Examples of quiz-creation websites include Hot Potatoes (n.d.), Quizlet (2024), Quizizz (2023), and Socrative (2024). These platforms also enable students to generate quizzes, which can be a useful activity for assessing metacognition. The quiz function of LMSs allows instructors to create automated assessments that students can access and submit online. Most platforms support a variety of item types, such as multiple-choice, true-false, yes-no, multiple-choice with multiple keys, sequencing, matching, fill-in-the-gap, short-answer, and essay. Short-answer items can be automatically graded if there are a limited number of predetermined responses, which the instructor types in when setting the quiz. Constructed responses, on the other hand, need to be graded by the instructor. However, most LMSs provide the option for instructors to add feedback, which students see when receiving their scores. Instructors can often view detailed reports after students complete a quiz, including statistics such as the highest and lowest scores, mean scores, standard deviation, average time spent on the quiz, item discrimination, and facility value (for more information on the meanings of these terms and on how statistics can improve assessments, see Chapter 14). Additionally, LMSs usually include a gradebook feature, where instructors and students can keep track of grades throughout the course.

Think-Pair-Share 13.4.2 Exploration   Conduct a web search for LMSs in your location. What questions would you need to find an answer to in order to decide whether you could use one with your students? List these questions (Hint: Some of the considerations overlap with the test specifications, or blueprint). Select one of the LMSs and evaluate it for a setting you are familiar with.

Online quiz tools tend to have a narrower scope than an LMS. They may include flashcards, selected-response quizzes such as matching and multiple-choice, and possibly a few other item types. Many of them are web-based, such as Quizlet, Quizizz, Socrative, Quizlet Live, and Kahoot! The latter two take a game-based approach to quizzes. The teacher, acting as a game-show host, sets the questions and displays them in the classroom, while the students, the game-show contenders, compete for first place on their own devices. In addition to the web-based tools, Hot Potatoes is notable freeware that can be downloaded to a teacher's or institution's computer, installed there, and hosted on their webpage. The software suite consists of five item types—JCloze (cloze or fill in the blank), JCross (crossword maker), JMatch, JMix (mixing the order of sentences), and JQuiz— (Hot Potatoes n.d.). There is also a sixth exercise type, the Masher, which combines as many of the other item types as desired[1].

Continuing our review of increasingly high-tech assessment tools of receptive language skills, technology has enabled **flexible item pathways**. In the assessment tools mentioned thus far, the order of items is either predetermined by the instructor or randomized by the program. Randomization has benefits from the perspective of test security. However, the benefits of flexible pathways go even further. According to the Office of Educational Technology of the US Department of Education, **computer-adaptive testing** has improved the ability of assessments to accurately estimate student knowledge and skills across the curriculum in a shorter testing session than would otherwise be necessary (2017). Computer-adaptive testing uses algorithms that adjust the difficulty of questions based on the student's responses during the test. For example, if the student answers a question correctly, a slightly more challenging item follows; if they answer incorrectly, the next item provides the student another opportunity to demonstrate their knowledge in a different way. Because adaptive testing targets content and test items that aim to match each student's

---

1 For a tutorial on how to create self-assessments in Hot Potatoes, JCloze, JCross, JMatch, JQuiz, JMix, see Tnteu (2020).

proficiency level, the adaptation leads to more accurate results for all students regardless of proficiency level, and in significantly less time. With a traditional paper-and-pencil or **fixed-path computerized test**, students would have to answer many more questions to achieve the same level of accuracy.

Did you know?   Perusall is a social learning tool designed to turn reading into a collective experience. It can be integrated with various LMSs, where instructors either upload any document that they own the rights to (such as their exercises, articles, syllabi, and textbooks) or legally arrange through their institution, bookstore, or Perusall to use any other readings (such as a book by another author). As students read, they annotate, pose questions to their classmates, provide and receive answers to questions, and learn through the engagement with the material and each other. The instructor can, but does not need to be involved. Based on its proprietary algorithm, Perusall then automatically grades students' contributions and engagement, though the instructor does have the ability to override the AI (Perusall.com 2024.; Introduction to Perusall 2021).

13.4.2   Speaking, Pronunciation, Fluency

Technology can offer numerous benefits in the assessment of oral language production. At the simplest level, recording devices (such as voice recorders, video cameras, and CDs) can record the outgoing prompt and/or stimulus passage to which the TT/student responds. This has the benefit of standardizing the input that the learner receives. The TT's/student's output can also be recorded for asynchronous rating, quality assurance, or rater training.

At a higher tech level, various technologies can assist in the improvement and assessment of pronunciation and fluency. **Text-to-speech software** as well as recordings with variable speeds can be set to play back speech at increasing speeds. Initially, learners can shadow speak/read aloud with the technological tool at a slower speed. Each subsequent time, the speed can be increased slightly while maintaining a focus on comprehensible pronunciation. In addition to varying the speed at which text is read aloud, most text-to-speech programs also make available male and female voices and numerous accents. Varying the voices, when available, can also train students to understand a wider variety of accents.

On the flip side, **speech-to-text technology** can also be beneficial in assessment. Dictation websites can type what they hear. Some of them, such as Dictation.io, can even do it in multiple languages. As a self-assessment tool, learners can dictate a text into the software, available on a smartphone or computer, and later compare what is written down with the original text. Any discrepancy can be brought to the teacher or a peer so that it becomes clear whether the source of the discrepancy is the learner's mispronunciation or inaccuracy in the program.

Speech-to-text, or automatic speech recognition, involves a computer processing human speech and creating readable text from it. The technology has been improving for more than 60 years. Common educational uses of this technology include live captioning of e-learning content and transcribing audio and video content, although automatic speech recognition is commonly used in call centers, finance, government, law, health care, military, retail, tourism, and media as well (Rev 2020).

Speech-to-text has accessibility benefits. Someone who cannot fully use their hands may prefer voice input for navigation, while a person with limited hearing might need transcripts of a video or podcast. Similarly, someone with a visual impairment might need a screen reader to understand the text on the screen. Speech-to-text makes all of this possible by helping platforms, websites, and apps to better understand natural human speech. Security concerns are addressed in multiple ways, such as training of employees and encryption of data at rest and during transmission through the cloud.

Think-Pair-Share 13.4.3 Exploration Conduct an internet search for any websites, programs, software, tools, applications, tests, etc. that automatically

a. turn text into speech, or read typed text aloud
b. recognize speech and turn it into text
c. assess spoken language

What are some of their appealing qualities? What questions do you have about these programs?

13.4.3 Writing

The assessment of writing has traditionally been characterized by low practicality. The teacher of a course in which students are required to write would assign a topic, the students would write in class or at home and submit their writing to the teacher, who, depending on the level, would spend the following days or weeks grading. Under optimal circumstances, the teacher would use a rating scale, which is well known to the teacher as well as the students. Typically, no new writing would be assigned until the teacher could work through the pile of papers and the students would receive— sometimes very delayed—feedback. Then, the cycle of writing, waiting, and feedback or grading would start anew. At other times, the students would write the subsequent assignment before having received feedback on the previous paper because the teacher is still buried under the previous pile. In some extreme cases, no feedback or grade would reach the students before the course would end. In earlier chapters, we have learned that productive skills, such as speaking and writing, can best be improved and assessed through direct (rather than indirect) practice and assessment. We have also learned that feedback is most beneficial if it is specific and prompt. These demands, however, are at odds with what most overworked classroom teachers are able to provide. While self- and peer-assessment are tools whose benefits far exceed freeing teachers up from the constant grading, at some point the students can benefit from the feedback of a more knowledgeable other.

It is the above challenge that technology-infused assessment is in the best position to address. As discussed earlier, instant grading is among the benefits of technology-based assessment. However, this pertains to not only the instant grading of selected-response items but also that of constructed-response assessment. Continued advances in AI, generally, and in its branch NLP, specifically, have made it possible for computer programs to process writing in real time and to provide automatic formative feedback.

Artificial intelligence (AI) "mimics the way a human would perform a task. AI systems achieve this through different techniques. **Machine learning**, for example, is a particular methodology of AI that involves teaching an algorithm to perform tasks by showing it lots of examples rather than by providing a series of rigidly predefined steps" (Grammarly 2024).

Natural language processing (NLP) "is a branch of AI that involves teaching machines to understand and process human language (English, for instance) and perform useful tasks, such as machine translation, sentiment analysis, essay scoring, and [...] writing enhancement" (Grammarly 2024).

One notable example is *Write and Improve* (W&I) by Cambridge English (2024b). This free online tool is aligned with the CEFR. After students self-select their level of proficiency as "beginner, intermediate, or advanced," they can choose from among dozens of prompts and start writing. Instructions specify the genre and word count of the response. Beginner prompts are sometimes accompanied by illustrations. Within seconds after the language learner submits a writing sample, W&I assigns a CEFR level and highlights sentences that need improvement.

Below is an example of one of the authors of this book responding to a beginner prompt in W&I. The task was to describe three accompanying pictures in 35–100 words. The writer has attempted to imitate the writing of a beginner writer who has mastered simple sentences in the Simple Present Tense and a few formulaic sequences such as "it is raining" and "at home" (see Figure 13.2).

After analyzing the writing sample, the W&I tool rated it as A1 and highlighted four sentences in lighter and one in darker color. The feedback did not provide more specificity as to the meaning of color coding, the nature of the problems, or how to correct them. A student would have to either know, ask a more proficient user of the language, such as a teacher, or revise the writing sample through trial and error. When testing the tool, we were able to revise our initial writing sample over a dozen times, without reaching any limit imposed by the W&I tool, if one exists.

Figure 13.3 demonstrates how one of the authors of this book has been able to revise the initial writing sample repeatedly to earn a rating in every CEFR band by the AI.

> Two boys play tennis. The weather is nice. The weather is bad. It is raining. Two boys have umbrella. They do not play tennis. Two boys play video game at home. They play tennis at home.

Figure 13.2   Cambridge English's Write and Improve.

1. After creating a free account in Cambridge English's (2024b) Write and Improve, we began by selecting the beginner level. Next, we selected one of the dozens of prompts. The prompt stated to describe the three pictures in 35–100 words. When we completed the following writing, we submitted it and received a CEFR rating (A1) and feedback as to which sentences should be revised (here underlined).

   Two boys play tennis. The weather is nice. The weather is bad. It is raining. Two boys have umbrella. They do not play tennis. Two boys play video game at home. They play tennis at home.

2. In the second round, we revised our writing sample. Our goal was to improve the highlighted sentences and in general to produce a writing sample that was more reflective of A2-level writing. Once we submitted the revision, the W&I tool rated the writing sample as A2 and marked a new set of sentences.

   Two boys are playing tennis and the weather is nice. Then the weather is bad because it is raining. The two boys have an umbrella. They are not playing tennis. Two boys are playing video game at home. They are playing tennis at home.

Figure 13.3   Cambridge English's Write and Improve A1-C2.

(Continued)

3. Again, we revised and resubmitted the paragraph. The new rating was B1 and different sentences were marked.

> On a tennis court in the city, two boys are playing tennis in nice weather. Suddenly the weather becomes bad. When it starts to rain, the two boys stand under their umbrella and they stop playing tennis. Finally, they go home and play a video game at home. The video game is tennis.

4. After the next round of revisions, a rating of B2 was awarded.

> On a sunny, though somewhat overcast day in the city, two friends decided to get together to play tennis. No sooner did one of them hit a serve, when the sky turned dangerously dark and the match got washed away by the rain. The boys quickly sought refuge under an umbrella while weighing their options. It did not take long for them to realize that the weather did not necessarily have to spoil their fun: they could play tennis and remain dry by playing a video game, in the comforts of their home. All's well that ends well.

5. Despite multiple attempts, further revisions resulted in no higher CEFR level than B2. Therefore, we returned to the landing page and identified our level as Advanced. We selected a new prompt from among the advanced topics. We were prompted to write an email between 220 and 260 words in response to the topic of proposing that the principal of my college invite a speaker.

> Dear Principal Smith:
>
> As per your request, I am writing to you with a proposal to celebrate the 100th anniversary of the College: to invite Ms. Greta Thunberg as a guest speaker. She would be the ideal candidate to open the celebrations at our College of Environmental Sciences. Ms. Thunberg, the Swedish climate activist, though still too young to have a university degree at the age of 19, has already received an honorary doctorate from a Canadian university. For the past four years, Ms. Thunberg has been the leading voice on the climate crisis. She has drawn crowds of tens of thousands. She has been invited to speak before the United States Congress and was even included in *Time Magazine's* list of the 100 most influential people in 2019.
>
> The event we are celebrating is not only the 100th anniversary of our university, but also our commitment to continue to be a leader in environmental education for the next 100 years. Nothing will accomplish this better than the presence of Greta Thunberg. She can connect with Generation Z, inspire them to take climate action seriously, and have far-reaching effects as our current students and alumni carry her ideas forward. The visit of such a celebrity is sure to be noticed by the local, national, and even international press, bringing global attention to our College.
>
> Therefore, for the above reasons, I believe that the College should open its centenary celebrations by Greta Thunberg, as its invited speaker.
>
> Yours sincerely.

Figure 13.3 (Cont'd)

6. The writing sample above, despite its minor flaws, was rated by the AI as C2 on the CEFR. However, it received only 2.5 out of 5 on being on topic. In other words, the AI must have expected to receive more words that it would have identified as directly relevant to this topic but failed to receive them. The word "principal" in the address was flagged as incorrect even though it was included in the prompt.

> Dear ☆ ? Principal Smith:

The *'s* after *Time Magazine* was marked as an unnecessary word.

> and was even included in Time Magazine ❗ s

The following sentence was highlighted without any explanation.

> plish this better than the presence of Greta Thunberg. She can connect with Generation Z, inspire them to take climate action seriously, and have far-reaching effects as our current students and alumni carry her ideas forward. The visit of such a celebrity is

7. Next, we removed a few formulaic sequences and turned some succinct phrases into clauses in order to produce the C1-level passage below.

Dear Principal Smith:

You requested and I am writing to you with a proposal to celebrate the 100th anniversary of the College: to invite Ms. Greta Thunberg as a guest speaker. Ms. Thunberg, the Swedish climate activist, is still too young to have a university degree because she is only 19, yet she has already received an honorary doctorate from a Canadian university. She would be the ideal candidate to open the celebrations at our College of Environmental Sciences. For the past four years, Ms. Thunberg has been an authority on the climate crisis. Tens of thousands of people listen to her. She has been invited to speak before the United States Congress and was even included in *Time Magazine's* list of the 100 most influential people.

The event we are celebrating is not only the 100th anniversary of our university, but also our commitment to continue to be a leader in education for the next 100 years. Nothing will accomplish this better than the presence of Greta Thunberg. She can connect with Generation Z, inspire them to take climate action seriously, and have far-reaching effects as our current students and alumni take her ideas forward. The visit of such a celebrity will definitely be noticed by the local, national, and even international press, bringing global attention to our university.

Figure 13.3 (Cont'd)

> Therefore, I believe that the College should open its centenary celebrations by Greta Thunberg, as its invited speaker.
>
> Yours sincerely,
>
> When the AI evaluated the above sample, and scored it as C1, it highlighted the same sentences as problematic as it had before.

Figure 13.3 (Cont'd)

Think-Pair-Share 13.4.4a Analysis and Application

a. Select one or two of the writing samples above. Based on how the W&I tool evaluated them, how might the construct of writing be defined by the AI[2]? (For a reminder of defining the construct, see Chapter 2).
b. Look up the writing scale (Overall Written Production) in the CEFR (Companion Volume 2020). Analyze each of the writing samples above in light of the corresponding level descriptions. If you were a human rater tasked with rating these writing samples, would your rating match those of the computer? Explain why or why not.
c. Select a rating scale of writing that you are familiar with.

   - Use the rating scale to evaluate one of the above writing samples.
   - How would you score it?
   - What feedback would you give to the writer?
   - Next, compare your score and feedback with those assigned by the W&I tool.
   - What are the similarities and differences?

Think-Pair-Share 13.4.4b Discovery Type the following keywords into a search engine and discover the latest websites that offer machine scoring of writing: *automated writing evaluation (AWE), automated essay scoring, automated essay grading software, essay rating tool, online writing evaluation, e-rater.* Explore two or three such tools in greater detail. For which context might they be useful and why? Are any available for the language that you (will) teach/assess?

Think-Pair-Share 13.4.4c Experiment Submit your own or your student's writing sample to one of the AWE websites. Examine the feedback you receive. How might this website be useful to you or your students?

Automated Writing Evaluation tools' algorithms are trained using corpora of written language. It is important, therefore, that the corpora be well chosen to "represent the tasks and discourse of the target language use domains" (Huawei and Aryadoust 2022, p. 19). For instance, if the corpora used to train the AI contain newspaper articles, the AWE will be more appropriate to rate the writing of students of journalism than that of young learners.

AWEs, however, are a black box, partially because the code is proprietary and partially because many of the decisions are made by the AI itself and even the programmers cannot have complete

---

2 This is not to imply that the proprietary technology behind this or any other automated evaluation tool is necessarily based on a definition of the construct that it assesses.

insight into its functioning. It is often unclear to users which corpora the AI is trained on. As the technology gains prevalence, an increasing number of studies are conducted on various qualities of test usefulness, such as their reliability, construct validity, and criterion-referenced validity. In their meta-analysis of AWE grading/marking systems, Huawei and Aryadoust (2022) argue that, based on the validity evidence in the reviewed studies, AWE technology is not yet ready to replace human raters. It is currently best used alongside human raters or in low-stakes, formative assessments.

Think-Pair-Share 13.4.4d Research-based Analysis Based on what you have learned about AWE, what is your informed opinion about the possibilities and limitations of humans vs. computers evaluating writing? Support your response with facts and sources.

Did you know? The Versant family of language assessments is fully automated. For instance, the Versant English Placement Test (VEPT) is a 50-minute-long four-skills test. It consists of nine parts: Read Aloud, Repeat, Sentence Builds, Conversations, Typing, Sentence Completion, Dictation, Passage Reconstruction, and Summary & Opinion. It can be taken on a computer that is connected to the internet or on one where the software resides on the computer. The entire test is scored within minutes by AI (Pearson English 2020; VersantTests 2019).

Think-Pair-Share 13.4.4e Application After watching the "Product Tour" of the VEPT online (VersantTests 2019), evaluate those qualities of test usefulness (VIP WAR) that you can. Which qualities are you not able to comment on based on watching the video? Of the qualities that you can evaluate, which ones appear high, which ones mid, and which ones low? Explain.

13.5 Multiliteracies

Although the preceding section delved into how technology can aid in the assessment of isolated or integrated language skills, increasingly language learners are called upon to apply their skills in a multiliterate manner (see Chapters 1 and 10 for more information on multiliteracies). Guided by the work of Kalantzis and Cope (2019) on Multiliteracies Theory and the Seven Affordances of New Technology, in order to assess students' multiliteracies, teachers can adopt the following strategies.

1. *Ubiquitous Learning*
   Assess students' ability to access and use assessment tools across various devices and locations. Consider the flexibility provided by technology in evaluating their understanding of concepts without being bound by traditional time and space constraints.
2. *Active Knowledge Making*
   Evaluate students' proficiency in creating and sharing digital artifacts. Assess their capability to actively engage in producing knowledge through the use of technology, moving beyond memorization to the application and synthesis of information.
3. *Multimodal Meanings*
   Design assessments that require students to express themselves through various multimedia elements. Evaluate their effectiveness in incorporating videos, experiments, or debates in meaningful ways to convey information, demonstrating a multimodal approach to communication.

4. *Recursive Feedback*

Assess students' responsiveness to immediate feedback mechanisms provided by digital assessment tools. Evaluate how well they utilize feedback from peers, experts, and teachers to iteratively improve their work, contributing to a recursive feedback loop.

5. *Collaborative Intelligence*

Evaluate students' collaborative skills in an online environment. Assess their ability to use technology for collaborative creation and assessment of knowledge, reflecting a collective intelligence approach to learning.

6. *Metacognition*

Assess students' metacognitive skills by evaluating their use of reflective technology tools. Examine their ability to reflect on experiences, learning processes, and the impact of technology on their understanding. Consider self-awareness and metacognitive skills in the assessment.

7. *Differentiated Learning*

Utilize adaptive assessment platforms to tailor assessments to individual learning needs. Evaluate students' proficiency in navigating various pathways and formats provided by technology, ensuring that educational outcomes are achieved through personalized approaches.

8. *Immersion in Texts*

Assess students' interactive experiences with texts facilitated by technology. Evaluate their ability to engage with diverse digital environments, demonstrating immersion in texts through interactive and meaningful interactions.

9. *Learners as Knowledge Makers*

Evaluate students' active contribution to knowledge creation using digital resources. Assess their ability to utilize infinite digital resources for research, exploration, and application in the creation of meaningful content.

10. *Multimodal Representation*

Assess students' proficiency in creating digital projects.

13.6 Further Considerations

In the previous pages, we have discussed how technology has affected the assessment of language skills, subskills, and multiliteracies. In the following, we explore the impact of technology on some overarching themes.

Think-Pair-Share 13.6 Review   Look for evidence in the chapter of the impact of technology on the timing, flexibility, and feedback and/or scoring of assessment. These are some overarching areas in which the role of technology in assessment can be most felt.

Further overarching themes include **item types, accessibility, security, and loss of jobs**.

13.6.1 Item types

Technology has enabled item types that are not possible on a paper-and-pencil language test. The Office of Educational Technology (2017) in the United States has identified the following:

- graphic response, to which learners respond by moving, arranging, or selecting graphic areas
- hot text, where students select or rearrange sentences or phrases within a passage

- performance-based assessments, in which students perform a series of complex tasks (2017)
- scenario-based assessments with computerized interlocutors (Purpura 2021)

13.6.2 Accessibility

Technology can have both a positive and negative impact on accessibility. On the positive end of the spectrum, technology enables the personalization of assessment, such as supporting students with disabilities through assistive technology, such as text-to-speech, speech-to-text (discussed earlier in this chapter), and a refreshable Braille display (n.d.); adjusting the font size, the volume, and the color contrast; and embedding bilingual dictionaries and glossaries. However, technology is a deterrent for examinees who are not used to it. Among refugees and the elderly, it is not uncommon to find someone either who has never used a computer before or who is afraid of using it. Compulsory computerized examinations usually begin with a tutorial on how to use a computer, a keyboard, and a mouse. Nevertheless, this is very little exposure and practice if one is not comfortable using them to some extent already.

13.6.3 Security

On the one hand, technology has reduced security concerns in assessment. It has eliminated the need for piles of secure test forms to be transported to test centers and then stored in a locked filing cabinet inside a locked office. In a classroom setting, there is less of a need for test papers to be guarded around the photocopier or to be stored in the teacher's desk. On the other hand, no technology is fraud-proof. To deter and prevent as many breaches of security as possible, during computerized assessment, a range of measures can be implemented. In a high-stakes testing center, TTs may be required to show a variety of picture identification such as a passport or driver license. They may be finger- or hand-printed. They may be photographed, their iris may be scanned, or their face may be scanned and compared against a picture ID. Inside the test center, in the computer lab, TTs are often seated in such a way that the proctor has a clear view of their screens. Monitoring takes place through a camera or by a human proctor who walks around. Cameras can be aimed at the computer screen, keyboard, and the TT's face. In case of suspicious TT behavior, a proctor may intervene and even invalidate the test.

The COVID-19 pandemic-induced closure of test centers and educational institutions has accelerated a trend in testing from home. When the student/TT and instructor/invigilator are not in the same room, technological tools can facilitate test security. As briefly mentioned in Chapter 12, there is software available for purchase that locks the computer screen or browser. A webcam tracks the TTs' eyes, monitors head and hand movements; a microphone detects voices and sounds in the student's environment; software locks the browser and desktop and inhibits common functionality on the computer, such as minimizing a browser window, printing a screen, or copying and pasting (Kanfer 2021; Kasen 2021; Stike 2021). In addition to the aforementioned browser locking solution, educational institutions and testing agencies often monitor test security with online proctors. The protocol here usually involves a series of pre-, while-, and post-test steps. Prior to the test, the TT identifies themselves by holding their picture ID close to their face and looking into the camera until the proctor has confirmed the TT's identity. Next, as briefly mentioned in Chapter 12, the TT performs a 360 scan of the room, directs their camera where instructed by the proctor, and proves that the room is free from unauthorized help. The proctor then monitors the TT during the exam and can instruct the TT to repeat the scan if any suspicious behavior is detected.

Think-Pair-Share 13.6a Exploration Conduct an internet search for test security measures common in your setting.

a. Search for the term: *browser lock software.*
b. Search for the terms: *online test proctor, AI proctor.*
c. Search for videos that demonstrate a room scan.

Apply your findings to your setting. Which, if any, of these technological tools are appropriate and practical for your setting? Discuss.

Think-Pair-Share 13.6b Exploration We began this section with the statement that no technology is cheat-proof.

a. Conduct an internet search for advice on how to cheat on exams to evade detection or by hacking into testing systems. Share your findings.
b. Discuss the implications of your findings narrowly (for your teaching and assessment setting) and broadly (for the trust stakeholders have in assessments).

At the intersection of rapid technological development and writing assessment, ChatGPT currently takes the place of honor. This chatbot can compose reasonably well-written responses to questions and prompts in numerous languages. For example, the following paragraphs were written by ChatGPT (see Figure 13.4). The prompt we gave it was "How can students cheat with ChatGPT?" In response, the AI wrote the following text within 4 seconds.

The follow-up question we typed into the chatbot was, "Does a plagiarism checker detect text generated by ChatGPT?" The answer was a logical, though probably an inaccurate, one (see Figure 13.5).

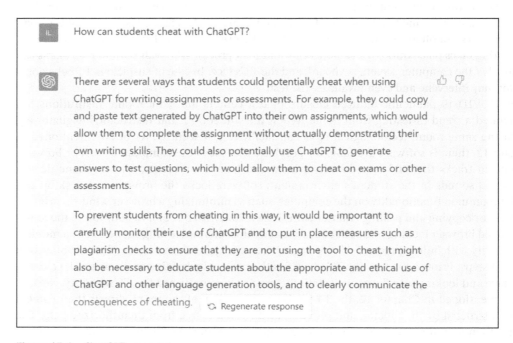

Figure 13.4 ChatGPT prompt 1.

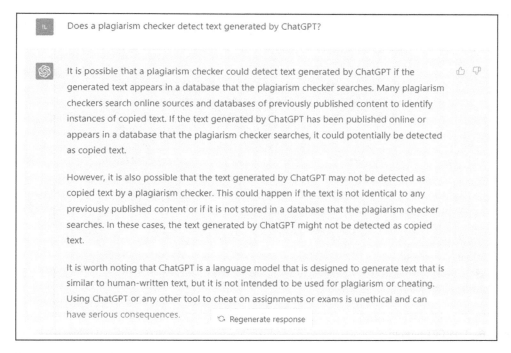

IL. Does a plagiarism checker detect text generated by ChatGPT?

It is possible that a plagiarism checker could detect text generated by ChatGPT if the generated text appears in a database that the plagiarism checker searches. Many plagiarism checkers search online sources and databases of previously published content to identify instances of copied text. If the text generated by ChatGPT has been published online or appears in a database that the plagiarism checker searches, it could potentially be detected as copied text.

However, it is also possible that the text generated by ChatGPT may not be detected as copied text by a plagiarism checker. This could happen if the text is not identical to any previously published content or if it is not stored in a database that the plagiarism checker searches. In these cases, the text generated by ChatGPT might not be detected as copied text.

It is worth noting that ChatGPT is a language model that is designed to generate text that is similar to human-written text, but it is not intended to be used for plagiarism or cheating. Using ChatGPT or any other tool to cheat on assignments or exams is unethical and can have serious consequences.

↻ Regenerate response

Figure 13.5 ChatGPT prompt 2. *Source:* Author created

If the abovementioned response were accurate, and text generated by a chatbot would be saved in a database or anywhere searchable, then a plagiarism detector would have a chance to detect it. Thus, we asked another follow-up question: "Is text generated by ChatGPT automatically saved, stored, or published somewhere by OpenAI?" To this, the chatbot produced the following response (see Figure 13.6).

The power of this and similar technologies speaks for itself. Their publication has generated vigorous discussion of their nature, potential, and mostly negative consequences (see O'Brien 2023; Schroeder 2022; Townsend 2023; Warner 2022). Alexander has been compiling an ongoing list of "Resources for exploring ChatGPT and Higher Education" (2022-ongoing). Efforts are even underway to create an AI detector that can recognize whether a text has been written by a chatbot or by a human (Cerullo 2023). The cat-and-mouse game between students wishing to outsmart the school system and representatives of said system has thus been taken to a whole new level. The full consequences will only unfold in the future. In the meantime, teachers who would like to assess their students' writing and ideas have few tools to ensure that their students are the ones producing specific ideas and writing. The best tool at their disposal is in-class writing, whether in a physical classroom face to face or in a remote, virtual classroom with live proctoring.

Think-Pair-Share 13.6c Investigation

a. Provide ChatGPT with a command in a language that you are proficient in. For instance, you may write, "Write an essay about the harmful effects of smoking." Evaluate the response generated by the chatbot. How proficient is the writing in the target language? How accurate is the content of the essay?

b. Ask ChatGPT to translate the above into another language that you are proficient in. Evaluate the proficiency of the translation produced by the chatbot.

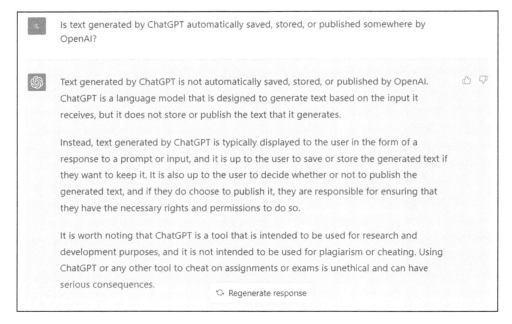

Figure 13.6 ChatGPT prompt 3.

Think-Pair-Share 13.6d Investigation

a. Play a game published in the *New York Times*: Follow this link: https://www.nytimes.com/interactive/2022/12/26/upshot/chatgpt-child-essays.html (Miller et al. 2022). Review the writing samples in the *New York Times* article, written in response to various prompts and try to determine whether they were written by a human child or by ChatGPT.
b. How accurate were your guesses?
c. What lessons can teachers of language and content areas learn about their ability to assess their students?

Think-Pair-Share 13.6e Investigation There are numerous alternatives to ChatGPT.

a. Conduct an internet search for other chatbots.
b. Assess the various chatbots' capabilities in the language you teach or assess. Do any of the technologies produce particularly good translations, texts, poems, or other answers to your queries?
c. For language professionals, what, if any, concerns might arise from this state of technology?
d. For language professionals, what, if any, opportunities might this technology offer?

Think-Pair-Share 13.6f Investigation Revisit Think-Pair-Share 12.5 on the English testing scandal in the United Kingdom that was uncovered in 2014. Re-read the articles and re-watch the videos with a focus on technology.

a. What role did technology play in contributing to the security breach?
b. What role did technology play in detecting the security breach?
c. What lessons can stakeholders in language assessment draw from the role technology can play in breaching test security and detecting its breach? Discuss.

Did you know?   In 2017, an Irish veterinarian failed a computer-scored oral English test she needed to remain in Australia. "While she blitzed all other components of the test including writing and reading, she failed to reach the minimum score immigration requires in oral fluency" (Australian Associated Press 2017).

1. According to Louise Kennedy, the test taker, "There's obviously a flaw in their computer software, when a person with perfect oral fluency cannot get enough points." (Australian Associated Press 2017)	2. "Pearson has categorically denied there is anything wrong with its computer-based test or the scoring engine trained to analyse candidates' responses...the immigration department set the bar very high for people seeking permanent residency." (Australian Associated Press 2017).	3. If a human rater inflates a test taker's score because, for instance, the rater recognizes that the test taker is a native speaker, then this is unfair human-rater bias. The human rater should not deviate from the rating scale regardless of who the test taker is.	4. Voice recognition technology that automatically assesses speaking has been trained on human ratings. It is able to measure aspects of fluency (such as pauses, silence, hesitations, speech rate, etc.). It has been designed to fairly and accurately rate without human bias.
5. It is the Australian government that set the bar too high if a native English speaker with two university degrees obtained in English is unable to earn a passing score.	6. A human rater would have recognized that the test taker was a native speaker of English and would probably have inflated her score.	7. Every test is a reflection of a single performance. Even native speakers' performance can be flawed at times. Being a native speaker does not guarantee a high score.	8. Native English speakers from one English-speaking country should be exempt from language proficiency exams when immigrating to another.

Figure 13.7   Opinions on the Irish vet's immigration to Australia. *Source:* https://tinyurl.com/speechbubbleicon

Think-Pair-Share 13.6g Evaluation   There has been no shortage of opinions on the case of the Irish vet whose oral English fluency was rated 74 (approximately B2 on the CEFR) instead of 79 (approximately C1), the minimum required by the Australian government for immigration. Evaluate the following arguments about the matter (see Figure 13.7). Which ones do you find compelling and why?

13.6.4   Loss of Jobs

Throughout the chapter, we have discussed numerous achievements of technology but also some of its unintended consequences. Loss of jobs is another such consequence. AI is going to continue to take away the jobs of language teachers and evaluators. One could argue that a portion of writing and speaking samples assessed by AI would never have been assigned by teachers or produced by learners because teachers would not have been able to evaluate them anyway. However, another portion of the writing and speech samples now rated by AI would once have been evaluated by human raters. In addition, as the quality of AI assessment improves and stakeholders' confidence in it grows, this trend of job losses will only continue.

13.7   Chapter Conclusion

This chapter provides an overview of the roles of no-tech, low-tech, and high-tech in assessment. We introduced concepts, terminology, tools, advantages, and disadvantages. The main purpose is to show what is possible and where educational technology is heading, encouraging the reader to explore the latest developments applicable to their setting.

We close with this online Language Testing Listserv post by Xiaoming Xi on the current state of AI assessment technology: "If you're a skeptic, then AI is better than you thought but if you're an optimist, then AI is not there yet" (2022).

Appendix 1 – Achievement Quiz of Chapter 13

(For discussion or writing prompts, see the Think-Pair-Share tasks in this chapter.)

Directions: For questions 1–4, select the response that best answers the question below. Questions 1–4 are worth 1 point each. For question 5, select all the answers that are correct. Question 5 is worth 2 points if entirely correct or 1 point partial credit regardless of the number of correct answers.

1. Language teachers who would like to ensure that it is the student and not a chatbot who is doing the assignment should _____.
   a. run student writing through a plagiarism checker
   b. avoid informing students about the technology
   c. have students hand-write their homework
   d. assign in-class writing assignments

2. According to experts, automated writing evaluation tools are mostly _____.
   a. effective when used in low-stakes assessments
   b. sophisticated enough to replace human raters
   c. valid and reliable for high-stakes assessment
   d. understood by programmers and researchers

3. A teacher who emphasizes her students' proficiency in multiliteracies may assess which evaluation criterion in an oral presentation?
   a. use of multimedia elements
   b. sensitivity to multiculturalism
   c. integration of multiple reliable sources
   d. triangulating through multiple measures

4. Advancements in technology have resulted in the following new item type.
   a. hot-text response
   b. pictures as options
   c. authentic assessment
   d. supply-cloze passages

5. Select all that apply. Speech-to-text technology includes which of the following benefits?
   a. is accessible across multiple platforms
   b. is accessible for learners with disabilities
   c. allows for self-, peer-, and teacher-assessments
   d. trains learners to understand a variety of accents

14

Improving Assessments Through Statistics

Chapter Overview

In this chapter, we introduce essential statistical concepts relevant to classroom teachers and item writers. We begin by highlighting teachers' ethical responsibility to their students. The discussion covers how basic statistical analyses can enhance teaching, learning, and assessment. We emphasize the importance of data-driven decision-making in one subsection. Overall, every teacher should possess a basic understanding of common statistical concepts. This knowledge enhances classroom tests and improves comprehension of standardized tests beyond statisticians working in test development and large organizations.

14.1 Chapter Objectives

1. Explain the purpose of using statistics in language assessment
2. Explain teachers' ethical responsibility in analyzing and improving assessments
3. Perform the most common statistical calculations
4. Summarize the complexities of data use for assessment
5. Recognize how correlation and causation differ

14.2 Statistics in Assessment

Think-Pair-Share 14.2a Background schema activation

a. In what (if any) ways in your <u>personal</u> life is statistics present?
b. As a second/foreign language teacher, when/where do you <u>professionally</u> need or foresee the need to know statistics?

Think-Pair-Share 14.2b

a. Reflect on your own experience as a teacher administering a specific classroom assessment. Where did the items come from?
b. After administering this assessment to your students and grading it, what steps did you take? You probably calculated their score and recorded it in the gradebook. Did you learn from the assessment experience in any way?

A Practical Guide to Language Assessment: How Do You Know That Your Students Are Learning? First Edition.
Ildiko Porter-Szucs et al.
© 2025 John Wiley & Sons, Inc. Published 2025 by John Wiley & Sons, Inc.

Teachers have an **ethical responsibility** to analyze and improve assessments. Analysis "provides a basis for accountability about the quality of an assessment" (Coombe et al. 2007, p. 158). Washback (the impact of assessment on teaching and learning) partially comes from the analysis of the assessment. In the classroom, we make decisions based on assessment results and those decisions affect students' lives in major and minor ways. Yet, according to Coombe et al. (2007), "the most frequently ignored phases of the assessment cycle are analysis, feedback, and reflection" (p. 158).

Analyses can provide teachers with **valuable information** (from Coombe et al. 2007, p. 159) such as

- the proficiency of individual students
- the abilities of all the students in the class
- the achievement of course goals
- the quality of teaching (a word of caution: be careful about correlating assessment scores with quality of teaching because many other factors may play a role as well) (even testing organizations whose assessments are used for this purpose by schools or policymakers caution against such use; their assessments were not designed to measure the quality of teaching)
- how well course and teaching activities have helped students learn
- if assessments reflect course aims and outcomes
- comparison of schools/classes that took the same assessment
- reliability of the test and its results
- whether the assessment discriminates (i.e. distinguishes between more and less able TTs)

Analysis provides a basis of accountability for the **quality of an assessment**. This is how one can tell whether an assessment is reliable and valid for specific context and use. Standardized testing organizations carry a heavy burden to produce quality assessments because their tests are often high stakes and impact a large group of TTs. To this effect, their statisticians perform numerous analyses for a variety of purposes, including ensuring test quality and security. Increasingly, they make a case for the quality of their tests with the Assessment Use Argument (for more information, see Chapter 2). However, even classroom teachers can—though often lack the time to—perform basic analyses to aid their teaching and their students' learning. Coombe et al. (2007) recommend the following analyses to help classroom teachers improve the quality of their assessments:

- calculate the overall frequency distribution of scores from every assessment
- check distribution against expectations for that type of assessment:
  - was this a diagnostic, achievement, etc. test and
  - what are our expectations going into it and
  - as we're analyzing the results, where are the results compared to our expectations
- use distribution to make final decision about cut points/cut scores (unless predetermined by upper administration)
- conduct item analysis for representative items and those with problems
- revise or reject items as needed
- recycle well-performing items
- use analysis results to inform students, own teaching, colleagues, administration, program revision (for positive washback; pp. 158–159).

14.3   Terms and Analyses

Item writers, test developers, and classroom teachers without the support of a team of statisticians can benefit from learning to conduct a few basic calculations. Some of them illuminate patterns in student performance. Others shed light on item performance.

14.3.1   Distributions and Frequencies

Frequency is the number of times the students received a particular score on a test.

For example, in a class of 15 students, on a quiz with a maximum score of 10, how many times did someone receive a score of 0 or 1 or 2 or ... 8 or 9 or 10?

The **frequency distribution table** is a list of all the students' scores in numerical order from lowest to highest. The table tells us how frequently each score appeared.

For example, in the above class of 15 students, the distribution of scores may look as follows:

Score	Frequency	Percentage (%)*
10	1	6.7
9	1	6.7
8	2	13.3
7	1	0
6	3	20
5	4	26.6
4	1	6.7
3	1	6.7
2	0	0
1	0	0
0	1	6.7

*For classes with large numbers of students, percentages may be helpful. The percentages here are approximate due to rounding. For instance, a score of zero occurred one time, so the percentage is 1/15 students = 0.0667 → times 100 = 6.667, rounded up = 6.7

Dispersion (variability or spread) is the degree to which scores differ from each other.[1]

Are the scores bunched together because almost everyone got the same score or are the scores wide apart? A similar concept is standard deviation, which will be introduced later. Unlike standard deviation, which is one score, dispersion is all the scores.

(Continued)

---

1   See Lane (n.d.) for definitions of central tendency, spread, shape, graphs.

(Continued)

For example, the mean of the following pairs of scores is 2.5 even if their spread is not the same:

$(5 + 0) \div 2 = 2.5$

$(2 + 3) \div 2 = 2.5$

$(1 + 4) \div 2 = 2.5$

Applied to a teaching situation, imagine that you teach three classes, with two students each. In the first class, one student earns 5 points and the other zero. Their average (mean) score is 2.5. In another class, one student earns 2 points and the other 3. Their mean is also 2.5. In the third class, one student earns 1 point and the other 4. Their mean score is also 2.5, yet the scores in the three classes are different. Thus, the mean can tell us some information but dispersion can give us more insight into the scores. Specifically, a wide spread may suggest highly differentiated learners or inconsistent teaching, etc. A narrow spread may suggest less differentiated learners, more uniform preparation, etc.

Pass Rate is the rate or percent of students who have passed. It is calculated by adding up the number of passing students (for example, all As, Bs, Cs, and Ds if these are passing scores) and dividing this number by the total number of students in the class.

For instance, if 14 out of 15 passed, then the pass rate is $14 \div 15 = 0.933 = 93.3\%$

Failure Rate is the opposite of the pass rate. It is calculated by adding up all the students with failing grades/marks (if F is the only failing grade, then everyone who got this is added up) and this number is divided by the total number of students in the class.

For instance, if 14 out of 15 students passed, then 1 failed. The failure rate is $1 \div 15 = 0.067 = 6.67\%$

Measures of Central Tendency comprise three ways to measure the middle of a distribution of scores: mean, median, and mode.

Mean is the arithmetic average; it gives us information about the average student's success on the assessment. Add up (take the sum, or total of) all the scores, and divide them by the number of scores. A low mean score means the assessment was hard. A high mean score means it was easy. Outliers (i.e. extremely high or low scores) influence the mean.

For example, if a class has three students and their scores on a 10-point quiz were 10, 8, and 5, the sum of the scores is $10 + 8 + 5 = 23$. Divide this by the number of students in the class, which is 3. Therefore, $23 \div 3 = 7.67$ out of 10 was the mean score of this class.

Calculate the mean for the whole test and for subsections. If a test assesses the four major skills (listening, speaking, reading, and writing), there will be a class mean for the entire test and separate means for each skill.

Median is the midpoint score when you arrange (put in order) scores from high to low.

In our example class of 15 students depicted in the frequency distribution table, the median score is 6; it's the score of the 8th student (there are seven students with higher and seven students with lower scores). This score is unaffected by outliers; therefore, it is more representative of the typical student. However, if there were an even number of students, for instance 16, the median would be the average of the 8th and 9th students. For example, if the 16th student's score was a 1, then the 8th and 9th scores would be 5 and 6. The median would be 5.5 (5 + 6 = 11, 11 ÷ 2 = 5.5).

Mode is the most frequently occurring score (the number that is the most common).

In the example class of 15 students displayed in the above frequency distribution table, the most frequently occurring score is 5 (four students earned a score of 5). If another student earned a 6, then both 5 and 6 would be the most frequent scores; therefore, both 5 and 6 would be the mode.

Think-Pair-Share 14.3a Application   Look at the following achievement test results and make a frequency table.

7, 7, 8, 9, 9, 10, 10, 11, 12, 12, 12, 13, 13, 13, 13, 14, 14, 14, 15, 15

Frequency Table for Class A

Score	Frequency	Percentage

Think-Pair-Share 14.3b Application   Using the numbers from Think-Pair-Share 14.3.a, what are the mean, median, and mode? And how can a teacher interpret these scores? What should the teacher's next steps be to help the students?

Think-Pair-Share 14.3c   Score reports of high-stakes standardized language assessments report the total score as well as section sub-scores. Figure 14.1 depicts an example from the TOEFL iBT. Why do you think the practice of reporting total and sub-scores is common? Why might it be useful?

Think-Pair-Share 14.3d   In their program admission requirements, many universities in English-speaking countries specify a minimum total score as well as minimum subsection scores on English-language tests required of applicants. One such example is Eastern Michigan University's MA TESOL program (2024). Why do you think this is the case?

Think-Pair-Share 14.3e   As of late, the score reports of some high-stakes standardized language assessments also report the TT's MyBest Scores, or so-called "superscores." These are the highest

Figure 14.1 ETS (2023). Total and section subscores. *Source:* https://tinyurl.com/ETSbest83

MyBest® **Scores**

Sum of Highest Section Scores	Reading (0–30)	Listening (0–30)	Speaking (0–30)	Writing (0–30)
86 out of 120	**22** Test Date Dec 16, 2023	**23** Test Date Mar 10, 2023	**21** Test Date Dec 16, 2023	**20** Test Date Jun 02, 2022

Figure 14.2 ETS (2023). MyBest Scores. *Source:* https://tinyurl.com/ETSbest86

subsection scores from multiple test-taking attempts within a specified time. Figure 14.2 depicts an example from the TOEFL iBT. Who might benefit from this practice? If you were responsible for your institution's admission of international students, would you accept superscores? Please explain.

Histograms are a type of bar graph that can be used to depict how well a group of students did on an assessment. The pattern shown is a curve of how well the group of students did on the test.

Norm- vs. criterion-referenced testing offers two distinct ways of drawing inferences about TTs' performance on a specific assessment. These test types differ in purpose, construction, items, and interpretation. Norm-referenced tests allow comparisons between individuals while criterion-referenced tests measure a TT's performance against a set of standards or criteria (Burkett 2018).

Norm-referenced tests (NRTs) compare students' or TTs' scores to each other. They sort students into high and low performers based on how others (the norm group) performed on the same assessment. Items target various proficiency levels. The scores are frequently expressed as a percentile.

The scores approximate a bell curve, which means that 50% of the students are above and 50% below the 50th percentile. In the bell curve below (A), the mean, median, and mode are the same. This is called a "normal" distribution.

A:

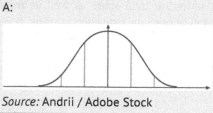

Source: Andrii / Adobe Stock

The cut score is often post-determined, in other words, after the test administration. This test does not lend itself well to tracking progress.

Uses of NRT: They are not used to show how much students have learned in a certain time. Instead, institutions often use NRTs for placement, to offer a limited number of spots to the top-performing students, or to **grade on a curve**. Curved grading is frequently used if the teacher cannot control the difficulty of a test but would like to ensure that at least some students earn As, Bs, Cs, etc. Then the teacher can select the top (for instance) 5% of students to receive an A, the next (for instance) 10% a B, etc. regardless of what score the students actually earned.

For example, if on a test out of 100 points the highest score was 60. If the cut scores for A vs. B vs. C, etc. had been decided in advance, then maybe nobody would have earned an A, B, or C and only those scoring 60 would have earned a D. Everyone else would have failed the test. If the instructor believes that the assessment may have been unusually difficult and the students should not be punished for it, then the instructor can decide that the top performers deserve the highest grade/mark. In that case, the instructor may post-determine that anyone who earned 55–60 would receive an A. The instructor has arrived at this calculation by comparing the students to each other, in other words, norm-referencing. Norm-referencing is common in competitive admission or in competition for an award. Only the top students will be rewarded with admission or the award, regardless if their top achievement is 100% or 80%. NRTs may be considered discriminatory, as the score is not related to the students' ability level but to who else was in competition.

Criterion-referenced tests (CRTs) are designed to determine if the students measure up against the criterion rather than other students, whether they have mastered the targeted skills. Multiple individual items may target the same proficiency level. CRTs have a narrower range of scores. The cut scores are pre-determined. CRTs are well suited to tracking progress.

When scores/grades/marks are assigned by criterion referencing, then the cut points are pre-determined. Potentially everyone may receive the same score. The reference point is the criterion, which could be the learning objectives. Typical CRTs are classroom tests, driving exams, certification exams. Many English proficiency tests such as the TOEFL and IELTS are CRT.

This is what an achievement test's histogram may look like in a class where most students learned the material well (see histogram B with skewed distribution toward higher grades).

B:

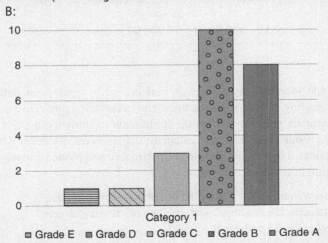

In order to plot grades on a histogram to visualize distribution in Excel, watch the tutorial by ECD Educational Technology Support (2012).

Standard Deviation (SD) is a measure of dispersion, how spread out a data set is, how closely scores are distributed around the mean. As demonstrated earlier, the mean can be the same with narrow, tightly clustered vs. widespread, scattered score points. In a class of three students, if the scores are 1, 5, or 9, the mean is 5. In another class of three students, if the scores are 4, 5, or 6, the mean is again 5. However, the SD is different. Using a standard deviation calculator, we see that the SD in the first case is 4, while in the second case is 1. The smaller the SD, the closer the numbers are to the mean, the more similarly the students performed.

Calculating SD can provide essential information for the classroom teacher. In the case of a class with a large SD, instruction will need to be differentiated to help those who have fallen behind to catch up while those who have achieved the learning objectives can be challenged. In the class where the SD is small, all students can receive the same level of instruction.

The SD may reveal a **bimodal distribution** (Glen 2013). This means that the SD has two peaks or two modes. This suggests two groups of students. Maybe one group who studied and another who did not, or one group who understood the material and another group who did not. The following is a histogram of a bimodal distribution (see histogram C).

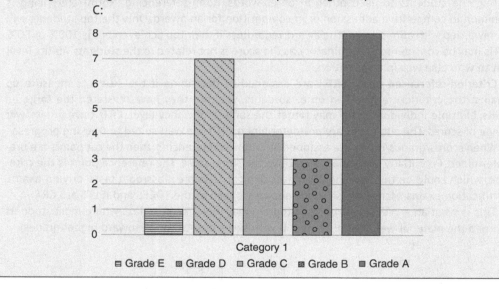

C:

Category 1

▤ Grade E   ▨ Grade D   ▢ Grade C   ▩ Grade B   ▦ Grade A

Think-Pair-Share 14.3f Practice   As a teacher, you primarily implement constructed-response assessments. After grading each assessment using the same rating procedure as usual, you calculate the mean to compare your current group of students to students in prior semesters and in other sections of the same class. You also calculate the standard deviation. On the most recent assessment, your standard deviation was unusually large, so you plotted a histogram. This showed a bimodal distribution in the class.

a. What does it mean that there is a bimodal distribution in your class?
b. How can you describe the students' performance on this assessment?
c. How will you as a teacher address the issue?

14.3.2 Item Statistics

Thus far, we have examined a group of students: a class or all TTs in a single test administration and the scores obtained by them. Now, we will turn our attention to the individual items on the assessment that the students or TTs took.

Item Analysis is used to check that individual test items are working appropriately. Good test items can be and frequently are recycled in a test bank. Faulty items (those that are not performing properly) need to be analyzed to understand why they are not working. It could be due to item violations or unexpected interpretations. Item violation means that the item itself is problematic, perhaps poorly written. Unexpected interpretation means that the item is well written, yet Ss are confused or tricked by it and the item is thus not fulfilling its role.

Item analysis is performed to avoid tests that are overall too easy or too hard and to remove unfair, biased, or otherwise problematic items. Item analysis takes place after test administration, when results are received. Even experienced item writers, despite doing their best to craft items to specifications, frequently struggle to hit the targeted level and write flawless items.

Item Difficulty or Facility Value (FV) is the proportion of correct responses. It is calculated by taking the number of students who answered correctly and dividing that number by the total number of students who answered. For instance, 100 students take a test of five items as depicted in the following table.

Item Number	Correctly Answered	Total Responses	Item Difficulty, or FV
1	95	100	0.95
2	48	100	0.48
3	13	100	0.13
4	29	100	0.29
5	83	100	0.83

There is some flexibility in what is considered an easy or hard item. Often an item with a FV of 0.8 and higher is considered easy while 0.3 and lower is considered hard. In other settings or situations, ≥ 0.95 is considered easy and ≤ 0.15 is considered hard. Both of these ranges can be considered appropriate for proficiency tests. On an achievement test, a FV of ≤ 0.5 might denote a difficult item since it means that only 50% of the students answered the item correctly even though they have studied it and all of them should know it.

The target FV for a proficiency test is 0.4–0.6. The test should start with easy items as confidence builders and finish with another one to end on a high note. Toward the middle, the items should become progressively harder. The way the test form is constructed, it should build up to the more challenging items.

The **Item Discrimination Index (ID)** examines if the item distinguishes, or discriminates, among stronger and weaker students / TTs. Stronger (sometimes called *more able*) and weaker (sometimes referred to as *less able*) only means the students' performance on the assessment in question. It does not suggest anything else the teacher may know about these students.

The possible range of ID is −1.0 to +1.0. Reliable items should discriminate at +0.30 or above. The closer the discrimination is to +1.0, the better.

When calculating ID, follow three steps.

1. Divide the class into high and low groups by setting aside the top 27% (or 25%) and the bottom 27% (or 25%) based on their overall score on the assessment. Ignore the middle 46% (or 50%).
2. For each item separately, count how many of the high group got the item right. From this, subtract how many in the low group got it right.
3. Divide the above number by the size of the top group that answered that item (i.e. 25% or 27% of the total students).

This method works best with 100+ students and less so with smaller numbers.

For example, 100 students took a test. The final score has been calculated and the students have been put in order from highest to lowest scores.

1. The top 25% (=25 students) and the bottom 25% (=25 students) are set aside for calculation. The middle 50% are ignored.
2. Examining item 1, 23 of the top 25 students answered item 1 correctly but only 5 out of the bottom 25 students did so. $23 - 5 = 18$
3. $18 \div 25 = 0.72$

This means that the ability of item 1 to discriminate among more and less able students is 0.72. This is considered a strong ID and a sign of a well-written item. In other words, a student who did well on the test overall had a high chance of keying this particular item; conversely, a student who did not do well on the test overall had a low chance of answering this item correctly.

Items that have an ID of <0.3 are problematic in some way. They need to be re-examined, revised, re-pilot-tested. Alternatively, they might need to be retired or rejected.

Items that have negative discrimination are highly problematic. A negative ID means that low performers did better on the item than did high performers. This often points to an incorrectly placed key, some error in the wording of the item, high-performers overthinking the item, or another source of confusion. Such an item needs to be reexamined, revised, re-piloted, or retired.

If an item's discrimination is zero—which can happen if everyone gets the item right or wrong—then the item does not help the instructor separate students into high-performing and low-performing groups. All students answering a question correctly is good news on an achievement test. On a proficiency test, however, such an item is a waste of time and space since it does not provide the tester with beneficial information about the TTs.

Note: Sometimes students skip an item on a test. Since ID is calculated separately for each item, in step 3 above the denominator in the division would need to be adjusted for the fewer students who attempted the test item.

Think-Pair-Share 14.3g Practice Consider the table below. How would you interpret the columns, rows, and each ID? What decision would you take about each item and why?

Item Number on Test	Difficulty for Top 27%	Difficulty for Bottom 27%	Item Discrimination Index
1	0.85	0.20	0.65
2	0.81	0.57	0.24
3	0.91	0.08	0.83
4	0.49	0.60	−0.11
5	1.0	1.0	0.00

Distractor Analysis/Distractor Efficiency investigates whether all options perform well and whether distractors attract students. In MCQs, options are either keys or distractors. Teachers and item writers need to ensure that all of the options serve a purpose. The Distractor Analysis calculates high- and low-performing groups. Create a table to show each item, total responses, low responses, and high responses. Any distractors with no responses should be changed because they do not appeal to any TTs; therefore, they do not serve a purpose. Every option should be attractive to some TTs: the key to those who have mastered the material, in the case of an achievement test for instance, and the distractors to those who did not. The items and options should never be confusing or tricky, just appealing to the low achievers. If any distractor is unappealing, then in effect the item is reduced from four options to three, thereby increasing the likelihood of someone guessing the key from 25% to 33%. A classroom teacher would do well to see which students found which option attractive, whether any patterns based on L1 or gender or age, etc. can be detected. Some options may be more attractive to one group of students than another.

Calculation:

Look at the response distribution of the top 27% (or quarter) and bottom 27% (or quarter) separately. → Start by looking at an item with high discrimination. Who was attracted to each option? High or low achievers? This gives the teacher insight into how these two groups of students are choosing among the alternatives. The teacher will know how to teach the topic differently in the future.

Think-Pair-Share 14.3h Practice Conduct a distractor analysis on the item below, which appeared on an achievement quiz for future English language teachers:

a. identify the stem, options, key, and distractors
b. understand what the numbers mean
c. decide what, if anything, you would do if this were an item in your class

Item Difficulty	Discrimination Index	1. Which of the sentences in the answer choices is in the Simple Present tense?		
0.50	+0.78	a. I won't take online classes.	2 respondents	20%
		b. I haven't taken online classes before.	0 respondents	0%
		c. I'm not taking online classes.	3 respondents	30%
		d. I don't usually take online classes.(* key)	5 respondents	50%
			10/10 respondents	

14.4   Use of Data

Did you know?   Data use, in part, originated in the United States as a consequence of the No Child Left Behind (NCLB) Act and has continued in the *ESSA* in which learning outcomes were defined in terms of results and attaining specified targets (Wayman, Spikes, and Volonnino 2013). This stimulated the use of data for informing teaching and learning in schools in the United States (Wayman, Jimerson, and Cho 2012), but at times, for accountability and compliance, rather than for continuous improvement (Hargreaves and Braun 2013). Policymakers have stressed the importance of data use to make education an evidence-based discipline (Mandinach and Schildkamp 2021).

Initially, the focus of data use was on accountability of learners but without accounting for differences in learning contexts. Later, the focus has shifted to continuous improvement, with consideration for students' individual needs and characteristics (Mandinach and Schildkamp 2021). The latter sociocultural paradigm allows for the consideration of more than test scores. "Educators need data, such as demographics, attendance, health, transportation, justice, motivation, home circumstances (i.e. homelessness, foster care, potential abuse, poverty), and special designations (i.e. disability, language learners, bullying) to contextualize student performance and behavior" (Mandinach and Schildkamp 2021, p. 2). With these additional sources of data, educators can improve the quality and process of decision-making.

Data use can benefit stakeholders if done well. According to Garner (2024), formative and summative classroom assessments inform teachers, parents, and students; assessment results can be used to improve teaching and learning (Marsh 2012; Schildkamp et al. 2019). Data from low- and high-stakes assessments, attendance, graduation rates, demographics, grades, finances, socioeconomics, etc. inform school personnel, districts, educational agencies, and other stakeholders external to schools. However, data that collect dust are worse than useless since their collection itself takes time and effort. Data-driven decision-making necessitates the analysis of data. Without analysis, decisions are often based on "opinions, assumptions, and anecdotal evidence" (Aguilar, as cited in Burroughs 2020, Why It's Important section, para.1). Similarly, data used for inappropriate purposes are highly problematic. Such can be the use of student test scores for teacher evaluations.

Data analysis and interpretation is an iterative process. It involves professional judgment (Schildkamp et al. 2019), as decision-makers filter data through their own lenses or "try to fit data into a frame that confirms their already pre-existing beliefs" (Kahneman and Frederick as cited in Mandinach and Schildkamp 2021, p. 3). Frequently, data are used solely for accountability and compliance purposes. The narrow use of data on raising standardized test scores reinforces a deficit mindset regarding students, a narrowing of the curriculum, and a restriction of teacher creativity (Mandinach and Schildkamp 2021). "The accountability pressure can also manifest itself in cultures where teachers feel the potential for retribution and punitive actions, shaming and blaming, especially when their students do not meet expectations, and therefore have little trust in data use" (Mandinach and Schildkamp 2021, p. 4). This could lead to a situation relayed to the authors by a recently graduated teacher who, at final exam time at a primary school, was told by a high-ranking school official to stand aside while the school official dictated the test answers to the whole class. The official unapologetically informed the young teacher that the reason for this form of academic dishonesty was the necessity to improve the school's accountability indicators. Similarly, English learners and low-performing students have been "disappeared" from schools, so that their test scores would not lower the school's performance indicators (Fernandez 2012). Such instances of manipulation, misuse, and abuse of data are not uncommon negative effects of accountability pressure.

In order for data use to be beneficial, based on their review of the scholarly literature, Mandinach and Schildkamp (2021) make the following recommendations.

- Do not start with data, but with clear and measurable goals.
- Triangulate different data sources, to capture the needs of diverse students.
- Collectively engage in a sense-making process, for example, in a data team.
- Connect professional judgment and data use to increase the quality of decision-making.
- Involve students in the process of data use.
- Conduct research into the role of students in the process of data use.
- Balance the use of data for accountability and continuous improvement.
- Assume an asset-based model for data use rather than a punitive, deficit approach that is based solely on accountability that tends to further marginalize the most challenged students.
- An increase in student achievement is an important goal for data use, but also focus on other important educational goals, such as well-being and equity.
- Acknowledge that data are diverse and that it is important to look beyond traditional indices.
- Use a combination of formal and informal data in the decision-making process.
- Align different types of data to the different kinds of decisions that need to be made to make actionable decisions to inform practice.

Think-Pair-Share 14.4a Application   First, think of a low-stakes formative assessment and answer the following questions. Next, think of a high-stakes summative assessment and answer the same questions below.

After you administer any form of assessment to your students, what do you do with the data you have collected? Has collecting data proven to be beneficial to your teaching practices? What, if any, data are you required to collect for stakeholders external to your classroom?

Remember! Frequently, the above exercise divides teachers into those who can readily relate to it (usually teachers of young learners in K-12 schools) and those who believe that these questions do not apply to them (usually teachers in other contexts, of adults, in higher education, etc.). It is important to remember the title of this book though: "How do you know that your students are learning?" You find out by completing the assessment cycle and after administering the assessment, examining its results, understanding whether the students have mastered the material, reviewing the items, and improving them as needed. Teachers regardless of their setting must take a close look at the assessment experience and the resulting data to effect positive washback and to advocate for learners.

Think-Pair-Share 14.4b Application   Select an assessment for language learners that carries medium- to high-stakes (for instance, ACCESS for ELLs in the United States or the Matura in Europe). Drawing on the aforementioned recommendations of Mandinach and Schildkamp (2021), discuss how the data from the assessment should be used.

Think-Pair-Share 14.4c Application   Examine the results of a test you have administered to your students. Perform the analyses on your assessment listed in Section 14.3.

14.5   Correlation vs. Causation

Think-Pair-Share 14.5a Background schema activation – Causation

a. Create up to three sentences that show causation using the word "because." One example might be, "Because Paulo studied the chapter, he did very well on the test." Which part is the cause and which is the effect?

b. Now analyze each of the sentences. Are the sentences true? Did the part that you identified as the cause really cause the part that you identified as the effect? Was it the only cause or just one of many potential causes? Explain.

Think-Pair-Share 14.5b Background schema activation – Correlation

a. Create up to three sentences that show a connection between events. Connecting words may include "at the same time, concurrently, meanwhile, before, after, coincidentally," etc. One example might be, "After the school purchased a new curriculum, the students' test scores increased.[2]"

b. Now analyze each of the sentences. What is the relationship between the two events? Does one cause the other? Are they coincidental? Are they related but not causally because of a third variable? Explain.

> The Australian Bureau of Statistics (n.d.) provides the following succinct yet accessible definition of these related concepts.
>
> **Correlation** is a statistical measure (expressed as a number) that describes the size and direction of a relationship between two or more variables. A correlation between variables, however, does not automatically mean that the change in one variable is the cause of the change in the values of the other variable.
>
> **Causation** indicates that one event is the result of the occurrence of the other event; i.e. there is a causal relationship between the two events. This is also referred to as "cause and effect."
>
> Theoretically, the difference between the two types of relationships is easy to identify … In practice, however, it remains difficult to clearly establish cause and effect, compared with establishing correlation.

The relationship between correlation and causation is akin to that of an insect and a bug. Every bug is an insect but not every insect is a bug. Similarly, in every causal relationship, there is correlation among the variables but not every correlation is necessarily causal.

---

2 The two variables (the school purchasing the new curriculum and the students' increased test scores) are likely correlated. In order to establish causation, an experiment could be set up where all other variables would need to be kept constant to see whether the purchasing of the new curriculum alone would lead to the increased test scores. It is not known whether the new curriculum was implemented and in what way. Was the school start and end date adjusted concurrently? Were the students better fed concurrently? Were the teachers retrained to implement the new curriculum and would other teachers with the same retraining but without the new curriculum have been more effective as well? Was the test on which the students did well also changed? Did the new curriculum teach to the test? All of these questions could point to other reasons why the relationship between the two variables might be correlational and not causal. Further, the relationship might be causal but not necessarily imply an improvement: the new curriculum may reflect learning objectives that are outdated or biased or problematic in some other way.

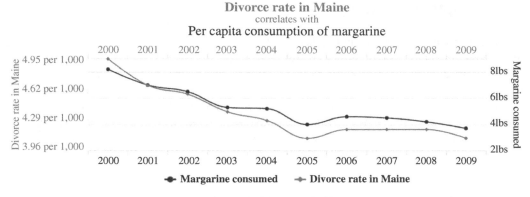

Figure 14.3 Example of spurious correlation. *Source:* https://tinyurl.com/correlationsgraph

There are situations when causation is clear. If we stand in the rain without a cover, we are going to get wet. If a fruit falls from the tree, it is going to fall down rather than up. If a novice student of a language with a different writing system is absent from class and doesn't study for the test, then they won't be able to read and understand the test.

There are also situations when a lack of causation is clear, even comical. Spurious Correlations (tylevigen.com, n.d.) is one of many websites that present two data sets that appear to be causally connected but are, in fact, unconnected. One example presented on this site is the steadily declining divorce rates in the US state of Maine between 2000 and 2009 and the similarly declining per-capita consumption of margarine over the same period (see Figure 14.3). The correlation between the two trends is 99.26%. The way the two trends are presented alongside each other suggests that one causes the other.

In other situations, however, it is less clear whether the relationship between variables is causal or correlational. In the example sentence above—Because Paulo studied the chapter, he did very well on the test—one might be quick to conclude that if Paulo studied and did well, then the relationship was clearly causal and the reverse—Because Paulo didn't study the chapter, he did very poorly on the test—must also be true. While this may be so, there may also be other reasons why Paulo did well on the test. He may have already known the material from another source; he may have picked it up during class and did not have to study; he may have copied his answers from a classmate; he may have guessed the answers; the teacher may have given away the correct answers, etc. The relationship of the reverse situation can also be questioned. Maybe Paulo did poorly on the test not because he didn't study (because he had mastered it during class) but because he was feeling unwell, or because the temperature or noise or smell in the classroom bothered him, or because he was tired or hungry or anxious about his home life, etc. When teachers interpret the results of assessments, they should consider carefully whether the results are, in fact, caused by the suspected causes.

Think-Pair-Share 14.5c Application   You have learned about the difference between causal and correlational relationships. Recalling situations from your teaching or learning, reflect on some that were causal and some that were correlational. Explain how you know. Could there have been other interpretations?

14.6   Chapter Conclusion

For classroom teachers, understanding basic statistical concepts is more crucial than performing calculations, except for specific situations. Teachers must calculate basic statistics (frequency, pass rate, mean, median, mode, dispersion) to assess student performance and analyze individual items (FV, item discrimination, distractor analysis). They ensure intra- and interrater reliability for constructed-response items and may set cut scores programmatically (standard setting) for class placements. Grading software can assist with item statistics. Statisticians handle complex calculations at high-stakes testing agencies. Understanding concepts and basic calculations enhances classroom assessments and comprehension of standardized tests.

Appendix 1 – Achievement Quiz of Chapter 14

(For discussion or writing prompts, see the Think-Pair-Share tasks in this chapter.)

Directions: Select the response that best answers each question below. Each question is worth 1 point.

1. What is the mode in the following set of scores?
   The class's test scores are as follows: 23, 42, 55, 59, 63, 63, and 64. The sum of these scores is 369. When you divide this total by the number of scores (7), the result is 52.71.
   a. 7
   b. 52.71
   c. 59
   d. 63

2. Ten students have taken the final exam. Select the pass rate if:
   A–D = pass
   E = fail

Grade	Frequency
A	5
B	3
C	0
D	1
E	1

   a. 0%
   b. 10%
   b. 90%
   c. 100%

3. The teacher has administered an assessment, and the facility value (difficulty) of item #1 is 0.93. After analyzing the results, the teacher wonders what to do with this item when teaching and assessing the same topic again in the future. The teacher should _____.
   a. revise it because it's too hard
   b. keep it as a confidence booster

    c. move it to the middle of the test

    d. keep it as a medium-difficulty item

4. The teacher has administered an assessment, and the discrimination of item #2 is –0.76. After analyzing the results, the teacher wonders what to do with this item when teaching and assessing the same topic again in the future. The teacher should _____.

    a. keep it because its value is close to –1.0

    b. reject it because it confuses strong students

    c. examine why the weak students did poorly on it

    d. move it to the last position to end on a high note

5. You are administering the final exam to your students. One of your students arrives a few minutes late for the test. He quickly sits down and starts working. When you calculate the results, you see that this student did not do as well on the assessment as you would have expected.

What kind of relationship exists between the student being late for the exam and his test results?

    a. causation

    b. correlation

15

Conclusion

In concluding this journey through the complexities of language assessment, we recognize it as a pursuit of understanding, empowerment, and transformation for educators across diverse contexts. As we reflect on the essential principles, practices, and challenges presented in this comprehensive guide, it becomes evident that language assessment is not merely a measure of student proficiency; it is a dynamic force shaping the very foundations of education.

We hope this book has fostered a deeper appreciation for the pivotal role assessment plays in showcasing language learning, while also enhancing readers' assessment literacy by equipping them with the necessary metalanguage to confidently engage in discussions about assessment concepts. In our multifaceted exploration of language assessment, we have delved into a myriad of concepts, spanning from foundational principles to practical applications in assessing learners across ages ranging from young children through adults, in a variety of educational settings worldwide. Our journey has traversed the spectrum of assessment methodologies, from traditional approaches to the development of AI-driven technology, equipping educators with the necessary tools for evaluating student learning. In the chapters dedicated to practical application, the structured approach invites readers to navigate the complexities of assessment with confidence. Chapter 4, in particular, sets this volume apart from the competition, as it serves as a practical guide for writing and evaluating assessments, emphasizing the importance of its concurrent study with other chapters. The integration of theory and practice, exemplified throughout this textbook, bridges the gap between abstract concepts and tangible tools, offering a roadmap for both preservice and in-service language teachers.

The curation of content from both seminal and cutting-edge research and further informed by the needs of students and alumni in our language-teacher education programs ensures that the insights and techniques presented here are not mere practical applications. The incorporation of TESOL's *6 Principles for Exemplary Teaching of English Learners* (Short et al. 2018) as well as that of the *Common European Framework of Reference for Languages: Teaching, Learning, and Assessment* (Council of Europe 2020) emphasizes the universal guidelines drawn from decades of research, anchoring this textbook in the evolving landscape of language education.

As we consider the global resonance of the call for comprehensive assessment education, it becomes clear that assessment literacy is a universal need. Whether in Chile, China, Czechia, or elsewhere, educators grapple with the weight of assessment terminology and the nuanced purposes of evaluation. We aspire for readers to glean insights into the significant responsibilities teachers and other stakeholders hold in the equitable and ethical development, design, implementation, and utilization of assessments. While we have furnished tips and tools to facilitate the creation of valid assessments, it's important to acknowledge that, akin to teaching, assessment is

A Practical Guide to Language Assessment: How Do You Know That Your Students Are Learning? First Edition.
Ildiko Porter-Szucs et al.

profoundly influenced by context and wields considerable impact on individuals. Therefore, we advocate for a thorough understanding of the purpose behind each assessment and the specific context in which it operates. This book stands as a testament to the transformative power of assessment education, aiming to dispel misconceptions and empower educators to make informed, responsible, and data-driven decisions with humanistic principles that prioritize integrity and accountability.

As we conclude this exploration, we envision this textbook not just as a static compilation of knowledge but as a dynamic resource fostering metacognition, enriching teaching experiences, and shaping a dynamic landscape for learning. We hope that every user of this book, whether a pre-service teacher, a seasoned educator, an assessment professional, or a policymaker, will find it to be the indispensable guide we intended it to be. Empowered by the insights gained, we trust that every reader will be equipped to confidently answer the crucial question: *How do you know that your students are learning?*

Appendices

Appendix A: Diagnostic Test
Appendix B: Achievement Test
Appendix C: Answer keys to diagnostic test, chapter quizzes, and the final achievement test

Appendix A: Diagnostic Test (Pre-Test)

Directions: Select the response that best answers each question below. Questions 1–30 are worth 1 point each. Questions 31 and 32 are worth 2 points each for entirely correct answers, 1 point each for partially correct answers, and 0 points each for entirely incorrect answers. Question 33 is primarily meant for readers in Canada and the United States and is optional for others.

1. Which type of test can be effectively used as a placement test by institutions?
   a. proficiency
   b. diagnostic
   c. achievement
   d. certification

2. In your class, you are measuring what your students have learned in Chapter 3 before moving on to Chapter 4 next week. You are administering _____.
   a. a direct test
   b. a placement test
   c. formative assessment
   d. summative assessment

3. A test that measures what it claims to measure is called _____.
   a. reliable
   b. valid
   c. authentic
   d. practical

4. When teachers spend their time teaching to the test instead of teaching content or language skills to their students, then the test has negative _____.
   a. washback
   b. construct
   c. purpose
   d. correlation

A Practical Guide to Language Assessment: How Do You Know That Your Students Are Learning? First Edition.
Ildiko Porter-Szucs et al.
© 2025 John Wiley & Sons, Inc. Published 2025 by John Wiley & Sons, Inc.

5. How does the "Design Statement" in the *Assessment Use Argument* assist test developers?
   a. by analyzing learners' proficiency according to content and language standards
   b. by justifying raw and scaled scores following test administration
   c. by providing guidance for operationalization, trialing, and assessment use stages during development
   d. by reporting the content-, construct-, criterion-, and consequential validity of tests to stakeholders

6. Your college requires that new applicants submit an official standardized language proficiency test score. If an applicant arrives with an institutional Test of English as a Foreign Language (TOEFL) score issued by the language school in your town, what would you, as the ESL director, do?
   a. although the applicant's TOEFL score does not meet the minimum admission requirement, you accept the score for admission based on trust in the language school
   b. because the applicant's TOEFL score does not meet the minimum admission requirement, you administer your institutional TOEFL test for a second chance
   c. require direct submission of the institutional TOEFL test results from the language school to your college
   d. require the official TOEFL test by Educational Testing Service (ETS), the makers of TOEFL, with scores sent to your college directly

7. You are teaching pronunciation at a language school. You would like to administer to your students a direct test of their pronunciation of a particular sound. What would you do? _____
   a. do a minimal-pair discrimination task where students circle the words containing the target sound
   b. have students silently read a text and underline everything that is pronounced with the target sound
   c. ask students to raise their hands whenever they hear you pronounce the target sound in a story
   d. have a conversation with the students and listen to their pronunciation of the target sound

8. When an item is based on a reading or listening stimulus, then the more difficult language should be found in the _____.
   a. key
   b. stem
   c. passage
   d. distractor

9. At your new job, you need to design an assessment tool for all the students at one proficiency level. You begin by _____.
   a. pilot testing
   b. crafting test items
   c. designing each task
   d. writing test specifications

10. From a learner's written language sample, what is the most precise method to determine the learner's proficiency level?
    a. by looking up the word frequencies in a corpus
    b. by assessing it in relation to a proficiency framework

   c. by comparing it with other language learners' samples
   d. by analyzing the writing with a readability calculator

11. The _____ the Type/Token ratio and the _____ the repetition of words, the harder the text is.
   a. lower, lower
   b. lower, higher
   c. higher, higher
   d. higher, lower

12. Which part of the brain is referred to as the switching station, for directing information in the brain?
   a. amygdala
   b. prefrontal cortex
   c. higher brain
   d. lower brain

13. A language learner with ADHD, a diagnosed disability, may receive which of the following accommodations, ensuring equity without changing the learning or assessment objectives on a reading comprehension test?
   a. using a text-to-speech program, which reads the article aloud
   b. reducing the number of multiple-choice response options
   c. giving the student a monolingual dictionary for the test
   d. completing the test in a distraction-free environment

14. You would like to assess your students' ability to participate in a two-way spoken event with transactional and evaluative elements, according to the CEFR. Which speech event will you have them engage in?
   a. obtaining goods and services in a shop
   b. a public announcement, such as a toast
   c. an informal discussion about feelings
   d. formal discussion, such as a debate

15. When a listener understands all the words but still does not understand the radio broadcast because of not knowing enough about the topic, which processing is lacking?
   a. bottom-up
   b. top-down
   c. one-way
   d. two-way

16. A teacher who focuses equally on how a student approaches essay writing as on the quality of the written essay is employing which method of teaching and assessment?
   a. dictocomp
   b. dictogloss
   c. product-focused
   d. process-focused

17. Your colleague would like to assess her students' reading comprehension. She decides to have the students write a summary of the reading passage. You warn her, however, that _____.
    a. her inter-rater reliability may be low if she knows whose summary she is grading
    b. she may not be able to separate the students' reading and writing performance
    c. this is an inauthentic task and should, therefore, be avoided
    d. this assessment is likely to produce negative washback

18. Your language program is transitioning to standards-based grading. What will be the basis for your grades?
    a. academic and nonacademic criteria
    b. indirect measures graded on a curve
    c. meeting specific evaluation criteria
    d. standards of behavior and attendance

19. Mrs. Jones is grading Sofi's paper and before assigning her a score of 7/10, she remembers how well Sofi performs in class. Mrs. Jones then bends her grade to 9/10. This is an example of _____.
    a. the halo effect
    b. relative grading
    c. positive washback
    d. absolute grading

20. When giving feedback in a written assignment, the teacher provides the correct answers next to the errors, this is an example of (the) _____.
    a. direct feedback
    b. indirect feedback
    c. hamburger principle
    d. global error correction

21. Vocabulary tests can be made more difficult by increasing the _____ in the text.
    a. word types
    b. word tokens
    c. number of formulaic sequences
    d. per-million word frequencies

22. Which of the following situations features a teacher/tester behaving unethically?
    a. A language learner is allowed to use a bilingual dictionary while taking a science test.
    b. A language student is marked down on a writing assignment for criticizing the government's foreign policy.
    c. A student with diagnosed dyslexia is given extra time on a French reading comprehension test.
    d. A teacher forgets to lock the drawer where the Portuguese final exams are kept.

23. On an internationally administered language test, you find the following test item:

    The weather in July is usually _____. a) hot b) cold c) rainy d) dry

    What concern might you have about this item? The item violates the principle of _____.
    a. accepted norms
    b. freedom from bias
    c. positive washback
    d. transparency

24. What is one recommendation for assessing students' multiliteracies according to Cope and Kalantzis (2015)?
    a. assessing the four skills both in isolation and in an integrated fashion
    b. implementing norm-referenced, summative assessments
    c. incorporating self- and peer-assessment with scaffolded peer feedback
    d. teaching and assessing young learners in multiple languages

25. Your students are taking an end-of-unit achievement test. Given the students' hard work and making great progress, which kind of distribution of scores do you hope to see?
    a. uniform
    b. bimodal
    c. bell-shaped
    d. skewed

26. After administering a multiple-choice test, you calculate item discrimination in order to differentiate between _____.
    a. test takers who answered the item correctly and test takers who did not
    b. items that were fair to all test takers and items that were not
    c. high-ability test takers and low-ability test takers
    d. easy items and difficult items on the test

27. The teacher has administered an assessment where the discrimination of item #2 is −0.76. What should the teacher do with this item after analyzing the results?
    a. move it to the last position to end positively
    b. reject it because it confuses strong students
    c. examine why the weak students did poorly on it
    d. keep it because its value is close to −1.0

28. Three of the following statements are true of bilinguals while one is a **misconception**. It is a misconception that bilinguals, when compared to monolinguals, _____.
    a. demonstrate better attention spans
    b. experience a delayed onset of dementia
    c. face an increased risk of specific language disorders
    d. overcome initial delay if educated in the second language

29. In three of the four sentences "take" is part of a formulaic sequence. Which sentence is the **exception**?
    a. The veins take the blood to the heart.
    b. I think I'm going to take next week off.
    c. Which class are you taking this semester?
    d. Why don't you take the warning seriously?

30. Speech-to-text technology **lacks** which of the following benefits?
    a. accessibility benefits for students with disabilities
    b. variable playback speeds for fluency development
    c. enabling both teachers and peers to analyze and correct mistakes
    d. availability on multiple platforms such as smartphones and computers

Select All That Apply (#31 and #32)

31. Which of the following are true of most young learners? They _____.
    a. are vulnerable
    b. are motivated by fun
    c. have a developing lower brain
    d. learn best through social interaction

32. Which of the following are reasons against testing young learners?
    a. damage to learning
    b. demotivation of students
    c. pursuit of scores
    d. absence of accountability

MATCHING to be completed by readers in Canada and the United States

33. Match the following list of characteristics with the Canadian and US school systems by writing the corresponding numbers next to the appropriate country. Note that some characteristics belong to both countries. (EL = English Learner)

    Canada: _____

    United States: _____
    1. An EL is someone whose L1 is not English.
    2. An EL is someone whose L1 is a significantly different variety of English.
    3. An EL is someone who is 3–21 years old.
    4. An EL is someone who is migratory.
    5. An EL is someone who is Native American or Alaska Native.
    6. An EL is someone who might be a child of both (un)lawful and (un)documented immigrants.
    7. A new EL takes an English language proficiency screener.
    8. An EL is entitled to English language development services.
    9. The Civil Rights Act (1964) forbids discrimination based on national origin.
    10. Lau v. Nichols (1974) affirms ELs' rights to overcome barriers to meaningful participation in educational programs.
    11. New students complete a home language survey.
    12. A screener test can be administered in the child's dominant language.

Appendix B: Achievement Test (Post-Test)

Directions: Select the response that best answers each question below. Questions 1–30 are worth 1 point each. Questions 31–32 are worth 2 points each for entirely correct answers, 1 point each for partially correct answers, and 0 points each for entirely incorrect answers. Question 33 is primarily meant for readers in Canada and the United States and is optional for others.

1. At a language teachers' conference in the publishers' exhibit area, you're looking at the latest offerings from test-development companies. You see a test booklet where all the items seem to be about question formation. You suspect that this test booklet is for a(n) _____ test.
   a. placement
   b. qualification
   c. proficiency
   d. achievement

2. Assessment *as* learning focuses on _____.
   a. low-stakes formative assessments (i.e. end-of-class exit tickets)
   b. low-stakes individual practices (i.e. students' self-awareness)
   c. standardized tests (e.g. IELTS, WIDA ACCESS, Goethe-Institut exams)
   d. standards-based, integrative assessments (e.g. all-skills achievement tests)

3. In your university's language program, you and a colleague are rating end-of-term portfolios for the two sections of your Level 2 class. To calibrate yourselves, you each rate Alex's portfolio: you award it 60 points while your colleague awards it 45 points. Your rating is an example of low _____.
   a. test validity
   b. intra-rater reliability
   c. inter-rater reliability
   d. criterion-related validity

4. After finishing a chapter on cats and dogs, students take an end-of-chapter test. Analysis of the test results reveals that students with cats and dogs outperformed those who do not have any pets. You suspect that the assessment might have a problem with _____.
   a. interactiveness
   b. authenticity
   c. construct validity
   d. indirect assessment

5. The *Assessment Use Argument* framework emphasizes the linkage among _____.
   a. rater-related reliability, learner-related reliability, and instrument-related reliability
   b. assessment performance, interpretation, and intended use
   c. test specifications, the blueprint, and the design statement
   d. practicality, authenticity, and interactiveness

6. In your new position, you and your language-teacher colleagues are responsible for designing an assessment tool. You begin by _____.
   a. pilot testing
   b. crafting test items

    c. designing each task

    d. writing test specifications

7. Which of the following is a minimal-pair discrimination item?

    a. let – led

    b. pen – pencil

    c. car – Toyota

    d. piece – peace

8. Which of the following responses is accurate for designing multiple-choice questions on a test of reading comprehension?

    a. Each item should be designed to measure a single construct.

    b. Items should assess prescriptively correct grammar points.

    c. To keep items short, extra wording should be in the options.

    d. The elicitation and response formats should be different.

9. Unlike _____ assessments, _____ assessments require the test taker to produce either writing or speech.

    a. formative, short-response

    b. summative, extended-response

    c. selected-response, constructed-response

    d. constructed-response, selected-response

10. Where can an item writer find inspiration for potential distractors?

    a. proficiency benchmarks

    b. learner speech samples

    c. readability measures

    d. language corpora

11. The lower the COCA frequency of a word, the more appropriate it is for a(n) _____ level learner.

    a. novice

    b. beginner

    c. intermediate

    d. advanced

12. In the brain, where does information go when a student is bored or afraid? It goes to the _____.

    a. amygdala

    b. lower brain

    c. prefrontal cortex

    d. switching station

13. In the United States, the broadest, most inclusive category of exceptional language learners consists of students with _____.

    a. disabilities, giftedness, and trauma

    b. visual, auditory, and speech impairments

    c. wheelchairs, guide dogs, and hearing aids

    d. physical, cognitive, and learning challenges

14. A language learner diagnosed with a hearing impairment may receive which of the following modifications, altering the learning or assessment objectives of a four-skills test?
    a. access to a bilingual dictionary
    b. exemption from the listening section of the test
    c. receiving a scribe to transcribe answers
    d. allowing extended time for completing the test

15. You would like to assess your students' ability to give information, or speak uninterrupted on a given topic, according to the CEFR. Which speech event will you have them engage in?
    a. a paired interpersonal interactional task
    b. a one-way transactional monologue
    c. understanding an interlocutor
    d. goal-oriented cooperation

16. When might you use dictogloss with your students?
    a. when intermediate adults need help paraphrasing a text
    b. when foreign-language learners need help with pronunciation
    c. when very young learners are learning to read and write
    d. when advanced students are learning to write an essay

17. The assessment of content knowledge of LESLLA learners in content-based settings needs to take place _____.
    a. after they have learned to read and write in their first language
    b. after they have learned to read and write in the target language
    c. through a translator, interpreter, pictures
    d. on tests with reduced questions and answers

18. Your language program is using absolute grading. What characterizes your grading?
    a. a predetermined numerical point system
    b. a quota for the number of each grade set in advance
    c. adjusting grades to maintain a specific class average
    d. deemphasizing grading through ungrading

19. How can teachers avoid the halo effect?
    a. by providing effective and timely feedback
    b. by keeping writing prompts short and clear
    c. by grading student writing anonymously
    d. by grading solely based on the rubric

20. Non-systematic "slips" due to problems with performing or demonstrating what the learner knows are called _____.
    a. errors
    b. mistakes
    c. macro issues
    d. stigmatizing issues

21. Which of the following tools can help teachers determine which words to teach?
    a. type-token ratio calculators
    b. lexical density calculators
    c. readability measures
    d. word lists

22. Browser lock software, 360 scans of a room, AI proctors are examples of _____.
    a. augmented reality
    b. security measures
    c. computer adaptation
    d. accessibility functions

23. On an internationally administered language test, you find the following test item in the section assessing knowledge of the cultures where the target language is spoken:

    The most popular sport is _____. a) cricket b) ice hockey c) rugby union d) association football

    This item violates which of the following principles?
    a. access and transparency
    b. positive washback
    c. freedom from bias
    d. doing no harm

24. Language teachers who are trying to ensure that it is their students, not a chatbot, doing the writing should _____.
    a. grade in-class writing assignments
    b. require students to handwrite their homework
    c. refrain from telling students about the technology
    d. use a plagiarism checker to review student writing

25. According to the New London Group (1996), what are the two aspects of multiliteracies pedagogy?
    a. cultivating awareness of contexts and skills in various modes of communication
    b. fostering language acquisition through the target language and translanguaging
    c. striving for a balanced approach between productive and receptive skills
    d. achieving a balance between norm- and criterion-referenced assessment

26. You plot the quiz results on a histogram and see a bimodal distribution of scores. What will you do the next day in class?
    a. revise the quiz items and re-administer the quiz
    b. differentiate instruction as you reteach the topic
    c. reteach the material to the whole class altogether
    d. celebrate the students' strong performance and move on

27. You understand the importance of triangulating assessments in your secondary-school language class. To achieve this, you will _____.
    a. require multiple oral presentations during the semester
    b. assess the students on a multiple-choice test, an oral presentation, and a role-play

    c. measure 2-3 learning objectives in each multiple-choice test item on the final exam

    d. utilize various evaluators for role-plays: teacher assessment, self-assessment, and peer-assessment

28. In a school setting, if something has not been taught and learned, it should not be assessed. Aside from diagnostic assessment, in which situation might an **exception** to the above general recommendation be allowed?

    a. in a content-focused class

    b. in a test-preparation class

    c. on an academic test

    d. on a final exam

29. Which of the following statements is a **misconception** about bilinguals? When compared to monolinguals, bilinguals _____.

    a. experience cognitive benefits

    b. can multitask more successfully

    c. underperform as emergent bilinguals

    d. experience linguistic delays for decades

30. In three of the four sentences "make" is part of a formulaic sequence. Which sentence is the **exception**?

    a. They made a model airplane.

    b. How much do you make at work?

    c. The economy is a make-or-break issue.

    d. Was the story about the monster made up?

Select All That Apply (#31 and #32)

31. Which of the following typically evoke a fight-flight-fear response in young learners?

    a. criticism

    b. competition

    c. boredom

    d. negativity

32. How do teachers maximize positive washback in young learner assessment?

    a. avoid self-assessment

    b. encourage and remind learners frequently

    c. use psychologically safe topics

    d. include peer interaction

MATCHING to be completed by readers in Canada and the United States

33. Match the following list of characteristics with the Canadian and US school systems by writing the corresponding numbers next to the appropriate country. Note that some characteristics belong to both countries. (EL = English Learner)

Canada: _____

United States: _____

1. An EL is someone whose L1 is not English.
2. An EL is someone whose L1 is a significantly different variety of English.
3. An EL is someone who is 3–21 years old.
4. An EL is someone who is migratory.
5. An EL is someone who is Native American or Alaska Native.
6. An EL is someone who might be a child of both (un)lawful and (un)documented immigrants.
7. A new EL takes an English language proficiency screener.
8. An EL is entitled to English language development services.
9. The Civil Rights Act (1964) forbids discrimination based on national origin.
10. Lau v. Nichols (1974) affirms ELs' rights to overcome barriers to meaningful participation in educational programs.
11. New students complete a home language survey.
12. A screener test can be administered in the child's dominant language.

Appendix C: Answer Keys

Diagnostic Test (Pre-Test) answer key: 1a, 2d, 3b, 4a, 5c, 6d, 7d, 8c, 9d, 10b, 11d, 12a, 13d, 14d, 15b, 16d, 17b, 18c, 19a, 20a, 21a, 22b, 23b, 24c, 25d, 26c, 27b, 28c, 29a, 30b; 31a,b,d; 32a,b,c; 33: Canada 1, 2, 6, 7, 8, 12; United States 1, 3, 4, 5, 6, 7, 8, 9, 10, 11

Chapter 1 answer key: 1d, 2c, 3b, 4d, 5T

Chapter 2 answer key: 1b, 2d, 3c, 4b, 5a

Chapter 3 answer key: 1. Answers will vary but may include: Who are the Ss/TTs? Who evaluates the assessment? Where are the Ss/TTs? Where does the test administration take place? Where does the scoring take place? Why are the Ss/TTs assessed? What is to be assessed? What is not to be assessed? How is the content assessed? How is the assessment scored? How long is the assessment? How frequently is it administered? When does the assessment take place?
2c, 3d, 4b, 5c

Chapter 5 answer key: 1c, 2a, 3a, 4c, 5b

Chapter 6 answer key: 1c; 2b; 3a; 4b, c, d; 5a, c, d

Chapter 7 answer key: 1a; 2a; 3c; 4b; 5 aC, cA, dB

Chapter 8 answer key: 1 False; 2d; 3a; 4a, b, c, d; 5 aA, aC, aD, bB, bE

Chapter 9 answer key: 1a, b, c; 2b; 3a; 4c; 5a

Chapter 10 answer key: 1a, 2c, 3d, 4a, 5 False

Chapter 11 answer key: 1c, 2d, 3a, 4b; 5aB, bC, dA

Chapter 12 answer key: 1a; 2a, c, d; 3a, b, c; 4b; 5c

Chapter 13 answer key: 1d, 2a, 3a, 4a; 5a, b, c

Chapter 14 answer key: 1d, 2c, 3b, 4b; 5b

Achievement Test (Post-Test) answer key: 1d, 2b, 3c, 4c, 5b, 6d, 7a, 8a, 9c, 10b, 11d, 12b, 13a, 14b, 15b, 16c, 17c, 18a, 19d, 20b, 21d, 22b, 23c, 24a, 25a, 26b, 27b, 28b, 29d, 30a; 31a,c,d; 32b,c,d; 33: Canada 1, 2, 6, 7, 8, 12; United States 1, 3, 4, 5, 6, 7, 8, 9, 10, 11

Glossary[1]

Absolute grading assessing work based on standards of performance described on a predetermined numerical point system

Accommodations changes made to classroom assignments or assessments or to the classroom environment or testing conditions that allow students to better demonstrate their knowledge and skills without being impeded by a disability, learning difference, or limited proficiency in English *[contrast with modifications]*

Achievement test or assessment a measurement to assess what the students have learned after the target element has been introduced, taught, and practiced

American Council on the Teaching of Foreign Languages (ACTFL) a US organization that developed descriptions of what individuals can do with language in terms of speaking, writing, listening, and reading in real-world situations in a spontaneous and non-rehearsed context

Analytic scoring providing separate scores for different criteria *[contrast with holistic scoring]*

Anchor items pretested test questions that are tried and true with great statistical properties

Assessment umbrella term for an appraisal or judgment of observable behavior; includes testing and measurement

  Assessment as learning (aka self- and peer-assessment): measures designed to enable the language learner to self-assess or peer-assess in order to develop metacognition and understand their own strengths and weaknesses, e.g. journals, reflection papers, self-/peer-assessment checklists

  Assessment for learning (aka formative assessment): informal, low-stakes measures, such as oral comprehension questions, ungraded classroom tasks, and exit tickets, used to help shape or form student learning and development and to improve instruction

  Assessment of learning (aka summative assessment): formal, planned measure used to sum up what students know, e.g. final exams; results have higher stakes than formative assessments

Assessment Use Argument (AUA) documentation of the development, use, and justification of an assessment in order to add accountability

Authenticity the degree to which the assessment task closely resembles a real-life task, outside of the teaching–learning–assessment situation

Automated Writing Evaluation (AWE) IT tool for assessing writing with algorithms that are trained using corpora of written language

---

1 An excellent glossary of terms in language assessment has been compiled for the British Council by Coombe (2018).

A Practical Guide to Language Assessment: How Do You Know That Your Students Are Learning? First Edition. Ildiko Porter-Szucs et al.
© 2025 John Wiley & Sons, Inc. Published 2025 by John Wiley & Sons, Inc.

Backwash (aka washback) the impact of assessment on teaching and learning, whether positive or negative

Benchmark the standard against which language production can be measured

Benchmark paper (aka exemplar): an example paper at a particular level, to be used by teachers, students, raters in conjunction with the rating rubric

Blueprint test specifications, or specs, that include the purpose, content, format, logistics, and scoring of a test; i.e. all features of the test development, administration, and scoring

Canadian Language Benchmarks (CLB) a descriptive scale of language ability in English as a Second Language (ESL) written as 12 benchmarks or reference points along a continuum from basic to advanced

Classroom assessment: any assessment administered in a classroom, by instructors, intended to see how much their students are learning

Cloze (aka cloze passage, cloze-deletion test) a fill-in-the blank passage

> **Conversational cloze** a fill-in-the blank passage in which words are missing from a dialogue
>
> **Fixed-ratio cloze, or systematic cloze** a fill-in-the blank passage in which the deletion typically occurs anywhere between every 5th and 10th word in each sentence; for instance, every 7th word is deleted
>
> **Rational, or unsystematic cloze** a fill-in-the blank passage in which specific parts of speech are deleted (such as three nouns, two verbs, four adjectives, etc.)
>
> **Select cloze** a fill-in-the blank passage in which options are presented for test takers to choose from
>
> **Supply cloze** a fill-in-the blank passage in which test takers must produce the missing words on their own

Common European Framework of Reference (CEFR) a set of standards developed by the Council of Europe for second and foreign language education

Comprehensive Adult Student Assessment Systems (CASAS) a US testing and curriculum tools system for preparing youth and adults with basic and academic skills

Content-related validity bias: a situation that occurs when the content of the assessment is more difficult for one group of students than another

Construct the characteristic or specific element you are attempting to measure

> **Construct irrelevance (or construct-irrelevant variance)** an irrelevant factor that hinders the interpretability of the TT's mastery of the construct because the item may measure something more or other than the targeted construct
>
> **Construct-validity bias** the extent to which an assessment fails to measure what it is intending to measure

Constructed-response test questions that provide a question or prompt for which an answer must be produced by the test taker, e.g. short answer (verbal or written), essay, oral presentation, fill-in-the-blank without a word bank, etc.

Correlation a statistical measure that describes the size and direction of a relationship between two or more variables

Criterion-referenced tests tests that measure a test taker's performance against a set of standards or criteria

Cross-text item a test question that requires the reading of more than one stimulus passage

Cut score (aka cut-off score, score cut point, boundary score) the minimum score accepted on an assessment for a test taker to pass or be considered for placement at a particular level

Diagnostic test a measurement tool to determine specific areas of strength and weakness before instruction

Dichotomous items test questions that contain two options

Direct assessment a measure of student learning that is based on the students' explicit demonstration of that learning, e.g. assessing speaking by having the student speak *[contrast with indirect assessment]*

Direct feedback explicit comments and correction of errors by the teacher *[contrast with indirect feedback]*

Discrete-skills test each skill is assessed in isolation

Dispersion (aka variability or spread) the degree to which scores differ from each other

Distractor incorrect option in a test item

Distractor analysis / distractor efficiency an investigation into whether all options in a multiple-choice item perform well and whether distractors attract students

Domains skill areas in language; traditionally reading, writing, listening, speaking

Dynamic Written Corrective Feedback (DWCF) a pedagogical approach for evaluating writing in which guided comments are provided in a quick and routine way

Elicitation (input) format the way the assessment question or prompt is posed to the test taker, be it oral, written, or multimodal

Ethics in language testing a set of guiding principles that ensures a standard of behavior that brings accountability and legitimacy to the field of language testing

Evaluation a value judgment with consequences that is placed on the measurement

Evaluation criterion in a rating scale, the component of speech or writing evaluated (e.g. pronunciation, fluency, vocabulary, grammar, spelling, organization, content, etc.)

Exit ticket an informal, formative, classroom assessment activity; in one version, students write on a paper their name, what they learned, and what is still unclear and submit it before leaving the class

Fairness in assessment equitable and meeting the needs of the students or test takers and the context so that the results are as valid and reliable as possible

Formal assessment official, planned assessment that can be formative or summative

Formative assessment informal, low stakes measurements, such as oral comprehension questions, ungraded classroom tasks, exit tickets, etc., used to help shape or form student learning and development and to improve instruction

Frequency the number of times the students received a particular score on a test

Frequency distribution table a list of all the students' scores in numerical order from lowest to highest

Global errors more severe errors that interfere with communication, e.g. structural or syntactic errors

Halo effect unfair rating behavior in which the rater is influenced by a test taker's previous performance

Histogram a type of bar graph that can be used to depict how well a group of students did on an assessment

Holistic scoring providing one overall score for groups of different assessment criteria, e.g. a single writing score rather than different subscores for each of: content, organization, coherence, vocabulary, grammar, and mechanics *[contrast with analytic scoring]*

Indirect assessment a measure of student learning that is not based on the students' explicit demonstration of that learning, e.g. assessing pronunciation by having the student identify words that rhyme *[contrast with direct assessment]*

Indirect feedback an indication that an error exists, and it is up to the student to correct it

Informal assessment unofficial, casual, often unplanned assessment that is formative

Information gap task a paired activity in which each partner receives different content about the same topic and must ask their partner for the content they are missing

Integrated test items test questions that assess performance based on information delivered through various modes—written and spoken, i.e. from both reading and listening passages

Integrative or integrated skills test skills are combined and measured in one assessment tool

Interactiveness the degree to which the learner's individual characteristics (language ability, topic knowledge, attitude, emotions, background schemata) are positively engaged by the assessment task

Interim measures practice progress tests or mock tests for high-stakes standardized tests used for formative purposes

Item test question

Item difficulty, or facility value the proportion of correct responses; it is calculated by taking the number of students who answered correctly and dividing that number by the total number of students who answered

Item discrimination index an examination of the item to determine if it distinguishes, or discriminates, among stronger and weaker students or test takers

Journal (aka log) assessment logs in which reflections, feelings, thoughts, steps, events, arguments, notes, vocabulary, etc. are captured by the individual; often assessment is based solely on completion or quantity rather than quality

Key the correct answer

Local errors small errors that do not interfere with reader comprehension of the message, though they may be distracting

Mean the arithmetic average; it gives us information about the average student's success on the assessment

Measures of central tendency the three ways to measure the middle of a distribution of scores: mean, median, and mode

Median the midpoint score when you arrange (put in order) scores from high to low

Mixed-up texts item a reading-comprehension question, for which a shorter text is interwoven with a longer text and the test taker must separate them based on coherence

Mode the most frequently occurring score (the number that is the most common)

Modifications changes in the expectation for student completion of grade-level standards, curriculum, instruction, and/or assessment that may alter the content of assessments, and what a test measures; as a result, modifications are not universally available and should only be used when they are explicitly named in a student's IEP

Multiple-trait scoring measuring a secondary and tertiary assessment criterion in addition to the primary criterion; the primary trait may be weighted more heavily than the other traits or all may be weighted equally

Needs analysis an evaluation of students' interests, strengths, and needs

Norm-referenced testing tests that allow comparisons between individuals; they sort students into high and low performers based on how others (the norm group) performed on the same assessment. Items target various proficiency levels; the scores are frequently expressed as a percentile

Norming (aka calibration) the process of achieving reliability among raters through familiarization of rating scale descriptors (benchmarking), followed by initial scoring of sample responses, followed by a comparison to actual scores and discussion of alignment of scores and descriptors, followed by subsequent round(s) of scoring until high inter-rater reliability is reached

Operational items questions on a test that have already been pretested and which count toward the final score

Option answer choices in selected-response items

Peer-assessment tool designed to enable the language learner to assess their peer's work or performance in order to develop metacognition and understand strengths and weaknesses, e.g. journals, reflection papers, peer-assessment checklists

Placement test or screener measurement tool that includes questions at a range of levels with the aim of sorting individuals into various proficiency levels

Plagiarism a form of academic dishonesty; using someone else's ideas or words without proper attribution

Portfolio a collection of student work with reflections, for formative or summative assessment

Practicality the degree to which money, time, personnel, and effort are required for the construction, administration, and evaluation of an assessment

Pretest items new test questions which are being tried out for the first time and do not count toward the final score

Primary-trait scoring measuring a single assessment criterion, which is deemed most important, such as topic development

Productive skills the ability to produce language output in the form of speaking, writing, and representing

Proficiency test measurement of language use, usually administered externally

Progress test or assessment a measurement administered at various points during a course to determine how much students are improving.

Rater the person (or computer program) that assigns ratings, or scores; this can also be the students' teacher, who assigns grades

Rating scale (aka rubric, scoring guide) see *rubric*

Raw scores the actual number of correct responses that test takers achieve on a form of a test

Receptive skills the ability to comprehend input in the form of listening, speaking, and viewing; no language is produced

Relative grading assessing work on a curve with predetermined percentages of grades allowed at each level

Reliability the consistency of a test score; repeatable over time; free from inconsistent fluctuations

    Inter-rater reliability the consistency of scores between different raters

    Intra-rater reliability the consistency of scores for a single rater no matter when the assessment is scored

    Instrument-related reliability the consistency of the score regardless of factors related to the assessment instrument and its administration, e.g. font size and room lighting

    Learner-related reliability the consistency of the score regardless of factors related to the learner (or test taker) other than proficiency in the language skills being measured, e.g. fatigue, anxiety, and familiarity with test format

    Rater reliability consistency of the score regardless of who rates the same performance and when

Response format the way the test taker produces language in response to the assessment question or prompt; it could be oral, written, nonverbal, or multimodal

Rubric (aka rating scale, scoring guide) a set of measurement criteria used to describe different levels of quality of performance at each score point

Scaled score the test result calculated through an equating process to ensure fairness among different forms of a test

Scoring guide see *rubric*

Selected-response item test questions that include options from which to choose the correct answer, e.g. multiple-choice, true/false, matching, and fill-in-the-blank from a word bank

Self-assessment tool designed to enable the language learner to assess their own work or performance in order to develop metacognition and understand their strengths and weaknesses, e.g. journals, reflection papers, self-assessment checklists

Sequencing (aka ordering) item a test question that requires the test taker to put given words or images in a particular order

Short answer item a test question for which the response can range in length from a single word to a few sentences; the prompt may be written, aural, or visual; the response may be written or oral

Single-point rubric a variation on the analytic rubric; separate assessment criteria are displayed and awarded separate scores, but only the target proficiency is described; the score points below and above are not described

Standard deviation a measure of dispersion, how spread out a data set is, how closely scores are distributed around the mean

Standardized assessment any assessment created, administered, and scored in a standards-based and systematic manner

Stem the statement or question part of a test item that provides the context for the question and the actual problem to solve

Stigmatizing errors errors or mistakes that are subjective, based on stereotypes, and depend on what irritates the interlocutor about the error or mistake

Stimulus an input text, e.g. reading or listening passage, or audio-visual (map, graph, image, video, etc.) on which assessment items are based

Summative assessment formal, planned measurement used to sum up what students know; results have higher stakes than formative assessments

Target element the piece or feature of language being assessed; e.g. the present perfect with *since* and *for*, the pronunciation of words ending in *-tion*, capital letters at the beginning of sentences; the unit of language targeted for instruction or assessment; units may include a vocabulary word, a formulaic sequence, a grammatical structure, a phoneme, a language function, language skill (e.g. paragraphing), etc.

Target language use (TLU) "situation or context in which the test taker will be using the language outside of the test itself" (Bachman and Palmer 1996, p. 18)

Test equating a calibration process conducted by a statistician to equalize or match up the difficulty levels of different versions of a test

Trait (primary, secondary) see *evaluation criterion*

Transparency in assessment clear and accessible information regarding assessment content, administration, use of results, etc.

Ungrading an assessment approach that emphasizes the learning process and replaces grades with meaningful comments on achievement

Validity the extent to which a test measures what it claims to measure

    Consequential validity all the after-effects of an assessment, such as promotion or placement decisions, social impact on the test-takers, etc.

    Construct validity the extent to which scores on an assessment instrument indicate underlying language ability in the target construct

Content validity the extent to which the content of the assessment reflects the content of the course, domain, general use of the target language

Criterion-related validity measures the positive correlation between the test taker's score in a skill on a well-established assessment against a new assessment tool

Face validity the degree to which the assessment appears to measure what it claims to measure

Predictive validity the correlation between the test taker's score on one assessment and the test taker's performance in a future situation

Washback (aka backwash) the impact of assessment on teaching and learning, whether positive or negative

WIDA previously stood for World Class Instructional Design and Assessment; a popular US educational and assessment framework for K-12 schools

Bibliography

100% Pure New Zealand (n.d.). *History*. https://www.newzealand.com/int/history/

Academic Success Media (2018). *Compass test practice: ESL*. https://compass-test-practice.com/esl.htm

Alberta Government (2013). *Alberta initiative for school improvement cycle 5 project summaries from public, separate, private, charter and francophone school authorities zones: 1–6*. https://open.alberta.ca/publications/aisi-cycle-5-project-summaries-from-public-separate-private-charter-and-francophone-school

Alberta Initiative for School Improvement (2009). *AISI Handbook for Cycle* 3, *2006-2009*. https://archive.org/details/ERIC_ED498246/page/n1/mode/2up

Alexander, B. (2022). *Resources for exploring ChatGPT and higher education*. https://bryanalexander.org/future-of-education/resources-for-exploring-chatgpt-and-higher-education/

American Council on the Teaching of Foreign Languages (ACTFL) (2024a). *Oral Proficiency Interview (OPI)*. https://www.actfl.org/assessments/postsecondary-assessments/opi

American Council on the Teaching of Foreign Languages (ACTFL) (2024b). *ACTFL assessments*. https://www.actfl.org/search?q=professional+development+assessment

American Council on the Teaching of Foreign Languages (ACTFL) (2024c). *ACTFL proficiency guidelines*. https://www.actfl.org/educator-resources/actfl-proficiency-guidelines?resources=view

American Speech-Language-Hearing Association (n.d.). *Module 1: what is dynamic assessment?* https://www.asha.org/practice/multicultural/dynamic-assessment/module-1/

Anderson, N.J. (2012). Metacognition: awareness of language learning. In: *Psychology for Language Learning* (eds. S. Mercer, S. Ryan and M. Williams), 169–187. London: Palgrave Macmillan.

Anderson, R. and Freebody, P. (1985). Vocabulary knowledge. In: *Theoretical Models and Processes of Reading*, 3e (eds. H. Singer and R. Ruddell), 343–371. Newark: International Reading Association.

Artiles, A.J., Rueda, R., Salazar, J.J., et al. (2005). Within-group diversity in minority disproportionate representation: English language learners in urban school districts. *Exceptional Children* 71 (3): 283–300.

Aryadoust, V. (2018). Communicative testing of listening. In: *The TESOL Encyclopedia of English Language Teaching* (eds. J.I. Liontas and M. DelliCarpini), Hoboken: Wiley Blackwell. doi: 10.1002/9781118784235.eelt0617.

Asher, J.J. (1969). The total physical response approach to second language learning. *The Modern Language Journal* 53 (1): 3–17.

Asthana, A. (2007). Call to ban all school exams for under-16s. *The Guardian*. https://www.theguardian.com/uk/2007/jun/10/sats.schools

Austen, J. (1813). *Pride and Prejudice* (ed. T. Egerton). Military Library, Whitehall.

A Practical Guide to Language Assessment: How Do You Know That Your Students Are Learning? First Edition.
Ildiko Porter-Szucs et al.
© 2025 John Wiley & Sons, Inc. Published 2025 by John Wiley & Sons, Inc.

Australian Associated Press (2017). Computer says no: Irish vet fails oral English test needed to stay in Australia. *The Guardian*. https://www.theguardian.com/australia-news/2017/aug/08/computer-says-no-irish-vet-fails-oral-english-test-needed-to-stay-in-australia

Australian Bureau of Statistics (n.d.). *Statistical language—correlation and causation*. https://www.abs.gov.au/statistics/understanding-statistics/statistical-terms-and-concepts/correlation-and-causation

Australian National Corpus (2023). *Australian National Corpus*. https://ausnc.org.au/

Avant STAMP (2024a). *Avant STAMP language proficiency tests*. https://avantassessment.com/stamp

Avant STAMP (2024b). *Sample tests*. https://avantassessment.com/sample-tests#4Se_Sample

Bachman, L. and Dambröck, B. (2018). *Language Assessment for Classroom Teachers*. Oxford: Oxford University Press.

Bachman, L.F. and Palmer, A.S. (1996). *Language Testing in Practice: Designing and Developing Useful Language Tests*. Oxford: Oxford University Press.

Bachman, L. and Palmer, A. (2010). *Language Assessment in Practice*. Oxford: Oxford University Press.

Ballantyne, K.G., Sanderman, A.R. and McLaughlin, N. (2008). *Dual Language Learners in the Early Years: Getting Ready to Succeed in School*. National Clearinghouse for English Language Acquisition.

Barbero, T. (2012). Assessment tools and practices in CLIL. In: *Assessment and Evaluation in CLIL* (ed. F. Quartapelle), 38–56. AECLIL-EACEA.

Barker, F. and Shaw, S. (2007). Linking language assessments for younger learners across proficiency levels (Phase 1). *Cambridge ESOL: Research Notes* 28: 14–18. https://www.cambridgeenglish.org/images/23147-research-notes-28.pdf

Barshay, J. (2019). New studies challenge the claim that black students are sent to special ed too much. *The Hechinger Report*. https://hechingerreport.org/new-studies-challenge-the-claim-that-black-students-are-sent-to-special-ed-too-much/

BBC Panorama (2014a). *UK student visa English testing scandal* [video]. Daily Motion. https://www.dailymotion.com/video/x1bx5uj

BBC Panorama (2014b). *The English test that ruined thousands of lives* [video]. YouTube. https://www.youtube.com/watch?v=cvotuj3wBsk

Beckett, G. H. and Slater, T. (2018). Technology-integrated project-based language learning. In: *The Encyclopedia of Applied Linguistics* (ed. C.A. Chapelle). Hoboken: Wiley-Blackwell. doi: 10.1002/9781405198431.wbeal1487.

Bennett, R. (2011). Children with two languages excel at school. *The Sunday Times*. https://www.thetimes.co.uk/article/children-with-two-languages-excel-at-school-sc8ftfsk8

BetterCloud (2016). How to find the readability score for your word document [video]. *YouTube*. https://www.youtube.com/watch?v=YnnB56gziRM

Bitchener, J. and Ferris, D. (2012). *Written Corrective Feedback in Second Language Acquisition and Writing*. Oxfordshire: Routledge. https://www-dawsonera-com.libproxy.nie.edu.sg/readonline/9780203832400/startPage/60

Black Cat (n.d.). *Black Cat English*. https://www.blackcat-cideb.com/en/

Blad, E. (2021). How two years of pandemic disruption could shake up the debate over standardized testing. *EducationWeek*. https://www.edweek.org/teaching-learning/how-two-years-of-pandemic-disruption-could-shake-up-the-debate-over-standardized-testing/2021/03

Blau, E.K. (1990). The effect of syntax, speed, and pauses on listening comprehension. *TESOL Quarterly* 24 (4): 746–753.

Blum, S. (ed.). (2020). *Ungrading: Why Rating Students Undermines Learning (and What to do Instead)*. Morgantown: West Virginia University Press.

Boas, I.V. (2018). Assessing speaking skills in the classroom. In: *The TESOL Encyclopedia of English Language Teaching* (eds. J.I. Liontas and M. DelliCarpini). Hoboken: Wiley-Blackwell. doi: 10.1002/9781118784235.eelt0246.

Bochner, J.H. and Walter, G.G. (2005). Evaluating deaf students, readiness to meet the English language and literacy demands of postsecondary educational programs. *The Journal of Deaf Studies and Deaf Education* 10 (3): 232–243. doi: 10/3/232/413358.

Brigham Young University (BYU) (n.d.a). *Corpus of Contemporary American English (COCA)*. https://www.english-corpora.org/coca/

Brigham Young University (BYU) (n.d.b). *British National Corpus*. https://www.english-corpora.org/bnc/

Brigham Young University (BYU) (n.d.c). *Corpus of Global Web-Based English (GloWbE)*. https://www.english-corpora.org/glowbe/

Brigham Young University (BYU) (n.d.d). *Corpus of News on the Web (NOW)*. https://www.english-corpora.org/now/

Brigham Young University (BYU) (n.d.e). *Corpora YouTube channel*. https://www.youtube.com/channel/UCy84tTzeJ0s8JLjf_wEiWUQ

British Council (2016). *Assessing writing: introducing language assessment* [video]. YouTube. https://www.youtube.com/watch?v=5-Tryu8KnIA

British Council (n.d.). *Genres*. Teaching English. https://www.teachingenglish.org.uk/professional-development/teachers/knowing-subject/d-h/genre#:~:text=Genre%20is%20a%20term%20used,set%20phrases%2C%20formality%20and%20purpose

Brown, H.D. and Abeywickrama, P. (2010). *Language Assessment: Principles and Classroom Practices*, 2e. London: Pearson Education.

Brown, H.D. and Abeywickrama, P. (2018). *Language Assessment: Principles and Classroom Practices*, 3e. London: Pearson.

Buck, G. (2000). Testing listening. In: *Language Testing Videos* [video] (ed. G. Fulcher). YouTube. https://www.youtube.com/watch?v=9Tad6Ti_P4Q

Burkett, T. (2018). Norm-referenced testing and criterion-referenced testing. *TESOL Encyclopedia*. doi: 10.1002/9781118784235.eelt0351.

Burlington Books (n.d.). http://www.burlingtonbooks.com/

Burroughs, A. (2020). *Why K-12 schools should establish a data-driven culture*. EdTech. https://edtechmagazine.com/k12/article/2020/04/why-k12-schools-should-establish-data-driven-culture-perfcon.

California Department of Education. (2024). California Assessment of Student Performance and Progress (CAASPP). *Assessments*. https://www.caaspp.org/

California's Multilingual Education Act of 2016 (2016). Proposition 58. *Official Voter Information Guide*. https://web.archive.org/web/20161016130224/http://voterguide.sos.ca.gov/en/propositions/58

Cambridge Boxhill Language Assessment Unit Trust (2024). *Occupational English Test (OET)*. https://oet.com/

Cambridge English Language Assessment (2024a). *Tests and exams*. https://www.cambridgeenglish.org/exams-and-tests/

Cambridge English Language Assessment (2024b). *Write and improve: improve your English writing online*. https://www.cambridgeenglish.org/learning-english/free-resources/write-and-improve/

Cameron, L. (2001). *Teaching Language to Young Learners*. Cambridge: Cambridge University Press.

Canadian Academic English Language (CAEL) (2024). *Paragon testing enterprises*. https://www.cael.ca/

Canadian English Language Proficiency Index Program (CELPIP) (2024). Paragon testing enterprises. *CELPIP Overview*. https://www.celpip.ca/take-celpip/overview/

Carless, D. (2007). Learning-oriented assessment: conceptual bases and practical implications. *Innovations in Education and Teaching International* 44 (1): 57–66. doi: 10.1080/14703290601081332.

Castañeda v. Pickard, 648 F. 2d 989 (5th Cir. 1981). https://web.stanford.edu/~hakuta/www/LAU/IAPolicy/IA1bCastanedaFullText.htm

CELBAN Centre (2021). *Test information.* https://www.celbancentre.ca/test-information.aspx

Center for Applied Linguistics (n.d.). *Sheltered Instruction Observation Protocol (SIOP) model.* https://cal.org/siop/about/

Centre for Canadian Language Benchmarks (CLB) (2012). *Canadian language benchmarks: English as a second language for adults.* https://www.canada.ca/content/dam/ircc/migration/ircc/english/pdf/pub/language-benchmarks.pdf

Certyfikat Polski (2024). *Egzamin z Języka Polskiego.* https://certyfikatpolski.pl/rejestracja-na-egzamin/

Cerullo, M. (2023). Princeton student says his new app helps teachers find ChatGPT cheats. *Money Watch.* https://www.cbsnews.com/news/chatgpt-princeton-student-gptzero-app-edward-tian/

Chan, S. (2017). Developing rating scales for integrated assessment tasks. *EALTA Webinar Slides.* http://www.ealta.eu.org/documents/resources/Webinar%202017_integrated%20scales_SC.pdf

Chang, A.C.-S. (2018). Speech rate in second language listening. In: *The TESOL Encyclopedia of English Language Teaching* (eds. J.I. Liontas and M. DelliCarpini). Wiley Blackwell. doi: 10.1002/9781118784235.eelt0576.

Chapelle, C. (1999). Construct definition and validity inquiry in SLA research. In: *Interfaces Between Second Language Acquisition and Language Testing Research* (eds. L.F. Bachman and A.D. Cohen), 32–77. Cambridge: Cambridge University Press. https://assets.cambridge.org/97805216/49636/excerpt/9780521649636_excerpt.pdf

ChatGPT (n.d.) https://chat.openai.com/chat

CHILDES Corpora (n.d.). *Child's language data exchange system: talk bank.* https://childes.talkbank.org/access/

Cho, Y. and Bridgeman, B. (2012). Relationship of TOEFL iBT® scores to academic performance: some evidence from American universities. *Language Testing* 29 (3): 421–442. doi: 10.1177/0265532211430368.

Choi, Y. (2020). Task-based language assessment. In: *The Encyclopedia of Applied Linguistics* (ed. C.A. Chapelle). Hoboken: Wiley Blackwell. doi: 10.1002/9781405198431

CitizensAcademyCleve (2011). *Think aloud* [video]. YouTube. https://www.youtube.com/watch?v=oi7RfnlkTL4

Civil Rights Act of 1964 (1964). *National archives identifier: 299891.* Enrolled Acts and Resolutions of Congress, 1789-2011; General Records of the United States Government, Record Group 11; National Archives Building, Washington, DC. https://www.docsteach.org/documents/document/civil-rights-act-of-1964

Clayton, V. (2016). The problem with the GRE. *The Atlantic.* https://www.theatlantic.com/education/archive/2016/03/the-problem-with-the-gre/471633/

Cohen, A.D. (1994). *Assessing Language Ability in the Classroom,* 2e. Boston, MA.: Heinle & Heinle.

College Board Accuplacer (2021). *WritePlacer ESL: guide with sample essays.* https://accuplacer.collegeboard.org/accuplacer/pdf/accuplacer-writeplacer-esl-sample-essays.pdf

Collier, C. (2011). *Seven Steps to Separating Difference from Disability.* Thousand Oaks, CA: Corwin.

Common Core State Standards Initiative (n.d.). *Standards in your state.* https://www.thecorestandards.org/standards-in-your-state/

Comprehensive Adult Student Assessment Systems (CASAS) (1992). *ESL model standards key.* https://www.casas.org/docs/pagecontents/1992_model_standards_key.pdf?Status=Master

Cook, A., Spinazzola, J., Ford, J., et al. (2005). Complex trauma in children and adolescents. *Psychiatric Annals* 35: 390–398. https://nursebuddha.files.wordpress.com/2011/12/complex-trauma-in-children.pdf

Coombe, C. (ed.). (2018). *An A to Z of Second Language Assessment: How Language Teachers Understand Assessment Concepts.* London: British Council. https://www.britishcouncil.org/sites/default/files/a_to_z_glossary_final.pdf

Coombe, C., Folse, K. and Hubley, N. (2007). *A Practical Guide to Assessing English Language Learners.* Ann Arbor: University of Michigan Press.

Cope, B. and Kalantzis, M. (2015). Assessment and pedagogy in the era of machine-mediated learning. In: *Education as Social Construction: Contributions to Theory, Research, and Practice* (eds. T. Dragonas, K.J. Gergen, S. McNamee and E. Tseliou), 350–374. Dublin, OH.: Worldshare Books.

Cope, B. and Kalantzis, M. (2017). Conceptualizing e-Learning. In: *E-Learning Ecologies: Principles for New Learning and Assessment* (eds. B. Cope and M. Kalantzis), 1–45. Oxfordshire: Routledge.

Corpus of Contemporary American English (COCA) (n.d.). Brigham Young University. https://www.english-corpora.org/coca/

Council of Europe (2009). *CEFR (Common European Framework of Reference) multilingual self-assessment grid for lower secondary* (middle schoolers). https://rm.coe.int/CoERMPublicCommon SearchServices/DisplayDCTMContent?documentId=0900001680492ff2

Council of Europe (2018). *CEFR: learning, teaching, assessment—companion volume* Strasbourg, France: Council of Europe Publishing. https://rm.coe.int/cefr-companion-volume-with-new-descriptors-2018/1680787989

Council of Europe (2020a). *Key concepts: mediation* [video]. Vimeo. https://player.vimeo.com/video/766431853

Council of Europe (2020b). *CEFR: Learning, teaching, assessment—companion volume.* Council of Europe Publishing. https://rm.coe.int/common-european-framework-of-reference-for-languages-learning-teaching/16809ea0d4

Council of Europe (2024a). *CEFR self-assessment grid.* https://www.coe.int/en/web/portfolio/self-assessment-grid

Council of Europe (2024b). *European language portfolio.* https://www.coe.int/en/web/portfolio

Councils of Ministers of Education, Canada (n.d.). *Overview.* https://www.cmec.ca/680/Elementary-Secondary_Education.html

Coxhead, A. (2000). A new academic word list. *TESOL Quarterly* 34 (2): 213–238. https://www.wgtn.ac.nz/lals/resources/academicwordlist

Coyle, D., Hood P. and Marsh D. (2010). *CLIL: Content and Language Integrated Learning.* Cambridge: Cambridge University Press.

Crawford, M.J.L. (2011). Lawmakers push to exempt English language learners from standardized test scores. *Capital News Service.* https://news.jrn.msu.edu/2011/09/lawmakers-push-to-exempt-english-language-learners-from-standardized-test-scores/

Creative Commons (n.d.). https://search.creativecommons.org/

Cummins, J. (1979). Cognitive/academic language proficiency, linguistic interdependence, the optimum age question and some other matters. *Working Papers on Bilingualism* 19: 121–129.

Daley, S. (2022). *Edtech.* Bultin. https://builtin.com/edtech

Davidson, F. and Lynch, B.K. (2002). *Testcraft: A Teacher's Guide to Writing and Using Language Test Specifications.* Connecticut: Yale University Press.

De Costa, P., Sterling, S., Lee, J., et al. (2021). Research tasks on ethics in applied linguistics. *Language Teaching* 54 (1): 58–70.

Debski, R. (2006). *Project-based language teaching with technology.* NCELTR. https://www.researchgate.net/publication/303792681_Project-based_language_teaching_with_technology

DELE Exam for Spanish (2019). Guía del examen DELE A1. https://examenes.cervantes.es/sites/default/files/DELE_A1_v2020_Gu%C3%ADa%20de%20examen.pdf

Deygers, B., Zeidler, B., Vilcu, D., et al. (2018). One framework to unite them all? Use of the CEFR in European university entrance policies. *Language Assessment Quarterly* 15 (1): 3–15.

Dictation.io. (2024). *Voice Dictation Online - Speech Recognition.* https://dictation.io/

Doiz, A., Lasagabaster, D. and Sierra, J.M. (eds.). (2012). *English-Medium Instruction at Universities: Global Challenges*. Bristol: Multilingual Matters.

Duolingo (2024). *Duolingo English test*. https://englishtest.duolingo.com/test_takers

Earl, L. (2006). *Rethinking classroom assessment with purpose in mind*. Manitoba Education, Citizenship and Youth. https://digitalcollection.gov.mb.ca/awweb/pdfopener?smd=1&did=12503&md=1

East, M. and King, C. (2012). L2 learners' engagement with high stakes listening tests: does technology have a beneficial role to play? *CALICO Journal* 29 (2): 208–223.

Eastern Michigan University (2024). *Teaching English to speakers of other languages/TESOL [M.A.]*. https://catalog.emich.edu/preview_program.php?catoid=40&poid=17622

ECD Educational Technology Support (2012). *Creating a frequency distribution of grades in excel* [video]. YouTube. https://www.youtube.com/watch?v=nsdYNAzLm3M

ECL European Consortium for the Certificate of Attainment in Modern Languages (n.d.). *Sample tests*. https://eclexam.eu/sample-tests/

EdPuzzle (n.d.). https://edpuzzle.com/

Educational Testing Service (ETS) (2007). *Test and score data summary for TOEFL® computer-based and paper-based tests*. https://www.ets.org/Media/Research/pdf/TOEFL-SUM-0506-CBT.pdf

Educational Testing Service (ETS) (2019). *TOEFL iBT test content*. https://www.ets.org/toefl/ibt/about/content/

Educational Testing Service (ETS) (2023). *Understanding your TOEFL iBT test scores*. https://www.ets.org/toefl/test-takers/ibt/scores/understand-scores.html

Educational Testing Service (ETS) (2024a). *Praxis tests*. https://www.ets.org/praxis/institutions/scores/interpret

Educational Testing Service (ETS) (2024b). *TOEIC test of English for international communication*. https://www.ets.org/toeic.html

Educational Testing Service (ETS) (2024c). *The TOEFL tests*. https://www.ets.org/toefl.html

Educational Testing Service (ETS) (2024d). *TOEFL iBT. Test of English as a foreign language*. https://www.ets.org/toefl/test-takers/ibt/about.html

Edutopia (2011). *Big thinkers: Judy Willis on the science of learning* [video]. YouTube. https://www.youtube.com/watch?v=J6FqAiAbUFs

EIKEN Foundation of Japan (n.d.). *EIKEN tests*. https://www.eiken.or.jp/eiken/en/eiken-tests/

EL Education (2016). *Austin's butterfly: models, critique, and descriptive feedback* [video]. Vimeo. https://modelsofexcellence.eleducation.org/resources/austins-butterfly

Ellis, R. (1997). *SLA research and language teaching*. Oxford: Oxford University Press.

Ellis, R., Loewen, S. and Erlam, R. (2006). Implicit and explicit corrective feedback and the acquisition of L2 grammar. *Studies in Second Language Acquisition* 25 (2): 243–272.

ELTE Origó (2024). *Origó for Hungarian*. https://www.onyc.hu/nyelvvizsga/

Encyclopaedia Britannica (n.d.). *History of Australia*. https://www.britannica.com/place/Australia/History

English, C.E. (1988). *The test of written English: a statistical analysis of validity and reliability* [Master's thesis, Portland State University, Paper 3757]. PDX Scholar. https://pdxscholar.library.pdx.edu/cgi/viewcontent.cgi?article=4767&context=open_access_etds

Escamilla, K., Hopewell, S., Butvilofsky, S., et al. (2014). *Biliteracy from the start: literacy squared in action*. Philadelphia, PA.: Caslon Publishing.

Eurocontrol (n.d.). *English Language Proficiency for Aeronautical Communication (ELPAC)*. https://elpac.eurocontrol.int/

Extensive Reading Foundation (n.d.). *Graded readers.* https://erfoundation.org/wordpress/graded-readers/

Fair Test (2007). *Examining the GRE: myths, misuses, and alternatives.* The National Center for Fair and Open Testing. https://www.fairtest.org/examining-gre-myths-misuses-and-alternatives

Feldman, J. (2019). *Grading for Equity: What it is, Why it Matters, and How it can Transform Schools and Classrooms.* Thousand Oaks: Corwin Press.

Feng, L., Huenerfauth, M., Jansche, M., et al. (2010). A comparison of features for automatic readability assessment. In: *Coling 2010 Posters* (eds. C-R Huang and D. Jurafsky) 276–284. https://aclanthology.org/C10-2032/

Fernandez, M. (2012). *Scandal of students who 'disappeared' at test time* [video]. NBC News. https://www.nbcnews.com/id/wbna49403687

Ferris, D. (2007). Preparing teachers to respond to student writing. *Journal of Second Language Writing* 16 (3): 165–193. https://www.sciencedirect.com/science/article/abs/pii/S1060374307000483?via%3Dihub

Ferris, D. (2014). Responding to student writing: teachers, philosophies and practices. *Assessing Writing* 19: 6–23.

Field, J. (2008). *Listening in the Language Classroom.* Cambridge: Cambridge University Press.

Fratiglioni, L., Paillard-Borg, S., and Winblad, B. (2004). An active and socially integrated lifestyle in late life might protect against dementia. *The Lancet. Neurology*, *3*(6), 343–353. https://doi.org/10.1016/S1474-4422(04)00767-7

Freeman, D. and Freeman, Y. (1988). *Sheltered English instruction.* Eric Digest ED301070. https://eric.ed.gov/?id=ED301070

French as a Second Language (2013). *Transforming French as a second language (*writing, oral *samples)* [video]. https://transformingfsl.ca/en/resources/samples-of-student-oral-and-written-production-based-on-cefr-levels/

French Institute Alliance Français (FIAF) (n.d.). *FIAF exams for French.* https://fiaf.org/exams/

Fulcher, G. (n.d.). *A test specification template (Popham's specplate).* https://languagetesting.info/ED7007/4/Specplate.pdf

Fulcher, G. (2009). *Rating scales and the halo effect.* https://languagetesting.info/features/halorating/rating.html

Galloway, N. and Rose, H. (2015). *Introducing Global Englishes.* Oxfordshire: Routledge Publishing.

Garner, I. (2024). *Data in education.* Learning A-Z: Part one of two. https://www.learninga-z.com/site/breakroom/data-in-education

Gentleman, A. (2020). Students wrongly accused of cheating in visa test take fight to Downing street. *TheGuardian.* https://www.theguardian.com/uk-news/2020/sep/24english-test-students-accused-of-cheating-send-letter-to-no-10

Gentleman, A. (2022). English test scandal: home office accused of 'shocking miscarriage of justice'. *The Guardian.* https://www.theguardian.com/uk-news/2022/feb/09/english-test-scandal-home-office-accused-of-shocking-miscarriage-of-justice

Gentleman, A. (2024a). English test scandal: students renew fight to clear names after 10 years. *The Guardian.* https://www.theguardian.com/uk-news/2024/feb/11/english-test-scandal-students-renew-fight-to-clear-names-after-10-years

Gentleman, A. (2024b). English test scandal: students wrongly accused of cheating launch legal action. *The Guardian.* https://www.theguardian.com/uk-news/2024/feb/19/english-test-scandal-students-wrongly-accused-of-cheating-launch-legal-action

George, T. (2021). *Consequences of mild, moderate & severe plagiarism*. Scribbr. https://www.scribbr.co.uk/preventing-plagiarism/consequences-of-plagiarism/

Giuffrida, A. (2020). Italian police investigate claims Luis Suárezs citizenship exam was rigged. *The Guardian*. https://www.theguardian.com/football/2020/sep/22/italian-police-investigate-claims-luis-suarez-citizenship-exam-rigged-barcelona-juventus

Glen, S. (2024). *Bimodal distribution: what is it?* From statistics how to. https://www.statisticshowto.com/what-is-a-bimodal-distribution/

Glossary of Education Reform (2013). *Continuous improvement*. https://www.edglossary.org/continuous-improvement/

Glossary of Education Reform: Learning standards (2014). *Great schools partnership*. https://www.edglossary.org/learning-standards/

Glossary of Education Reform: Standardized test (2014). *Great schools partnership*. https://www.edglossary.org/standardized-test/

Goethe-Institut (2009a). *Deutsch-Test Für Zuwanderer A2-B1*. https://www.goethe.de/resources/files/pdf209/dtz_pruefungshandbuch.pdf

Goethe-Institut (2009b). The CEFR grids for writing, developed by ALTE members [writing samples]. https://www.eaquals.org/wp-content/uploads/German-samples-Goethe-Institute.pdf

Goethe-Institut (2024). *German examinations*. https://www.goethe.de/en/spr/kup/prf.html

Goh, C.M. (2018). Cognition, metacognition and L2 listening. In: *Handbook of Research in Second Language Teaching and Learning*, 3 (ed. E. Hinkel), Oxfordshire: Taylor and Francis.

Gonzalez, J. (2021). *Build it together: co-constructing success criteria with students*. Cult of Pedagogy Website. https://www.cultofpedagogy.com/co-constructing-success-criteria/

Gorter D. and Cenoz, J. (2017). Language education policy and multilingual assessment. *Language and Education*, 31 (3): 231–248. doi: 10.1080/09500782.2016.1261892.

Gottlieb, M. (1995). Nurturing student learning through portfolios. *TESOL Journal*, 5 (1): 12–14.

Gottlieb, M. (2006). *Assessing English Language Learners*. Thousand Oaks: Corwin Press.

Gottlieb, M. (2016). *Assessing English Language Learners: Bridges to Educational Equity*, 2e. Thousand Oaks: Corwin.

Government of Alberta (2019). Literacy: definition, components and elements of the progressions. https://education.alberta.ca/media/3069627/definition-components-and-elements-literacy.pdf

Government of Canada (2024). *Find free newcomer services near you*. https://www.cic.gc.ca/english/newcomers/services/index.asp#table1caption

Grammarly (2024). *How we use AI to enhance your writing*. https://www.grammarly.com/blog/how-grammarly-uses-ai/#:~:text=Grammarly%27s%20AI%20system%20combines%20machine,even%20paragraphs%20or%20full%20texts

GrapeSEED English for Children (2024). https://grapeseed.com/grapeseed/us

Gray, J. (2006). *A study of cultural content in the British ELT global coursebook: a cultural studies approach* [Doctoral Dissertation, University of London]. University College London. https://discovery.ucl.ac.uk/id/eprint/10023103/1/514195.pdf

Gunning Fog Index (2024). *What is the Gunning Fog Index?* https://www.webfx.com/tools/read-able/gunning-fog/

Gutierrez-Clellen, V. and Peña, E.D. (2001). Dynamic assessment of diverse children. *Language, Speech, and Hearing Services in Schools*, 32 (4): 212–224. doi: 10.1044/0161-1461(2001/019).

Hamp-Lyons, L. (1991). Basic concepts. In: *Assessing Second Language Writing in Academic Contexts* (ed. L. Hamp-Lyons). 5–15. Ablex.

Hanover Research (2014). *Impact of formative assessment and learning intentions on student achievement*. http://www.hanoverresearch.com/media/The-Impact-of-Formative-Assessment-and-Learning-Intentions-on-Student-Achievement.pdf

Hargreaves, A. and Braun, H. (2013). *Data-driven improvement and accountability*. National Education Policy Center. http://nepc.colorado.edu/publication/data-driven-improvement-accountability/

Harris, B., Plucker, J.A., Rapp, K.E., et al. (2009). Identifying gifted and talented English language learners: a case study. *Journal for the Education of the Gifted*, 32 (3): 368–393. http://files.eric.ed.gov/fulltext/EJ835865.pdf

Hashimoto, B.J. (2016). *Rethinking vocabulary size tests: frequency versus item difficulty*. (Publication No. 5958) [Master's thesis, Brigham Young University]. Scholars Archive. https://scholarsarchive.byu.edu/etd/5958

Hasselgren, A. (2000). The assessment of the English ability of young learners in Norwegian schools: an innovative approach. *Language Testing*, 17 (2): 261–277. doi: 10.1177/026553220001700209.

Hasselgreen, A. (2003). *Bergen 'Can Do' project*, Council of Europe Publishing. https://www.ecml.at/Portals/1/documents/ECML-resources/pub221E2003_Hasselgreen.pdf?ver=2018-04-17-115104-580

Haukås, Å., Bjørke, C., and Dypedahl, M. (eds.), (2018). *Metacognition in Language Learning and Teaching*. Oxfordshire: Routledge.

Helbling Readers (n.d.). https://www.helbling.com/int/en/helbling-readers

Hernandez, C. (2024). Tips for teaching English language learners who are blind or visually impaired. *Paths to Literacy*. https://www.pathstoliteracy.org/tips-teaching-english-language-learners-who-are-blind-or-visually-impaired/

Hiebert, E.H., Scott, J.A., Castaneda, R., et al. (2019). An analysis of the features of words that influence vocabulary difficulty. *Education Sciences*, 9 (8): 1–24. https://www.mdpi.com/2227-7102/9/1/8

Holland, P.W., Dorans, N.J., and Petersen, N.S. (2006). 6 Equating test scores. In *Handbook of Statistics: Psychometrics* (eds. C. R. Rao and S. Sinharay), 26: 169–203. doi: 10.1016/S0169-7161(06)26006-1.

Hot Potatoes (n.d.). Version 7. Half-Baked Software Inc. https://hotpot.uvic.ca/

Hougen, M. (2014). *Evidence-based reading instruction for adolescents, grades 6-12* (Document No. IC-13). University of Florida, Collaboration for Effective Educator, Development, Accountability, and Reform Center website: http://ceedar.education.ufl.edu/tools/innovation-configurations/

HSK Chinese Test Services (2018). *Chinese proficiency test*. https://www.chinesetest.cn/HSK

Huawei, S., and Aryadoust, V. (2022). A systemic review of automated writing evaluation systems. *Education and Information Technologies* 28: 771–795. doi: 10.1007/s10639-022-11200-7.

Hughes, A. (2003). *Testing for Language Teachers*, 2e. Cambridge: Cambridge University Press.

iClicker (2024). *Macmillan Learning Company*. https://www.iclicker.com/

Inclusion Canada (2017). *Linguistically responsive education*. http://www.inclusioncanada.net/english languagedevelopment.html

Individuals with Disabilities Education Act (IDEA) (2024). https://sites.ed.gov/idea/

International Baccalaureate (IB) Middle Years Programme (2014). *Language acquisition guide*. https://curryib.com/wp-content/uploads/2018/10/language-acquisition.pdf

International Civil Aviation Organization (ICAO) (2021). *ICAO English test*. The English Centre https://englishcentre.eu/#icao

International Civil Aviation Organization (ICAO) (n.d.). *ICAO language proficiency descriptors*. Mayflower College. https://www.maycoll.co.uk/pdfs/onlinelearning/icaodescriptors.pdf

International Council of Professors of Educational Administration. https://files.eric.ed.gov/fulltext/EJ1204463.pdf

International English Language Testing System (IELTS) (2023). British Council; IDP IELTS; and Cambridge University Press & Assessment. https://www.cambridgeenglish.org/exams-and-tests/ielts/

International English Language Testing System (IELTS) (2023). *IELTS scoring in detail*. https://ielts.org/take-a-test/preparation-resources/understanding-your-score/ielts-scoring-in-detail

International English Language Testing System (IELTS) (2024). *IELTS test types*. British Council; IDP IELTS; and Cambridge University Press & Assessment. https://ielts.org/take-a-test/test-types

International Language Testing Association (ILTA) (2018). *Code of ethics for language testers*. https://www.iltaonline.com/page/CodeofEthics

Ionnaou-Georgiou, S. and Pavlou, P. (2003). *Assessing Young Learners*. Oxford: Oxford University Press.

Izgi, U. and Seker, B.S. (2012). Comparing different readability formulas on the examples of science-technology and social science textbooks. *Procedia—Social and Behavioral Sciences* 46: 178–182. https://www.sciencedirect.com/science/article/pii/S1877042812012189

Japan *Act for Eliminating Discrimination against Persons with Disabilities, Act No. 65 of June 26, 2013*. https://www.japaneselawtranslation.go.jp/en/laws/view/3052/en

Japanese Language Proficiency Test (JLPT) (2012). *Japan foundation*. Japan Educational Exchanges and Services. https://www.jlpt.jp/e/

Jim Casey Youth Opportunities Initiative (2011). *The adolescent brain: new research and its implications for young people transitioning from foster care*. https://www.aecf.org/resources/the-adolescent-brain-foster-care

Justus Liebig Gießen University, Germany (2023). *Corpus linguistics help*. https://www.uni-giessen.de/en/faculties/f05/engl/ling/clhelp/dl/list_of_corpora

Kagan, S. (n.d.). *The power of pair work*. Kagan Online Magazine, 64. Kagan Publishing. https://www.kaganonline.com

Kahoot! (2024). Kahoot! https://kahoot.com/

Kalantzis, M. and Cope, B. (2019). *Multiliteracies and learning by design: meaning making* [video]. YouTube. https://www.youtube.com/playlist?list=PLV_zfgB7n1yT9RohZn1ev49XY88l_EyCN

Kan, V., Lai, K. C., Kirkpatrick, A., et al. (2011). *Fine-tuning Hong Kong's medium of instruction policy*. The Hong Kong Institute of Education.

Kanfer, J. (2021). All about Respondus lockdown browser: how it detects cheating. *LearnPar*. https://learnpar.com/respondus-lockdown-browser/

Kaplan, L. (n.d.). *Inuit or Eskimo: which name to use?* Alaska Native Language Center. https://www.uaf.edu/anlc/research-and-resources/resources/archives/inuit_or_eskimo.php

Kasen, J. (2021). How to cheat Respondus lockdown browser: bypass around hacks. *GradeBees*. https://gradebees.com/cheating-respondus-lockdown-browser/

Katakowski, D., Koceski, S., Toohey, S., and Whitmore, S. (2018). *Oakland schools guidance: separating difference from disability in English learners who struggle*. https://drive.google.com/file/d/17K_lJbmr4xkSbr-dkk-RoVcg4wiM923W/view?usp=sharing

Kiru, E. and Cooc, N. (2018). A comparative analysis of access to education for students with disabilities in Brazil, Canada, and South Africa. *Journal International Special Needs Education*, 21 (2): 34–44. https://files.eric.ed.gov/fulltext/EJ1198901.pdf

Klein, L. (2018). *Making the most of 'continuous improvement' in state ESSA plans*. https://www.edweek.org/policy-politics/q-a-making-the-most-of-continuous-improvement-in-state-essa-plans/2018/06

Klieger, D.M., Bridgeman, B., Tannenbaum, R.J., et al. (2018). *The validity of GRE general test scores for predicting academic performance at US law schools*. ETS Research Report RR-18-26. https://www.ets.org/research/policy_research_reports/publications/report/2018/jzfw.html

Knoch, U. (2009). Diagnostic assessment of writing: A comparison of two rating scales. *Language Testing* 26 (2): 275–304.

Kohn, A. (1999). From degrading to de-grading. *High School Magazine*. http://www.alfiekohn.org/article/degrading-de-grading/

Krashen, S.D. (1982). *Principles and Practice in Second Language Acquisition*. Oxford: Pergamon Press. http://www.sdkrashen.com/content/books/principles_and_practice.pdf

Kunnan, A.J. (2004). Test fairness. In: *European Language Testing in a Global Context* (eds. M. Milanovic and C. Weir), 27–48. Cambridge: Cambridge University Press.

Kunnan, A.J. (2008). Towards a model of test evaluation: using the test fairness and wider context frameworks. In: *Multilingualism and Assessment: Achieving Transparency, Assuring Quality, Sustaining Diversity* (eds. L. Taylor and C. Weir). Papers from the ALTE Conference in Berlin, Germany. 229–251. Cambridge: Cambridge University Press.

Kurzer, K. (2018). Dynamic written corrective feedback in developmental multilingual writing classes. *TESOL Quarterly* 52 (1): 5–33. http://www.jstor.org/stable/44984810

Kuzborska, I. (2018). Interactive reading strategies. In: *The TESOL Encyclopedia of English Language Teaching* (eds. J. I. Liontas and M. DelliCarpini). Wiley Blackwell. doi: 10.1002/9781118784235. eelt0475.

Lane, D.M. (n.d.). *Describing univariate data*. HyperStat online statistics textbook (Chapter 2). https://davidmlane.com/hyperstat/desc_univ.html

Larsen-Freeman, D. (1997). Grammar and its teaching: Challenging the myths. *ERIC digest, 1–7*. ERIC clearinghouse on languages and linguistics. ED406829. https://files.eric.ed.gov/fulltext/ED406829.pdf

Larsen-Freeman, D. and Celce-Murcia, M. (2016). *The Grammar Book*, 3e. National Geographic Learning, Cengage Learning.

Lau v. Nichols, 414 U.S. 563 (1974). https://www.britannica.com/topic/Lau-v-Nichols

Learnalberta (2024a). *Supporting English as an additional language learners: tools, strategies resources*, [videos]. https://www.learnalberta.ca/content/eslapb/video.html

Learnalberta (2024b). *Supporting English as an additional language learners: tools, strategies, resources* [writing samples]. https://www.learnalberta.ca/content/eslapb/writing_samples.html

Leech, G. (2001). *The role of frequency in ELT: new corpus evidence brings a re-appraisal*. In: ELT in China 2001: Papers presented at the 3rd International Symposium on ELT in China. Foreign Language Teaching and Research Press, Beijing, 1–23. https://pdfs.semanticscholar.org/3e5d/b409321ae7c0341dd18fc5f3a356e6469568.pdf

Lehman, E., De Jong, D., and Baron, M. (2018). *Investigating the Relationship of Standards-Based Grades vs. Traditional-Based Grades to Results of the Scholastic Math Inventory at the Middle School Level*. Education Leadership Review of Doctoral Research, Vol. 6. https://files.eric.ed.gov/fulltext/EJ1204463.pdf

Levesque. (2015). Testing is necessary to expand opportunity for all. *New York Times*. https://www.nytimes.com/roomfordebate/2015/05/04/is-testing-students-the-answer-to-americas-education-woes.

Levine, L.N., Lukens, L. and Smallwood, B.A. (2013). *The GO TO strategies: scaffolding options for teachers of English language learners, K-12*. For Project EXCELL, a partnership between the University of Missouri-Kansas City and North Kansas City Schools, funded by the US Department of Education, PR Number T195N070316. https://ez.cal.org/cal_user/what-we-do/projects/project-excell/the-go-to-strategies

Lexile Text Analyzer (2024). https://hub.lexile.com/analyzer

Liang, J. (2014). Toward a three-step pedagogy for fostering self-assessment in a second language writing classroom. *The CATESOL Journal* 26 (1): 100–119.

Linnarud, M. (1986). *Lexis in composition: a performance analysis of Swedish learners, written English.* Liber Förlag.

Literacy Education and Second Language Learning for Adults (LESLLA) (2019). *Vision.* http://web. archive.org/web/20240117173351/https://www.leslla.org/our-vision

Lynn, B. (2018). German students protest unfair English exam. *Voice of America* (VOA). https://learning english.voanews.com/a/german-students-protest-unfair-english-exam/4378236.html

Macknish, C. (2010). *Academic and Professional Writing for Teachers.* New York: McGraw Hill.

Mandinach, E.B. and Schildkamp, K. (2021). Misconceptions about data-based decision making in education: an exploration of the literature. *Studies in Educational Evaluation* 69.pp. 1–10. doi: 10.1016/j.stueduc.2020.100842.

Marian, V. and Shook, A. (2012). The cognitive benefits of being bilingual. *Cerebrum.* PMID: 23447799; PMCID: PMC3583091. https://www.ncbi.nlm.nih.gov/pmc/articles/PMC3583091/

Maritime English Test (n.d.). *Online English language testing.* Marlins. https://marlins.co.uk/ maritime-english/

Marsh, D., Zając, M., Gołębiowska, H., et al. (2009). *Profile report bilingual education (English) in Poland: Overview of practice in selected schools.* CODN, British Council Poland, University of Jyväskylä, Warszawa. https://web.archive.org/web/20210301115606/https://www.researchgate.net/ profile/Anna-Czura/publication/314869723_Bilingual_Education_and_the_Emergence_of_CLIL_ in_Poland/links/58c6c0f0a6fdcc5bd3c5c3af/Bilingual-Education-and-the-Emergence-of-CLIL-in-Poland.pdf

Marsh, J.A. (2012). Interventions promoting educators' use of data: research insights and gaps. *Teachers College Record* 114 (1): 1–15.

Marzano Resources (n.d.). *Tips from Dr. Marzano.* https://www.marzanoresources.com/resources/tips/ slgtsbg_tips_archive/

Mayflower College (n.d.). *Benchmark test for English aviation (b-TEA).* https://www.maycoll.co.uk/ aviation-english/benchmark_test_of_english_for_aviation.htm

McBride, K. (2011). The effect of rate of speech and distributed practice on the development of listening comprehension. *Computer Assisted Language Learning* 24 (2): 131–54.

McDowell-Wahpekeche, D. (2021). Which is correct? Native American, American Indian or Indigenous? *The Oklahoman.* https://www.oklahoman.com/story/special/2021/04/22/what-do-native-people-prefer-called/4831284001/

McGill University, Canada (2024). *Undergraduate grading scale and grade point average.* https://www. mcgill.ca/dise/about/resources/instructor-resources/undergrading

McInerney, M. and McKlindon, A. (2014). *Unlocking the door to learning: trauma-informed classrooms & transformational schools.* Educational Law Center, 1–24. https://www.elc-pa.org/wp-content/ uploads/2015/06/Trauma-Informed-in-Schools-Classrooms-FINAL-December2014-2.pdf

McKay, P. (2006). *Assessing Young Language Learners.* Cambridge: Cambridge University Press.

McTighe, J. and Ferrara, S. (1998). *Assessing learning in the classroom.* Student Assessment Series. National Education Association. https://files.eric.ed.gov/fulltext/ED429989.pdf

Menken, K., Hudson, T. and Leung, C. (2014). Symposium: language assessment in standards-based education reform. *TESOL Quarterly*, 48 (3): Special topic issue: K-12 standards-based educational reform: implications for English language learner populations, 586–614.

Merriam-Webster Dictionary (2024). https://www.merriam-webster.com/

MetaMetrics (2024a). *The lexile framework for reading.* https://lexile.com/educators/tools-to-support-reading-at-school/tools-to-determine-a-books-complexity/the-lexile-analyzer/

MetaMetrics (2024b). *Lexile case studies.* Lexile Framework for Reading. https://lexile.com/education-companies/education-company-lexile-case-studies/

MetaMetrics (2024c). *How do lexile measures relate to grade levels?* Lexile Framework for Reading. https://lexile.com/parents-students/measuring-growth-lexile-measures/evaluating-performance-by-grade/

Mewald, C., Gassner, O. and Sigott, G. (2009). E8 speaking test specifications version October 09. https://web.archive.org/web/20240627070115/https://www.aau.at/wp-content/uploads/2017/09/E8_Speaking_Specifications.pdf

Meyer, A.N.D. (2011). *The positive and negative effects of testing in lifelong learning.* Dissertation, Rice University. https://scholarship.rice.edu/handle/1911/70351

Meyers, C. and Holt, S. (1997). *Pronunciation diagnosis & training* [video]. Aspen Productions. https://www.youtube.com/playlist?list=PL2zgxdcd6elRxSsgow9tgKNmWKvRWipy0

Michigan Corpus of Academic Spoken English (MICASE). (n.d.). University of Michigan. https://quod.lib.umich.edu/cgi/c/corpus/corpus?c=micase;page=simple

Michigan Corpus of Upper Level Student Papers (MICUSP) (n.d.). English Language Institute, University of Michigan. https://eli-corpus.lsa.umich.edu/main

Michigan Language Assessment (2013). *Examination for the certificate of competency in English (ECCE) speaking test sample.* https://www.youtube.com/watch?v=cN2FoaeEwIc

Michigan Language Assessment (2014). *Examination for the certificate of proficiency in English (ECPE): sample speaking test* [video]. YouTube. https://www.youtube.com/watch?v=FIY4ZoODfeg

Michigan Language Assessment (2015). *Graduate student instructor oral English test* (GSI OET). https://michiganassessment.org/michigan-tests/gsi-oet/

Michigan Language Assessment (2024). https://michiganassessment.org/

Michigan Language Assessment (n.d.). *Michigan young learner exam (MYLE) Bronze details.* https://michiganassessment.org/michigan-tests/myle/myle-bronze-details/

Michigan State University (MSU) (2024). *MSU English language examinations.* https://www.msu-exams.gr/en/content/about-msu-exams

Miller, C.C., Playford, A., Buchanan, L., et al. (2022). Did a fourth grader write this? Or the new chatbot? *The New York Times.* https://www.nytimes.com/interactive/2022/12/26/upshot/chatgpt-child-essays.html

Ministry of Education, Culture, Sports, Science and Technology (MEXT), Japan (n.d.). *Special needs education.* https://www.mext.go.jp/en/policy/education/elsec/title02/detail02/1373858.htm#:~:text=Special%20Needs%20Education%20is%20education,their%20independence%20and%20social%20participation

Minnesota Literacy Council (2020). *Classroom videos: classroom activities for adult ESL learners.* https://www.literacymn.org/classroom-videos

Monaghan, P., Chang, Y-N., Welbourne, S., et al. (2017). Exploring the relations between word frequency, language exposure, and bilingualism in a computational model of reading. *Journal of Memory and Language* 93, 1–21. https://www.sciencedirect.com/science/article/pii/S0749596X16300730

Moneta-Koehler, L., Brown, A.M., Petrie, K.A., et al. (2017). The limitations of the GRE in predicting success in biomedical graduate school. *PLoS One* 12 (1): e0166742. https://www.ncbi.nlm.nih.gov/pmc/articles/PMC5226333/

Mosteller, F. (1989). The "muddiest point in the lecture" as a feedback device. *On Teaching and Learning: The Journal of the Harvard-Danforth Center* 3: 10–21.

Mott-Smith, J. A., Tomaš, Z., and Kostka, I. (2017). *Teaching effective source use: classroom approaches that work.* Ann Arbor: University of Michigan Press.

M-STEP Michigan Student Test of Educational Progress. (2024). *M-STEP Summative.* https://www.michigan.gov/mde/Services/Student-Assessment/m-step

M-STEP Michigan Student Test of Educational Progress (2024). https://www.michigan.gov/mde/Services/Student-Assessment/m-step

Natcorp (n.d.). *British National Corpus (BNC)*. http://www.natcorp.ox.ac.uk/

Nation, P. (1990). *Vocabulary tests*. Victoria University of Wellington, New Zealand. https://www.wgtn.ac.nz/lals/resources/paul-nations-resources/vocabulary-tests

National Association for the Education of Young Children (2009). *Where we stand on assessing young English learners*. https://www.naeyc.org/sites/default/files/globally-shared/downloads/PDFs/resources/position-statements/WWSEnglishLanguageLearnersWeb%20%282%29.pdf

National Center for Educational Statistics. (2024). English Learners in Public Schools. https://nces.ed.gov/programs/coe/indicator/cgf

National Institute of Education Singapore (2001). *Corpus of spoken Singapore English interviews*. https://videoweb.nie.edu.sg/phonetic/niecsse/interviews.htm

NCSSFL-ACTFL (2019). *LinguaFolio*. American Council on the Teaching of Foreign Languages. https://ncssfl.org/linguafolio-materials/

NCSSFL-ACTFL (2024a). *Can-do statements for use with LinguaFolio*. American Council on the Teaching of Foreign Languages. https://ncssfl.org/linguafolio-linguagrow/2017-can-do-statements/

NCSSFL-ACTFL (2024b). *Can-do statements*. American Council on the Teaching of Foreign Languages. https://www.actfl.org/educator-resources/ncssfl-actfl-can-do-statements

Nemeroff, C.B. (2016). Paradise lost: the neurobiological and clinical consequences of child abuse and neglect. *Neuron*, 89 (5): 892–909. doi: 10.1016/j.neuron.2016.01.019.

New London Group (1996). A pedagogy of multiliteracies: designing social futures. *Harvard Educational Review* 66 (1): 60–92. http://newarcproject.pbworks.com/f/Pedagogy+of+Multiliteracies_New+London+Group.pdf

North Atlantic Treaty Organization (NATO) (2010). *Standardization agreement (STANAG) 6001 NTG Edition 4 Language proficiency levels*. https://www.natobilc.org/documents/LanguageTesting/NU-ST%206001%20NTG%20ED4.pdf

Oakland Schools (n.d.). *Curricular units: all courses*. https://oaklandk12-public.rubiconatlas.org/Atlas/Public/View/Default

O'Brien, M. (2023). EXPLAINER: What is ChatGPT and why are schools blocking it? *AP*. https://apnews.com/article/what-is-chat-gpt-ac4967a4fb41fda31c4d27f015e32660

Ockey, G.J. (2018). Oral language proficiency tests. In: *The TESOL Encyclopedia of English Language Teaching* (eds. J.I. Liontas and M. DelliCarpini) Hoboken: Wiley Blackwell. doi: 10.1002/9781118784235.eelt0234.

Ogle, D.M. (1986). K-W-L: a teaching model that develops active reading of expository text. *Reading Teacher* 39: 564–570.

O'Malley, J.M. and Pierce, L.V. (1996). *Authentic Assessment for English Language Learners: Practical Approaches for Teachers*. Addison-Wesley Publishing Company.

Ontario Human Rights Code (1962). http://www.ohrc.on.ca/en/ontario-human-rights-code

Ontario Human Rights Commission Report (2002). *The opportunity to succeed: achieving barrier-free access for students with disabilities*. http://www.ohrc.on.ca/en/book/export/html/2470

Ontario Ministry of Education (2007a). *English language learners ESL and ELD programs and services: policies and procedures for Ontario elementary and secondary schools, kindergarten to grade 12*. https://web.archive.org/web/20230411080456/https://www.edu.gov.on.ca/eng/document/esleldprograms/esleldprograms.pdf

Ontario Ministry of Education (2007b). *Supporting English language learners in kindergarten: a practical guide for Ontario educators*. https://web.archive.org/web/20220901070021/https://www.edu.gov.on.ca/eng/document/kindergarten/kindergartenELL.pdf

van Oosten, P., Tanghe, D. and Hoste, V. (2010). *Towards an improved methodology for automated readability prediction.* Proceedings of the International Conference on Language Resources and Evaluation. LREC 2010, 17-23 May, Valletta, Malta. https://biblio.ugent.be/publication/1055826/file/1055827.pdf

Organization for Economic Cooperation and Development (OECD) (n.d.). *Programme for International Student Assessment: PISA.* http://www.oecd.org/pisa/

Orr, M. (2002). The FCE speaking test: using rater reports to help interpret test scores. *System* 30 (2): 143–154.

O'Sullivan, B. (2012). A brief history of language testing. In: *A Cambridge Guide to Second Language Assessment* (eds. C. Coomb, P. Davidson, B. O'Sullivan and S. Stoynoff). 9–19. Cambridge: Cambridge University Press.

Otus (2022). *Standards based grading: everything you need to know.* https://otus.com/guides/standards-based-grading/

Oxford, R. (2016). *Teaching and Researching Language Learning Strategies: Self-Regulation in Context.* Oxfordshire: Routledge Oxford University Press (2012). *List of corpora and databases.* https://fdslive.oup.com/www.oup.com/uscompanion/us/static/companion.websites/nevalainen/70_List_corpora_and_databases_Reviewed.pdf

Pearson Education (2019). *Versant English placement test* [video]. YouTube. https://www.youtube.com/watch?v=w3mUDKaoNC4&t=190s

Pearson Education (2022). *Versant English placement test: test description and validation summary.* https://www.pearson.com/content/dam/one-dot-com/one-dot-com/english/SupportingDocs/Versant/ValidationSummary/VEPT-TestDescription-ValidationSummary.pdf

Pearson Education (2023). *Our tests.* https://www.pearson.com/languages/en-us/hr-professionals/versant/our-tests.html

Pearson English (2020). *Getting to know versant English placement test + remote monitoring with Andrew Khan* [video]. YouTube. https://www.youtube.com/watch?v=Jh9JcfVALHY

Penguin ELT Readers (2024). https://www.penguinreaders.co.uk/

Perusall (2021). *Introduction to Perusall* [video]. YouTube. https://www.youtube.com/watch?v=_PfAcOD2erk

Perusall (2024). https://www.perusall.com/

Plakans, L. and Gebril, A. (2015). *Assessment Myths: Applying Second Language Research to Classroom Teaching.* New York: University of Michigan Press.

Plickers (2022). https://get.plickers.com/

Plyler v. Doe (1982). https://legaldictionary.net/plyler-v-doe/

Polio, C. and Glew, M. (1996). ESL writing assessment prompts: how students choose. *Journal of Second Language Writing* 5 (1): 35–49.

Pont, B. (2013). *Learning standards, teaching standards and standards for school principals: a comparative study.* OECD Education Working Papers No. 99. http://www.oecd.org/official documents/publicdisplaydocumentpdf/?cote=EDU/WKP(2013)14&docLanguage=En

Popham, J. (1997). What's wrong—and what's right—with rubrics. *Educational Leadership*, 55 (2): 72–75.

Porter-Szucs, I. (2014). *Assessing the speaking of LESLLA, SLIFE, and community college students.* Expanding our Perspectives: From the Classroom to the Community. Selected Proceedings of the 2014 Michigan Teachers of English to Speakers of Other Languages Conference, 42–52. Grand Rapids: Michigan.

Porter-Szucs, I., Macknish, C., and DeCicco, B. (2016). *The CaMLA speaking test: face-to-face vs. audio delivery.* CaMLA Working Papers 2016-02. Cambridge Michigan Language Assessment.

https://michiganassessment.org/wp-content/uploads/220/02/20.02.pdf.Res_.TheCaMLASpeaking Test-FacetoFacevs.AudioDelivery.pdf

Porter-Szucs, I. (2018). Process approach versus product approach. In: *The TESOL Encyclopedia of English Language Teaching* (eds. J.I. Liontas and M. DelliCarpini). Hoboken: Wiley Blackwell. doi: 10.1002/9781118784235.eelt0612.

Preliminary SAT (PSAT) (2024). *College Board and National Merit Scholarship Corporation (NMSC)*. https://satsuite.collegeboard.org/psat-nmsqt

Princeton University (2019). *Voces de Princeton*. https://voces.princeton.edu/

Progress (n.d.). Pearson. https://www.pearson.com/english/catalogue/assessment/progress.html

PTE Academic Tests (2024). Pearson. https://www.pearsonpte.com/pte-academic

Public Domain Vectors (2024). https://publicdomainvectors.org/

Purdue University (2024). *ELL language portraits*. College of Education. https://education.purdue.edu/elllps/ell-language-portraits/

Purpura, J.E. (2004). *Assessing grammar*. Cambridge: Cambridge University Press.

Purpura, J.E. (2021). A rationale for using a scenario-based assessment to measure competency-based, situated second and foreign language proficiency. In: *Évaluation des acquisitions langagières: du formatif au certificatif, mediAzioni* (eds. M. Masperi, C. Cervini and Y. Bardière) 32, A54–A96. https://mediazioni.sitlec.unibo.it/

Purpura, J.E. (2022). *Using a learning-oriented assessment framework to reimagine classroom assessments* [Webinar]. YouTube. https://www.youtube.com/watch?v=S5hO4sP5XxI

Quartapelle, F. and Schameitat, B. (2012). Teaching and learning with CLIL. In: *Assessment and Evaluation in CLIL* (ed. F. Quartapelle). 29–37. AECLIL-EACEA.

Quizizz (2023). https://quizizz.com/home-v1?lng=en

Quizlet (2024). https://quizlet.com/

Read, J. (2000). *Assessing vocabulary*. Cambridge: Cambridge University Press.

Readability Formulas (2023). *Learn how to use readability formulas*. https://readabilityformulas.com/learn-how-to-use-the-flesch-kincaid-grade-level/

Readable Blog (2024). *How to choose the right readability formula*. https://readable.com/blog/how-to-choose-the-right-readability-formula/

Reading Rockets (2024). *Think-alouds*. https://www.readingrockets.org/strategies/think_alouds

Refreshable Braille Displays (n.d.). American Foundation for the Blind. https://www.afb.org/node/16207/refreshable-braille-displays

Renandya, W.A. and Widodo, H.P. (eds.). (2016.) *English Language Teaching Today: Linking Theory and Practice*. New York: Springer International. doi: 10.1007/978-3-319-38834-2.

Rennert, C. (2023). *Language skills as a prerequisite for certain degree programmes*. Technische Universität Dresden. https://tu-dresden.de/studium/vor-dem-studium/bewerbung/studienvorausset zungen/sprachvoraussetzungen?set_language=en.

Reuneker, A. (2017). *Lexical Diversity Measurements*. https://www.reuneker.nl/files/ld/#

Rev (2020). *Speech to text report on how businesses use speech to text services*. https://www.rev.com/blog/speech-to-text-report#

RMIT University (n.d.). Academic word list tool. https://learninglab.rmit.edu.au/content/academic-word-list-tool.html

Ruhr Universität Bochum (2023). *The corpus of Black and coloured South African English in contact*. https://www.ruhr-uni-bochum.de/engling/research/sa/corpus.html.en

Ross, S. (2008). *The "stair method" of grading*. Flickr. https://www.flickr.com/photos/ragesoss/2159598710/

Sackstein, S. (2021). *Assessing with respect: everyday practices that meet students, social and emotional needs*. ASDC.

Sadeghi, K. (2018). Comprehension processes. In: *The TESOL Encyclopedia of English Language Teaching* (eds. J.I. Liontas and M. DelliCarpini). Hoboken: Wiley Blackwell. doi: 10.1002/978111878 4235.eelt0468.

Sánchez, M.T., Parker, C., Akbayin, B., et al. (2010). *Processes and challenges in identifying learning disabilities among students who are English language learners in three New York State districts.* Institute of Education Sciences, National Center for Education Evaluation and Regional Assistance, no. 085. https://ies.ed.gov/ncee/edlabs/regions/northeast/pdf/REL_2010085.pdf

Sanchez Zinny, G. (2015). Latin America's wake-up call on global school tests. *BBC.* https://www.bbc.com/news/business-32161854

Schildkamp, K., Poortman, C.L., Ebbeler, J., et al. (2019). How school leaders can build effective data teams: five building blocks for a new wave of data-informed decision making. *Journal of Educational Change* 20: 283–325. doi: 10.1007/s10833-019-09345-3.

Schoepp, K. (2018). Predictive validity of the IELTS in an English as a medium of instruction environment. *Higher Education Quarterly* 72 (4): 271–285. doi: 10.1111/hequ.12163.

Scholastic ELT (2024). https://shop.scholastic.co.uk/elt

Schroeder, R. (2022). Deconstructing ChatGPT on the future of continuing education. *Inside Higher Ed.* https://www.insidehighered.com/digital-learning/blogs/online-trending-now/deconstructing-chatgpt-future-continuing-education

Schweitzer, K. (2019). *Understanding scaled scores.* ThoughtCo. https://www.thoughtco.com/understanding-scaled-scores-4161300

Selinker, L. (1972). Interlanguage. *IRAL: International Review of Applied Linguistics in Language Teaching* 10 (3): 209–231.

Serrano, D. and Scardina, K. (2018). *Improving the identification of English learner students for talented and gifted programs.* Regional Educational Laboratory Northwest. https://ies.ed.gov/ncee/edlabs/regions/northwest/pdf/el-tag-infographic.pdf

Shehadeh, A. (2018). Task-based language assessment. In: *The TESOL Encyclopedia of English Language Teaching* (eds. J.I. Liontas and M. DelliCarpini). Hoboken: Wiley Blackwell. doi: 10.1002/9781118784235.eelt0379.

Shimono, T.R. (2018). L2 reading fluency progression using timed reading and repeated oral reading. *Reading in a Foreign Language* 30 (1): 152–179. https://files.eric.ed.gov/fulltext/EJ1176224.pdf

Shockey, L., and Cavar, M. (2013). Roadrunners and eagles. *Research in Language* 11 (1): 97–102. doi: 10.2478/v10015-012-0012-x.

Short, D.J., Becker, H., Cloud, N., et al. (2018). *The 6 principles for exemplary teaching of English learners: Grades K-12.* Alexandria: TESOL Press.

Shukla, P. (2019). *Simon says game for children* [video]. https://www.youtube.com/watch?v=90GBmR LMtfM

Sketch Engine (n.d.). *Corpora by language.* Lexical Computing. https://www.sketchengine.eu/corpora-and-languages/

Snow, M.A. (2001). Content-based and immersion models for second and foreign language teaching. In: *Teaching English as a Second or Foreign Language*, 3e (ed. M. Celce-Murcia), 303–318). Boston, MA.: Heinle & Heinle.

Socrative (2024). https://www.socrative.com/

Special Education Promotion Law, Republic of Korea (1994). Japanese Society for Rehabilitation of Persons with Disabilities (JSRPD). https://www.dinf.ne.jp/doc/english/intl/z15/z15007le/z1500748.html

SpeechTexter (2024). https://www.speechtexter.com/

Splendid Learning (2024). *Flo-Joe: writing class makeovers.* https://www.flo-joe.co.uk/fce/students/writing/makeover/archive.htm

Spurious Correlations. (2014). https://www.tylervigen.com/spurious-correlations

Statistics Canada. (2019, September 30). Annual Demographic Estimates: Canada, Provinces and Territories 2019. https://www150.statcan.gc.ca/n1/en/pub/91-215-x/91-215-x2019001-eng.pdf?st=FD33htP1

Stecklow, S. and Dudley, R. (2017). College Board tightens SAT exam security, but key risk remains. *Reuters.* https://www.reuters.com/article/us-college-sat-security/college-board-tightens-sat-exam-security-but-key-risk-remains-idUSKBN1612AB/

Stike, T. (2021). *What is browser lockdown software?* Honorlock. https://honorlock.com/blog/what-is-browser-lockdown-software/

Stommel, J. (2020). How to ungrade. In: *Ungrading: Why Rating Students Undermines Learning (and What to do Instead)* (ed. S. Blum), 25–41. Morgantown: West Virginia University Press.

Supporting English Language Learners in Kindergarten (2007). https://www.edu.gov.on.ca/eng/document/kindergarten/kindergartenell.pdf

Swain, M. (1985). Communicative competence: some roles of comprehensible input and comprehensible output in its development. In: *Input in Second Language Acquisition* (eds. S. Gass and C. Madden), 235–53. New York: Newbury House.

Swan, M. and Smith, B. (eds.). (2001). *Learner English: A Teacher's Guide to Interference and Other Problems*, 2e. Cambridge: Cambridge University Press.

Swartz, C.W., Hanlon, S.T., Stenner, A.J., et al. (2011). *Text complexity of English international newspapers preparing for college and career.* White paper. MetaMetrics. https://metametricsinc.com/research-publications/text-complexity-english-international-newspapers/

TalkTyper. (2018). *Free speech to text dictation software in a browser.* https://talktyper.com/

Tauroza, S. and Allison, D. (1990). Speech rates in British English. *Applied Linguistics* 11 (1): 90–105.

TED Talks (n.d.). *Ideas worth spreading.* https://www.ted.com/

Test of English as a Foreign Language (TOEFL) (n.d.). Educational Testing Service. https://www.ets.org/toefl.html

Test of English as a Foreign Language (TOEFL) iBT (n.d.). *Test of English as a foreign language.* Educational Testing Service. https://www.ets.org/toefl/test-takers/ibt.html

TOEIC (n.d.). *Test of English for international communication.* Educational Testing Service. https://www.ets.org/toeic/

TOLES Advanced (2024). *Test of legal English skills.* Hellenic American Union. http://www.hau.gr/?i=examinations.en.description-of-the-toles-advanced

Testing of Arabic as a Foreign Language (TOAFL) (2022). Al-Arabiyya Institute. https://toafl.com/al-arabiyya-test-online-arabic-a1-c2-certificate-acc-cefr

The Bell Foundation (2024). *Great idea: dictogloss.* https://www.bell-foundation.org.uk/eal-programme/guidance/effective-teaching-of-eal-learners/great-ideas/dictogloss/#:~:text=Dictogloss%20is%20a%20type%20of,but%20with%20familiar%20subject%20content

Thornbury, S. (2005). *How to teach speaking.* London: Pearson.

Tnteu, J. (2020). *How to use hot potatoes: jcloze, jcross, jmatch, jquiz, jmix* [video]. YouTube. https://www.youtube.com/watch?v=cgaw1A_h_KE

Tomaš, Z. and Shapiro, S. (2021). From crisis to opportunity: turning questions about "Plagiarism" into conversations about linguistically responsive pedagogy. *TESOL Quarterly* 55 (4): 1102–1113. doi: 10.1002/tesq.3082.

Tonkinson, R. and Brendt, R.M. (2024). Australian Aboriginal peoples. *Encyclopaedia Britannica.* https://www.britannica.com/topic/Australian-Aboriginal

Tophat Glossary (n.d.). *Educational technology.* https://tophat.com/glossary/e/educational-technology/

Toulmin, S.E. (2003). *The Uses of Argument.* Cambridge: Cambridge University Press.

Townsend, C. (2023). *ChatGPT essays and more: how teachers and schools are dealing with AI writing: is artificial intelligence an academic tool for good or evil?* Mashable. https://mashable.com/article/chatgpt-ai-essays-classroom-materials-teachers-react

Tracktest (2024). *Tracktest English.* https://tracktest.eu/

Trinh, M. P. (2022). Teaching a difficult subject? Try gamifying your classroom. *Nature.* https://www.nature.com/articles/d41586-022-01945-z

Trinh, M.P. and Savvides, M. (2022). *Course stories, episode #1: Adventures in stats: a gamified online course* [Podcast]. Arizona State University. https://teachonline.asu.edu/2022/02/course-stories-episode-1-adventures-in-stats-a-gamified-online-course/

Trinity College London (2024). *Integrated skills in English (ITS).* https://www.trinitycollege.com/site/?id=3192

Truscott, J. (1996). The case against grammar correction in L2 writing classes. *Language Learning* 46: 327–369.

Turner, C.E. and Purpura, J.E. (2016). Learning-oriented assessment in second and foreign language classrooms. In: *Handbook of Second Language Assessment* (eds. D. Tsagari and J. Banerjee). 255–272. Berlin: De Gruyter.

United Nations (2024). *Instruments and mechanisms.* https://www.ohchr.org/en/instruments-and-mechanisms

Université catholique de Louvain (2023). *Learner corpora around the world.* Centre for English Corpus Linguistics. https://uclouvain.be/en/research-institutes/ilc/cecl/learner-corpora-around-the-world.html

University of Chicago (n.d.). *Reading Spanish for research purposes.* https://summer.uchicago.edu/course/spanish-reading-spanish-research-purposes

University of Hawaii (n.d.). *2018-19 Catalog: French courses.* http://www.catalog.hawaii.edu/courses/departments/fr.htm

University of Oslo, Norway (n.d.). *Grading scale.* https://www.uio.no/english/studies/examinations/grades/grade-descriptions/od-karakterskala.pdf

University of Wisconsin-Madison (n.d.). *Reading and translation courses.* https://web.archive.org/web/20230606052537/https://continuingstudies.wisc.edu/languages/languages-reading-translation/

Ur, P. (1996). *A Course in Language Teaching: Practice and Theory.* Cambridge: Cambridge University Press.

Ure, J. (1971). Lexical density and register differentiation. *Contemporary Educational Psychology* (5): 96–104.

US Citizenship and Immigration Services (USCIS) (n.d,). *Civics test* (archived). https://www.uscis.gov/citizenship/2020test

US Citizenship and Immigration Services (USCIS) (2021). *Civics test questions for American citizenship.* https://www.uscis.gov/sites/default/files/document/crc/M_1778.pdf

US Citizenship and Immigration Services (USCIS) (2021). *USCIS reverts to the 2008 version of the naturalization civics test.* https://www.uscis.gov/news/news-releases/uscis-reverts-to-the-2008-version-of-the-naturalization-civics-test

US Department of Education (1965). *Elementary and secondary education act of 1965*: H. R. 2362, 89th Cong., 1st sess., Public law 89-10. Reports, bills, debate and act. [Washington]: [US Govt. Print. Off.].

US Department of Education (2015a). *Elementary and Secondary Education Act (ESEA).* https://www2.ed.gov/about/inits/ed/non-public-education/essa.html

US Department of Education (2015b). *Every Student Succeeds Act (ESSA).* https://www.ed.gov/laws-and-policy/laws-preschool-grade-12-education/every-student-succeeds-act-essa

US Department of Education (2016a). *Office of English Language Acquisition English Learner toolkit for state and local education agencies (SEAs and LEAs)* (Chapter 1). https://www2.ed.gov/about/offices/list/oela/english-learner-toolkit/chap1.pdf

US Department of Education (2016b). Office of English Language Acquisition EL toolkit;. https://ncela.ed.gov/educator-support/toolkits/english-learner-toolkit

US Department of Education (n.d.). *About IDEA* (Individuals with Disabilities Education Act) https://sites.ed.gov/idea/about-idea/

US Department of State English Language Teaching Methods (n.d.). *Shaping the way we teach English* [video]. YouTube. https://www.youtube.com/playlist?list=PL7BlTIDdOgZKXgMkfUsDGoFp5HH97TP_8

US Government Contact Center (n.d.). *Branches of the US government.* https://www.usa.gov/branches-of-government

US Immigration and Customs Enforcement (ICE) (2024). *Mission.* https://www.ice.gov/

Using English (2024). *Text analyzer—text analysis tool.* https://www.usingenglish.com/resources/text-statistics/

Vandergrift, L. and Goh, C.C.M. (2012). *Teaching and learning second language listening: metacognition in action.* Oxfordshire: Routledge.

Versant Arabic Test. (2019). Pearson. https://www.pearson.com/content/dam/one-dot-com/one-dot-com/english/SupportingDocs/Versant/DataSheets/Product-Info-Sheet-Versant-Arabic-Test.pdf

Versant English Tests (2023). *Tests.* Pearson. https://www.pearson.com/languages/hr-professionals/versant.html

Versant English Placement Test (n.d.). Pearson. https://www.pearson.com/english/versant.html

Versant Tests (2019). *Versant English placement test—product tour* [video]. YouTube. https://www.youtube.com/watch?v=w3mUDKaoNC4

Victoria State Government (n.d.). *Self-assessment of reading: draft pupil checklist.* https://cpb-ap-se2.wpmucdn.com/global2.vic.edu.au/dist/d/30223/files/2013/11/Reading-assessment-record_self-178i0qx.pdf

Virginia International University (2019). *Grading system and GPA.* https://web.archive.org/web/20191215210752/https://www.viu.edu/academics/registrars-office/grading-system-gpa/

VoiceNotebook (2016). https://voicenotebook.com/

Wagner High School (n.d.). *Tier 2 and tier 3 vocabulary terms.* Common Core State Standards. https://www.wagnerhigh.net/pdf/Tier_2%20AND%20Tier%203_Common%20Core_Volcabulary_Terms.pdf

Waldek, S. and Dobrijevic, D. (2024). *Northern lights (aurora borealis): what they are & how to see them.* Space.com. https://www.space.com/15139-northern-lights-auroras-earth-facts-sdcmp.html

Wallace, M.P. and Qin, C.Y. (2021). Language classroom assessment fairness: perceptions from students. *LEARN Journal: Language Education and Acquisition Research Network* 14 (1): 492–521. https://so04.tci-thaijo.org/index.php/LEARN/index

Walters, F.S. (2016). *CLIC Workshop.* https://bpb-us-e1.wpmucdn.com/blogs.rice.edu/dist/7/6535/files/2016/06/SPECS_handout-1z6c75z.pdf

Warner, J. (2022). Freaking out about ChatGPT—Part I: artificial intelligence can crank out passable student essays in seconds. What are we going to do? *Inside Higher Ed.* https://www.insidehighered.com/blogs/just-visiting/freaking-out-about-chatgpt%E2%80%94part-i

Washington State University Office of Assessment for Curricular Effectiveness (2020). *Quick guide to norming on student work for program-level assessment.* https://ace.wsu.edu/documents/2015/03/rubrics-norming.pdf/

Watson, R. (2014). Student visa system fraud exposed in BBC investigation. *BBC Panorama.* https://www.bbc.com/news/uk-26024375

Wayman, J.C., Jimerson, J.B. and Cho, V. (2012). Organizational considerations in establishing the data-informed district. *School Effectiveness and School Improvement* 23 (2): 159–178. doi: 10.1080/09243453.2011.652124.

Wayman, J.C., Spikes, D. and Volonnino, M. (2013). Implementation of a data initiative in the NCLB era. In: *Data-Based Decision Making in Education: Challenges and Opportunities* (eds. K. Schildkamp, M.K. Lai and L. Earl), 135–153. doi: 10.1007/978-94-007-4816-3_8.

Weigle, S.C. (2002). *Assessing Writing*. Cambridge: Cambridge University Press.

Weigle, S.C., Lamison, B. and Peters, K. (2000). *Topic selection on a standardized writing assessment*. Miami Florida, USA: Paper presented at Southeast Regional TESOL.

Welner, K. (2015). The testing regime in US schools isn't working. *New York Times*. https://www.nytimes.com/roomfordebate/2015/05/04/is-testing-students-the-answer-to-americas-education-woes

WIDA (2007). *English language proficiency standards. PreKindergarten through grade 5*. Board of Regents of the University of Wisconsin System on behalf of the WIDA Consortium. https://wida.wisc.edu/resources/english-language-proficiency-standards-prekindergarten-through-grade-5-2007-edition

WIDA (2015). *WIDA focus on: SLIFE: students with Limited or interrupted formal education*. https://wida.wisc.edu/sites/default/files/resource/FocusOn-SLIFE.pdf

WIDA (2020). *Overview of WIDA 2020 standards* [video]. YouTube. https://www.youtube.com/watch?v=E794aTuyHng

WIDA (2024a) *Kindergarten ACCESS placement test*. University of Wisconsin-Madison. https://wida.wisc.edu/assess/access/kindergarten

WIDA (2024b). *Proven tools and support to help educators and multilingual learners succeed*. https://wida.wisc.edu/

Wigglesworth, G. and Elder, C. (2010). An investigation of the effectiveness and validity of planning time in speaking test tasks. *Language Assessment Quarterly* 7 (1), pp. 1-24. doi: 10.1080/15434300903031779.

Willis, J. and Willis, M. (2020). *Research-based strategies to ignite student learning: insights from neuroscience and the classroom*. Alexandria: ASCD.

Winke, P. and Zhang, X. (2019). How a third-grade reading retention law will affect ELLs in Michigan, and a call for research on child ELL reading development. *TESOL Quarterly* 53 (2): 529–542.

Wolfe, J. Shanmugaraj, N. and Sipe, J. (2016). Grammatical versus pragmatic error: employer perceptions of nonnative and native English speakers. *Business and Professional Communication Quarterly* 79 (4): 397–415. doi: 10.1177/2329490616671133.

Wray, A. (2000). Formulaic sequences in second language teaching: principle and practice. *Applied Linguistics* 21: 463–489.

Wray, A. (2002). *Formulaic language and the lexicon*. Cambridge: Cambridge University Press.

Wright, W. (2023). *Landmark court rulings regarding English language learners*. Colorin Colorado. https://www.colorincolorado.org/article/landmark-court-rulings-regarding-english-language-learners

WriteReader (2024). https://www.writereader.com/en

Xi, X. (2022). Opinion on the current state of AI assessment technology [online forum post]. *LTEST-L Language Testing Listserv*. https://www.iltaonline.com/page/ListServe

Yang, Y. (2017). TEM test for English majors-band 8 in China. *Journal of Language Teaching and Research* 8 (6): 1229–1233.

Yow, W.Q. (2015). *CHILDES English-Mandarin Singapore Corpus*. https://childes.talkbank.org/access/Biling/Singapore.html

Yule, G. and Tarone, E. (1997). Investigating communication strategies in L2 reference: pros and cons. In: *Communication Strategies: Psycholinguistic and Sociolinguistic Perspectives* (eds. G. Kasper, and E. Kellerman), 17–30. London: Longman.

Zaki, H. and Porter-Szucs, I. (2016). *Beyond the borders of traditional feedback on ESL writing* [conference presentation]. International TESOL Convention, Baltimore, MD, USA. https://www.academia.edu/2413860 4/Beyond_the_Borders_of_Traditional_Feedback_on_ESL_Writing_presentation_given_at_the_2016_TESOL_Convention_in_Baltimore_MD

Zehler, A., Fleischman, H. Hopstock, P., Stephenson, T., et al. (2003). *Descriptive study of services to LEP students and LEP students with disabilities policy report: summary of findings related to LEP and SPED-LEP students*. Development Associates, Inc. http://onlineresources.wnylc.net/pb/orcdocs/LARC_Resources/LEPTopics/ED/DescriptiveStudyofServicestoLEPStudentsandLEPStudentswith Disabilities.pdf

Zhang, L. (2022). Test review: college English test–spoken English test (Cet-Set). *Studies in Language Assessment* 11 (21): 164–180. https://arts.unimelb.edu.au/__data/assets/pdf_file/0008/4396265/SiLA_11.2_Test-review.pdf

Zhao, Y. (1997). The effects of listeners' control of speech rate on second language comprehension. *Applied Linguistics* 18: 49–68.

Zipgrade. (2024). *Getting Started Tutorial*. https://www.zipgrade.com/

Zwick, M.J. (2018). Measuring reading fluency. In: *The TESOL Encyclopedia of English Language Teaching* (eds. J.I. Liontas and M. DelliCarpini). Hoboken: Wiley Blackwell. doi: 10.1002/978111878 4235.eelt0495.

Index